HENRY'S SHADOW

HENRY'S SHADOW

THE LIFE AND TIMES OF JOHN MORTON

Ashley Wood

AMBERLEY

First published 2025

Amberley Publishing
The Hill, Stroud
Gloucestershire, GL5 4EP

www.amberley-books.com

British Library Cataloguing in Publication Data.
A catalogue record for this book is available from the British Library.

ISBN 978 1 3981 2010 5 (hardback)
ISBN 978 1 3981 2011 2 (ebook)

1 2 3 4 5 6 7 8 9 10

Typeset in 10.5pt on 13.5pt Sabon.
Typesetting by SJmagic DESIGN SERVICES, India.
Printed in the UK.

Contents

Preface

An interest in John Morton began way back with my schoolboy fascination for the Wars of the Roses. Why was this cleric, this strawberry grower, a threat to the life of Richard III? How did he persuade the Duke of Buckingham, after the King the most important man in the country, to rebel in favour of Henry Tudor? Such questions have niggled over the years and here is an attempt to answer these and other puzzles from this mist-shrouded age. There is so often an absence of hard evidence as to what happened, how it happened, or why, inviting hypotheses, deduction, and speculation. Even where there is contemporary documentation, it tends to be scanty, biased, contradictory, or simply downright suspicious.

The primary sources, almost all of which were assembled decades after the events they describe, include conversations which could not have been witnessed or, if they were, all the witnesses were long dead. There are also traits, some stronger than others, of political bias, misogyny, and personal bias which muddy understanding.

For this period historians have great difficulty in agreeing facts. This is something which makes the times so interesting and entertaining, but which can be frustrating. Take a very simple example: Richard, Duke of Gloucester and Henry, Duke of Buckingham meet Anthony, Earl Rivers and Lord Richard Grey on the road to London after Edward IV's death. But where and in what order?

Paul Murray Kendall has Rivers arriving at Northampton where he and Gloucester quaff some ale together, Buckingham turns up later. Rivers is arrested the next morning, held at Northampton, and Gloucester and Buckingham go on to Stony Stratford to arrest Lord Grey and secure the boy King Edward V. All then return to Northampton.

Michael Hicks has Rivers and Grey both arrested in Northampton. Edward is found at Grafton Manor with Sir Thomas Vaughan (also arrested) from where he is moved south to Stony Stratford.

A J Pollard has Rivers arrested at Northampton and then taken back to Stony Stratford where Grey and Vaughan are also arrested.

Alison Weir has Rivers and Grey arrested at Northampton. Rivers is detained there but Grey is taken back to Stony Stratford to be re-arrested in front of the King.

Dan Jones sees Rivers and Grey arrested on the journey with Gloucester and Buckingham from Northampton to Stony Stratford.

There are further permutations.

The aim here is not to look for a consensus or a middle ground, but to simply offer what seems most probable, taking the tale forward rather than working back from a predetermined conclusion.

Many histories debate the pros and cons of contesting arguments and interpretations, with narrative seen as of secondary importance. Or the prejudices and reliability of individual chroniclers are closely weighed. Here, narrative rules the roost. Contesting arguments may be introduced, but this is only where it helpfully illuminates character and motivation. That said, my own interpretations and opinions inevitably filter through, particularly where evidence is weak or absent.

Please keep in mind that I have tried to avoid adopting a position where absence of contemporary evidence, no smoking gun if you will, is held sufficient reason to conclude that something simply didn't happen. Often, no written evidence remains over such a long period of time, or, if it does, it may be simply political propaganda. That said, this is a Lancastrian view of the fifteenth century and is distinct from the more prevalent Yorkist apologias.

As an attempt to construct John Morton's story, where possible I have tried to present it from his eyes, on his terms, and without too much concern as to how others may have interpreted his actions. Certainly, the vox-pop never seemed to have bothered him in the least. A man of his time, he possessed many virtues. There were also unpleasant attributes to his character. But then he lived in unpleasant times.

It is a story pretty much devoid of humour. Evidence of humour in Morton is, at best, dry; drier than I can find much to smile about. His rebus, or ornamental device, was of a bird or mor (think 'moorhen') on a wine barrel or tun. Advertising was alive and well 600 years ago, but it wasn't that witty. There is also little or no reference to sex. No evidence exists on Morton's views on or, indeed, engagement with, sex of any sort. It seems likely that he had a highly romanticised view of women but little personal interaction with them other than a courtly or protective relationship. He would probably have subscribed to the Church's teachings of the time for clerics, but there are suggestions that he was not uncomfortable translating those with a liberal outlook.

The bibliography is simply a list of my own readings on and around the subject matter. Inclusion suggests these books have something interesting to say, but I don't necessarily agree with what they are saying.

And what is Henry's Shadow? In part it is the shadow of Henry V over the English psyche and a motivator to John Morton; in part John Morton himself becomes the shadow of Henry VII; and the shadow is also the ghost of Henry IV insidiously impressing an acceptance of usurpation on the fifteenth-century body politic.

Endings: Knole Park, Sevenoaks, 15 September 1500[1]

Early afternoon autumnal light seeps through wooden shutters, creating streaks of silver grey on dark oak panelling and reaching the bright, heavy tapestries. The room is dominated by a four-poster bed under an ornate canopy hung from the ceiling. Propped up on plumped pillows to assist his laboured breathing is a frail old man with long, wispy, grey hair crowned by a crimson velvet cap.

John Morton is dying.

Any freshness in the air has been long suffocated by incense and other smells striving to keep bad humours at bay. In the bedroom doorway stand two dour doctors, quietly conferring, though without hope or purpose. Observers. Witnesses, if you will. In the antechamber are gathered more witnesses, though these have greater affinity with the dying man. There is John Fyneux, Chief Justice of the King's Bench and an executor to John Morton's will; Hugh Peyntwyn, Archdeacon of Canterbury; Henry Edyall, Archdeacon of Rochester; William Barons, a rising star who will become Master of the Rolls and Bishop of London; Robert Turberville, a relative on Morton's mother's side; and a handful of other notables – who are there more to ensure the surrender of the Great Seal as ordered by the King the day before than to afford comfort at the end.[2] Nonetheless, it is an impressive gathering of the good if not the great. The King, his seat stable but dynasty still juvenile, will not take risk with disease. And rightly so. Only 43 years old, he is starting to develop the tuberculosis that will finish him by the end of the decade. For now, Henry VII is protected within Woodstock Palace, Oxfordshire, and stays there.

The observers discreetly take sips of fortified wine believing its antiseptic properties will help counter any ill effects of infected air. And for simply something to do during the wait.

John Morton knows that he is dying. The octogenarian has been sinking since the beginning of the previous winter and it is clear, even to him, that his body is well beyond providing a frame for the next. A most precise and forward-thinking man, he made his final will at Canterbury on 16 June and then travelled up to Knole, where he has always felt most comfortable, on 26 August, continuing to work until just four days ago.

He is not frightened of death, although being the most hated man in England, twice declared a traitor, a spy master, aiding the fall of an anointed king and the rise of a usurper, perhaps he should be. On the other hand, he is Archbishop of Canterbury, a Cardinal of Rome, Lord Chancellor, a leading scholar and lawyer, and innovator. It would be uncharacteristic if he had doubts about the life everlasting and his place therein. It is the apparent contradictions of his life which attest to his conservatism: service, order and family are his mainstays regardless of risk or reward, steadfastness his most elevated virtue.

The process of dying is of concern to him, though. He is gripped by a malarial infection bringing increasingly debilitating bouts of shivering and fever and now that infection has spread to his liver to show jaundice, not only in his eyes, but in his skin. Lucidity and consciousness come and go. Are these best strived for, or surrendered?

2

Beginnings: Milborne Styleham Manor Farm, Dorset

The boy John was brought up to put his family, his religion, and his king before all other considerations, although there might be some flexibility in which took precedence at any particular time.[1] As a boy, unsurprisingly reflecting the national mood, his fixation would be very much on his king, Henry V, whose exploits in France, particularly on the battlefield at Agincourt, stirred the imagination and ambition. National identity was forged by the desire and ability to outdo the French.

A preoccupation with the King as super-hero was also embedded by repeated telling of the campaign around the evening fireside as he, and his younger brothers grew up. The stories would sometimes feature John's great-uncle, Robert Morton.[2]

The tale would always be told well, with few embellishments other than added gruesomeness as the boys got older. Henry's campaign of 1415 against the French sought to establish his claim to the French throne (although there was always the possibility of compromise on the table if the price was right – but this would not be part of the story). Having taken Harfleur, the English were in a quandary over the next move in the campaign.[3] The siege of the town and sickness had cut numbers considerably – casualties were about 1,600, reducing Henry's army down to around 9,600 fighting men. Those beyond active service together with the bones of those of rank who had perished were shipped home. The traditional fighting season was moving on and there was a need to bring matters to a resolution, so a challenge to combat had been sent out to the French, but after a week and a day, they had failed to materialise. In short, Henry had to make something happen as disease and lack of food debilitated English bodies and spirits and a fight with the French seemed the best, if not only, option.

The decision was taken to leave 1,200 to defend Harfleur and the rest, 8,400 knights, men-at-arms and archers, would march the 140 or so miles to Calais: hoping to draw the French to a fight on the way. In all, they were some 11,000 souls including non-combatants, with victuals for eight days – 7 days marching and one day for battle. The wisdom of the decision to march was made clear the day before the vanguard left Harfleur when a terrible storm struck, which destroyed many of the English ships; a reminder of the perils of travel by sea.

The army set off in three sections, known as 'battles'. Robert Morton was in the vanguard, commanded by Edward, Duke of York, in whose affinity Robert had been for many years.[4] They marched out late evening. The King, commanding the main battle, left early the next morning, followed by the reserve.

After two weeks marching, they were still 40 miles short of their destination. Followed and harried by the French it took many long detours to find fords across swollen rivers. Life was dominated by the weather. It was cruel, with heavy rains, strong winds and cold nights. In a wretched state, they were weak, starving, soaked beyond soaking, dragging themselves through sucking mud. It was a foolish man who was not frightened for their situation.

It is now the day before the Feast of St Crispin and St Crispian and the vanguard are seeking a route to cross the River Ternoise. Continually harassed by the French, they eventually reach the town of Blangy to find the enemy attempting to destroy the bridge. Without a second thought, the Duke leads a charge upon the French troops to secure the crossing.

On the far side, the ground ascends from the river to a high ridge and then a plateau, which is out of sight. Scouts are sent out to survey the route forward but soon return with the blood drained from their faces. They have sighted the massive French army just ahead. On receiving news of the situation, King Henry hastens ahead of the main battle to join his vanguard and, reviewing things for himself, brings forward the whole force drawn up in battle order facing the French. The view of the enemy shows them to outnumber the English by at least three to one and with the prospect of further troops reinforcing their number. Both sides weigh each other up. Soldiers begin to pray and make their confessions to the priests.

Sunset comes, so it is evident that there will be no battle until the next day. And then it rains. By St Peter and St Paul, how it rains! How, after the soakings received over the past fortnight, there was any more water up in the heavens was beyond understanding! The English make camp outside a village called Maisoncelle. The leaders hold council and lodge within the village while the army hastily constructs shelters, or the men simply lay on the ground under hedges and trees, all the while listening to the unrelenting beat of the rain. All are soaked through and cold with it. The urgency is in keeping bows, bow strings, and arrows dry so that they are fit for the next day's action.

Most cannot sleep; anticipating death in the morning they offer up prayers throughout the night for the forgiveness of sins, for survival, or at least a quick dispatch. It was God's answer to those prayers, so they would say, through the righteousness of the King's cause, his leadership and, incredibly, the rain which now tormented them, that would determine the matter.

The French are encamped little more than half a mile from the English front. Henry orders complete silence throughout the night so that all are alert to any movement by the enemy. Such is the danger from a possible surprise attack that any man-at-arms making a noise will forfeit horse and armour. Anyone of lower rank will have an ear cut off. Thankfully, there is no report of any such penalties invoked. Bonfires are lit to keep watch by. These were wise precautions: one advance on the English lines by a large contingent of Frenchmen was seen off smartly by the archers.

At first light they attend Mass and then, still quiet, assemble battle lines. To the front, a ploughed field is saturated by the night's rain. Woods flank each side, confining the French line, which takes up the whole width of open ground. There is no way to Calais other than through the enemy lines. The vanguard takes up the right-hand battle with the village of Tramecourt beyond the woods. The reserve battle, under Thomas, Lord Camoys, takes up the left wing with Agincourt lying beyond the woods on their side. Henry, with the main battle, takes centre. This provides a full, if shallow, front to the French.

Henry issues an order for the baggage train to be drawn up nearer the battle lines and releases all French prisoners on parole that they will not take up arms and will surrender themselves again if England wins the day.

As the vanguard's archers hammer in their protective stakes, 200 slip away into the woods to the right to hide and wait. A similar trap is set on the left flank. Meanwhile, Henry rides his white horse along the entire front, raising spirits for the coming fight. Though most cannot hear him, the sight of the king in royal tunic with a crown on his helmet inspires many by his courage in his flagrant exposure to the enemy.

The English need to draw the French attack. Weak and malnourished, time is not on their side and the threat of French reinforcements arriving continues to worry. Three hours pass and nothing happens. Henry decides to press the matter and, contrary to accepted military wisdom, has all men-at-arms dismount ready to advance banners on foot. No one is going to flee the field.[5]

On cue, Sir Thomas Erpingham, who had command of the archers' deployment, rides out onto the field with two men-at-arms, throws his white baton into the air yelling, 'Now. Strike!'[6] At this, the whole army runs forward: nobles, men-at-arms and archers. Wearing leather jackets rather than plate armour, the nimble archers get within range of the enemy while most of the French are unready or out of position. Each archer could fire off a dozen arrows a minute and up to 1,000 each second are let loose on the Frenchmen and their horses. There is something spellbinding in the release of thousands of arrows. First, there is the reverberation in the ear of that twanging release of the bowstrings. Then the eerie whistling of the arrows' flight: if silence had a sound, this would be it. And then the shock of the thud as the arrows make impact.

There is an instant charge against the archers in Robert Morton's wing but, being relatively few in number, the French receive a hail of arrows that cause their horses and riders to fall into the mud, leaving riderless horses running off to disrupt their own vanguard.

Reassembling, the enemy then mount their attack directly on the three commanders and it is the vanguard battle that receives the fiercest French assault. But, as their horses charge, the archers who had been hidden in the woods let fly a barrage. Turning to face those in the trees, the French are then assailed by the archers remaining within the battle, who advance on them and catch them in a crossfire. Dead and dying men and horses, many crushed and suffocated, pile up one on the other until they are two spears' high. Now, though, the archers are running out of arrows and must resort to hand-to-hand fighting where the French men-at-arms hold the advantage. It was here that the greatest number of English fell – nearly ninety, including the Duke of York, the Earl of Suffolk and Sir Richard Kyghley.[7]

Robert Morton does not see Duke Edward fall: fighting for his own life and with the din of battle it is simply slaughter and survive. But the English troops are rallied by Sir Gilbert Umphraville and Sir John Cornwaille and the line does not break.[8] Slowly the French are forced back: except now with the pile of dead behind them there is nowhere to retreat to. The heavy clay holds fast both horses and men. So, the English fall on them in a frenzy with sword and poleaxe, butchering those French not already dead from arrows or being crushed or suffocated by their own countrymen. And then – after little more than an hour – it is over. The day is Henry's.

Not quite over though – as John would learn later in life.

There is no time to rest and re-gather strength. Although tiredness, shock, and the horror of what had been endured and delivered to the enemy were very real, the overriding emotion was elation at what had been achieved. Tempering that, the English had no idea whether the French could somehow regroup and attack once more. So they had to press on to Calais as soon as possible.

Marching on to safety, Robert Morton would have been able to glean news of other episodes and acts of heroism from the battlefield. No doubt the most talked about figure was Henry himself, striking with the disfigurement on his right cheek where an arrow had entered his face at the battle of Shrewsbury and standing astride his brother, the Duke of Gloucester, who had fallen with a wound to his groin, fighting off Frenchmen until friendly arms could help young Humphrey to safety.[9]

His victory provides the bargaining position for the Treaty of Troyes in 1420, which recognised Henry as heir to the French throne, further secured by his marriage to the 18-year-old Princess Catherine. It is a strange coincidence that her older sister, Isabelle, was wife to Richard II, deposed by Henry's father, and went on to marry Charles, Duke of Orleans, England's most prestigious prisoner from Agincourt.[10]

The heroes and values absorbed in our early years tend to stay with us and help form our future self. So it was for John Morton. His ambition to serve his king, right or wrong, had been forged. It did not take long for a self-realisation that this service would be with the application of intelligence rather than with martial skills. This would make him stand out in the crowd rather than be subsumed by it.

The Lancastrian claim to the English throne, let alone the French throne, was down to force and circumstance rather than strict legality. Henry was king *de facto* rather than *de jure*. His father, Henry IV, had usurped the throne from his cousin Richard II and then had him murdered. Richard descended from the first son of Edward III while Henry was only descended from the fourth son. This provided the descendants of the second and third sons with strong claims against him. The wars with France were regarded by Henry V as essential to secure the legitimacy of his line as successors to Edward III, universally regarded as the greatest king of England. Not only that, but Edward also had a stronger claim to the Capetian French crown than the incumbent Valois line. So, paradoxically, the validity of the Valois claim for France was remarkably like that of Lancaster for England. But such fine arguments were settled on battlefields, in the game of thrones rather than in law courts, the rewards of violent success far exceeded those of honesty and truthful argument and were more speedily obtained. Might is right, and reasoned justification sought after the event, and if you challenged the status quo, you did so with your life on the line.

Henry's opportunity to press his claim in France came in large part from the mental weakness of the French King Charles VI and the deep and often violent divisions between the leading French families. A mad or weak monarch and recalcitrant factions would be constants in the English body politic for most of Morton's public life.

Two other lessons to be learned from the 1415 campaign were the use of spies and of diplomacy, which Henry put to good use. His agent, Philip Morgan, did much to ensure that neither John the Fearless of Burgundy nor Philippe of Charolais took part at Agincourt.[11] Similarly, agents John Hovyngham and Simon Flete helped keep the Duke of Brittany neutral.[12] The lack of effective leadership within France also meant the Duke of Berry and the Duke of Anjou failed to turn up.

At the battle of Agincourt, the English baggage train does not have sufficient time to get its act together and move from Maisoncelle to the rear of Henry's lines when ordered. It is attacked by a force of some 600 locals led by a handful of French knights. Most of the English flee, including the clerics, leaving the crowd to plunder cash and treasure (not least the English crown) but if the aim was also to distract and confuse the English battle lines, it failed as it was too far away to be noticed. The baggage train had been guarded by only ten men-at-arms and twelve archers, so there was no capacity for effective resistance. One of those guarding the train was a Morton. Thomas Morton was a Clerk of the Wardrobe, responsible for logistics, and had personally provided and paid for three archers to join the army.[13] Nothing seems to be heard of him after Agincourt and it is probable that he fell there, his corpse burned with other dead Englishmen in a barn at Maisoncelle (along with at least a few live French prisoners). The lower ranks received no memorial. Henry needed to cover the miles to Calais as quickly as possible in case of pursuit and further attack, so the dead received minimal consideration.

Which leads us to the greatest omission from the tale as it was probably conveyed to the Morton children: Henry orders the slaughter of prisoners. To be clear, battlefield prisoners are men of sufficient rank with potential to provide ransom. Wounded or trapped soldiers with no salvage value will be despatched there and then with a blade to the throat or an axe to the brain. Chivalry, if it ever existed outside of Arthurian romances, is a sham.

With the fighting seemingly over, the English trawled the field seeking battle bonuses. Suddenly a shout went up that the French were regrouping and about to make another attack. This was the French reserve, including their crossbowmen, and could have numbered some

3,000 men – apparently advancing. In fact, with most of their leadership dead or captured, no attack came, and they fell back and dispersed. But Henry panicked. He needed not only survival, but a decisive victory to protect his dynasty and to carry forward his ambitions over the French throne. This meant he had to protect his men. His true feelings towards the low ranks was exposed in the callous neglect his soldiers received on reaching Calais. Not only were the men exhausted physically and mentally but his archers had spent all their arrows. He needed to ensure that the French leadership could not reunite with this potentially threatening force and to focus his own troops' concentration on the perceived peril rather than the promise of profit. His solution to the situation was to order all prisoners, except those of royal blood, to be put to death immediately.

The English leaders on the field showed a reluctance to carry out this order. This could have been a matter of chivalry or, like as not, a reluctance to throw away some recompense for their campaign costs. Henry's response was to give the task to an esquire with 200 archers under his command. It is possible that up to 400 prisoners were killed but the actual number is impossible to determine. However, some 800 prisoners are known to have been taken for ransom and not killed.

How is it that this action did not diminish Henry's image as hero in the eyes of John Morton or, indeed, the English generally? It received little condemnation from chroniclers on either side. There were numerous examples of such barbarities from the past and, as mentioned, any concern here is not for the ordinary soldier but for the comfort or insurance of 'chivalric' protocols enjoyed by the higher classes should they become captured in battle. Edward III, for the English the epitome of what is a true king, had also ordered the killing of prisoners on the battlefield of Crécy in 1346. Behaviour towards prisoners in the Crusades was even worse.

Henry was a contemporary national hero for a contemporary England. All heroes are flawed to some extent, even superheroes. Henry behaved with chivalry to those who were not confronting or contradicting him. On the battlefield though, his thoughts and actions were for 'Total War' with no compromise. In the eyes of those wanting to believe in him, this was the admirable trait of 'resolution': even when he showed greater psychopathic tendencies at Caen and Rouen.[14]

Any criticism of him as a Christian also failed to challenge his conscience. The Commandments may say 'Thou shalt not kill' but Moses killed as many Egyptians as he could literally shake a stick at. It seemed the Commandment only applied to not killing one's own. Like Moses, Henry was God's instrument and winning proved God's blessing on his actions.

He also had no empathy for women. Ordering that any woman found within three miles of his army on the Agincourt campaign should have her left arm broken suggests a peculiar misogyny. Even Catherine had value only as the key to his dynastic ambitions, not as a person, although this was not in itself particularly unusual in royal marriages.

Henry was a winner and, as a contemporary hero. he had no peers. He had seized the nation's imagination and that of John Morton to bind their allegiance to the House of Lancaster.

3

The Road to Oxford

By any measure, John Morton had an exceptionally good childhood. These were pastorally as well as educationally and physically formative years.

Home was a modest manor house (meaning modest by manor house standards – alongside the church, it was the most commanding building in the parish) with ashlar elevations, some rendered cob to timber framework, and a stone slate roof, first built by John's grandfather William Morton of Harworth and gradually extended. The hall was the principal room featuring a large open fire, with kitchen and buttery off. Servants would sleep in the hall. The family and guests would have their accommodation on the first floor.

Milborne Styleham Manor stood on the east side of the brook, which separated it from the village of Milborne St Andrew, its compact Norman church being but 300 yards distant. To the south is the Iron-Age hill fort known as Weatherby Castle, and all around the district are tumuli indicating an ancient importance.

The farm was held in tenancy from Cerne Abbey. Sheep were the main source of income and the gravelly soil also provided wheat, oats, and barley which, with some oxen, horses, cattle, and some pigs and chickens, along with a home vegetable garden, kept the family in most of the staple foods and supplied a general prosperity.

The family is well-respected and of good repute, a reputation that is valued and not taken lightly. They are part of the rising class of the gentry: landed persons of local influence and importance, including a scattering of knights, members of parliament, and so on. John's ancestors include a Sheriff of Nottingham, and a Secretary to Edward III. His uncle, William, lives in Cerne and will become its Member of Parliament for some years.

Richard, his father, is a genial gentleman farmer with a sound knowledge of agriculture, his land, and the markets into which he sells. Galvanised by his religious values and governed by the seasons, he has a dispassionate interest in what goes on outside of a twenty-mile radius of the farm, but he desires his offspring to take up wider participation according to their talents.

Elizabeth, his mother, comes from an important local family from nearby Bere. Her father is Richard Turberville and her mother Celia Beauchamp, granddaughter of John, second Baron Beauchamp, who owned several manors in Somerset.[1] While his middle two brothers take mostly after Richard, John is more akin to his mother, both physically with his long face and angular jaw line, and mentally, with an energetic and assimilating mind.

In addition to Milborne Styleham Manor, the Mortons held land on the adjoining Milborne St Andrew Manor, also from Cerne Abbey. There is an element of irony in this. Cerne Abbey obtained the manor of Milborne St Andrew in 1403 having received it from Sir Humphrey Stafford in return for a daily mass for him and his wife, together with other spiritual benefits and services. Sir Humphrey was certainly someone needing a sponsor for supplications to his God. He also had big issues with the Beauchamp family.

In keeping with many of his contemporaries, Humphrey was an arrogant bully, apathetic towards others, short-tempered and quick to violence. In 1400, just sixteen years old, he murdered Richard Merston (brother of a future MP for Worcester) and went on the run, pursued by Thomas Beauchamp, 12th Earl of Warwick. Thomas died that same year, so Humphrey was able to elude justice for the time being, seeking to ingratiate himself with God via Cerne Abbey and the Crown by serving Henry, Prince of Wales, fighting in the battle of Shrewsbury in 1403. As reward for the latter action, he received a royal pardon in 1404. Not only that, but he also received the royal appointment of Rider of Feckenham Forest, in Worcestershire. Here, his character re-emerged, and he fell out with William Beauchamp, Lord Abergavenny, who protested that Humphrey had broken into his property at Feckenham, trespassed on his land and assaulted his servants. Not only that, but he had to be restrained from harassing John Brace, one of Beauchamp's retinue and another future Worcestershire MP. Through all of this, though, he retained Henry's favour and eventually reconciled himself with the Beauchamps, joining the 13th Earl of Warwick on the 1417 expedition to France and, it seems, dying there in 1419, age 35. An atonement of sorts, a balancing of the scales.

It is industry and piety that define the Morton family. John develops a good understanding of agriculture and land management with daily hands-on chores commensurate with his age. He develops a physicality and stamina which belies his moderate, wiry frame. Like all young men of his class, he learns to ride a horse well and gains a proficiency in hunting, archery, and swordsmanship. But it is his development in logic, mathematics and languages that impresses most, and with this his confidence in communicating with others grows.

The Mortons have four sons.[2] Amiable and intelligent, the parents have great ambition for their children. Richard is two years younger than John and will become High Sheriff of Somerset and Dorset. William, one year younger again, will become MP for Shaftesbury. There is a gap of some eight years to Thomas, the youngest. It would be unfair to call him a 'mistake', but that wouldn't necessarily be incorrect. Perhaps a 'surprise'. He will rise to be Archdeacon of Ely.

The order and routine afforded by a farming life, disturbed only by the occasionally trying quiddities of Nature, is embraced. It is echoed by the order and routine of religion. The church of St Andrew is attended by all the family whenever a service is held. If the vicar is serving the other half of his living at Dewlish, two miles away, then appropriate prayers are performed in the house. The stability and security afforded by such certainties provide John Morton with pleasure, comfort, and a sense of place.

St Andrew was a small church, comprising nave, porch, and a tower. Although attendance at church was not compulsory it was certainly expected for Sunday Mass and the celebration of feast days. The congregation all stood in the nave, there being no pews or seats, and services were all read in Latin, which most people did not understand. The absence of seating ensures no one from the hardworking farming community dozes off. What keeps them coming is not the fear of God and authority alone, but also that this is the gathering at which both local news and news from outside the immediate community can be shared and discussed.

Six miles away is another church dedicated to St Andrew, this one at Bloxworth; the living of which was also in the gift of Cerne Abbey. The incumbents of both churches were eager for the patronage of parents looking to their sons' betterment through private tutoring. Few ordained ministers found their benefices capable of providing financial support for all their needs and would draw much of their income from working the church lands and owning some livestock. As tutors, they would prioritise a basic grounding in Latin, English, and French, together with the fundamentals of grammar, logic, and rhetoric. There was also great emphasis on reciting religious services and on good manners and how to conduct oneself. All the Morton children show intelligence, but it is John who demonstrates a singular ability to absorb, recall, and analyse, which suggests his is a special future to be cultivated and supported.

Outside of the Mortons' world, trouble is brewing that will underpin all of John's adult life. The country is in a time of increasing uncertainty. Henry V dies in 1422 so close to reaching his desire of gaining the French throne but, in the event, ingloriously falling to dysentery and cancer of the rectum.[3] His son and heir, Henry VI, is nine months old. So, although Henry has left an heir, he has failed to see the child come of age, creating a vacuum in government. Until the infant is old enough to take command of his inheritance, a protectorate is established to oversee his interests.

The infant King's great-uncles are appointed his guardians. Henry Beaufort is the Bishop of Winchester and 47 years old at the time. He is ambitious, avaricious, and ruthless. Thomas Beaufort is Duke of Exeter, 45 years old, but he will not survive long enough to have a significant impact on events or the King's development.

Henry V's brother, John, the Duke of Bedford, is Regent of France and Normandy. At 33 he is a competent politician and soldier and, for his times and family, level-headed. The younger brother, Humphrey, Duke of Gloucester, is 32. He is volatile and aggressive, no peacemaker, but is nonetheless cultured and a notable supporter of the arts. Humphrey is made Protector of England but, because of his character, only whilst John is out of the country. It is universally acknowledged that Bedford is the main man.

The decisions of the protectorate are subject to the approval of the King's Council (something of particular importance later in Morton's career). If they can all work together until the new king reaches his majority, then there may be hope for unity and peace. This aspiration is quickly cast into doubt.

There is mounting conflict, both political and personal, in Council, evidenced from 1424, led by the pro-Armagnac Humphrey of Gloucester on the one side (later adopting a line of no concessions to the French) and the pro-Burgundy Henry Beaufort on the other (later adopting a position seeking peace with the French). The argument between the parties is essentially about who controls the young King and, thereby, the wealth of the Crown. This is expressed through war with France and how personal wealth can be maintained and increased. When Thomas of Exeter dies in 1426, the discord within the Council escalates.

The French wars were particularly expensive. The income derived from the captured lands was insufficient to meet the costs of maintaining them. Martial and diplomatic reverses abroad have frustrated any ambitions for peace or for promoting trade, requiring an increasing tax burden with no visible prospect of seeing a return on the investment or compensation for hardships endured. On the other hand, there are many in the country who consider the legacy of Henry V and the honour of England beyond monetary value.

To raise money above what parliament will grant or the royal estates provide, it is necessary for the Crown to take loans. The laws of usury prohibit the charging of high rates of interest. To get past this, a loan is taken out for a certain sum – let's say, £1,000. But only £750 is handed over to the person borrowing. Nonetheless, he must pay back the full £1,000 on a prescribed day. This is seen as the price for purchasing a loan rather than the payment of interest. There is always a way around restrictions if you are powerful enough. An interest rate or discount of 25–33% would not be unusual for the Lancastrian crown.

The Bishop of Winchester was a major creditor of the Crown in this way and had used the process to gain possession of the King's jewels, pawned at a heavily discounted rate. Being not only one of the King's guardians, but also Chancellor of the Exchequer, Bishop Beaufort has little difficulty in arranging this.

Mudslinging between the two, uncle and great-uncle, reaches such a point that in late 1425 Gloucester suspects an imminent coup by Winchester and persuades the City of London to close its gates against the Bishop and his armed retinue. Henry Chichele, Archbishop of Canterbury, arbitrates a peace before violence gets out of hand, providing time for Bedford to return from France. Bedford then asserts his authority over the factions and a profoundly embarrassed Winchester is forced to publicly declare his loyalty to Henry VI and also to resign his Chancellorship.

These events illustrate, if such is needed, the dysfunctional nature of the royal family and the governing classes. Seeds of disrespect or, alternatively, emulation of their lordships' values, are sown within the lower orders. The national pride generated (rightly or wrongly) by success in France will dissipate as that success disintegrates. And after 1426, the English conquest of France does indeed start to break up. Under the inspiring Joan of Arc, the Dauphin and the Duke of Orleans raise the siege of Orleans and the Dauphin is crowned Charles VII, King of France, age twenty-five, at Reims in 1429. In the same year, Henry VI is crowned King of England at eight years of age in Westminster Abbey. This is a very young age for coronation but is seen as politically important as a step towards rebutting Charles' coronation.

Joan was captured by the Burgundians at Compiègne in 1430, sold to the English and burnt as a heretic. Henry travels to Paris the next year where he is also crowned King of France, but it is a weak gesture. The English are fighting on too many fronts, at too great an expense and with too many ambitions.

The writing is plainly on the wall for those English ambitions when, in 1435, at the Council of Arras, Philip of Burgundy reaches an accommodation with Charles VII and the Armagnacs. He is formally released from his oaths to support the English, and Henry V's Treaty of Troyes, which established his claim to the French throne, thus becomes unenforceable. When Henry VI, not yet fourteen years old, receives a note from Burgundy breaking off the alliance with England, and no longer addressing him as the King of France, the royal adolescent bursts into tears. There doesn't seem to be anything else that he can do.

Within the English church, the power of Rome is in decline and subject to challenge. The people retain and demonstrate faith in their religion but faith in their religion's institutions is not on such firm footings. The Great Western Schism of the Roman Catholic Church has ended and there is now just a single Supreme Pontiff.[4] But the criticisms propounded by John Wycliffe and the Lollard movement have taken root and persist, particularly in the north of the country, into the early part of the next century. The name 'lollards' comes from the Dutch word meaning 'to mutter' and was likely applied to the sect because they continually read from the scriptures in their worship. They sought a simpler, evangelical lifestyle close to that lived by Jesus and anticipated Martin Luther and the Reformation. Their message was an attack on practices within the church that they beleived did not properly reflect the Law of God. So, the transubstantiation of wine and wafer into the actual blood and body of Christ; the sale or adoration of relics; penance; excommunication; indulgences; all came under fire and contested the divinity of the Pope and the income of the Church. As heretics, they were particularly pursued by Henry V and driven underground.

The Statutes of Provisors and Premunire were a cause of friction between Rome and England. These Acts of Parliament were passed between 1306 and 1351 but were now so widely applied as to affect both the capacity of the Pope to gain income and to exert unrestrained authority within the English church. Appointments to church benefices or the transfer from one post to another (called 'translations') were exclusively the gift of the papacy and, particularly at the level of bishop or archbishop, could generate some very attractive 'fees'. The filling of ecclesiastical benefices was now increasingly made by the English church independent of papal direction: in particular, this created a career path in which the Crown could promote and reward its brightest officials within the civil service. One effect was to reduce, if not eliminate, the appointment of bishops from overseas or with overseas allegiances. The premunire laws made it an offence to appeal to or obey a foreign court or authority, as this would challenge the supremacy of the Crown. Thus, papal jurisdiction in England was diminished.

In 1427, the Bishop of Winchester is elevated to Cardinal by the Pope. This brings him under attack from Gloucester once again. There is an argument that a man should not hold the rank of a cardinal and a bishop at the same time. To do so would put him in potential conflict between his obligation to the Pope and to the Crown. There was some precedent for this argument from 1278 and 1368, when the archbishopric of Canterbury had been resigned on the incumbent taking up cardinalship. The application of this argument so alarmed Henry Beaufort, who feared possible impeachment as a traitor, that it steered him to avoid trouble with Parliament by resigning the Chancellorship.

None of all this impacts on ordinary lives in rural Dorset though, as much as the economy and the weather.

The manorial system is in terminal decline and coming towards its end in many if not most parts of the country. Leasehold, or copyhold, becomes the new relationship, whereby the lord of the manor receives rent instead of customary services. The old villein or cottager becomes a waged labourer, many moving away to the towns. This is accelerated as sheep farming leads to the enclosure of arable land for pasture and to consequent widespread evictions. These are the most radical changes in society for the past 500 years and enable the rising power of the gentry.

The structural changes within society have been brought about by the decline in population resulting from the Pestilence, which started in the middle of the previous century and continued as sporadic outbreaks throughout the 1400s.[5] Adult life expectancy is shortened until the middle of the next century. The population decline is particularly noticeable in Dorset relative to its neighbours, and its recovery is slower. This was certainly within the purview of the Mortons, as the upheavals brought about the desertion of forty-two villages in their county.

As the workforce shrank and labour costs rose, marginal land was taken out of cultivation and given over to pasture. By 1450, the arable area in the country had shrunk by a third.[6] Output of all crops fell in the first half of the fifteenth century, not helped by some extreme weather events, and Gross Domestic Product fell. Prices were rising but real wages, especially outside the towns, fell. Poverty and starvation were the result.

The production and export of wool, for so long the bedrock of English prosperity, was in decline. The production of cloth, however, was very much in the ascendancy, its lifeblood in cottage industry, and north Dorset, in the Shaftesbury area and on towards Salisbury, gained a reputation for it.

The challenges of these changes on the community, the landscape, and the national spirit would have been picked up on by John Morton. His core conservatism would not deter his intellect from seeking to understand the dynamic of what was happening – and seek to put it to profitable use.

In the spring of 1435, changes occurred in the Morton family. With the supporting escort of brothers John and Richard, William walks the short distance from Manor Farm to the church. It is his wedding day. He is fifteen years old. His bride is fourteen.[7] She is also in early pregnancy.[8] In their footsteps, the rest of the family follow, together with friends and those who cannot not be invited. Everyone is in good humour. The marriage has been arranged between the families and would not have been formalised for a while yet, but the accelerated timetable has evidently suited the respective, as well as the prospective, parents.

On this joyful day, the groom and his family entourage gather around the vicar of St Andrew's at the church porch. The sound of Morris Men's bells, whistles, drums, and sticks beating time herald the bridal party, led by one of the dancers holding high a branch of rosemary, an aid to remembering the marriage vows. Those vows are exchanged in front of all, and the groom presents a simple ring to his bride. All then enter the nave of the church where a table is laid out with drinks for everyone, alongside the bride's dowry and guests' gifts.

By evening, the wedding feast and celebrations held at the Manor Farm have concluded and, to much noise and acclaim, the married couple had been sent off to their bedroom. The boisterous games continue unabashed, increased ale consumption making up for any departing guests.

It is also at this time that the path to John Morton's future opens up. While his brothers seem well suited and content with a farming life, John has long shown a restless ambition for wider horizons and more cerebral challenges, and these have not been discouraged by his parents. In particular, he aspires to a career in law, which, at this time, requires admission to the priesthood.

Family discussions have determined that although the route to university and the legal profession necessitates becoming a priest, becoming a monk would be too restrictive of future possibilities. So it is that John's father has been in communication with his landlord, Abbot John Winterbourne at Cerne, and he is happy for John to attend the abbey to receive tuition to bring his education up to the standard required for university entrance. His actual placement in the abbey is deferred until the following year to help the family construct an extension to house William and his new family and to fill gaps in the farm's workload, which his brother's distractions as a new husband and father will inevitably entail.

When the time is right, Abbot Winterbourne agrees to sponsor Morton's application to Oxford, at a college of his choosing, even though the abbey itself is Benedictine. Cerne Abbey is only thirteen miles from Milborne Styleham, so Morton can be released from time to time for home visits – particularly at key points on the farming calendar.

Other than a few visits to Bere, where his maternal grandparents live, Cerne is the furthest John has travelled from home and this is his first experience of being free from family life. There are occasional pangs of homesickness. To his surprise, he particularly misses playing with his nephew Robert, William's son, and seeing him grow up. There is a close bond between John and his nephew, which develops and holds right through their adult lives. But the shining compensation for these losses is the unrestricted access he enjoys to the abbey's notable library of books and manuscripts. Not least among these are the muniments setting out the abbey's land rights and privileges, their rents, and services due, and all those matters which make up practical property law as it affects the clergy.

He is soon settled in to life within the abbey's cloistered community and takes comfort in deferring his move from home as the severe three-month winter from December 1435 had made his services particularly valuable to the family. Not that winters over the next few years will be any kinder. Hard frosts cause buildings to collapse and even the River Thames freezes over. There are violent storms, food shortages, plague and an earthquake. But abbey life provides shelter from the worst of these ravages.

He was greeted on arrival by a new abbot, John Godmanston, Abbot Winterbourne having died shortly before Morton's journey up from Milborne Styleham.[9] Abbot Godmanston will be invaluable in planning Morton's learning programme whilst at the abbey and promoting him to Oxford. There is no entrance examination to the university, only recommendation. The relationship with the abbey will be valued throughout his life and his life entrusted to it on at least one occasion.

The black habit of the Benedictine monks was by far the most widely recognised of all the brotherhoods. Someone seeking to be admitted into the order would be required to undertake five years' conversion before final vows could be taken. Life as a Benedictine was strict in that it was based on obedience, self-sufficiency, self-denial, and a regular routine. But it was also liberal in its outlook compared to many other cloisters and provided a self-supporting community founded on worship, manual labour, and study.

For John, the day would normally start with a service (Prime) at around 06:00; although the monks would have started their day at 02:00. There would then be further services at 09:00 (Tierce), 12:00 (Sext), 15:00 (Nones), 18:00 (Vespers), and at 21:00 (Compline), after which all would retire to bed. Meals were built around this routine. The first meal taken sitting down was directly after the mid-day service and was called 'prandium' or 'early dinner'. Taken in the refectory, the food would be plentiful and varied, sourced from the abbey's grounds. Up until the noon meal, time would be spent in manual labour: farming, gardening, cooking, cleaning, and repairing. Gardening, growing fruits, vegetables, and herbs will engage John for his lifetime. Cultivating fruits such as damsons, gooseberries, strawberries, medlars and raspberries proves particularly satisfying, as well as medicinal herbs such as absinthe, catnip, henbane and mandrake. After prandium, John would undertake lessons in grammar and languages until Nones. That would be followed by refreshment – perhaps a glass of beer and a piece of bread. Some discussion of scripture or philosophy might take the afternoon through to Vespers, which preceded supper, a meal similar to prandium. Then, a couple of hours reading before Compline and the day's end. Tomorrow will be the same. As will tomorrow. And tomorrow.

At Cerne, John cemented his love for an orderly existence and communal society where the reassurance of ritual and repetition provided a framework for constructive meditation. At the same time though, that very predictability in life reinforced his yearning for engagement with the wider world to test his skills and ambition. He became fluent in Latin and French. He learned the finer points of debate and rhetoric. Skills in organisation were honed. Basics of property and church law were assimilated. He was ready for the challenge of university.

True to his word, Abbot Godmanston recommended Morton to Balliol College and, now in his early twenties, he is accepted there to begin studies in law, both civil and canon. There are other links to Oxford University. It is a patron of the living of Bere (close to home and where his mother hales from) and also of Winterbourne-Kingston, which is where the late Abbot Winterbourne came from. Such ties, no matter how loose, carry weight in these times.

And, of course, Henry V's brother Humphrey of Gloucester was educated at Balliol, which adds to its attractiveness. It also boasted, if that is the right word, the heretic and enemy of monasteries John Wycliffe as a sometime Master.[10] Both alumni spoke of the college's reputation for a humanist approach to education, particularly alluring to Morton's aspirations in law.

4

Early Oxford Days

They would have talked about the possibility of journeying by water: Weymouth wasn't far away for a boat to London and then up the Thames to Oxford. But overland by horse was preferred. The journey from Milborne St Andrew to the university was just over a hundred miles and normally took four to five days, depending on the weather and state of the highway or lane travelled. Morton was alert to the benefits of maximising free time in the city to accustom himself to his new environment, and – never being one to hide his light under a bushel – early arrival might offer an opportunity to acquaint himself with some key academics without alienating his peers. In short, he was both excited and anxious.

He would travel light, with a single change of clothing, a cape and cap, and some money to see him through his early terms. Balliol College provides a bursary which includes board within the college hall (a bed in shared rooms for which he must supply mattress, pillow, and blankets, forwarded on in a chest also containing extra clothing).

New landscapes and passing towns and villages hold his attention. The route is reasonably straightforward: the Dorchester road to Salisbury and Old Sarum, north and east in the direction of Silchester but striking off due north at Highclere Castle to the university town. Morton is soon able to join up with other travellers on the road and, for mutual safety, they journey together. Not quite a Chaucerian band, they become strung out from time to time but keep well in sight of each other. Along the way he no doubt ruminates upon the significant changes of the past few years and how these may determine the agendas and controversies he will engage with in his new life.

He had learned of shifts in the balance of power and changes in policy. The Duke of Bedford had died back in 1435 at the time of the collapse of the Anglo-Burgundian alliance and a new accord between Burgundy and the French crown and Armagnac group. This made Humphrey, Duke of Gloucester, heir presumptive at forty-five years of age. But his aggressive policies against France lose out to the peace negotiations favoured by the sixty-year-old Bishop of Winchester. This shift had been supported by the assumption of full royal powers by the pacific sixteen-year-old Henry VI in 1437. Pragmatic diplomacy was also a result of the fall of Paris to Charles VII the previous year, and the re-cementing of the 'auld alliance' between Scotland and France giving the former confidence for border raids on the northern marches.[1] Although early English setbacks are countered, claims on the French throne cannot be continued long through lack of military or financial capacity.[2] For now, a truce is reached between England and France.

He also considers other news broadcast across the country that same year. Queen Catherine, the King's mother, had died in Bermondsey Abbey aged only thirty-six; apparently in childbirth but also due to stress because her secret husband, Owen Tudor, had been seized by Humphrey of Gloucester and imprisoned on the grounds that the marriage (made, in 1429 and producing six children) was unlawful and potentially traitorous. King Henry was unforgiving of Gloucester for the treatment of his mother and went on not only to pardon Owen and confer knighthood on him, but also took responsibility for the education and welfare of his two half-brothers, Edmund and Jasper.[3] The generation of Henry V was fast slipping away.

The weather is kind, the way is good, rider and horse are strong, and they sight Oxford on the fourth day. Its size and its accumulation of churches meet expectations, but the diorama soon deteriorates with the decay and desolation outside the town walls. Post-plague regrowth has been slow. Oxford is no longer a meeting place for the great councils of state, and it has lost its position as the high point for navigation on the Thames to Henley. Its importance as a county and market town has substantially declined and, with that, its population, prosperity, and the demand for property. Only the university is of significance, and it is the university that controls the town.

Not only that, but the number of students within the university has also fallen dramatically and although now recovering, is a little over 1,000, not counting an additional couple of thousand 'grammar-school boys'. This deficit in the number of students required to keep government and church supplied with capable administrators is of concern to the state institutions and is no doubt why Morton has effectively received a free scholarship which would otherwise have been received by someone whose family was less able to provide support. The bishops in convocation in 1438 have called upon the patrons of benefices to give preference to university graduates to help stimulate entrance not only to colleges but also to grammar schools. Education for advancement is Oxford's main industry. But the university does itself provide employment and its wage levels are good for good staff.

Morton's first responsibility on arriving at Balliol would be to attend to his horse, paddocks and stable block being found off Broad Street, which the college fronts, and up Magdalen Street. That done, he can then pass through the college grounds, which provide gardens, walks, and areas for socialising and contemplation, to seek out his accommodation.

Balliol has a history going back over 150 years, founded in 1282 by the dowager Lady Dervorguilla in memory of her husband John de Balliol, with traditions, rights and rules that are jealously and stringently imposed and enforced.[4]

Within the college grounds is a small stone chapel with leaded roof. Balliol has its own priest, and students are expected to hear Mass each day. Meals are taken in a separate refectory: basic except on high days, but good sustenance – or so it is promised. There are Bible readings at each meal to add a little seasoning to the fare and aid digestion. All conversation between students and teachers is in Latin. The gates are locked from nine in the evening to eight in the morning – which reduces the opportunities for mischief both by college residents and those without.

If not on this stroll through the grounds then most likely on one in the next few days, Morton would have the opportunity to meet the class of important contemporaries he was anxious to get acquainted with, such as Archdeacon William Grey, Richard Bole, and Nicholas Saxton, Fellows of Balliol all seeking their Doctorates.[5]

Grey, in particular, is a rising star for Morton to watch, who has a yearning for Chancellorship of the University. Archdeacon Grey's father was Sir Thomas Grey, one of those executed for plotting the murder of Henry V at his embarkation from Southampton to France and Agincourt. Yet his position is restored notwithstanding the treachery in his family, and he is impressively wealthy.

Whatever the course of Morton's passage through the college grounds he would arrive in the front quadrangle, giving access to the library, the Master's residence, the Fellows' rooms, and the main hall – where most of his work will be undertaken. Finally, there is Old Balliol Hall, which provides the student quarters.

Off the Hall's passageway is Morton's modest room, shared with three others. The room is occupied by four bed frames and each occupant's chest and little else. Underneath their beds students stow away their sword and dagger as they are prohibited from being worn on college grounds. With the general mediaeval aversion to daily washing and periodic flatulence from student diets the close confines would not prove particularly enjoyable.

Morton would first check the content of the large chest which preceded his arrival and remove the bed clothes, then fill his mattress with straw from a communal supply outside the Hall. His attention would then turn to his gown – known as a cappa clausa – which he dons. Surely stiffening to a pose of moral and physical rectitude he takes the measure of what is now his daily garb. As its name suggests, it is a closed cape save for slits for the arms to come through. Full length, of a sober black cloth, it also has benefit of a hood with a short liripipe, a kind of tail, to keep it in position. He surely feels the moment to be significant.

His final task of induction would be to meet the Master of the college who had his own lodging house on the other side of the quadrangle. In fact, this proved to be just a single room, though big enough to accommodate a large bed, a desk doubling as a dining table, and a scattering of wooden chairs and stools around a sizeable fireplace.

The Master is William Brandon who provides Morton with a formal welcome to Balliol and administers the prescribed oaths requiring students to live to the rules and standards of the college, after which they discuss John's study plan and the generalities of college life.

In particular, Master Brandon would hold forth on one of the particular worries facing the university's administration, but also students generally. Not only the university but also government are concerned that too many see Oxford simply as a stepping-stone to the continental universities and higher preferment (this would include Messrs Grey, Bole and Saxton). There were also unhealthy and often violent rivalries and feuds in Oxford to be avoided. These could be between town and students, northerners and southerners, the religious colleges versus the secular, art students versus jurists. Rather than any real differences of opinion or ideals, they more often than not came down to young men needing to assert their position in the pack, leaving aside their intellect and fuelling their fire with fermented apples or barley.

Morton would also be warned to guard against voices criticising the university, and indeed Balliol, for conservatism and a slow take up of the ideas flowing from the Italians, French, and Germans. This was not because the administrators are deaf and blind to them, but because of a perceived need to re-establish Oxford's reputation for orthodoxy. Oxford scholars are regarded with suspicion by the church when it comes to awarding preferments and the Henrician government is also wary of new thought. This is a direct consequence of Oxford's association with the ideas promulgated by Wycliffe and his followers, the Lollards. So, while novel and testing ideas are nourishment within the colleges, the policy is not to air them outside. At least, not until Oxford's standing within society at large is stable. Whilst the university does have many liberal friends within government, such as Archbishop Chicheley and the Duke of Gloucester, overall, those holding power do not like change or the unorthodox.

This sort of thinking is in line with Morton's instincts. He draws both strength and comfort from the known and certain. He also believes that the operation of law depends on all trusting in that certainty and stability. So, it is essential that practitioners of law hold the common trust in its administration. Laws may need to be refined or changed to reflect changes in society, but they need that basic understanding and acceptance to be effective.

Brandon would also induct Morton into the ways the university is run. Oxford scholars have immunity from lay jurisdiction, and the Chancellor, or his deputy, deal with all matters criminal and civil concerning students excepting murder and riot. In many respects the university's powers are greater than those of the town.

The Chancellor is elected, usually for a term of two years, by an assembly of teaching or regent masters or who meet collectively as a Congregation, which is the supreme governing body. The Congregation has evolved into two groups who meet separately as well as together. The largest faculty in the university is that of the arts. They have the highest number of masters and are generally younger than their peers in the other faculties. They make up what is known as the Black Congregation and, not unnaturally, seek collectively to impose themselves on decision making. The balance of the Congregation is made up of the faculties of theology, civil law, canon law, and medicine.

Under the Chancellor are two Proctors. These are elected annually. They supervise teaching, examinations, organise ceremonial life, police the university, administer finance and draw up annual accounts. They are the wheels which keep the university in motion. The Proctors then have agents, their Beadles, who are also elected by the Congregation. The Chancellor's deputy is appointed from time to time to help process cases before his court. The deputy is known as the Commissary, or sometimes vice-Chancellor.

As for the structuring of Morton's course, the degree Bachelor is to provide proof of a grounding in grammar, logic, rhetoric, and mathematics. Over the next twelve months he will practise disputations with his fellow students on a range of topics. Then he will be examined at Responsions, when he will present a thesis on an agreed theme. Finally, the determination of the degree will follow attendance at a set of lectures on set books.

After that he would then be able to seek a Master of Arts degree. The last piece of advice he would receive from this interview would be to work hard, avoid distractions, keep physically fit – Oxford being prone to damp air and mists – which is precisely what Morton intended doing.

Life as a student was not easy. Morton would share a bedroom with three others, sleeping on his straw-filled mattress. The food they had was poor. Bread was often bad in substance, colour, and taste. Beer was weak and sometimes unfit for human consumption. Food such as fish or meat could be three or four days old. In the town, overpricing was common. Keeping the body fit, healthy and nourished took clever planning.

But head down, chin up, both at the same time, and he sails through his Bachelor degree to gain acceptance to begin a course for a MA degree at the age of twenty-three.

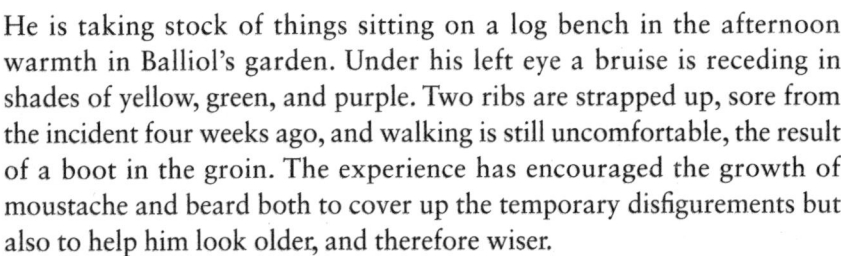

The Making of a Lawyer: Oxford, 1447

He is taking stock of things sitting on a log bench in the afternoon warmth in Balliol's garden. Under his left eye a bruise is receding in shades of yellow, green, and purple. Two ribs are strapped up, sore from the incident four weeks ago, and walking is still uncomfortable, the result of a boot in the groin. The experience has encouraged the growth of moustache and beard both to cover up the temporary disfigurements but also to help him look older, and therefore wiser.

Coming towards the last parts of his studies for the Master's degree, Morton had been surprised and moved to find himself, at twenty-nine, nominated by Chancellor Robert Thwaites to the position of Commissary (or vice-Chancellor), which he took up in late 1446 under the new Chancellor Gilbert Kymer. Kymer was a physician and was Dean of Wimborne Minster in Dorset. He had a distinguished academic career being a past proctor of the university, Principal of Hart Hall, and twice Chancellor of Oxford. He would go on to become Dean of Salisbury Cathedral, and from being physician to Humphrey of Gloucester to physician for Henry VI in 1455.

The chief task of the vice-Chancellor was to sit giving judgement in the Chancellor's Court. Much of this work was administrative: for example, processing and determining wills and probate. An early case, though slightly out of the ordinary, offered little promise of excitement. But excitement it surely delivered. It concerned a matter of precedence between the arts and law faculties, reflecting the gradual decline in dominance of the Black Congregation in the administration of university affairs. The case for the law faculty was presented with some passion by William Vowell and Edmund Martyn who were expecting a favourable decision from Morton, as his ambitions for a law career were well known.[1] Acting against those expectations was Morton's ensconcement in the status quo unless clear evidence proved it unsound, and his refusal to put personal preference before his sense of justice. Obscene cries of anger prefaced Vowell and then Martyn leaping across the Chancellor's bench to bring Morton to the floor, laying into him with fist and foot.

The Court bailiffs pulled the belligerents away as quickly as possible, leaving Morton not only physically hurt but shaken, confounded that seemingly intelligent men could react with violence over what was in essence a matter of form rather than principle.

The two have now been brought back before him. As they are close to completing their degrees, he decides not to send them down, but they are fined both to cover his medical fees and as punishment. The fine totals thirty-three shillings and four pence – the equivalent of nine weeks' wages for a skilled labourer.

Morton's garden contemplations are fuelled by, rather than focussed on, this incident. The anger, frustration, intolerance, are not unique but appear to be a growing reflection of and reaction to changes and disappointments in society that show few signs of resolution. Other than fight in an increasingly futile French war, there are no obvious logical outlets for an alpha-male.

At the commencement of Morton's path to a Master's degree, violence among Oxford students had been rife, perhaps no more so than in August 1441 when 60 well-armed southerners raided White Hall in Turl Street, which mainly accommodated northerners. The window of Master William Wytham, a Doctor of Law, was smashed and when he opened the college door to cries of 'Scottish dogs!' 200 arrows were allegedly fired into it.

The following day, the university Chancellor and the town mayor called for calm but come early afternoon, two groups clashed at Broadgates and many of the southerners were beaten up if they did not flee into hiding. Another group of southerners and Welshmen were chased by northern vigilantes, killing one by an arrow through the neck. There were similar disturbances in London and elsewhere – as if coordinated. It was certainly a time when the mind could construct conspiracy theories. Not least because of what happened the preceding month.

The supernatural was taken seriously. Pre-Christian beliefs, nearly 1500 years on, continued to gnaw at men's minds. Where the church could adopt, adapt, and exploit ancient customs and superstitions, they were tolerated. Where it could not, their manifestation became witchcraft.

So, holy relics obtained superpowers and became fetishes. Man-made images of holy figures could provide miraculous cures. The worship of saints reached such an intensity as to bring compliance with the Second Commandment into doubt. The mysticism of the Mass manipulated and massaged. These displays of superstition represented conformity.

The 'old ways' were frowned upon, but in England, unlike mainland Europe, witchcraft was rarely subject to serious punishment. The notion of a witch making a pact with the Devil for her powers developed in the late Middle Ages through the Roman church: but England was outside Roman law and had no Inquisition. It was not until the 16th century that a more intolerant attitude took hold, witchcraft being made a statutory offence in 1542. If dabbling with witchcraft and the supernatural led to more heinous crimes though, then the civil law could swing firmly into action.

By 1440, the influence of Humphrey, Duke of Gloucester, was waning as the warlike stance of his late brother Henry, from whom he had taken up the baton, also lost favour in the face of the more non-combative, diplomatic philosophy of the new king and those closest to him. He had become an anachronism, and his enemies were squaring up to remove him. And the rug was to be pulled from under his feet by his wife.

Eleanor Cobham was Humphrey's second wife. It was not a marriage that was popular with the populace. His first marriage to Jacqueline of Hainault in 1422 fizzled out three years later when Humphrey failed to wrest her territory from the Duke of Burgundy and he returned alone to England to begin an affair with Eleanor, a lady-in-waiting to his wife. The marriage to Jacqueline was annulled in 1428 and Humphrey wed Eleanor.

Not only was the manner of the marriage disapproved of, but Eleanor proved to be arrogant and ambitious even by the standards of 15th-century aristocracy. When John, Duke of Bedford died in 1435, Humphrey became heir presumptive to the throne, which meant that Eleanor stood in line to be queen. Anxious to discover if and when she might be queen, she sought the astrological skills of three of her household, who forecast that Henry would become ill in 1441 and she would indeed be crowned. Added to this, she obtained potions from a renowned witch, Margery Jourdemayne – the Witch of Eye – to ensure she could provide Humphrey with an heir.[2]

This reached the ears of the King's court. How, it is not clear. The three men involved were all clerics, illustrating how close the supernatural could be to orthodox religion, although astrology was perceived as a science rather than superstition. Roger Bolingbroke, an Oxford scholar, was Eleanor's personal clerk; Thomas Southwell was her personal physician and a canon of St Stephen's, Westminster; and John Home was her chaplain and canon of Hereford. The fate of the first two was not good, but Home received a pardon and continued to hold his position at Hereford until his death in 1473. Was it he who leaked the conspiracy? Perhaps to Gloucester's great adversary, William de la Pole, the Duke of Suffolk, an ally of Cardinal Beaufort?

The three were interrogated by Suffolk and by John Beaufort, Duke of Somerset. Eleanor took sanctuary in Westminster Abbey but was forced out. At her trial she implicated the Witch of Eye who had form, having been released from a charge of witchcraft ten years previously on her word that she would desist from the practice. For seeking the death of the King, Bolingbroke was hung drawn and quartered. Southwell took poison in the Tower of London before the death sentence was carried out. Margery was burnt at the stake. Eleanor had to do three days public penance after which her marriage to Humphrey was annulled, her property made forfeit, and she was moved from prison to prison until her death in 1457. And Humphrey's standing was irreparably undermined.

The scandal was talked about extensively in Oxford over many years, not least because Thomas Southwell had a close relationship with the present Chancellor, Gilbert Kymer. They had been joint petitioners for the foundation of a London college of physicians and surgeons back in 1423 and on its formation in 1424, Kymer was its first Master and Southwell one of its two wardens.

As Gloucester's position declined, the old warrior class, or 'patriotic party', became embodied in Richard, Duke of York. In many ways he was the iconic magnate of the Middle Ages. Charismatic, courageous, uncompromising, unpleasant, murderous, born of a father who lost his head and destined to lose his own. He also fathered so many children that it is a wonder he had time to involve himself in warfare. Seven survived to adulthood out of thirteen that were legitimate. Though that tally was far behind that of his father-in-law, Ralph Neville, Earl of Westmorland, who had twenty-three legitimate children, albeit from two wives.

Richard was the richest man in the country next to the king. He was Earl of March, with land in most counties but concentrated on the Welsh border – the 'march'. He was also Earl of Ulster with lordships in Clare, Connaught, and Trim in County Meath. He was able to retain the lands of his traitorous father the Earl of Cambridge, and then following the death of his uncle at Agincourt took the dukedom of York. In 1436, two years before he married, his annual income was as much as £7,000; Henry VI's lands were producing £8,400 a year.

He was twenty-seven years old when he married Cecily Neville, 'the Rose of Raby', in 1438. She was aged twenty-three, with a fiery temper and a renowned ego. They were a good match.

Richard had strong hereditary links to Edward III. His mother, Anne Mortimer, was a direct descendant of Edward's second son, Lionel, Duke of Clarence. His father was the son of Edward's fourth surviving son, Edmund Duke of York. Cecily's mother was Joan Beaufort, daughter of John of Gaunt, Edward's third son and Henry VI's great-grandfather. His claim to the throne would eventually and fatally eat into him.

York's first major appointment was in 1436 as Lieutenant of France, shortly after the death of the Duke of Bedford. Underfunded, inexperienced, he was out of his depth and could only watch the loss of Paris and so asked to be released from the command. Returning to England he became part of the Duke of Gloucester's party, their values being those of Edward III and Henry V. In 1441 he was reinstated as Lieutenant of France, but the Council had little confidence in him, although they were too fearful of his rank and power to recall him. They decided to send over John Beaufort, Duke of Somerset, commanding a large army which not only undermined York's efforts and authority but, adding insult to injury, Somerset had received £25,000 towards his costs while York was funding his army from his own pocket. Somerset proved to be a complete incompetent and in 1444 returned home in disgrace and committed suicide. York burnished an unending hatred of the Beaufort clan and their party together with everything they stood for as a result.

The 'peace party' represented by Cardinal Beaufort was more in tune with the mind of Henry VI and, as a result, held dominance at Council. Henry was deeply religious, paying much more than lip service to Christian values, unlike most of his peers – and that includes the non-secular. He was also prudish and squeamish, but he had moral fortitude. As with most men of power, particularly those with absolute power, he was receptive to those who put forward proposals which aligned with his own thinking and embraced them as friends. Nonetheless, he tried to keep everyone content whatever their position. His tragedy would be that the several antagonists within his Council could not be reconciled even if they had such a potential disposition in their character.

As Gloucester's influence declined because he was out of step, and out of favour, Beaufort's influence and capacity declined because of his age and health. In 1445 he was seventy-one. The man who would replace him as leader of the 'peace party' was William de la Pole, Earl (later Duke) of Suffolk, thirty-nine years old at that time. For a proponent of peace, Suffolk had an impressive military background, having fought for seventeen years in France for both Henry V and Henry VI. But he had concluded that England's position in France was unsustainable and that the country's long-term interests would be best served by withdrawing on well negotiated terms to establish strong trading relations with its neighbour across the Channel. Sadly, Suffolk's diplomatic skills fell short of his military ones. He had ability but was short on wisdom. In particular, he failed to grasp that as England's military position weakened, so the French willingness to make peace weakened. And, like many royal favourites, he aimed too high and would pay the price. Charming and intelligent, he was also manipulative, vindictive, scheming, self-seeking, and murderous.

In 1442, Henry attained his majority and being twenty-one years old it was decided that he needed a wife; for the sake of peace, a French wife. Suffolk and his close colleague Adam de Moleynes, Dean of Salisbury, went to France in search of a suitable bride, but Charles VII was not interested in a match between Henry and one of his own daughters: instead, Margaret, daughter of Rene, Duke of Anjou and self-styled King of Sicily, Naples, and Hungary, was put forward.[3] Suffolk and Moleynes 'negotiated' the terms for a marriage, which were revealed to be for little more than a two-year truce and no dowry of any substance, as Rene may have had titles, but he had no money.

Henry and Margaret were betrothed by proxy in 1444 and Suffolk used his time not only to brief Margaret on her new home but also to ingratiate himself with her as a friend, in order to strengthen his access to the King. She is coached, if not groomed.

When Margaret of Anjou arrived in England in 1445 for her marriage and coronation, she was only fifteen years old. Brought up in Italy, she is an attractive blonde, intelligent, well versed in languages, self willed, and strong in temperament. Henry and the Council were pleased. So much so that Suffolk was elevated to the rank of marquess, enabling him to take precedence over the other earls. He was also awarded the wardship of Lady Margaret Beaufort, the late Duke of Somerset's two-year-old daughter (who will become the mother of Henry VII). Moleynes was also rewarded, being translated to Bishop of Chichester.

By settling the marriage without first resolving the peace issue, Suffolk displayed his weakness at diplomacy. He returned home with a penniless bride for his king and merely the prolongation of a truce for his country. That is not to say anyone could have done better, but those who seek applause when things go right must take the blows when things go wrong. And things did go wrong.

With or without the knowledge or consent of the King, but certainly without the knowledge of Council, Suffolk and Moleynes attempted to gain better terms for a peace by engaging in secret discussions with the

French for returning Maine and Anjou to them. Suffolk had been the custodian of the Duke of Orleans and had developed a friendship with Orleans' illegitimate son, the Count of Dunois, and considered them as allies to broker a peace.

This came to little, though, other than extending the truce into 1447, while Henry promised to release Maine and Le Mans. Both sides procrastinate and frustrations give way to a rearmament for fresh hostilities.

Margaret is perceived as a potent part of the peace process and when it is seen to flounder she loses favour with the people. She will also be cast as an instigator of the resignation of English lands to France. This is a misplaced criticism. She is aware that it is the wish of her husband and his key advisers to secure peace and rid themselves of the cost of maintaining estates which produce no income. She would be aware that loss of these lands, if they were supporting the English treasury, would act against her personal interests. Her support and advocacy of the policy seems rational and proper for a queen in an age when women are considered by most men to be, as Aristotle put it, 'defective males'.

She is fiercely partisan by nature. The growing weakness of Henry, both physically and mentally, sees the Lancastrian party build around her as being the best route to the King. Suffolk leads this party along with Edmund Beaufort, 2nd Duke of Somerset, Lord Scales, Lord Saye, and the Bishop of Salisbury. She will take all steps to guard the rights of the Crown and crush those who are held up to be her husband's enemies.

She is also aware, and made to be aware, that until she produces an heir for Henry then the Duke of Gloucester is still next in line to the throne.

Suffolk is alive to the necessity for him to crush the war party if his peace plans, which require surrender of French lands, are to go through. The first step is to remove Gloucester. Using Margaret and the members of his circle within Council, Suffolk poisons Henry's mind against his uncle, and from 1446 Gloucester no longer attends Council meetings. By the next year, Gloucester is completely isolated and at the Bury St Edmunds parliament is accused of treason by Suffolk, Moleynes, and others of their party. He is arrested and three days later dies of an alleged stroke: 'the son of a king, brother of a king, and uncle of a king' was apparently overcome by shame and grief – though rumours suggested Suffolk had a hand in poisoning him or having him suffocated under a pile of feather mattresses.

Gloucester's illegitimate son, Arthur Plantagenet, is also arrested and is convicted of treason. It is clear to anyone, even Henry, that this is a trumped-up charge, and he is pardoned. Though by July he is dead: poisoned. Gloucester's lands go mainly to Margaret. The next requirement will be to see that Richard of York is out of the circle of influence.

A few weeks later, Cardinal Beaufort dies at Winchester.

As Vice-Chancellor of the university, Morton receives both real news together with rumour and gossip on the shifting political world soon after the event. This is particularly so when the subject of the news is a great benefactor of Oxford, such as Humphrey of Gloucester. He and his colleagues are also aware of the growing favour of Cambridge university with the house of Lancaster and its purse.

As his knowledge of contemporary politics deepens, so does his concern for the future. As long as the Crown is secure and respected, and the rule of law prevails, then he has confidence that divisions will heal.

Although the country is troubled, the Morton family prospers. William Morton has gained a second son, Thomas. John's brother Richard has also married. His wife is Edith Turberville. Although of the same surname as the Mortons' mother, Elizabeth is not so closely related as to precipitate any claim of consanguinity. But thoughts of home are suppressed by the need to focus now on achieving his Master's degree.

Rising and Falling Tides: Oxford, 1448–1452

John Morton's delight in gardening is lifelong and he is to be found sitting on his favoured bench within Balliol's gardens, a place in which he secretes himself regularly for contemplative solitude. The college chapel or any one of Oxford's prolific churches would provide similar calm, possibly with greater privacy, but a consecrated building doesn't seem appropriate for thoughts which are not particularly religious. This is possibly the last occasion Morton will relax in this favourite spot.

It is 1448, and not only has Morton been awarded the degree of Master of Arts for civil law, but he has been ordained a priest. Not to put too fine a point on it, this latter decision opens the door to potential income and advancement which would not otherwise be possible. It is a firm foot across the threshold of the establishment. He may be admired for being honest and upright, but even he is self-aware of an avarice and ambition and can see no moral or practical reason for curbing those traits. If the meek are to inherit the earth they certainly need strong legal minds free from the temptations of corruption to plead their case.

Obtaining a Master's degree is no mean feat, taking eight years studying to regulations formalised in 1431. It requires a complete training in the seven sciences and three philosophies: grammar, rhetoric, logic, arithmetic, music, geometry, astronomy, and the natural, moral, and metaphysical philosophies.

To move forward and gain his doctorate requires some changes, chiefly motivated by the need to support himself financially. If he is to advance, he cannot do so as a pauper.

Balliol does not provide financial support to those taking a degree at doctorate level. That is the rule. As part of their Statute, it is, effectively, a rule written in stone. His Master's degree provides opportunity to gain some income from lecturing and teaching within the grammar school system and he also holds the position of proctor within the university, which allows him to practise law in the Chancellor's Court for the administration and resolution of local complaints. This leads him to secure a Fellowship with Peckwater Hall, the foremost school of civil law in Oxford.[1] The award of MA was followed by 'inception', the practical expression of one's achievement. This included attending a school, such as Peckwater, and delivering a series of lectures as a teaching or 'regent' master. Lectures were strictly on prescribed books and in a set manner. The text was read first, its meaning then explained, special passages noted, and questions then raised and discussed. All regent masters were required to lecture for two years after inception. During the same period, they also had to attend the university Congregation by which degrees were granted.

But when it comes to his Doctorate, Morton prefers to undertake this at the relatively new college of All Souls.[2] All Souls was founded only ten years before to commemorate the victims of the Hundred Years' War with France. It might be considered a high-risk decision by someone who appeared to be orthodox and conservative. Except that the founders of the college were possibly two of the most orthodox and conservative members of society: King Henry VI and Henry Chichele, Archbishop of Canterbury – two people Morton looked to in order to effect his advancement.

In addition to its founders' religious aims, the real attraction was its academic aim, which was to provide for advanced study in the higher degrees of theology, law (including 'canon' or church law), and medicine. Those admitted had to have had at least three years' study in another university college – so all were mature students, most with a bachelor's degree at minimum. The aim was to prepare its students for an active life in church or government: as Chichele put it 'an unarmed militia' to restore and maintain good order and a strong national identity. This perfectly mirrors Morton's own philosophy.

But government and the rule of law is falling apart.

Following the return to England of the Duke of York, the role of Lieutenant of France rested with Edmund Beaufort, which he held until 1449, being created Duke of Somerset in 1448 at the age of forty-two. Somerset was a cousin to both Henry and to York – the former he sought to control and the latter he hated unreservedly. Like his brother, the previous Duke of Somerset, Edmund seemed a magnet for failure.

He secured great patronage from Henry. Although Beaufort was the head of one of England's highest ranked families, his fortune was slight compared to, say, York. Henry bestowed on him many offices to bring his worth to about half of York's, but this only served to increase jealousy among his peers and more generally. He also managed to fall out with the Earl of Warwick, driving him and others of the Neville family towards York's side.

He was appointed to replace York as Commander in France in 1448 and the next year warfare erupted in Normandy. Subsequent military failures exposed him to criticism from the York camp: thirty fortified towns fall by the end of August. In part, this is caused by the failure of the military establishment to recognise that French artillery had made English archers outdated. The English had also become complacent. They had no intelligence operatives and believed their own mythology from earlier battles. Most humiliating was the surrender to the French in September of Rouen, the capital of Normandy, without even a token siege taking place. Harfleur was next, then lands in Anjou, Maine and all Normandy around the Seine. By the summer of 1450, nearly all the English possessions in northern France were lost and, by 1453, so would English possessions in southern France.

As so often with hated political figures, either the villain had his pedigree assailed or, failing that, personal scandalous behaviour would be broadcast. In the case of Somerset, he would be linked to illicit affairs with Henry VI's mother and then his wife. There seems little doubt that he could charm and turn a lady's head, but sexual liaison is difficult, if not impossible, to substantiate.

In England, the government is controlled by Suffolk and his party, and they have the Queen with them, pressing for the release of French lands. Somerset's succession of failures suggests to some that there may be a traitorous conspiracy here.

Criticism and sniping at Suffolk and Somerset originates with York and the Nevilles. So it is that the pressure to see York removed increases. Adam Moleynes, Bishop of Chichester, and now a Privy Councillor, openly accused York in parliament of defrauding soldiers in Normandy of their pay. York was able to prove this a lie by providing witness from accountants that disbursements had been properly made and by showing that Moleynes had bribed soldiers to give perjured substance to his claims. In the event, the Council was not going to come down on Moleynes as, essentially, he was speaking for them as a whole, but nor could they condemn York on an obviously trumped-up charge.

A means was at last constructed by Suffolk to rid the Privy Council of York's presence so that they could advance or even conclude their policies. York was 'promoted' to Lieutenant of Ireland. Duke Richard managed to defer setting off to Ireland for a year and a half but had to make the journey in 1449. He went with a large bodyguard, for Suffolk's agents, including Sir Thomas Stanley, were dispatched to despatch him. He reached Ireland nonetheless unharmed and found a good reception there, his governance ensuring a sound base of Yorkist support for future years.

The Suffolk party encouraged profiteering, oppression, and manipulation of the law against the interests of the gentry. Lawyers were employed to actively seek out defects in land titles and if that failed, then outright thuggery and violence were not shied away from. The perversion of the law, failure to pay returning soldiers (and sailors) from collapsing France, and the disintegration of law and order in many parts of the country expressed itself in riot and rebellion against a morally and financially bankrupt government.

York and his party were about to effect revenge.

The first to succumb is Adam de Moleynes. His failure to secure the impeachment of York, and his exposure to widespread criticism for the loss of French territory by his association with Suffolk, lead him to re-evaluate his position both as a politician and as a churchman. He decides to resign from the affairs of state in 1449 and go on a religious pilgrimage. His pilgrimage is to begin by taking a ship from Portsmouth. This is an unfortunate choice for embarkation. Portsmouth is suffering from the loss of trade with French ports and the town's economic malaise is squarely placed on the shoulders of Suffolk and his henchman, the malign Moleynes. He arrives on 9 January 1450 at the Hospital of Saint Nicholas and Saint John the Baptist, a well-known resting place for travellers and pilgrims entering or leaving the port.[3] Word soon spreads of his arrival and a large mob of angry residents, inflamed by agents of York, drag him from the building to butcher him on the beach.[4] Such is the desire for retribution for this murder of one of their own that the Privy Council secures the excommunication of the whole town by John Stafford, Archbishop of Canterbury. The crime is seen as so appalling that the excommunication is not lifted until 1509, almost sixty years later.

Next on the list for the chop, literally, is Suffolk. Other than the King and Queen, he has no support in Council or in parliament due to the widespread outcry against him and the policies which he had effected. That he has taken no actions without the agreement and consent of Council or parliament will not save him from the populist voice. So it is that less than three weeks after Moleynes' murder Suffolk is the subject of an impeachment petition from the Commons. By February he is indicted on eight charges, including conspiracy to depose Henry in favour of his own son John, criminal mismanagement of French affairs, and subverting justice. It is also said that he has met with the Count of Dunois (son of the Duke of Orleans) giving secrets of English defences in France to help the French recover their land in exchange for an invasion force to help Suffolk achieve his ambition at home. Charges of treason have little evidence to suggest credibility, but it is clear that parliament will insist on his execution: if only to excuse themselves. Henry intervenes and uses the royal prerogative to impose banishment for five years rather than see his friend and leading minister put to death.

Suffolk, silly man, escaping London by the skin of his teeth, waits six weeks within his castle at Wingfield before setting off to Calais from Ipswich. This is certainly long enough for York to be advised of his situation and for a plan of action to be put in place. Suffolk is intercepted by a small squadron of ships headed by *Nicholas of the Tower* ('of the Tower' being the contemporary equivalent to HMS, a royal ship). The *Nicholas* is commanded by Robert Wennington of Dartmouth. Suffolk is persuaded off his own ship, given a mock trial, and his head is then hacked off with half a dozen strokes of a rusty sword wielded by an Irishman (and so rumoured to be one of York's new followers).

Public fury at corruption in government is also aimed at corruption within the clergy. There was a general sense of hostility towards those bishops and others who provide no example of Christian values, who happily collect money from their see yet fail to visit their churches, preferring to stay attached to court life. One such is William Ayscough, Bishop of Salisbury, and a friend of Suffolk. He had joined Henry and Margaret in marriage. He was also one of the examiners of Eleanor Cobham and so associated with the fall of the Duke of Gloucester. So incensed are his 'flock' that on a rare visit to his diocese at Edington, he is dragged out of the church after finishing Mass and beaten to death.

At the same time, a more serious expression of discontent is taking place with the march of Kentish men on Blackheath, the doorstep to London. Under the nominal leadership of Jack Cade, this is no Peasants' Revolt but includes much support from the respectable middle-class, who are directing their protest towards oppressive and corrupt officials rather than landowners. They are also expressing grievance at the consequences from the loss of land in France which has seriously disrupted trade. Some 5,000 men make camp on the heath while their demands are conveyed to the King. It is not Henry's intention to give way to the mob, but he does make reconciliatory noises and goes so far as to set up a commission to root out any and all extortioners, traitors and villains, very much the action of a government's pretending to act. One apparent concession, though, is to arrest the universally detested James

Fiennes, Lord Saye and Sele, the government's treasurer and Warden of the Cinque Ports, and confine him to the Tower. Nerves within the establishment are very much on tenterhooks as Cade is styling himself 'John Mortimer', suggesting the presence of the Duke of York behind, or at least aligned with, the rebellion and flagging up his potential claim to the throne.[5]

None of the government's weak promises satisfy the rebels and they march through London, dragging out from custody Lord Saye and his son-in-law William Cromer, sheriff of Kent, to behead them and then mutilate their bodies.[6] This display of barbarity coupled with widespread looting turn the Londoners against Cade's cause and after some heavy night fighting the rioters disperse. Cade himself, tracked down and killed, is described as Irish born – again offering a link to York. He is further discredited posthumously as having murdered a pregnant woman, of dabbling in the occult, and of using several aliases.

There is general jubilation across the country at the fall of Suffolk, Ayscough (his murderers were given a royal pardon following public pressure), and Saye. Within the establishment, including church and academics, there is only concern at the total breakdown in law and order.

Sensible to the general situation, York returns to England and lands with a considerable force in Wales on 7 September and marches to London. Returning without the King's express permission, his action is not unreasonably viewed with high suspicion and is a direct confrontation between Lancastrian and Yorkist parties. Such is the level of alarm that Somerset is recalled from France and made Constable of England. The Council also sends out emissaries calling for its supporters to waylay and frustrate York's progress. One victim of this is Sir William Tresham, a former Speaker of the Commons, who is ambushed and murdered on his way to meet up with York.[7]

York evades his enemies and, advancing his purpose as that simply of a reformer loyal to the King, he arrives at London at the head of some 50,000 men on 27 September. Although he does not have the trust and support of the Lords, he does command a majority in the Commons and the goodwill of the people. This is more than can be said for Somerset, who has to be held in the Tower for his own safety.

York's position is strengthened by the election of his chamberlain Sir William Oldhall as Speaker of the Commons. He presses to regain his seat in the Council and is given a relatively minor post. He stands his ground as a reformer calling for better government and prosecution of those who lost northern France (meaning Somerset, whom he has determined to destroy). But his political credibility and trust in his motives remains weak. Somerset leaves the Tower in April and is invested as Captain of Calais. An attempt to get the Commons to name York as heir to the throne is treated with derision and the mover of the petition, Thomas Young, MP for Bristol, consigned to the Tower.[8] With no hope of advancing his cause, York sits tight in Ludlow Castle to the end of 1451. Plotting.

The university Congregation is in session. It is the very beginning of January, and a letter has been received from the Duke of York. A similar letter has been dispatched to the other leading towns and cities of England outlining the Duke's motivation for mobilising his troops to move on London, confront the King, and secure the removal of false advisors. The letter protests his loyalty to the King and calls on citizens not to be concerned for their safety or security. Of course, the effect is to create those concerns in no small measure.

Gilbert Kymer, Chancellor of the university, has read out the letter to all (though those present already know of its content). Kymer is visibly enraged by the letter and perhaps because his academic interests are medicine and theology, his lesser logic and legal instincts take him off course from time to time. His anger at this latest manifestation of the breakdown of order originates not only in his personal investment in helping restore orthodoxy but reflects that he is a dean of Salisbury cathedral and could have been present when Bishop Ayscough was murdered. As Kymer's Vice-Chancellor, Morton has to provide input as to how York's letter should be dealt with, his Chancellor being in obvious need of legal support.

The Congregation knows it is on dangerous ground and seeks to adopt a neutral position by considering the content of the letter in the context of its lawfulness rather than any sympathies or sensibilities to recent events, or any political partisanship held.

York's protests that his only intention is to see the removal of bad advisors and return the country to government which is honest and incorrupt make it clear that this includes the removal of Somerset at the least. The very fact that so large an army is being raised to present a petition suggests it is not being moved to London for reasons of safety but for reasons of intimidation and confrontation. Further, it is being raised and moved without consent or authority. Similarly, York's return from Ireland was without recall from the King and was not done to protect the crown but to enforce a petition which would restore the Duke to the Privy Council.

There is no evidence of overwhelming support for the Duke of York's position, least of all among his peers. He stands at the head of a minority. Avoiding judgement on conjecture and rumour, there is nonetheless a trail of circumstantial evidence to put all on alert that York's supporters are suggesting he has a claim on the throne, even if he denies any such intention. Moving an army towards the King without his command or consent must be considered impeachable and a risk to the common good.

Henry has been acclaimed king by all the peers of this land; by York himself. He is king and, unless he is declared a tyrant, then king he is. From whom he takes counsel is his prerogative: he is to receive counsel from reason and wisdom, not force of arms.

And so the Congregation resolves simply to note the letter but pass it on to the King's Council and inform them that it has not received accord or acclaim within the university. The last thing any of those in Congregation want is loss or diminution of royal favour if their future is to remain financially sustainable.

John Morton is radiantly happy. He is decked out in the gown of a Doctor of Law with the elite stalked cap on his head, the price of his inception being 10 pence. He walks through the main thoroughfares of Oxford with his 17-year-old nephew Robert who came up to university in 1450, enjoying an early entry partly in the light cast on him by his uncle. They are going to celebrate John's admission, but in a rather unusual way.

Celebrating his own Master's degree at this time is 20-year-old George Neville of Balliol college.[9] George is someone John knows well: both being highly proficient in getting to know everyone. The difference is that George is the youngest brother of Richard Neville, Earl of Warwick. And George is also incredibly rich and keen to demonstrate that as widely as possible. George's celebrations are spread over two days with sit-down lunches for 600 on the first day and 300 on the second. Both Mortons have been invited to day one of the celebrations and the ever-frugal John decides that this will do nicely for his own celebration. Although John's parents are not particularly old, neither is sufficiently fit to endure the journey up from Dorset or leave the farm for any length of time. So, uncle and nephew will mark the event in the generous company of those others attending.

In addition to his teaching roles, Morton received his first preferment within the church in 1450 as a sub-dean to Lincoln cathedral. The position is not onerous but does provide a small supplement to his income and, most important, a foot on the first rung of ecclesiastical acknowledgement. The essence of the role is to receive and review faculty recommendations and offer legal advice as to whether a faculty (being permission to carry out any work on church land or buildings) is appropriate.

With the indulgences provided by George Neville's extreme celebrations comes the opportunity to strike up new acquaintances, and through the introduction of Chancellor Kymer these include Thomas Bourchier, Bishop of Ely, and his brother Henry, Viscount Bourchier.[10]

The Bishop is in his mid-forties, and the Viscount a year or two younger. Thomas displays an appreciation of the good life, as does Henry, although he is evidently more muscular and a soldier. Their lineage is from Edward III on their mother's side. These are exactly the sort of people Morton wants to know and be known by.

It is evident that Morton's qualities are circulating within the right circles and patronage soon follows with John being elected Principal of Peckwater Inn at the commencement of the academic year. This will provide him with status, a good salary, and good lodgings. He is now truly ascending the ladder.

While Oxford celebrated, York was long on the march. The issue of his manifesto, followed up with a further letter of demands in February, amounted to a declaration of war on Somerset who is blamed for a personal vendetta against him and for the loss of further territories in France. He falls short of speaking against the King.

With the removal of Suffolk, Somerset has been the principal minister and he is seen to be particularly close to Queen Margaret. Between them they appear in command of the King's mind. Attempts to topple Somerset through the Commons in 1451 had failed, so direct action appeared to be York's only clear option.

The King's forces moved to intercept York but this they failed to do, although London refused to open its gates to him. So, York swung through Kent to reach Deptford on the east side of the capital. Although he found some sympathy from the men of Kent, they did not rally and join him. Notwithstanding the general pardon after Cade's rebellion, there had been ruthless reprisals exacted and they had no stomach for further retribution.

At Blackheath, he met the King's force – larger than his own – and negotiations were opened. York's first demand was that Somerset should be brought to trial. Henry agreed to this and, on the strength of the King's word, York disbanded his army and attended Henry's tent to continue negotiations. Here, though, he finds he has been set up. Somerset stands there as assured as ever. Clearly, no one's word holds true, and no one trusts anyone anymore. And after Cade's rebellion, York has no credence or credit with the King or the royal party. To his astonishment he is taken to London and kept under virtual house arrest, but he is spared further jeopardy by the rumour that his son Edward, a boy of ten, is marching on London with ten thousand men. York is forced to swear an oath to keep the peace, to raise no troops, and to be obedient to the King. Only then is he allowed to return home, to Fotheringhay, where his wife is pregnant with their third son, to be named Richard. There's a prophetic irony: Richard, the third.

Catatonia, 1453–1455

Oxford is frequently visited by plague, causing an exodus of academics from the city to outlying farms and sanctuaries within their estates. It would be commonplace to see John and Robert Morton taking the opportunity during one such visitation to exercise their horses with an unlaboured morning hack, during which they would inevitably converse and reflect on personal and political developments. Their debates and confidences would bind a trust in each other which would last a lifetime.

John is still assimilating recent elevations within the establishment. Thanks to the recommendation of Cerne Abbey, he has been appointed to the living of Bloxworth, which will provide opportunity for more frequent visits home to Milborne St Andrew. In addition, he has been made rector of Shellingford, about 17 miles south-west of Oxford.[1] For this, he has received a papal dispensation allowing him to hold two 'incompatible' benefices with the ability to exchange or switch these as he wishes. The church prohibited the holding of 'pluralist' benefices unless they were physically adjoining, but dispensations were fairly easy to obtain. Of no less importance in the recognition of his standing and skills, Morton has been appointed to audit the accounts of the university's proctors. Both his reputation and finances are looking up. From Boars Hill they would be able to pause and take in the view of the ubiquitous mist blanketing the river valley: a first-class vector for disease, plague or not.

Morton finds Robert an excellent companion. Not the greatest mind for new ideas, nor the most ambitious, but he is thoughtful, loyal, an orderly administrator, a good listener and, most important, a keeper of secrets.

So it is that he can share and reflect on sensitive news with his nephew. There is a growing concern among the King's medical advisors that his personality is changing as a result of the stresses placed on him from threats to his throne, real or imaginary, from the loss of his lands in France and the widespread challenges to his appointed councillors and the general peace. The outcome is that whereas he has always been seen as meditative, peaceful, and desiring accommodation, he is now displaying a violent temper, is fearful and vindictive.

Recalling the Cade rebellion, the Archbishops of Canterbury and York alongside the Duke of Buckingham and Viscount Beaumont assured the rebels that the King would listen and respond to their grievances. Henry's 'response' was to bring his army onto Blackheath with anything but clemency on his mind. With the men of Kent fled from the field and in real danger of being hunted down, Henry was moved back to Westminster and then to Kenilworth. Many assumed that this was to keep the King safe from the rebels. But it was to keep the rebels safe from the King. The Queen remained in London and, through the good brokerage of John Kemp, Archbishop of York, a general pardon was issued.

By now, the King is wholly suspicious of everything the Duke of York says or does. He is not interested in York's assertions of good faith but in forcing his submission by threat of armed suppression. Again, the Queen strives to keep the doors open and regularly bestows gifts and goodwill upon him. But there has been no indication that the estrangement between York and his sovereign is nearer to resolution. Behind all that is presented for public consumption, York was very lucky not to lose his head at the Deptford confrontation, so livid was Henry. It seems that the fears, paranoia, anger, and intolerance exhibited from time to time by his father and also his maternal grandfather have risen to the surface.

But York's ambitions may soon receive a check. It is believed that the Queen is expecting a child. Hopefully, this will prove to be the case and a public announcement can be made in the late spring, the end of September being the anticipated time of the birth. This news has already been released to some, including the Duchess of York, who has met with the Queen, expressing her delight: not least because it will remove suspicions of her husband and lead to true reconciliation.

Queen Margaret is indeed pregnant. Henry is overjoyed and bestows a handsome pension of £40 a year on Sir Richard Tunstall, the Esquire of the Body who brings the news to him. He also sends Margaret a jewel to keep with her during her confinement. But the joy does not last. The suspicions about York's intentions multiply as the birth of an heir will, in Henry's mind, side-line Richard's perceived aspirations and may make him more deadly. The pressures on Henry's mental wellbeing become unbearable by the summer. July sees the loss of Gascony and the effective end of the Hundred Years' War at the battle of Castillon, where John Talbot, Earl of Shrewsbury is killed alongside his son, Lord de Lisle.[2]

This means England's possessions in France amount to no more than Calais and about 120 square miles surrounding it. At home, a feud in the north between the younger members of the Neville and Percy families is breaking out into warfare. It is too much for the fragile king to bear.

It is 10 August. Henry is at Clarendon, near Salisbury. His gentlemen of the body find him in a trance-like state, completely uncommunicative, with no sense of time or place, profoundly inert with no physical coordination, and total absence of memory. He is in an unresponsive stupor. Surgeons apply ointments, cordials, suppositories, shave his head, remove haemorrhoids: even exorcism is tried. There is no response.

Somerset covers up what has happened to provide time for a possible recovery and decide what to do next. He is also aware that without Henry to shield him he is in a vulnerable position, as he receives almost universal blame for the French disaster. Henry is quietly moved from Clarendon to Windsor.

It is thought that the King's illness may be derived from his maternal grandfather, Charles VI of France, through his mother Catherine of Valois, Charles being known as Charles the Mad with numerous psychotic episodes well recorded throughout his life. These included extreme impatience, speech impediments, amnesia, refusing to bathe for five months, killing four of his servants, and most memorably, believing he was made of glass.

With Henry incapacitated, Margaret is moved from Greenwich to Westminster on 10 September by barge up the Thames for her lying-in, the traditional long bed rest before and after giving birth. This is a full month before the actual birth, suggesting the term may have run over that anticipated by a week or two. She is accompanied on her river journey by the Mayor and aldermen of London, with Somerset and Buckingham. York is not in London so there is no question of him being snubbed.

The birth takes place on 13 October, and the baby is baptised Edward the very next day by the Bishop of Winchester, with Somerset, the Duchess of Buckingham, and Cardinal Kemp, Archbishop of Canterbury and Chancellor, as godparents.

There is a clear need for a Regent while the King is incapacitated, which Somerset cannot resist indefinitely, particularly as Henry's plight becomes more widely known. A Council is called for November, but York is not at first invited. However, a belated invitation is issued on 23 October. The signatories suggest that Margaret may have had some input in correcting the snub: all but one of those signing were not particularly York supporters – and Somerset's moniker was missing. At the same time, Margaret continues to show favour to Somerset, suggesting that she is still hopeful of some reconciliation between the lords, but more likely she is trying to sweeten both camps to bolster her own case for the regency.

Any thoughts of reconciliation are, of course, delusional. York has come to resolve his vendetta. As Council opens, John Mowbray, Duke of Norfolk, denounces Somerset as a traitor and, after long debate, Somerset is arrested on 23 November and sent to the Tower.[3] He is neither formally charged with any crime, nor brought to trial.

Margaret comes to the not unreasonable conclusion that the long-term security of the Lancastrian dynasty, and in particular the safety and security of her son, requires a working unity between the lords of the realm. To achieve this, she seeks to create a consensus built around herself as Regent. There is one precedent for a queen becoming regent working under advice of a Council. In 1253, Henry III named his wife, Eleanor, Regent while he was abroad. Like Margaret, Eleanor was not particularly liked, but the difference was she had several children including a son who, at fourteen, was well into his teenage years. Margaret has only one child, and but a few months old. After more than four weeks' debate, Council decides to back a man in preference to a woman. In fact, there seems little appetite for either candidate or for the option of governance by Council with no regent.

On 15 March 1454, Edward is created Prince of Wales and Earl of Chester. The apparent haste to bestow these titles is to ensure the income flow from the royal Welsh estates goes directly into the royal coffers without diversion to the protectorate.

On 27 March, York is named Lord Protector. He swears to protect Edward's rights and also Margaret's. However, there is a swift development of factionalism on the Council. John Kemp, Archbishop of Canterbury and Chancellor, dies before the Council decision is given. Some say that his death has been brought on by bullying from the Duke of Norfolk. Richard Neville, Earl of Salisbury, is made Chancellor and Thomas Bourchier is elevated to Archbishop of Canterbury.

The challenge by York for the protectorate and, with it, the crystallisation of his threat to her family's interests, causes Margaret to turn her back on pacification and she resolves to build up a royal Lancastrian party to bring down York and his affinity. The She-Wolf is born.

But York's protectorate lasts only ten months. On 25 December, Henry regains his senses. Somerset is released from the Tower with the Duke of Buckingham, Earl of Wiltshire and Lord Roos acting as surety on 4 February 1455, and two days later York formally resigns his office to the King at Greenwich. A Council meeting is called for 4 March to resolve outstanding issues. The first thing the King does is to discharge Somerset from his bail conditions, and he becomes head of the government once again. Rubbing salt into the wound, the captaincy of Calais is taken from York and transferred back to Somerset. Somerset and York are then instructed to submit their differences to arbitration. A few days later, Salisbury has to resign the chancellorship to Archbishop Bourchier. Wiltshire is made Treasurer.

And so, all of York's work is dismantled. He and his followers are clearly without hope of political influence and are also facing the likelihood of retribution from Somerset. They therefore withdraw from court and immediately begin gathering an army.

Another Council is summoned for 25 May at Leicester, to discuss the provision of safety to the King's person. York's party assume that this was called to bring them fully to heel and cement Somerset's victory, so they decide to intercept Henry's force en route: they would maintain that the aim was to secure a fair hearing – though how this would not be seen as a direct challenge to the King's authority and the legitimacy of the Council is difficult to argue. In fact, the King, Somerset, and the King's advisors interpret it exactly as such a challenge, motivated by an attempt to usurp the throne.

The two forces meet at St Albans. York, the Earl of Warwick, and the Earl of Salisbury arrive with perhaps as many as 7,000 men between them. York insists that Somerset is handed over to him. Clearly, this is an impossible demand and an affront to the King. Henry calls upon York to fall back but he refuses. The two armies engage within the town and the result is a devastating loss for the Lancastrians. Somerset, Northumberland, Lord Clifford, and Buckingham's eldest son are all killed. Buckingham himself, Dorset and Devon are all wounded and taken prisoner. And to crown it all, Henry is wounded as an arrow grazes his neck and he is likewise taken prisoner. The Yorkist army enters London with the King to the fore, to demonstrate that there is no threat to the sovereign. Henry's nerve and emotions are in shreds, as he expected to be put to the sword at St Albans when found.

York was in a dilemma. It was clear to him, and everyone else, that he had no power except when he was backed by an armed force. On the other hand, if he raised his sword before his enemies made their move he would be condemned as the aggressor. Any move he does make requires justification to the public and indeed to God. His support came principally from kinsmen by marriage: Salisbury, Warwick, and Norfolk. Londoners also favoured him, not least because he promised greater stability and more trade. The rest of the country supports the King though, notwithstanding his incompetence. An outright declaration of a bid for the throne risks loss of credibility and reputation and could weaken the ties he has with many potential supporters. He needs to be careful and canny.

In London, York is made Constable of England and Warwick is elevated to Captain of Calais. By the end of the year, Henry relapses under the strain, although he is not so severely afflicted as before. York regains the Protectorship, albeit with reluctance from the Lords who are under pressure from the Commons. But the King's recovery is soon in coming; being sufficiently competent by February 1456 he attends parliament to relieve York of his role as Protector.

Power rests with whoever controls the crown, and it is Margaret who exercises that control. She is the glue that holds the Lancastrian party together. The relationship with York is one of complete loathing with no room for reconciliation. Both know that one or other must be destroyed. So, Margaret moves Henry and the court from London to Kenilworth, both parties taking steps to court allies and build up their strengths.

Advancements, 1456

By 1456, Morton was spending time chiefly between Oxford and Bloxham, although increasingly he was finding himself pursuing civil and canonical cases in London, sometimes as advocate and sometimes sitting in judgement. Typically, his skills were put to use in the administration of estates such as wills, probate, and other family matters. He was well aware that his case load and his role in the courts was guided by the patronage of Thomas Bourchier as much as by the recommendation of past clients and those within the legal fraternity.

Bourchier prioritised stability in both church and government and had little difficulty in recognising an inter-dependence between the two. He held a pragmatic outlook, his eye being on long term interests. In contrast to the rising star in the church, George Neville (recently created Bishop of Exeter at the age of twenty-five on the recommendation of the Protector), he was seen as a safe pair of hands, unlikely to innovate or take risks, steady and without ostentation.

Morton practised in several courts, but it was in the Court of Arches that his skills were fully appreciated, and his knowledge of canon law displayed to best advantage. The Court of Arches was principally, though not exclusively, the court of appeal through which the Archbishop of Canterbury exercised control over his ecclesiastical province except for two northern episcopal sees controlled by the Archbishop of York. The court sat at the church of St Mary le Bow on London's Cheapside and gained its name from the arched windows in the church crypt.[1] An important function was to scrutinise the bishops' courts, and the limits of the rights and duties of the archbishop towards his bishops would create some bitter disputes for Morton towards the end of his career. The administration of vacant sees was another major function of the Court of Arches.

The ecclesiastical courts heard cases relating to probate and wills, family matters, and those which would fall in the jurisdiction of admiralty courts. Morton acted as advocate, even giving judgement on such cases. Advocates were all doctors of law and were similar in many respects to modern barristers. They would organise themselves into a loose society eventually to become known as Doctors' Commons. Morton was soon regarded as the leading advocate within this world and became known as 'the well sounding bell of St Mary's', gaining not only in reputation but in fees earned.

It is stiflingly hot. Even by the Thames there is little respite from the heat, nor a breeze to be caught. Crossing London Bridge, Morton notes no movement of boats other than those propelled by oar, and their progress is listless. He is overdressed for the weather, and he is sweating too much for comfort, results of both the weather and the meeting before him.

From the bridge he turns right into Clink Street, tall warehouses and wharves on the riverside, and on the left his destination, Winchester House, the London residence of William Waynflete, Bishop of Winchester. The air is cooler in the shade of the buildings either side of the street, but at the same time there is an oppressiveness about the place. Within the cluster of buildings are several brothels or 'stews', owned and leased out by the bishop himself and controlled by published 'Ordinances touching the governance of stewholders in Southwark under the direction of the Bishop of Winchester'. Break the rules for doing business and fines will follow. The cellars of Winchester House also provide prison accommodation – 'the Clink' becomes a byword for the jails of London.

In the early part of the year, Morton was commissioned by the King to lead an investigation into allegations that the incumbent warden of St John the Baptist Hospital in Oxford had sold off the religious vestments and ornaments. It was made clear early on that his real client was Waynflete, who was hoping eventually to acquire the hospital to complete the founding of a new college within the university – to become Magdalen College.

Bishop Winchester was wedded to the establishment and promotion of educational institutions, a passion which had brought him close to the King, who had similar interests. Waynflete's rise was first to be noted in 1442 when, at the age of forty-six, he became provost of Eton College. Acclaimed historically as Eton's first headmaster, he held the post until 1447 when he was elevated to the bishopric of Winchester. He played the part of an intermediary for the King in Cade's rebellion and in the confrontation with York at Deptford, displaying no little courage. William Waynflete is a master at ingratiating himself with both Henry and Margaret, a key figure in their inner circle. So, for Morton, he is a client to impress.

The Oxford hospital administered to the spiritual and physical needs of the sick, but not the incurable. Its statutes also prohibited interference in its business by religious authorities, which was the necessity for Morton's investigation to be authorised by the King himself.

Morton delivered his report direct to the Bishop. With a small secretariat he had interviewed the warden, Richard Vyse, at the hospital. Vyse was elected warden sixteen years previously, was of good character, wedded to the cause of the institution he served, but overwhelmed by the lack of adequate funds to meet its obligations to its brethren or the sick to whom it administered. In particular, the physical upkeep of the building left much to be desired and there was no prospect of attracting the necessary capital to bring it to a condition satisfactory for its purpose. All this was put to Morton by Father Vyse and evidenced by his own inspection of the building and the hospital's accounts.

Father Vyse also admitted that he had used the hospital's vestments and ornaments as security for a loan to pay for urgent repairs to the building necessary to halt structural decay. He had acknowledged that this was an improper action but was hoping to redeem the security in a short period of time. Unfortunately, it was very unlikely that this would prove possible.

Vyse was a good man with valuable experience, an otherwise unblemished record and the capability to provide useful and loyal service in the future. It was therefore Morton's recommendation that the hospital be formally closed, that Father Vyse resign his position; that the hospital be transferred to Bishop Waynflete for the foundation and extension of Magdalen College as a seat of learning within the university of Oxford; but also that Father Vyse be installed as parson to the vacancy at All Saints church, Fawley, within Waynflete's diocese. The solution to the problem was precisely what the Bishop wanted to hear and his delight would soon be expressed with a career-changing recommendation.

Morton though would have been, at least for a time, uncomfortable in his role in something that was certainly the best result for all parties but yet the outcome was pre-determined, and he had gone along with that. Sometimes you just have to go with the inevitable and make the best of it. That is part and parcel of the political world, he tells himself.

It was only weeks until Winchester's promise of patronage became a reality. Morton was in Oxford when he received a summons to come straight away to the royal court at Coventry. Tying up some loose ends at Peckwater, packing saddle bags (including his best gown and hat to display his academic and legal standing), and making the 60-mile journey, he is in Coventry three days later. On 26 September, he is riding out with the Bishop of Winchester to the royal residence at Cheylesmore Manor to be formally appointed as Chancellor of the Duchy of Cornwall.

The post is to effectively manage and account for Prince Edward's estate. This is a role of great significance in these uncertain times as the royal family needs to protect its interests, financially, politically, and constitutionally. Under Morton will be an appointed team for him to work to with, and there will be a Council for the Prince drawn up by the New Year to which he will report and make recommendations.

The Manor House is a pleasing timber frame and rendered stone building with mullion windows, the house formed around an inner courtyard and set in extensive formal gardens. It is a favourite retreat for the royal family and he meets them all – but it is the twenty-seven-year-old Queen Margaret who particularly cements his loyalty and with whom he will build a strong and trusting working relationship. Morton is nearly forty but has never had a direct, meaningful conversation with any woman outside of his family before – let alone a queen. He is captivated.

Morton learns that changes are afoot within the government as the royal party anticipate an escalation in lawlessness and violence from York's followers. Among these changes will be Bishop Waynflete replacing Archbishop Bourchier as Chancellor. This is not because any disloyalty has been expressed by the Archbishop, but he has cooperated with York in the past and his brother, Viscount Bourchier, is married to York's sister. The Viscount himself is also being replaced as treasurer by the Earl of Shrewsbury. The King does not want to place any man in a situation where loyalties become strained or tested.

If, as he had so often claimed, York's sole aim was to remove the late Duke of Somerset as the King's chief advisor, then he should have been satisfied by his murder at St Albans. But now there seems little if any doubt that, with the help of his affinity, he means not only to force himself into that same position but also to hazard taking the crown itself.

At the Coventry Great Council a few weeks later, the new chancellor and treasurer are formally appointed. York is said to have left the council on good terms with Henry but that may be superficial or even false. More tangible is an open brawl between Somerset's men and those of York – leaving four dead in Coventry's streets – Somerset the evident aggressor seeking vengeance for his father's death.[2]

Preparations for War, 1457–1458

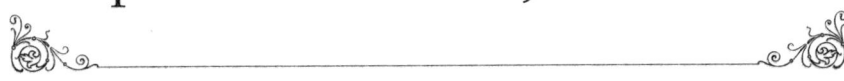

On the same day as Morton receives his appointment, Robert Whittingham is made Receiver-General.[1] Changes continue within the royal circle. Margaret's chancellor, Lawrence Booth, replaces the dying Thomas Liseux as Keeper of the Privy Seal shortly after. Booth will go on to become Bishop of Durham later in the year and, under Edward IV, Archbishop of York, succeeding George Neville. Viscount Beaumont is made the Prince's chief steward, Giles St Lo keeper of the prince's wardrobe, and Thomas Throckmorton the Prince's attorney-general.

At the end of January, a formal council is appointed for the management of Prince Edward's possessions and affairs until he comes of age. It is a veritable *Who's Who* of Lancastrian supporters: Booth; Waynflete; Reginald Boulers, Bishop of Coventry; John Stanbury, Bishop of Hereford; Henry Stafford, Buckingham's heir; Shrewsbury; Wiltshire; Beaumont; Thomas, Lord Stanley; and John Sutton, Baron Dudley.

Both sides seek foreign support to supplement their cause. York made an early attempt to find an accommodation with the Duke of Alencon, but the conspiracy was discovered by Charles VII and Alencon was arrested, so it came to nothing. But it did show, once again, that York and his party, by independently negotiating with foreign powers, were active traitors against the Crown. York then sought an alliance with Burgundy using Warwick and Calais as a base for advancing negotiations. Margaret, in turn, seeks support from Scotland and from her uncle, Charles VII.

There had been a truce between England and Scotland from 1453, but which was to expire in 1457. Negotiations started with James II to agree an extension, but behind the scenes the Scots were also sounded out for future help against York. There was hope in this discreet enquiry as York was a past ally of the Earl of Douglas – anything but a friend to the House of Stuart. The Earl, whose title had been made forfeit in 1455, resided in England and (illustrating some of the inconsistencies of the time) was receiving an annuity of £500 a year from Henry. The Stuart king also led a raid into England in August 1459 while negotiations were continuing. As it was, the truce was formally extended from September 1459 to 1468.

French negotiations had less success. Warwick had received word in 1457 that an attack was being planned on Calais. As a precaution, he increased the garrison's provisions from the Kent ports so that any attack or siege could be repelled. The French decided to leave Calais alone in the circumstances but instead strike at its source of supplies.

A squadron of French ships cross the Channel under the command of Piers de Breze, seneschal of Anjou, Poitou, and Normandy, and sack Sandwich, after which they move down the coast to burn Sutton Pool, Plymouth. They then land at Fowey, Cornwall, to burn and pillage, attacking Place House where they are famously repulsed by Elizabeth Treffrey who, in the absence of her husband, organises boiling lead to be poured onto the invaders.[2]

It is unfortunate for Margaret that de Breze is, and is perceived as, a personal friend. He was instrumental in the arrangement of Margaret's marriage to Henry, and she has stayed in touch with him, not least because he is close to Charles. De Breze was an adventurer though and, not unlike Warwick, had an eye – and an itch – for action. He had raided the Yorkshire coast as far back as 1451. Rumour suggested that Margaret encouraged the raid on Sandwich, although it is difficult to see what she might have gained from this.

Because of the Sandwich debacle, Henry Holland, Duke of Exeter, loses his position as Captain of the Sea to Warwick, who is commissioned for three years, and he proves to be particularly successful in his exploits. When appointed Captain of Calais, Richard Neville was only twenty-nine years old. Calais was a heavily fortified town and held England's only professional army: in all garrisoning some 2,000 men. The harbour town was further protected by the dominant Tower of Risban, and by castles at Guines and Hammes. Warwick quickly impresses merchants on both sides of the Channel in his new role, making particular friends of the ports back in England and he takes the time to learn navigation and the art of marine warfare.

Reappointed as Lieutenant of Ireland, York refuses to go, knowing full well that this is an unsubtle attempt to keep him away from the King and Council. Not only that, but he senses a good possibility that once out of the country he will not be allowed to return.

News comes, not wholly unexpected, that Richard Morton is dying, and that John should journey back to Milborne Styleham in haste if he is to say a proper goodbye to his father. The decision is made, for them rather than by them, that Robert shall remain in Oxford as he is in the last six months of his studies to gain a Master's degree. So it is that Morton returns to the family home alone. Sadly, he arrives too late.

The body of 72-year-old Richard has been washed and shrouded and lies in state in the church, surrounded by candles, everything draped in black. The laying in state is a tradition to ensure all in the community can confirm the death. A mass is said for the soul of the deceased, after which the burial takes place. Cremation is not an option as it is considered a desecration of the body and is not permitted by the church. After the burial there is a large meal for guests, the supervision of which has helped keep his mother distracted from her grief. Bread and cheese are also provided for the poor who attend as professional mourners – they also receive a black robe, as is custom.

As may be expected with a farming family, things have changed little since John's last visit and, not least because this is a wake, conversations inevitably concentrate on anecdotes from the past. One notable change is that William has a new wife, his first – Robert's mother – having died in childbirth some ten years earlier. In fact, Robert has yet to meet his stepmother as William has been re-married less than a year, his studies keeping him in Oxford.

The affairs of church and Council are pressing, and John sets out on his return journey without a lengthy stay. He is to do a circular route as his first leg, taking in Maiden Newton, then Bloxworth and finally Cerne Abbas, where he proposes to stay the night. Morton has only recently been appointed rector at St Mary's church, Maiden Newton, and is keen to become acquainted with it and its vicar. He has accumulated sufficient additional appointments to make his financial situation more than healthy: these include prebends at Dinder in the diocese of Bath and Wells; Corringham in the diocese of Lincoln; together with Fordington and Writhlington in the diocese of Salisbury.[3]

After an hour at Maiden Newton and another at Bloxworth, Morton arrives at Cerne Abbey mid-afternoon where he would meet the new incumbent, Abbot John Hellyer, sharing his fears that civil war is looming. Tension has been heightened by a series of slanderous attacks against the royal family.

Two days before York was compelled by the King to resign his second protectorate in the preceding year, the apprentice lawyer John Helton was hung drawn and quartered for circulating bills claiming that Prince Edward was a changeling and not born of the Queen at all. It was only

March of this year that the Council of London warned its businessmen not to engage in spreading rumours about the Queen and the Prince. Then there is a commission to be sent into Norfolk this very month to investigate possible slanders against the honour of the Queen and the Prince, whose findings are awaited.[4]

Morton may believe that war is inevitable, but Henry is not prepared to give up on peace and calls for a Great Council to be held at Westminster. It is as a result of this Council that John finds himself standing in a throng of Londoners on Ludgate Hill close to St Paul's Cathedral.

All the lords arrived for the Council with large escorts, in some cases closer to being small armies, each body of men wearing tabards and badges identifying their allegiance, and heavily armed. For a time, the likelihood of serious violence simmered and even now, with the council formally closed and a pacification of the peers reached, hostile stares between these kitted out potential combatants lining either side of the thoroughfare are blatant. The Mayor's stewards give some assurance of control and the sound of heraldic trumpets coming up from Fleet Street help to defuse the situation further.

At the council, where Morton was present as an observer with the aim of engaging in a private review of the political picture later, the King lost no time in making it clear to all that his patience was done, and this would be the last opportunity for those present to come together and work for the common good and the rule of law. In fact, he was now laying down the law. St Albans must never be repeated. If it was, there would be no further pardons and he didn't feel the need to spell out the consequences of that. So, York, Salisbury, Warwick and their affiliates were ordered to found and fund a chantry at the monastery of St Albans for the souls of those killed there and, additionally, to compensate the families of the dead. This they agree to do. In addition, the King calls for a public demonstration of reconciliation on the next day, 25 March, Lady Day, which shall be named a Love Day.[5]

It is this parade of 'peace in our time' that the capital's citizens, the peers' pikemen, and Morton await sight of, coming up behind the heralds and a contingent of the royal bodyguard. Arm in arm are Somerset and Salisbury (killer of his father), Exeter and Warwick, then the King in full royal regalia, and the Queen hand-in-hand with York. They enter the cathedral where this miraculous accord is celebrated in a High Mass administered by Thomas Bourchier. The professed peace and harmony are a complete sham of course, and evaporate wholly within months.

Next came a personal bombshell.

Two months after Robert gains his Master's degree he seeks out John's help, the latter having been in London on business and away from Oxford. At the time of his graduation he became 'acquainted' with a novice at the Benedictine abbey of Godstow, a short distance from Balliol. The abbey has a reputation for slackness, shall we say, in the discourse between its sisterhood and outsiders, particularly men of the cloth. The outcome is that Robert finds himself a prospective father. Robert is adamant on accepting the child as his own and maintaining it and the mother.

From Robert's position, he is committed to a life and career within the church and so marriage is out of the question. However, it is acceptable and not uncommon within the church for a priest to acknowledge a child and for the mother to take on the platonic duties of a housekeeper. Even bishops are known to have sired and raised children in this manner.

The mother must leave the abbey as soon as possible. The baby will need to be born away from Oxford and raised to a sufficient age of independence from its mother. In fact, the child will become a valued and cherished member of the Morton family and gains acknowledgement in Morton's Will as 'Robert son of Robert'.

Robert has received the benefice of All Saints' church at Huntingdon which will provide sufficient income for him to meet their costs and John acts as go-between in arranging for the mother to have and raise the child at Milborne St Andrew until an appropriate time when they can join Robert, once he has cemented a good living for them all.

As a bonus, William's second wife produced a son, Thomas, the year after Robert junior's birth, and they enjoyed their early years together.

Warwick has spent his time as both Captain of the Sea and Captain of Calais wisely, correctly seeing this duality of responsibility essential to any move on the King's government. He put particular effort into refitting ships in Calais's harbour, building up an efficient, well-equipped fleet.

Scouting ships are regularly sent out into the Channel and on 28 May, prophetically, twenty-eight Spanish ships are sighted. As Spain is an ally of Charles VII, Warwick puts his fleet to sea and after a six-hour engagement, almost a quarter of the Spanish ships are taken – providing a great boost to his fame and reputation at home. The English are ever jubilant at bringing adversity upon commercial rivals, even if legitimacy is a little dubious.

The reaction from home, and the spoils won (helping the financial costs he is incurring and for which there is scant hope of receiving recompense from the royal coffers) increase his boldness. Unfortunately, he falls victim to his self-cultivated image as the most renowned of Englishmen and seizes a Hanseatic fleet of Lubeck carrying salt.[6] This creates a major embarrassment for Henry and his government as the German/Baltic League is a friend of England. While the London, and English commercial concerns generally, avoid censure of Warwick for the time being, a move to see him replaced by Somerset is ignited within Council, particularly by Margaret and those close to her.

This is not the only display of arrogant rashness on the part of Warwick. Deluded by his self-confidence and self-estimation, without any authority he tries to arrange marriages, simultaneously, for a French or Burgundian bride for the Prince of Wales. His schemes blow up in his face and the resulting embarrassment is a further motive for Margaret to seek his removal.

Warwick's acts of virtual piracy – particularly his seizure of the Lubeck salt ships – and other crimes see him recalled to Westminster in October to account for his actions before the King's Council. With a typical display of arrogance, he arrives on 9 November with a large contingent of retainers, each in a red tunic displaying his emblem of the ragged staff. Soon after he enters the court chamber from the main hall, an argument breaks out between his men and a sizeable crowd of court servants – described by some as 'cooks and scullery boys'. Later reports say someone had drawn a dagger or brandished a meat cleaver. Such is the noise that Warwick emerges from the chamber and perceives he and his men are in danger of their lives. There is no report of members of the court party also going into the hall. Warwick and his bodyguard fight their way out of the building and flee in their barges down river, thence back to Calais via Warwick Castle. Each party accuses the other of staging the event. It is as though each side is seeking to build up sufficient justification to take the final step towards extinction of the other.

There follows a formal demand that Warwick surrenders the Captaincy of Calais, which he refuses to do unless his authority is rescinded by parliament who, he declares, conferred the position on him and is therefore the only body who can take it from him.

It is clear that an armed resolution will be the only outcome and in December the Staple Merchants are exempted from shipping tax in return for a loan to the Crown. This is as much about trying to get Calais (the Staplers' most significant centre of operations) on board with the King's party and away from Warwick as it is about securing war funds. As it happened, the Company lent to any English king with whom they could strike a profitable deal. In funds, the Lancastrians stockpile pikes and leaded clubs, along with some serpentines, or light cannon.

10

Rebellion, 1459–1460

The King continues to strengthen his position, in late spring of 1459 ordering the repair of the royal castles along the Thames valley and buying in 3,000 bows and sheaves of arrows for the Tower. At the same time, no overt cause for complaint is given to the Yorkist party. Between the fracas with Warwick at Westminster and August, York is appointed to forty-two royal commissions of the peace, Salisbury thirteen, and Warwick sixteen. Not only that, but in June Salisbury receives payment of £1,578 for his services as Warden of the West March.

A Council is called at Coventry in the summer at which the Yorkist faction and its sympathisers are conspicuous by their absence, either making their intentions clear or suspecting a trap. The latter is certainly the message they want to convey to the world in general. For the King's part, he only issues a censure of the absentees but, with business done, moves to Nottingham where he starts to raise a force in earnest. The Queen remains at Coventry, from where she is also gathering an army, all to wear Prince Edward's swan badge. Morton is with the Queen and Prince Edward and notes all that is happening, continuing his duties as Chancellor of the Duchy of Cornwall administering the flow of funds into Edward's treasury.

The Duke of York is assembling men at his fortress at Ludlow and calls for Salisbury and Warwick to meet him there with as many men as they can muster. This is all so swiftly constructed after the Coventry Council that it is likely that both sides were hatching their plans even then, or more likely before.

Salisbury puts together a substantial force at his Middleham base in the north: at least 3,000 men and possibly as many as 7,000. Extracting a pledge from all 'to take full part with York' he sets out for Ludlow with his army.

The Queen is made fully aware of Salisbury's move and is prompt in sending out her own force under James Tuchet, Lord Audley and John Sutton, Lord Dudley, with some 8,000 troops to intercept, either to secure a dispersal or engage and force the issue. The two armies meet at Blore Heath near Market Drayton, Staffordshire, on 23 September. There is no way that Salisbury and his followers are peacefully going home, and the consequence is that it is the Yorkists who prevail. Audley is killed on the battlefield[1] and Dudley is captured, the royal army fleeing in disarray. The only disappointment for Salisbury is that his two youngest sons, John and Thomas Neville, let the blood rush to their heads in the excitement of victory and are captured while chasing after the escaping royal forces. At thirty and twenty-eight respectively, perhaps they should have known better. They are imprisoned at Chester Castle where they will remain for a year. With nightfall, Salisbury marches on to Ludlow.

Meanwhile, Warwick has assembled some 500 professional men-at-arms on the promise that they will not be called upon to act directly against the King. With him is Calais Captain Andrew Trollope. Leaving Calais under the command of William Neville, Lord Fauconberg, the army sails across the Channel to Sandwich, very much a Warwick safe haven. He issues a manifesto on landing to plead the old case that they only sought to remove the King's bad councillors and restore peace and justice to the country, having no antagonism towards the King himself. The fact that this was a military offensive which simply sought to replace one set of self-centred interests with another was not something they thought would be realised or understood by the people at large. The manifesto added, somewhat sinisterly, that anyone who did not support the Yorkist cause was, by definition, evil and should be punished accordingly.

Warwick moves up through the heart of the country during the end of September via London to Ludlow. He is not opposed along his route but neither does he attract supporters to his band. Perhaps he should read something into this.

Immediately on Warwick reaching Ludlow, yet another protestation of loyalty was drawn up and sent to Henry who responded with another offer of pardon except for Salisbury and a few others who had been attainted after taking up arms against him at Blore Heath. The offer was rejected and, as Henry's army came closer, the rebels drew up battle lines at Ludford, on the opposite side of the River Teme to Ludlow. On 13 October, Henry's full force is in place. A further offer of pardon is made and again it is rejected.

The Yorkist leadership – perhaps mindful of the men of Calais asserting that they will not fight against the King – have started rumours that Henry is dead. They have even brought in witnesses to attest to his demise and hold a mass for his soul. On learning of this, Henry reveals himself and has a few rounds of cannon fired off to demonstrate strength and resolution. This is enough to cause Andrew Trollope and most of the Calais contingent to defect after dusk, leaving the Yorkists without their best trained troops and with their strengths, strategy and secrets all now known to their enemy, as Trollope had been privy to it all.

The Yorkist leaders consult and decide that their position is precarious and probably lost, so they decide to flee. Those lords who can make a run for freedom, but some surrender to the King's mercy. The common soldiers disperse. Most of those surrendering receive a pardon of life and will later, with the consent of parliament, be given a general pardon, protecting their land and goods from forfeiture. Some known ringleaders with a history of unlawfulness and rebellion are executed.

The fugitive lords make haste into Wales and decide to split up. York, with his eldest son, Edmund, Earl of Rutland, together with Lord Clinton sail to Dublin where they are warmly welcomed. The others – Warwick, Salisbury, York's second son, Edward, Earl of March, along with Sir John Wenlock – take a longer journey, their whereabouts unknown to the King's party until mid-November.

Their immediate destination is the north Devon coast, guided to the manor house of John Dynham. Here they are hidden and well provided for by Dynham's widowed mother, Joanna, who is remembered and rewarded by Edward two years later after his return to England. Dynham spends the next couple of days gathering sufficient funds to buy a small boat and hire a crew, whereupon they hoist sail. Their first call is Guernsey, where they wait to ensure that Fauconberg still has control of Calais. On receiving a reply in the affirmative, they proceed to safety, arriving on 2 November.

With the rebels having fled Ludlow, the castle and several nearby villages within York's lordship were laid waste, giving vent to the rage of Henry and Margaret against the rebellion. Henry's anger is particularly inflamed by the way in which his offers of pardon were rejected: directly calling into question his honesty, capacity and intent. Buildings were stripped bare, and soldiers were given the freedom to loot, get intoxicated, and molest women with impunity. Yet York's wife, Cecily, and her two youngest sons George and Richard were treated well. Cecily was placed in the protective custody of her sister Anne Neville, Duchess of Buckingham, and godmother to Prince Edward. This is not to suggest that Cecily was held in confinement, she moved between the houses of friends and relatives seemingly at ease. Cecily was also granted

1,000 marks per annum from her husband's forfeited lands for the upkeep of her family.

The King eventually falls back to Coventry and a parliament is called there for 20 November, the business being to determine the retribution to be brought down on those rebels who had not sought pardon. It will become known by the Yorkists as the Parliament of Devils.

John Morton is appointed to a commission of seven served with the task of drawing up a Bill of Attainder against the leaders of the rebellion. The commission is headed by Sir John Fortescue, sixty-five years old, a knowledgeable and well-respected legal mind, and Chief Justice on the King's Bench.[2] Of the other five members, Thomas Thorpe is the most vociferous being a past Speaker of the Commons. He also has a personal grudge against York. In 1454, while Speaker he was ordered by the King to seize some arms being stored by the Duke. Unfortunately, the King became ill, and York had Thorpe imprisoned for a year. On his release, he regained favour immediately and was made Chancellor of the Exchequer, only to fall once again under false allegations from York, using him as a scapegoat for St Albans with claims that he had intercepted messages to the King which might have prevented violence. Royal favour was once again secured in 1457, and now the time for revenge had arrived.[3]

The bill cites twenty-four people for levying war against the king at Blore Heath and at Ludford.[4] A further three are cited, including the Countess of Salisbury, for plotting the King's death. The full fury of the indictment is reserved for York, of course. The commission wastes no time in setting out the several royal favours bestowed on York, and also on Salisbury and Warwick, and then proceeds to itemise each of York's crimes in full. They include reference to Cade's rebellion and its support of the Duke's claim; his ill-concealed attempts to force his ideas and influence on the King; stirring up rebellion in 1452; breaking three solemn oaths of loyalty; the killing of political rivals at St Albans; and then the latest armed insurrection.

Morton, Fortescue and Thorpe, with co-authorship from Lawrence Booth, Bishop of Durham, also produced a pamphlet *Somnium Vigilantis* as a defence of the bill and to help explain it to a wider audience. This would be the first time an Act of Attainder is passed by parliament. The pamphlet presents a fictitious court case giving both sides of the argument but as expected, concluding that it is only the King's authority and the supremacy of law that can guarantee the stability of the state.

The commission, including Morton, is in a fierce mood and argues that there should be no clemency shown towards any of these named traitors, who stand to lose both life and property. This includes a complete bar on their heirs gaining any inheritance. The vehemence expressed in the drafting of this Attainder will put John Morton high on the Yorkist hit-list.

This is the first parliament called in over three years and is the first that Morton has experienced. It is opened by William Waynflete, John's client and benefactor, as Chancellor. He preaches a sermon on peace and justice and how one supports the other. While those present were keen to see the condemnation of York and his supporters, it was clear that the King wanted to retain the royal prerogative to pardon. In part, this may have been a result of the actions of his troops after Ludlow preying on his conscience. It may also have been because there was the potential for monetary and political gain from restoring at least some of the minor rebels rather than creating a different pack of over-mighty lords by having to distribute their holdings between fewer peers.

Before parliament was dissolved on 20 December, the sixty-six members of the Lords present, including the bishops, were required to take yet another oath of loyalty: not just to Henry but to Margaret and Prince Edward as well. The Act of Attainder was now, it was hoped, a precedent – understood by all as capable of resurrection if further rebellion should arise.

Some of the forfeited estates are distributed to those who are close to Henry or who need their loyalty cemented to the royal house. So Owen Tudor, Henry's stepfather, receives an annuity from Clinton's estate and the Earl of Pembroke, the King's half-brother, makes gains, as do the Dukes of Exeter and Buckingham, the Earl of Douglas, Thomas Thorpe and others. But most lands are kept in hand for the time being at least.

It was not enough to simply attaint the rebel leaders. Immediate action was needed to completely neutralise them and ensure no repetition of their treasons. As a first step, Lord Rivers and the Sheriff of Kent were commissioned to put Kent on alert to the possibility of a further invasion from Calais and to seize all ships found which belonged to Warwick, and some were indeed captured anchoring in Sandwich harbour. The Duke of Somerset was also given the Captaincy of Calais and provided with six week's wages for 1,000 men to take it. Andrew Trollope would have put the royal party on alert that Lord Fauconberg probably had command of Calais, even if Warwick had not yet managed to return there. Thomas Thorpe, Sir Gervase Clifton, and John Judde (Master of the King's Ordnance) were put in funds to fit out ships and secure armaments. As ever, things failed to go as planned.

Approaching Calais, Somerset's fleet is greeted by guns firing from both the town and from Risban Tower. He makes a landing near Escalles to the west and marches to the English garrison at Guines, to which he is admitted on promise of payment of long overdue wages. That is the least of Somerset's problems. Three supply ships sent to reinforce him, either by accident or design, end up in Warwick's hands, losing him men and material.

Somerset's men clashed with troops from Calais almost daily, but their losses were the greater. In the absence of reinforcements their position grew the more precarious. Moreover, Calais continued to attract trade, including the English wool of the Merchant Staplers. The commercial treaty between England and Burgundy expired in 1439 and the English failed to expedite negotiations to extend it. This gave Philip the excuse he needed to make a three-month truce with Warwick to give him some breathing space – not least in closing one eye at forays from the men of Calais crossing Burgundian territory to loot from the French.

Meanwhile, Henry's moves against York were also getting nowhere. On 4 December, the Earl of Wiltshire (also Earl of Ormond) was named Lieutenant of Ireland in York's place: not that this had any effect, as the Irish parliament not only continued to recognise York but allowed him to set up a mint and appointed his son Rutland as Chancellor of Ireland. Wiltshire sent his representative, William Overy, to serve writs for York's arrest, only for him to be arrested and then executed. Not being able to raise an army, Henry let it be known that he would support the native Irish if they rose to conquer the English held territories, but with no result. York could not be shifted.

The King's councillors were well aware that they had to do more: not least for Somerset, whose situation was deteriorating daily. So they appointed Lord Rivers and Sir Gervase Clifton to mount Somerset's relief. On 10 December men are mustered at Sandwich, the plan being for Clifton to guard the sea with Rivers pressing on to Guines and then Calais. Once again, everything goes horribly wrong.

The men of Kent, and in particular those of Sandwich, were keeping Warwick informed of everything that was going on. So it was that on 15 January, as Rivers' fleet was near ready to set sail, Warwick sent out John Dynham, Sir John Wenlock, and a band of Sandwich men who took possession of the town capturing Rivers, his wife, and his son Sir Anthony Woodville, asleep in their beds. They returned to Calais with the whole fleet, its provisions and men, and their noble captives.

The government is thrown into disarray, fearing that a full-scale invasion is imminent. A council meeting is held at Westminster (although the King is in Leicester) and commissions of array are ordered in several key areas of the country. There is also an increase in the suppression of Yorkist sympathisers or suspected sympathisers, with imprisonments and executions. Not least among these moves is the siege of Denbigh Castle by Jasper Tudor, now Earl of Pembroke. While Kent, Sussex and Norfolk are seen as the most likely landing areas for the Calais lords, Wales was the obvious destination for York.

But it is money, or the lack of it, that dictates what can be achieved. Parliament had only recently been dissolved so it would be difficult and embarrassing to consider recalling it for more taxes. It would also be difficult, if not impossible, to squeeze more out of the merchants, as they had already provided a large loan and their trade through Calais was now prohibited. A plea is made to the church for cash, but the response will take time. So a wider appeal for loans, secured against revenue from assets forfeited by the rebels, and from future taxes such as 'tunnage and poundage' is made.[5] This has a measure of success but falls well short of what is hoped for or needed.

There is still no relief for Somerset. The seas cannot be effectively patrolled. Henry reaches Westminster on 3 March but then comes even more distressful news. On 16 March, with twenty-six ships, Warwick meets up with York at Waterford.

Activity in England now becomes frenzied but is disorganised and ineffective. The fitting out of ships is accelerated and by late April – with Warwick still plotting with York in Ireland – the fleets are ready to sail under the Duke of Exeter and the Devonian adventurer Sir Baldwin Fulford. Their orders are to intercept and destroy Warwick on his return to Calais, but until he starts his journey back to Calais they can do nothing but continue to try to patrol the seas. A highly secret request to the same purpose is also sent by Margaret to Pierre de Breze.

With over £5,000 owed to his men in back-pay, Somerset has to take the opportunity for the recovery of Calais while Warwick is away. But an attack on 23 April fails, with greater losses to the attackers.

Tensions continue to mount, and these find expression in increasing repression, most notably of the people of Newbury in Berkshire, but anyone with a link to York or the other rebel lords is a likely candidate for confiscation, imprisonment or extermination. Not only that, the affinity of London to the King's cause is severely tested by the interference with trade and the imprisonment and, effectively, holding to ransom of Venetian traders for failing to hand over their flotilla to the royal fleet. To counter disaffection, rumours are spread that the French are considering taking advantage of the situation to mount their own invasion of England, but there is nothing to substantiate this to encourage belief. The rebels have the whip-hand for propaganda against a government with little direction, few ideas and no money.

After two months of strategic discussions with York, Warwick makes his return to Calais. Yet another disastrous folly ensues. He is sighted off the coast of Cornwall and his way blocked and outnumbered by Exeter's fleet. He signals that he is ready for a fight but amazingly, Exeter's ships back off and return to Dartmouth, leaving the way clear to Calais. How could this come about? Yet again, it is the result of lack of money. Exeter's fleet was on the point of mutiny and without any wages were not prepared to put their lives on the line for more empty promises. A significant opportunity to remove the chance of success by the Yorkist camp had gone.

With all this happening, Somerset's plight had not been forgotten and on 23 May reinforcements were commissioned to be raised at Sandwich under the command of Osbert Mundeford. Unfortunately, and Somerset seems entirely without good fortune, not only were lessons not learned from the previous raid on Sandwich, but the assembly of boats and troops took place precisely as the Calais lords began their offensive with a raid to establish a beach-head for the main force of Warwick, Salisbury, and March. The assault on Sandwich is by both land and sea, and led by John Dynham, Sir John Wenlock, and Lord Fauconberg. It is almost a reprise of the January adventure, although Dynham suffers a badly wounded leg this time which will hinder him for the rest of his life. But Mundeford is captured and taken back to Calais where he is beheaded a short while after; a recent resident of the town, he was treated as a traitor to Warwick's cause. Fauconberg remains in Sandwich to secure the foothold and marshal the raising of Yorkist supporters. With the loss of reinforcement yet again, Somerset's position was now virtually hopeless.

Word is spreading of the impending assault. On 22 June, John Judde, Master of the King's Ordnance, is murdered outside St Albans travelling from London with thirty carts loaded with cannon, gunpowder, lances, axes, and other weaponry destined for Henry's fortifications. Judde was also responsible for seizing the armoury of the Duke of York and for fitting out Somerset's ships ready for sailing to Calais.

On 26 June the Calais lords and 2,000 troops land at Sandwich.

11

Loss and Retribution, 1460

The sandstone walls of Kenilworth Castle secure the favourite residence of the Lancastrian line. About five miles south of Coventry, the twelfth-century fortress was developed to provide palatial accommodation by Henry's great-grandfather, John of Gaunt. It is perfectly situated for access to the Midlands and the Welsh marches, and only a hundred miles from London.

Morton would be found in a quiet recess off the Great Hall, busily engaged in drafting letters calling for support and steadfastness from the towns, gentry and nobility across the country to meet the threat posed by the traitors and their growing army moving up from the south.[1] The alarm also needs to be raised with the west coast defences and those of Wales as a coordinated invasion with the Duke of York has to be expected. He is one of a small group of servants to the court who are being directed in their work by Queen Margaret. Also at the castle is, of course, the seven-year-old Prince Edward, as well as twenty-nine-year-old Henry Holland, Duke of Exeter, who is in command of the castle's defences.[2]

The King left Kenilworth immediately on receiving word of the rebels' advance, taking with him the royal arsenal that had been assembled there. Heading the royal army with him were the Duke of Buckingham; John Talbot, Earl of Shrewsbury; Lord Edmund Grey of Ruthin; Viscount John Beaumont; and Thomas Percy, Lord Egremont.

It is known that Warwick, Salisbury, Fauconberg, and March advanced from Sandwich to reach Canterbury with an army strongly reinforced by the turbulent men of Kent. Canterbury had been specifically strengthened against a possible invasion with orders to hold out against allcomers. Its captains offered no resistance, however, and greeted the rebels into the city. Although Archbishop Bourchier was in London, engaged in convocation with his bishops, it seemed unlikely that the seat of his see would give way to Warwick so easily without his collusion. In retrospect, Morton could appreciate why the King and his advisors had been so wary of him at the end of York's protectorate. At the same time, to confuse matters, he is the half-brother of the Duke of Buckingham, now leading the King's army.

Morton muses on the way family ties are being pulled apart or seemingly strengthened by these conflicts. Speculating on potential political strategies is becoming a necessity for any governmental role. For some, loyalty and family are quite evidently their principal values; for some it is the long-term sense of the common good; for others it is about power and wealth. His thoughts run to those who have ridden out seeking battle and for whom he gives silent prayer. John Beaumont is well known to him as he is on Prince Edward's council, and they regularly converse. At fifty-one, he is eight years older than Morton, is amiable, intelligent, and unswervingly loyal to the King's cause. His second wife, Katherine Strangways, is the sister of Salisbury and aunt to Warwick.

Humphrey Stafford, Duke of Buckingham, is a very different person. The oldest of the army's leaders at fifty-seven, he has great experience as a warrior but also a long-held reputation as a peacemaker: though that predisposition has been put behind him in recent times and he is now anything but a pacifier. Those who come up against him now find him unlikeable, harsh, and ill-tempered. He enjoys the full confidence of King and Queen. Like Beaumont though, he is another related to the Nevilles by marriage, his wife Anne being a sister of Cecily, Duchess of York.

Of the other leaders, forty-six-year-old Shrewsbury is Buckingham's son-in-law. He once got on well with Warwick, but a long-standing dislike of York developed into an understanding of the Duke's brooding treachery, and he moved across to the royal cause. A period as Lord High Treasurer saw him oversee the collapse of economic prosperity in the country.

Edmund Grey, forty-four, has little to recommend him except his pedigree as a great-grandson of John of Gaunt, grand-nephew of Henry IV. His wife is a daughter of the Earl of Northumberland. He was one of three accused of treason in 1457 by the priest Robert Colynson, but nothing was proven. And last there is thirty-seven-year-old Thomas Percy, Lord Egremont; a thug and leader in the Percy-Neville feud seemingly intent above all things to disassociate himself from his mother, Eleanor Neville, sister of the Duchess of York and the Duchess of Buckingham.

Morton must snap himself away from his thoughts and press on with his urgent letters.

There is an emissary calling for an audience with the Queen. An Italian friar, Lorenzo of Florence, has a message and a letter to deliver. He is acting on behalf of the papal legate, Francesco Coppini, Bishop of Terni, who has taken up the Yorkist cause and is riding with the invading army.[3] Or rather, a safe distance behind it.

Coppini is known to Margaret. Early in the previous year, he sought to enlist Henry's support for a crusade against the Turks, which was being proposed by the new pope, Pius II. Henry was invited to send delegates to a conference (known as a diet) of princes at Mantua to discuss and plan the invasion, but because of the civil war developing in England, he was unable to spare any nobles and only sent two priests. This was considered highly disrespectful and swung the sympathies of Pius, and his legate, away from the Lancastrians. Seeing where the wind was blowing, Warwick went out of his way to cultivate a relationship with Coppini, who was looking for pledges of support against Normandy and Gascony on behalf of the Duke of Burgundy. Warwick was keen to secure help to form an alliance with Burgundy, Dauphin Louis (now completely alienated from his father), and with Francesco Sforza, Duke of Milan. Such an alliance would provide York with assistance in his long-term aim to renew war with France.

There is little doubt of York's intention towards the throne. Even a relative stranger and newcomer to the conflict like Coppini understood it and reported back to Pius that Warwick referred to Henry as a dolt and a fool, and that York should be on the throne if there was any justice. Warwick declared that the Yorkists would drive their foes from the King's side and govern the kingdom themselves. The King would be sovereign in name alone. Coppini also reported back on Warwick's claims of infidelity by Margaret and Prince Edward's legitimacy. The papal court has no doubt that it is Warwick's intention to depose Henry.

Lorenzo begins his address to Margaret. Exeter and Morton are in attendance. His demeanour and delivery do not display the humility a queen might expect, and it is clear he is not endearing himself to her. He begins by updating Margaret on the rebel's progress, stressing their gains with no show of sympathy for Henry's situation.

Moving on from Canterbury, the rebel army reached London on 2 July having grown to some 20,000. Like Canterbury, London had orders to resist, but like Canterbury, they welcomed Warwick with acclaim. Lorenzo stressed the popularity of Warwick, particularly with communities who were dependent upon trade, who saw him as their champion. Lorenzo is almost gleeful in imparting that Lord Audley and Edward Brooke, 6th Baron Cobham, were among the recruits to the Yorkist side.[4]

The leaders went to St Paul's on the day after their arrival at the city and met the southern clergy who were in convocation there and to whom they justify their actions, present their goals, and continue to pledge allegiance to the King. There is no dissent from the bishops; some, such as Thomas Bourchier, William Grey (Ely), and – of course – George Neville, actively join Warwick's train.

Lorenzo then offers a letter to Margaret. He informs her that it is a copy of a letter from Coppini delivered to Henry at Northampton, where his troops are entrenched outside the town walls. Margaret coldly declines to take the letter but motions Morton to do so, asking him to read it out loud.

The letter says that the writer prays for a peaceful resolution of the conflict and stresses that he is with the Yorkist army having no other choice. But this is disingenuous and there follows a poorly veiled threat that unless the Yorkist demands are met, then any violence will be Henry's fault. 'You can prevent this war if you will, and if you do not, you will be guilty in the sight of God in that awful Day of Judgment.' Clearly, this is intolerable not only for Henry but also Margaret. It would be impossible in law for any king to take the blame for the consequences of suppressing revolution. The inference has to be that to take such blame Henry would need to be no longer king.

Morton is quick to give the friar a short and vociferous lesson on the rights of kings and how to properly address a queen to boot. The berated cleric leaves without another word, not with his tail between his legs but steely and purposeful.

The next day– it is 10 July – and another messenger gallops into Kenilworth in the late evening rain. While equerries attend to his exhausted horse, the rider runs to the Great Hall where he is met by Morton and after a basic debriefing, servants are sent to summon the Queen and Exeter. The news could hardly be worse. The Yorkists have seized the day at Northampton. They have also seized the King. Buckingham, Shrewsbury, Egremont, and Beaumont are all dead.

The Lancastrian prospects looked good at the start. The men were well entrenched within ditch and behind hedge protecting the Delapre Abbey deer park just to the south of the town, and the royal cannon were also deployed there. Early attempts to speak to the King by the clergy accompanying Warwick's army were denied. Henry was notably affected by the stress of the situation and was kept comfortable in his tent at the rear of the battle lines.

The armies clashed in the early afternoon. Heavy rains had caused the ditches to flood, the powder charges of the cannon were soaked and the guns failed to fire. Yet the Lancastrians retained an advantage. Until, that is, Grey of Ruthin betrayed his peers, letting the troops of Edward, Earl of March, breach the defences and roll over the centre and left of the royal army in a flanking attack. Henry was captured in his tent, where Warwick knelt before him and proclaimed his loyalty. Many seeking to escape the carnage of the battlefield were drowned in the swollen waters of the River Nene.

Also reported is the resignation of William Waynflete as Chancellor, who returned the Great Seal to Henry in his tent at Northampton. There is suspicion that the Bishop of Winchester had some knowledge that the Yorkists would succeed at Northampton and, having presided over the parliament which attainted the rebel leaders, sought to distance himself from the Lancastrian cause. Certainly, he came to no harm under the Yorkist regime. Did he have pre-knowledge of Grey's defection? Or did he surrender to pressure from the other bishops who had shown support for Warwick?

The audience at Kenilworth are frozen by shock and by the jeopardy which is no more than thirty-five miles from their door. It is Margaret who comes out of their communal stupor first, surprising them with a clear plan, no doubt driven by an instinctive need to protect her family, particularly her son. Logic tells her that as long as the Prince of Wales is alive and free then there is little danger to Henry since his death would automatically transfer the crown to Prince Edward. Conversely, if Edward is killed then Henry's chance for survival is minimal. The urgent need is therefore to put distance between themselves and their enemies.

The decision agreed upon is to take flight to Wales and reassess the situation when they have time and safety on their side. They will be safer and faster if they travel as a small group: Margaret and Edward, Exeter, Morton, and no more than a handful of guards. The castle will be held by a skeleton force and the remainder sent north to provide notice of events to the Earl of Northumberland.

The night is spent gathering up jewels, money, clothing and supplies ready for departure at dawn, at which time the small band heads westward in light rain towards the Welsh border with Harlech Castle their destination, 140 miles away. They cover just over half that distance without incident, other than the discomfort of riding along mud tracks in heavy rain, when just outside the market town of Malpas they are waylaid by John Cleger, one of Lord Stanley's men, leading a patrol along the border marches. The bad weather and the distraction of a sacrificed baggage train help the pursued avoid capture and they eventually reach their refuge.[5] They do not stay long though, preferring to travel on to Denbigh Castle, which is occupied by Henry's stepfather and step-brother, Owen and Jasper Tudor. Here Margaret feels safe enough to begin planning actions to free Henry and exact revenge – or, from her perspective, justice. It is also much more accessible to her loyal base in Cheshire, Lancashire, and the northern lords.

Warwick and his army remained at Northampton for three days before setting out back to London with King Henry, once the dead were accounted for and buried. Having seemingly secured the support of the bishops for their manifesto, it is important that they present themselves as suitably subservient to both Church and Crown.

Salisbury and Cobham had remained in London, laying siege to the Tower where Lord Scales, Lord Hungerford and others were holding out and causing damage by launching fireballs into the City. The attack on the Tower was both from the land and from the River Thames, and there was intermittent cannon fire from both sides. However, just as the Lancastrian government continually experienced difficulties in raising money to pay their troops, so the Yorkists ran into the same problem. So much so that they feared a mutiny by the mariners and boatmen involved in the siege and had to make special payments on 9 and 11 July to keep a grip on the Tower. In fact, arguments over wages were such that on the 10th, the blockade was breached by Sir Thomas Browne and others who were able to get much wanted supplies to the besieged. However, Warwick's return to the capital with the King on 16 July signified the futility of further resistance. Scales and Hungerford secured a promise of safe conduct and the Tower was surrendered three days later.

Not believing that his life would be spared, Lord Scales decided to make his escape. He was spotted and hacked to death by watermen. Sir Thomas Browne and five of his accomplices in breaking the blockade were executed on a charge of treason on the 29th. It didn't help them that they served under the Duke of Exeter when he was Constable of the Tower, for the Yorkists had a particular hatred of him. John Archer, a former servant of Exeter, was also executed.

Of the rest, Thomas Thorpe tried to escape but was caught and imprisoned, first at Newgate and then at the Marshalsea. Lord Hungerford, and Sir Edmund Hampden were allowed their freedom and went north looking to join Margaret.[6] The Earl of Kendal, John, Baron Lovell, Lord de la Warr, Lord de Vesey and Sir Gervase Clifton chose to join the Yorkists.[7]

The proclamations of the London populace made it abundantly clear that their support and favour were with Warwick and Henry. Neither York, nor indeed Margaret, commanded much love from the city.

Henry is accommodated in the Bishop of London's Palace at St Paul's. After a couple of weeks settling in, the leaders of the rebellion take Henry on a pilgrimage to Canterbury and the shrine of St Thomas a Becket.

During the pilgrimage, an order is issued in the name of the Council for castles in Wales to surrender, but this is simply ignored.

Richard, Duke of York, eventually landed in England at Redcliffe, Cheshire (amazingly, only thirty-five miles from Denbigh). It is 8 September – nearly two months since the battle of Northampton. York travels south at a painfully slow pace as if on a royal progress. His intentions towards the throne become more evident. As if to ensure there is no doubt, his armorial bearings display the royal arms. There is certainly a lot of sympathy towards the Yorkist complaints, their cries for justice and the reinstatement of their lands and titles, but little or no support for a coup. Warwick had ridden out to meet up with York at Shrewsbury and had apprised him of the London mood, making it clear that a light touch would be needed to win the propaganda war. In the meantime, rumours were being circulated by Warwick's men that continued to deny the legitimacy of Prince Edward, and also that troops from Cheshire and the Midlands were being recruited to the Lancastrian cause on promise of being permitted to loot the richer south-eastern counties.

In anticipation of York's arrival, a parliament had been called for 7 October. Henry, who had been staying at Greenwich and Eltham for hunting and other pastimes since the return from the pilgrimage, was moved to Westminster Palace where he resided in the Queen's Apartments.

The first business for parliament was to repeal the Act of Attainder. It was then necessary to confirm appointments within the Council and other rewards to key supporters. The Bishop of Exeter was made Chancellor, Viscount Bourchier became Treasurer, and the Earl of March and John, Lord Wenlock joined the Council. Other elevations include John Neville to King's Chamberlain, and Salisbury to Great Chamberlain of England; John Dynham is made Chancellor of Ireland; Warwick becomes Constable of Dover Castle and Warden of the Cinq Ports. And Francesco Coppini is granted a licence to become an English bishop to pave the way for nomination as a cardinal.

On 10 October, York arrives in London and theatrically enters parliament at Westminster. He has decided to cast subtlety aside and act wholly in character. Not only that, but everyone needs to be aware that he is nobody's puppet: particularly not a Neville puppet. Before him is carried his vertical sword pointing upwards to the roof and he strides to the vacant throne on which he places his hand, symbolically claiming it for himself. Those present are stunned into silence. York is expecting thunderous applause and acknowledgement. Nothing. Frustrated and angry, he storms out. Only as far as the King's Apartments though, which had been made up for him, suggesting Warwick's hand in a piece of propaganda. Though Henry was resident in the neighbouring Queen's apartments, York avoided meeting with him.

What followed were heated discussions over three weeks to try to square the circle over York's claim. There were many objections. These included the several oaths that had been taken to be true to Henry – and his family. Acts of Parliament had confirmed the legitimacy of the Lancastrian claim to the throne descending through its male heirs, and the assertion of Henry IV that he had taken the Crown by right of inheritance from Henry III had been upheld. York's claim to have a stronger right of inheritance was rejected. But a politically acceptable compromise had to be reached. In the end, while the lords and bishops were unwilling to break their oaths in respect of Henry, they found their way to overlook their sworn affinity to Prince Edward. So, on 25 October it was announced by George Neville, Lord Chancellor, that while Henry would continue as King, York – or his successor – would take the throne after his death. Henry conceded, thereby disinheriting his son, who also lost his title Prince of Wales, which was transferred to York. York was confirmed as Protector, giving him control of government.

It is said that Henry signed his agreement to this betrayal of his family without duress, but his mind was frayed. He was returned to the Bishop of London's care.

Prince Edward's disinheritance is conveyed to Margaret and her small court by the priest Lorenzo of Florence, acting on behalf of Coppini. To no one's surprise, she receives the news with unbridled fury and dismay. But when he presents a letter from Henry calling on her to join him in London her mood becomes ice cold, and Lorenzo is simply dismissed and told to wait for letters to take back to London.

When the Florentine has left, Margaret reveals that before she parted with Henry they had agreed on the use of a particular flourish to his signature if any correspondence from him was freely written with no coercion. The letter received via Lorenzo was not signed with that flourish. That proved, if proof be needed, that Henry was being held as a prisoner and the accommodation of York could therefore be denied legitimacy.

On instruction, Morton sets about drawing up a letter to the Council purporting to come from the eight-year-old Edward. Similar letters are also issued in the names of Margaret and of Jasper Tudor. The Prince's letter begins by denouncing York as an evil, oath-breaking traitor who has blinded the lords with untruths, setting them against his royal person. York has laid claim to the throne with lies and pretence. Aware of Yorkist propaganda, Morton includes an undertaking that the city will not be despoiled or looted by any Lancastrian soldiers under pain of 'extreme punishment'. But it does press the point that the only way Edward and his mother will return to London will be at the head of a large military force to free the King and bring traitors to justice. This letter is read to Council on 2 December. A similar letter from the Earl of Northumberland arrives soon after.

At the same time, letters are sent out from Margaret calling for an army to gather at Kingston upon Hull to rescue the King and by mid-December about 15,000 had been assembled, the largest contingents provided by the Earl of Northumberland, the Earl of Devon, as well as Percies, Dacres, Cliffords, and the northern Nevilles. They were also joined by the Duke of Somerset.

The Yorkists obviously know exactly where Margaret and Prince Edward are, and it will only be a matter of time before they make an effort to capture or kill them. Up to now, they have been distracted and perhaps have underestimated the Queen's resolve and ability. What have those distractions been from such an important objective?

From the moment the Scots heard of the Calais lords landing at Sandwich they seized the opportunity to cross the border and laid siege to Roxburgh Castle. There was an attempt to mask the continuation of ubiquitous border raids by alleging that this was to assist the Yorkist cause, but that was quickly denied by Warwick's party as any such link up would damage them more than it could help. In fact, Salisbury was instructed to raise a relief army for the besieged castle.

Scottish peers were as capable of stupid actions as their English counterparts and so it was that on 3 August, King James II managed to put himself next to a Flemish cannon at the siege, which exploded, killing him instantly. The Scots continued with the siege of the castle though, and five days later captured and dismantled it. They then went on to do the same to Wark Castle, after which they decided to call a halt to hostilities and discuss terms for a peace.

The new king of Scotland was the eight-year-old James III, the country under the regency of his mother, Mary of Guelders.

Having achieved a level of stability for the Yorkist situation in England, Warwick returned briefly to Calais and the Duke of Somerset finally had to surrender Guines. However, Somerset engineered an escape through France with aid from Charles VII, who was aware that the Burgundians and Yorkists were colluding over a possible invasion of his country. Charles would also provide assurances of safe conduct to Margaret and Prince Edward.

Somerset reaches England on 21 September and establishes himself at Corfe Castle, Dorset (less than twenty miles from Milborne St Andrew) and by December he is with the Earl of Northumberland, having raised a thousand men from the south-west.

Margaret considers her next move and concludes that she should travel to Scotland to seek help. Morton will go with her, but Exeter will join the northern lords and keep her in touch with their progress as well as any news on Yorkist movements.

The royal party return to Harlech and take a boat up the west coast to the River Nith, navigating the river to Dumfries and then to Lincluden Priory, arriving in early December. They have also decided to take the priest Lorenzo with them; not that they have suddenly found him charming, but perhaps he will have value in either conveying their side of the argument in the civil war or, if not, he might be a useful vector for disseminating false news of their intentions to the Yorkists.

Margaret and her small group were greeted well by twenty-six-year-old Mary of Guelders, four years her junior. Mary held the regency of the Scottish crown as one of a council of seven. She was convivial towards her guests but cautious, and with no money but only the promise provided by her growing army in the north of England, Margaret was not in a strong bargaining position. Charles VII pressed Mary to do what she could to assist the Lancastrians, who were also supported by her chief advisor James Kennedy, Bishop of St Andrews. But Mary was the great-niece of Philip the Good, Duke of Burgundy, who was hosting Charles's disaffected son, the Dauphin Louis, and both were building a relationship with the Yorkists with an eye on a joint attack on France. As this relationship developed, Mary's sympathies for the Lancastrian cause diminished.

While Margaret and Mary bonded, Morton built an understanding – a friendship even – with Kennedy, appreciating the older prelate's religious priorities which combined with a reforming outlook. An accommodation of sorts was achieved. Mary promised Margaret some troops and provisions and Margaret proposed to recommend to Henry and his council the betrothal of Prince Edward to Mary's daughter, another Margaret. Discussions progressed at a leisurely but business-like pace with due reverence and relaxations over the Christmas period but were swiftly brought to a conclusion in the New Year with the arrival of the astonishing news that the Duke of York and the Earl of Salisbury were dead.

12

Rota Fortunae

Richard, Duke of York was the personification of misplaced self-belief. If the Lancastrians lost the battle òf Northampton being understrength and finding themselves in bad circumstances, York lost the battle of Wakefield by being understrength and creating bad circumstances for himself.

News had reached London by late November 1460 of the assembly of an army in the north by Henry Percy, Earl of Northumberland and his cohorts. There was also a steady stream of complaints of pillaging of the estates and tenants of York and Salisbury. The Yorkists had taken their eye off the ball as they wrestled with Council and parliament to resolve the matter of succession after Henry, but now this had been achieved York and Salisbury decided they would go themselves to teach these plunderers a lesson. This decision was also reinforced by jealousy as to the level of popularity and influence enjoyed by Warwick.

With Warwick and Norfolk left behind to safeguard London, the two lords, along with York's son the Earl of Rutland, left London on 9 December with about 6,000 men. Having seen supporters flock to Warwick's banner on the march from Sandwich to London, they anticipated adding to their army on their journey north. However, not only were they marching through the Midlands, which was strong on Lancastrian sympathies, but they were also without the charisma of a Warwick. So their army never grew to the strength required. Setting out from London at the same time, Edward, the Earl of March, took a force westward towards Wales, aiming to recruit and join up with his father later.

The biggest mistake was in underestimating the strength and determination of the enemy. A force of up to 15,000 awaited them. York and his men reached Sandal Castle at Wakefield on 21 December where they spent the Christmas holiday. On 30 December, a contingent left the castle to forage for food in the neighbourhood and were attacked by Lancastrians. Without hesitation, York and Salisbury led the garrison out to rescue their colleagues, only to find themselves outnumbered by nearly three to one. York and Rutland fell on the battlefield. Also lost were William Bonville, Lord Harington, Salisbury's son-in-law; Sir Thomas Harington; Sir Thomas Neville, a son of Salisbury; eighteen-year-old Sir Edward Bourchier; Sir James Pickering; Sir Harry Radford, and Sir Thomas Parr, either on the field of battle or succumbing later.[1] Salisbury was taken prisoner to nearby Pontefract. He pled for his life on promise of paying a large fine but was dragged from his cell the next morning and beheaded, Thomas Holland, bastard son of the Duke of Exeter, the executioner.

York had sent a message to March calling on him to come to Sandal. If he had waited in the castle for his son's arrival the outcome may have been different. With their blood lust up, the victorious lords authorised the mutilation of the corpses of their enemies, which was not the best of ways to win over the undecided but not out of tune with the times. The leaders' heads were put on spikes over the gates to the city of York, to greet Margaret on her arrival there on 20 January.

The grisly sight did not deflect Margaret; there was still much to do. Her mind was focussed on the necessary march to London to rescue the King. It was now the heart of winter and food for the army was in short supply, made more critical by the exceptional rainfall throughout 1460 which had severely reduced the harvest. The Yorkists also ensured that supplies from the south did not reach their enemies. Pillaging became a necessity, and this fuelled the fears of the southerners. The Lancastrians were well aware they would receive little support, not least because no response had been forthcoming to any of the letters sent to the city and to Council. The speed of Margaret's response to the news of Wakefield meant that the number of Scottish troops accompanying her was smaller than it could have been, but their very presence added colour to tales of wild barbarians from the north descending on the civilisation of the Home Counties.

Morton watched the long, stretched-out columns with a sense of anticipation and excitement but also a growing concern at the extent to which pillaging was increasing. The sheer quantity of supplies needed to keep an army of this size was one thing (to march and fight a soldier required a substantial intake of meat, dairy produce, bread and other grain foods, and ale – although few vegetables) but it was noticeable that many were taking chattels, even plate from churches.

For almost four weeks the Lancastrian army moved south, its foraging parties raiding and scavenging ever wider, and the fear generated by their activities, the unusual talk and accents of Scottish, Welsh, and northerners generally, and simply that they were 'strangers', preceded them always.

On 16 February the army reached Dunstable, about thirty-seven miles from London, when the first resistance was met resulting in a small skirmish. Though easily dealt with, it is remembered because of its leader, a local butcher, who hanged himself in the shame of his defeat.

The next day, St Albans was reached where Warwick's army was found to be re-setting its battle lines. The Yorkist scouts had failed to detect the Lancastrian army and, assuming he had the benefit of time, Warwick was repositioning his troops when the enemy fell upon him in a flanking manoeuvre. The impact of the surprise caused the Yorkists to flee; their predicament, as so frequently in this war, once again worsened by a defection – this time by the Kent captain Sir Henry Lovelace switching to Margaret's side.[2] That is not to say that fighting was anything but ferocious and some 3,000 were left dead on the battlefield, most of whom were Yorkists.

Warwick had brought Henry with him from London. This was to stress that the King was under his protection, if not under his command. Warwick was unable to be a king himself, but he wanted his power to be unquestioned. The defeat at St Albans was the first step in the dismantling of that power. But it also proved to signal the dismantling of the Lancastrians.

In the confusion of the battle, Warwick and the Duke of Norfolk fled westward with an eye to joining up with Edward, Earl of March, who had earlier set out for Wales. The King was completely forgotten in this chaos, and he took the opportunity of sending one of his attendants, Thomas Hoo, to let Margaret know of his presence and good health.[3] Margaret, Prince Edward, along with Morton and others, were situated safely away from the battlefield and it was Northumberland who received the message, who then arranged to have Henry brought to Lord Clifford's tent for the family reunion. The royal family embraced with no little emotion, after which Morton stepped forward with his book of set prayers, or orisons, which he read while Henry conferred knighthood on some thirty individuals. First was the eight-year-old Edward resplendent in a suit of brigandines, that is steel plates covered with a heavy purple velvet and offset with gold ornamentation. After Edward is knighted, the honour is bestowed by the boy-prince on supporters such as Thomas Tresham, Speaker of the last parliament, Robert Whittingham, Prince Edward's Receiver-General, and not least, Andrew Trollope. Brought forward with the assistance of a colleague, Trollope had trod on a caltrop during the battle. This was a device of four metal spikes arranged such that when it was cast to the ground, one spike would always point upwards. Their primary deployment was against cavalry and dozens would be cast in front of battlelines for protection. Notwithstanding his injury, Trollope claimed fifteen kills at the battle. No one contradicted him.

Then, two knights are brought into the tent, their hands bound behind them with rope. They are sixty-eight-year-old Baron William Bonville and sixty-five-year-old Sir Thomas Kyriell. Bonville was an Agincourt veteran and had conducted a twenty-four-year feud with Thomas Courtney, Earl of Devon. Kyriell, another soldier of Henry V, had been elevated to the Order of the Garter by Warwick just eight days earlier. They had been guarding Henry during the battle and stayed with the King after the Yorkist army broke and fled to ensure his safety, expecting a pardon for themselves. Instead, Devon accused them of treason and their fate was soon sealed. As part of his induction into kingly behaviour, Prince Edward was made president of the court trying these ill-fated prisoners and was called upon to pronounce how they should die, to which he replied beheading, and they were duly taken outside and their heads lopped off.

This was widely regarded as a cruel and unjust action as it undoubtedly was, since their hopes for pardon appear to have come from words given by Henry himself. Justice is replaced by vendetta. This is common to both sides, but it is particularly damaging to the Lancastrian cause and their relationship with London. Morton struggled with this for only a short while. The bottom line for him was that Bonville and Kyriell were traitors. They had taken up arms against their king. To that extent, their sentence was merciful and befitting men of rank: they could have been hung, drawn and quartered.

The escalating viciousness in the civil war was of concern to the conscience. Morton would have been aware that it was he who read the orisons because there were no bishops present, all prelates having either declared for the Yorkists or simply kept their distance from the political and military scene. The return of the King also presented a conundrum as to who was commanding the royal forces. Henry, though seemingly physically healthy, was certainly not the man Morton had met five years previously at Coventry. Whilst he was aware and active in religious and ceremonial duties – and, by all accounts, in his favourite pastimes of hunting in its various forms – political discussions saw his inner light visibly turn off, pupils dilate, and head sag. His ability to engage trust and project leadership were much diminished.

Margaret was no longer able to direct actions herself, being a woman and therefore subservient to her husband. Her goal of securing the release of the King had succeeded and now it was expected that she would step back; which, in practice, put command in the hands of Northumberland,

Somerset, and their peers. However, the Queen would continue to be driven by her need to protect her son and his inheritance.

The immediate urgency was to secure the support of London, but also to provide sustenance for the army, which was drained of strength and morale in the winter weather. Soldiers continued to take food from whoever and wherever they could. Not only that, but books and manuscripts were looted to fuel fires and plate and chalices stolen from churches and abbeys. Abbot John Whethamstede of St Albans' Benedictine monastery successfully pleaded for Henry to issue an order against plundering, only for offenders to argue that Margaret had authorised their actions in lieu of wages. This situation quickly filtered through to London, adding to citizens' fears of a northern mob and illustrating the decline in authority of the Crown over its own forces.

The imperative for decisive action was also impelled by news from the West Country.

As Warwick prepared to move north to engage Margaret's army, Edward, Earl of March headed westward to raise volunteers to the Yorkist cause and also to engage with any Lancastrian forces along the Welsh border. At just short of 6ft 4in, the nineteen-year-old Edward cuts a striking figure. With a genial disposition, unless crossed, he is a lively and charismatic magnet to followers. Not only that, but he leads a band of talented and seasoned soldiers. These include John Tuchet, Baron Audley, sixty-one-year-old John, Lord Wenlock, Walter Deveraux, William Herbert, William Hastings and Humphrey Stafford.[4]

The Earl of Wiltshire and the king's half-brother, Sir Jasper Tudor, Earl of Pembroke, had recently arrived in Wales by sea at Milford Haven with a contingent of Frenchmen, Bretons, and Irish. They soon joined Sir Owen Tudor, Henry's stepfather, leading a sizeable Welsh army, and together moved eastward.

Anticipating their route in the winter weather, Edward based his army at Wigmore Castle and on receiving confirmation that the Lancastrians were approaching, advanced to meet them at Mortimer's Cross, some four miles away. Here, on 2 February, the Yorkists imposed a heavy defeat on their enemy and Jasper Tudor and Wiltshire fled.[5] Some 2,000 Lancastrian lives were lost at Mortimer's Cross, and possibly half that number of Yorkists. The battle brought Edward to the fore, no longer the apprentice of Warwick.

The victory also provided Edward the opportunity to exact some revenge for the death of his father and younger brother at Wakefield. Among those captured was Owen Tudor. Tudor was anticipating his freedom on payment of a ransom or fine, but that hope was soon dispelled and he was summarily beheaded. Joining him on the block in Hereford marketplace were nine other leaders. This mass execution failed to attract the concern or censure that would follow a similar action at St Albans ten days later by the Lancastrians.

The Lancastrians had moved a further ten miles south to Barnet but were still ten miles from the City of London. It is John Morton who steps forward to suggest that a letter be sent to the common council of London requesting they be admitted to the city and, in the meantime, that supplies be sent to feed the army to prevent plundering. The Londoners agree to send out supplies but seek greater assurances on what will happen if the Lancastrian army is allowed entrance into the capital. To this purpose they send out a delegation on 19 February comprising the Duchess of Bedford, the Duchess of Buckingham, and Lady Scales. Although their brief is to talk to both King and Queen, it is obvious from the choice of delegates that it is Margaret who is regarded as the decision maker. Bedford and Scales had both been in Margaret's escort from France and were well known to her, Scales remaining an attendant to the Queen. The Duchess of Buckingham, of course, was godmother to Prince Edward and a long-time friend. Here is yet another pointer to the King's lack of competence.

The next day, the delegation returns to London with a firm promise against pillaging in the city, but words of goodwill are qualified with the equally firm promise that it is the intention of Henry and Margaret to punish 'the evil doers'. The reaction of London and Londoners is not favourable to the Lancastrians. They simply do not like or trust the northerners and fear retribution, they are anxious over the beheadings carried out at St Albans and what precedent they might set, and – like the Lancastrians – they are now aware that Warwick and the balance of his army have met up with Edward of March and they are now travelling eastward.

Carts laden with food for the Lancastrian troops are destroyed by the Londoners. Lancastrians Sir Baldwin Fulford and Sir Alexander Hody are attacked at Westminster.[6] A delegation from Henry is allowed to enter London to assess the city's feelings towards the Lancastrians on 22 February under Sir Edmund Hampden, Sir John Heron, and Sir Robert Whittingham.[7] What they found confirmed that London was not willing to acclaim the Lancastrians and allow them access. With no supplies or financial aid, the ongoing winter weather, and the prospect of a large Yorkist force arriving soon, the Lancastrians decided to retire north, having no capacity for a further battle.

Edward and his army arrived at London and with his leading supporters was admitted into the city on 26 February to acclaim and celebrations. He had met up with Warwick and his men at Chipping Norton, about seventy miles west of St Albans.

A momentous decision had to be made. Since the Yorkists no longer had hold of Henry, they lacked any legitimacy to govern the country. With York's death their logic is that the accord which made him heir to Henry's crown should now pass to Edward. At the same time, York's death also permitted them to break that accord and Edward could now claim the throne in his own right by bloodline. If they do not claim the throne, then the only alternative is to flee the country. The claim to the throne by right is, of course, a weak one: not least because Henry still lives. But Edward offers a vigour and vitality that Henry cannot match and his popularity, at least in the south-east, is high. He has also just won an important battle, whereas Warwick has just lost one. His presence has also driven the Lancastrians with their barbarous hordes from the very gates of London, saving it from ransack.

On 1 March, George Neville, Bishop of Exeter and Chancellor of England, creates momentum for the case in a speech to a crowd of thousands outside the city walls at Clerkenwell, by which he secures popular consent to usurp Henry with Edward. The propaganda campaign continues and the Council's blessing to Edward's claim is obtained on 3 March, and he is then sworn in as King the next day by Archbishop Bourchier. He had yet to be anointed and crowned but was now acknowledged as King Edward IV.

There was no time to celebrate though. If Edward was to impose and sustain his authority on the whole of the country, he needed to conclusively defeat his enemies in battle. His first action therefore was to call on the leading families in southern England below the River Trent and to issue Commissions of Array to county sheriffs to recruit men and join him on his journey north to crush his enemies.

In particular, Edward announced that he would pardon any adherent of Henry VI if they submitted within ten days except for persons having land worth a hundred or more marks a year or, especially, twenty-two people named as traitors: which list included Doctor John Morton.

It was 46-year-old John Mowbray, Duke of Norfolk, who set off from London first to raise men from East Anglia on 5 March. On the 7th, it was Warwick's turn, and he took a sizeable force into the West and Midlands drawing in considerable reinforcements to his cause. Not only that, but he also captured Thomas, Bastard of Exeter, who had beheaded Warwick's father at Pontefract, and took satisfaction in taking his head at Coventry. Lord Fauconberg, now fifty-seven, set out with the vanguard of the army on 11 March and Edward followed two days later with the supply wagons. Despite severe winter weather and a shortage of provisions – not least because they were travelling in the wake of the Lancastrian army – the Yorkists' march averaged twelve miles a day.

The royal party had retired to York, the capital of northern England, which they reached on 12 March, the main army coming on behind them, and they began calling on families throughout the north to provide military aid. Moving as quickly as possible, they hoped to ensure that the impending showdown took place on their 'home' territory and as far from the Yorkist base of London and the Southeast as possible.

Morton, appointed as Archdeacon of Norwich the previous year, had been given permission to leave the retiring army to go to Norwich cathedral so that he could formally occupy the position, being inducted by Bishop Walter Hart.[8] When he caught up with the royal army, he decided to stay with it rather than press on to join the King and Queen at York and fell in with James Butler, Earl of Wiltshire, who presented him with a sword and dagger; hoping that he wouldn't need the use of them but that they would provide some insurance should matters prove hazardous.

Not long after, they crossed the River Aire at Ferrybridge, just beyond Pontefract. With the army safely on the north bank, the Lancastrians demolished the bridge and moved off to encamp about eight miles away near the village of Towton. This was their chosen battlefield and their 50,000 troops settled down as best they could to await the enemy.

The full Yorkist army, with the exception of Norfolk and his 5,000 men who were still struggling to catch up, reached the river on 28 March, the day before Palm Sunday. Their number is not far short of the Lancastrian force. Keen to minimise delay, not least because of the dreadful weather and limited food supplies, Edward ordered a new bridge to be built. Construction work continued through the night and by early morning it was complete. Their industry had been under observation by the Lancastrians though, and at first light a strong column of about 500 horsemen under John, Lord Clifford, charged the bridge and captured it.[9] There followed a short, fierce fight in which John Radcliffe, Lord Fitzwalter, who was in command of the bridge detachment, received mortal wounds and Warwick's half-brother was killed. Warwick himself was injured in the retaking of the bridge when hit by an arrow in his leg, but the Yorkists won the encounter and drove the Lancastrians back towards their main army, Clifford being killed in the retreat with an arrow to his neck.

The Lancastrian lines are drawn up on a half-mile wide plateau which falls away into a valley known as Dintingdale. To their left is marshy ground and to their right a narrow but deep stream named Cock Beck. There appears little option for the Yorkists but to mount a full-frontal attack. In overall command of the Lancastrians is Somerset and, with Trollope, he holds the right wing. Northumberland holds the left, and Exeter the reserve.

From this position of advantage, Morton at first hears and then sees the advancing Yorkists. Even though he knows he is surrounded by one of the largest armies assembled in England, and that they hold the high ground, yet he is in awe of the spectacle before him. Subconscious thoughts of Agincourt would begin to rise. Then, as the Yorkist front advances up the side of the valley, a fierce wind shifts to drive sleet and snow directly into the faces of the Lancastrian archers who are holding the plateau ridge. The winter storm is so blinding that the archers' arrows have little effect, in contrast to those of the Yorkists who are firing with the wind behind them. And then the Yorkists are on the plateau in brutal hand-to-hand fighting. Accompanied by the sounds of swords, poleaxes, and maces clashing against armour, and by screams where armour is penetrated, Morton retires to the rear lines.

The battle is in the balance until the afternoon. Then the Duke of Norfolk arrives with his reinforcements, who provide a flanking movement against a pressed Lancastrian line. It is too much for the Lancastrian soldiers. Their nerve breaks and a chaotic stampede begins in the direction of York. The result is devastation as the Yorkists pursue and butcher. Hundreds are drowned trying to ford the Cock Beck or, further north, the River Wharfe at Tadcaster where the Lancastrians had destroyed the bridge in anticipation of a flanking movement by their enemies. Indeed, at the latter location a new bridge was formed – from the dead bodies of the drowned.

Morton had been numbed by what was happening in front of him but was pulled out of his shock when Wiltshire raced past, urging him to follow and flee. As his senses returned, Morton put both heels to his horse. In the corner of his eye he perceived a figure running towards him and he caught a glimpse of the man wearing Warwick's badge of the Ragged Staff. He pulled his sword, swinging downwards, and felt the impact as contact was made. He galloped on into the swirling snow without looking back.

The loss of Lancastrian leaders at Towton seriously diminishes the strength of the King's party. The Earl of Northumberland (mortally wounded fleeing the battlefield); Randolph, Baron Dacre of Gillesland (killed by an arrow to the head): Baron John Neville (killed with Clifford after Ferrybridge), Lionel, Baron Welles: and Sir Ralph Bigod, are all felled. And perhaps the greatest loss is Andrew Trollope.

In the wake of the battle, Edward displays the ruthless streak that will secure his throne against all-comers and, by exceeding any previous examples of war criminality, sets the tone for his successors. Forty-two captured knights and lords are summarily executed. The order of the day had been to take no prisoners.

Those fleeing the battlefield, whether lord or common soldier, are hunted down leaving bodies scattered over an area of six miles by three. It is estimated that 20,000 Lancastrians died at Towton and 8,000 Yorkists.

Somerset was riding hard and reached York ahead of his pursuers. On hearing news of the disaster, Henry, Margaret and Edward flee to Scotland, arriving there in April, joined by Exeter, Lord Roos, Sir Robert Whittingham, Sir John Fortescue and others.

Edward entered York the day following the battle. His first action was to take down the heads of his father, brother, Salisbury and the other Yorkist leaders at Wakefield from Micklegate Bar, replacing them with the heads of the Lancastrian fallen. These included the badly injured Earl of Devon, who was dragged out of his bed to be executed.

Morton sits in the gloom of his prison cell within the Tower of London. It is furnished with two wooden stools, one for him and the second for any visitor or inquisitor needing it. There is a small desk, a straw bed, and a slops bucket. The little room enjoys no ventilation other than a grille in the heavy wooden door, but there is a modest open fire to combat the chill and damp. Considering Morton is not of the aristocracy, it is generous accommodation.

His mind drifts back to the flight from Towton through the blinding snowstorm, which with nightfall aided escape. After a time, it seemed safe to slow down to walking pace. Indeed, it was necessary as the horses were having a hard time of it. Four had made it through together: Morton, Wiltshire, Sir Ralph Plumpton, and Doctor Ralph Makerel.[10] They decided to press on north-westward seeking to eventually find a boat to take them to the safety of Scotland. They nearly made it.

Over the course of a week, they put some 120 miles behind them to reach Cockermouth, just 10 miles from the coast. Whether their movements had been noted and reported, or whether it was just bad luck, they were captured by a patrol from Carlisle under the command of the Sheriff of Cumberland, Richard Salkeld.[11] The prisoners were then transported to the eastern coast to Newcastle where Edward was surveying the northern extremity of those parts safe for the Yorkist regime and making plans for bringing the rest of the country under control up to the Scottish border.

It was with the greatest trepidation that the four were brought before Edward on 1 May, who arrived in Newcastle a few days after their incarceration. They were made well aware that he had already executed forty-two captured Lancastrian leaders since Towton as well as having sanctioned the slaughter of hundreds of common soldiers. James Butler, who had established a reputation for leading from the back, was swiftly judged and executed, Morton and his two companions being compelled to watch the beheading.

Sir William Plumpton had seen enough and agreed to pay a bond of £2,000 and swear allegiance to Edward. He was given a full pardon the next year. Morton would not submit however and, in any event, neither he nor Makerel had the wherewithal to give their bond. On 10 May, Edward appointed his close friend, Sir William Hastings, to lead a commission investigating Morton's 'treasons' committed in York: effectively an inquiry into his actions, initiatives and relationship with Henry and Margaret.[12] In the meantime, Morton, Makerel, and, in a casket, Wiltshire's head were sent south to London and the Tower.

And so, forty-five-year-old Morton contemplates what future he may have. If indeed he has a future. Certainly, all his income, his positions, and his reputation are gone. Not least, he is at risk of a traitor's death of being hung, cut down alive, disembowelled, and axed into quarters. His King, his Queen and the legitimate heir to the throne are all alive though, so denying them – even should it mean death – is no option.

A silent recitation of Psalm Three would have been appropriate to his situation:

Lord, how my enemies have increased!
Many are rising up against me.
Many are saying of my soul,
"There is no salvation for him in God." Selah.
But You, Lord, are a shield around me,
My glory, and the One who lifts my head.

The next that is known is that Morton escapes his imprisonment. There is no record of how this escape was achieved but, given that his confinement is in what was regarded as the most secure royal residence and prison in the country, inside help would seem essential. Given also that Morton is not capable of affording a bribe such inside help would need to have been from the highest quarters.

The obvious candidate for John's liberator is his patron Archbishop Bourchier using the auspices of his brother, Viscount Bourchier, who also happens to be Constable of the Tower.[13] There is also the 'old school' tie of Oxford University, which ensures he is joined by Ralph Makerel.

13

Intrigue in France and Scotland, 1461–1463

A three-masted trading ship gently eased into Dieppe. Its cargo unloaded, it stayed at the dock overnight, to be reloaded with goods in the morning which it would take on down the coast to Portugal. In the early hours, two fugitives noiselessly disembarked. Only too aware that they had no safe conduct papers, Morton and Makerel decided to travel north until they could find a small fishing boat which would take them across to Scotland to rejoin the Lancastrians. They had been provided with a small amount of currency and were able to purchase food and cider to keep their strength up. On their third day on Normandy soil, they have travelled nearly twenty miles to arrive at the town of Eu, just two miles inland from the sea. Although still in no little peril, for the Count of Eu is the Charles of Artois who was a prisoner of the English for twenty-three years following Agincourt, they take this first practical opportunity to give thanks for their deliverance at the Church of Notre-Dame et Saint-Laurent. It doesn't take long for the two to learn that there are high-ranking Englishmen in the town.

Cautious, for these could be Yorkists, they discover they are among friends: it is the Duke of Somerset, Robert, Lord Hungerford and Sir Robert Whittingham on a mission from Queen Margaret. They have come from Scotland with a request for support – a treaty of peaceful relations, a loan of 20,000 crowns, and an army with which to press the Yorkists. They have already sent a messenger to Charles VII to receive them, and have sent similar letters to Charles, Count of Maine, to Pierre de Breze, and other French lords. It is Somerset's intention to strike out alone to see his friend the Count of Charolais and, through him, Dauphin Louis. They are able to catch up with the news.

On arrival in Scotland, the royal party were first accommodated at Linlithgow Palace, about fifteen miles west of Edinburgh, while a more permanent residence was fitted out for them at the Dominican convent in the capital. There was a price to pay for Scottish sanctuary though, and that was to relinquish Berwick, which Henry did on 25 April. He also agreed to cede Carlisle if the Scots could take possession of it.

After Towton, the Lancastrian cause became heavily dependent on the support of foreign powers, particularly Scotland and France. The level of that support depended entirely on the politics of the moment: the extent to which they wanted to embarrass Yorkist England or frustrate any threatening diplomatic or military schemes the English might be considering aligning themselves with.

This was immediately evident in efforts by Edward, Philip of Burgundy, Dauphin Louis, and indeed the leading lords of Scotland to prevent any alliance with the Lancastrians. But the promise of Berwick was too great an offer to turn down.

Putting Berwick, and indeed Carlisle, in Scottish hands was an essential part of the Lancastrian plan for striking back at Edward, as it secured the border from the Yorkists, making incursion from Northumbrian fortresses feasible and with a route for supplies or to safety kept open.

Edward was well aware of the need to subdue opposition in the north and to remove Henry, Margaret and Prince Edward one way or another if his crown was to be secure and peace and order returned to the country. So he left Warwick and John Neville, now promoted to Lord Montagu, to stem any action by either the Lancastrians or the Scots and also William Herbert, now Lord Herbert, to bring Wales to heel. Newcastle was left in the hands of Fauconberg, who also commanded the fleet, which was constantly patrolling the coast and routes to France.

The Lancastrian move was not long in the waiting. With Berwick resolved, the Scots and the English refugees began a siege of Carlisle in June. The siege could not be maintained though, and the town was relieved by Montagu. Warwick also challenged a raiding party on Durham made by Roos and Fortescue, sending them packing.

It was agreed that there was little, if anything, Morton and Makerel could do in France and so they made immediate steps to get to Scotland. Additional funds from Hungerford, with the warning of many English patrol ships up and down the coast, provided them sufficient to hire a small boat and crew to get them to Edinburgh.

This was a fortunate decision for Morton. The messenger that Hungerford had sent to Charles soon returned with the concerning news that the French king had just died, apparently of blood poisoning from an infected jaw. This meant that the Dauphin, no friend to the Lancastrian cause to date, was to be enthroned as Louis XI.

Somerset was found to have no papers of safe conduct and was held in custody at Arques, some six miles inland from Dieppe, while Hungerford and Whittingham are detained in Dieppe itself, albeit able to move freely within the town.

Meanwhile, Edward had slowly moved west and south, visiting many towns as a procession towards his formal crowning in London and he arrived at Shene, Richmond on 12 June. Edward formally entered London on 26 June when he bestowed twenty-eight knighthoods that included his brothers, George and Richard.

The coronation duly took place two days later, and in spectacular fashion, at Westminster Abbey, Thomas Bourchier, Archbishop of Canterbury anointing Edward and placing the crown of the Confessor on his head – delivered up by brother William, Viscount Bourchier.

After the coronation there are more rewards distributed to Edward's chief supporters. William Hastings becomes Lord Hastings and King's Chamberlain, Sir William Herbert becomes Lord Herbert, Sir Walter Deveraux is elevated to Lord Ferrers, Sir Humphrey Stafford is Earl of Devon, John Tiptoft the Earl of Worcester, and Henry Bourchier is Earl of Essex.

But time could not be spent long on the trappings of power and priority had to be given to its exercise. At Calais, Hammes Castle would hold out against the Yorkists until the autumn. In the Channel, Pierre de Breze had already taken advantage of the situation, leading a French force to occupy Jersey as early as May (although he was recalled by the new king, Louis). But it was Wales that became the point of focus against the Lancastrians.

Lords Herbert and Ferrers were instructed to raise an army on the marches, and Philip Harveys, Master of the King's Ordnance, was approaching Hereford with cannon and other weaponry in train by mid-August. The army was ordered to meet Edward at Hereford on 8 September, but the King did not arrive until nine days later due to a week's sojourn at Bristol, where he also witnessed the execution of Sir Baldwin Fulford, who had tried to intercept Warwick between Ireland and Calais. This is another example of Edward's enjoyment of revenge on his enemies. With his eyes on advancing that revenge, Edward then decided to concentrate his mind on the Westminster parliament called for early November and he left the Welsh problem entirely to Herbert and Ferrers. They made Pembroke castle their first target, which Sir John Scudamore surrendered on 30 September and by 4 October all the Welsh castles were in Yorkist hands except Carreg Cennen (which held out until May 1462) and Harlech (until 1468).[1] Lords Exeter and Pembroke fled the country in October and Welsh resistance was then, to all intents and purposes, inconsequential.

Edward's first parliament began on 4 November 1461, two days after which 46-year-old John Mowbray, Duke of Norfolk died, a personal and political loss to the King. The meaty business of the parliament did not start until its ninth day when Edward's hereditary right to the crown was confirmed and the Lancastrian kings declared usurpers. The next obvious step in proceedings was to remove the attainder against the leading Yorkists and a new Act of Attainder against the Lancastrians was presented and passed. Those attainted were headed by Henry, Margaret and Prince Edward. Because attainder resulted in the legal forfeiture of property, the list of other Lancastrian leaders and supporters included many who had died in the conflict to date. Within this list was cited 'John Morton, late Parson of Blokesworth in the Shire of Dorset, Clerk' and a reward of £100 posted for his capture.

When Morton reached Scotland and the royal court, strategies were under review. Margaret and Prince Edward were still at Edinburgh, but Henry had relocated to Kirkcudbright. They were close to poverty, their subsistence dependent upon charity. Both Edward and Burgundy were increasing pressure on the Scottish council to sever their support of the Lancastrians. Not only that, but the Scots saw Edward's position as increasingly secure and were thinking about negotiating a truce with him. So it was that in August, Edward had authorised negotiations with Burgundy for a truce and trade agreement and also allowed Warwick to settle a truce with Scotland.

At the same time, kingship had moderated the view of Louis of France towards both Edward and Burgundy, and he signalled a more favourable disposition towards Henry and Margaret. His quarrels with his late father were no longer of relevance and he saw his best interests lay in keeping both England and Scotland in a state of agitation. So, at the beginning of October, Louis received Somerset, Hungerford and Whittingham at Tours: they gained little, but were allowed to return to Scotland.

It was evident that with no prospect of an independent income, and a leaning of the Scots to an accommodation with Edward, something bold had to be done to advance the Lancastrian cause. Having sat out the winter, Margaret set sail in April 1462 to talk directly to Louis, armed with a letter of authority signed by Henry to negotiate, and accompanied by an escort and staff of suitable size – which included John Morton, who had been elevated to the post of Keeper of the Privy Seal. They made landfall in Brittany on 16 April and were well received by Duke Francis II, developing a relationship which would prove particularly beneficial later. Meetings were also held with Margaret's father and Pierre de Breze and, having been joined in June by Jasper Tudor, Earl of Pembroke, and Sir John Fortescue, an audience was eventually obtained with Louis XI at Chinon, Touraine, on 23 June.

The Lancastrian offer was born out of desperation: without tangible support from Louis their cause was lost. The limits to which they would go were discussed thoroughly before the meeting, but they were gossamer. Louis knew this and proved willing to provide just enough to ensure that Edward didn't have the capacity to get involved in French affairs.

Essentially, Calais was mortgaged to Louis for the sum of 20,000 francs (notwithstanding the fact that the Lancastrians did not hold it). If Henry regained Calais, then, within a year either the loan would be repaid, or Calais handed over – on payment of a further 40,000 crowns. This was wrapped up in a 100-year truce and mutual aid package, added to which Louis released Piers de Breze to lead 800 men and forty-two ships to invade Northumberland. Morton was a signatory to this agreement.

Unlike most of his contemporaries in the power struggle, Morton was keen both to learn from the enemy and to work on their weaknesses. From any distance it was clear that the Yorkists led in the propaganda war and were no slouches when it came to distributing stories that people wanted to hear rather than the truth; stories which worked on their prejudices and beliefs. Fake news.

One way of frustrating the Yorkists and causing them to spend scarce resources from their war-chest was to spread false claims of impending invasion or insurrection. So it was that in the summer of 1462 Morton planted rumour of an impending Spanish invasion of England, this reaching the ears of Edward himself. Perhaps enjoying the importance bestowed by a £100 reward on his head, he added the detail that leading the attack in Norfolk would be Margaret's brother John, Duke of Calabria, and himself. His humour was never less than dry.

Not all the stories floating around at the time were planted or false. No less a person than John de Vere, Earl of Oxford, his son Aubrey and Sir Thomas Tudenham, were executed for leading a plot to assassinate Edward. Aubrey and Thomas were beheaded, but for Oxford, unusual for a peer of the realm, the punishment was disembowelment and castration, his organs being burned before him, and only then his head struck off.

Morton arrived back in Scotland with Margaret's small army in mid-October. It was the Lancastrians' intention to use the castles of Bamburgh,

Dunstanburgh, and Alnwick as their bases for attacks. But first they had to be wrested from Yorkist hands. Reunited with Henry, they moved down the coast in the French ships, landing near Bamburgh, the castle surrendering with little argument and left in the charge of Somerset. Dunstanburgh also quickly went over to the Lancastrians and Alnwick gave up after only a short siege. But the anticipated and necessary rising of local lords and landowners to Henry's cause failed to materialise.

The response was strong and swift. Not only did Warwick advance on Northumberland, but Edward also marched north – with one of the largest armies assembled in England. The Lancastrian commanders decided to hurry back to Scotland to raise reinforcements for what was evidently an inadequate force to keep their foothold.

Unfortunately, the weather once again failed to smile on Henry's cause and storms smashed into their fleet, wrecking four ships. Henry, Margaret and Breze were able to get to Berwick on 3 November in an open fishing boat, having come close to drowning as their ship sank. The other three ships which were lost were driven onto the rocks and some 400 of the French soldiers were stranded on Lindisfarne island and quickly surrendered in the face of fierce Yorkist action.

Having gone as far as Durham, Edward became seriously unwell with measles and was compelled to hand over all command of military action to Warwick, who commenced the siege of Bamburgh, Dunstanburgh, and Alnwick on 10 December. Although the Earl of Angus and Breze were assembling a Scottish force to relieve the besieged castles, this was unknown to them. Reduced to eating their own horses, on 27 December both Bamburgh and Dunstanburgh decided to surrender and as a condition of the surrender both Somerset and Sir Ralph Percy were required to swear an oath of allegiance to Edward. To prove his loyalty, Somerset joined the action against Alnwick, and Percy was put in charge of the two castles. Those who would not swear allegiance, notably Jasper Tudor and Lord Roos, were awarded safe custody to go back into Scotland.

On 5 January 1463 the Scots did arrive at Alnwick. What they found was a depleted, disenchanted English force suffering from cold and hunger. Edward's inability to support what was originally such a large army caused many to be discharged and sent home. They also discovered that Warwick, like themselves, wanted to avoid a pitched battle. So Lord Hungerford was allowed to march out of the castle to withdraw across the border with his rescuers. The next day the English retook possession of Alnwick.

A recurring theme on the borders, nothing stays certain. In March, following Warwick's journey back south having concluded that he had sufficiently consolidated Edward's position, Sir Ralph Percy broke his oath and switched sides to let a combined French and Scottish army back into Bamburgh and Dunstanburgh. And in May, Sir Ralph Grey, Constable of Alnwick, decided to surrender that castle, too, in a spate of bad temper having had his leadership talents apparently overlooked.

Had Warwick been too generous in his conditions of surrender? This was not a question the Lancastrians were about to spend much time on, but they certainly saw an opportunity to exploit. An attempt was made to gain Norham Castle, south-west of Berwick, relying on Scottish troops in the main, but this proved unsuccessful. The failure at Norham pressed home a feeling of disillusionment among the English Lancastrians and Breze in particular despaired at the unwillingness of the Scots to engage in battle, their heart seemingly only in raiding. Henry did not feel the same and was content to remain in Northumberland, based at Bamburgh, sticking to the original plan of stirring things up from the castles he held.

Margaret had had enough of this forlorn adventure however, and on 3 July she set sail with Prince Edward, Breze, Exeter, Fortescue, Whittingham, Makerel, and Morton, together with the remaining French soldiers in four balinger ships for Sluys in Holland.[2] They would never see Henry again.

14
Wilderness Years 1463–1470

Edward and Louis had grown weary of the time and cost spent on assuaging the suspicions and disagreements between them and were looking to reach an accommodation: not least so that they could focus that time and cost on other pressing issues. So delegations were proposed to meet, under the chairmanship of Burgundy, at St Omer, about 32 miles south-east of Calais to discuss the possibility of a truce. This would, if successful, bind each party to provide no assistance to the enemies of the other. Margaret had it as her objective to frustrate this conference, and she was particularly spitting fire as the proposed truce would effectively tear up the agreement that she had recently agreed with Louis herself.

As soon as Margaret reached Sluys, she and her entourage made their way as quickly as possible to Bruges where they were generously received by Charles, Count of Charolais, who was related on his mother's side to John of Gaunt and thereby the Lancastrians. It was his father, Philip of Burgundy, that Margaret had in her sights, though. Philip was reluctant to engage with her, but persistence paid off and an audience was given at St. Pol, 100 miles away, on 31 August. It was a journey not without hazards, passing within reach of Calais patrols. Despite the enmity between Burgundy and the Lancastrians over the years, Philip was duly respectful in listening to her, but he was as resolute as Louis or Edward to see a truce agreed. The best he was able to do was provide her with 1,000 crowns, and then she and her followers had to leave, retracing their route to Bruges.

With nowhere else to go, Philip provided the English expats with an armed escort to a chateau at Koeur-la-Petite belonging to Margaret's father, near St Mihiel-en-Bar, 230 miles distant, located on the River Meuse and 55 miles south of Luxembourg. This was to be the hub for some 200 Lancastrian exiles for the next seven years, who continued to agitate against Edward's regime but in a state of poverty.

The truce between France and England was completed in October, at least for a year, at Hesdin and in December a similar understanding was reached between England and Scotland. Henry had been residing in Edinburgh, but now the risks of remaining there were too great, and he travelled back to Bamburgh. From there, he wrote to Margaret in February 1464 requiring his affinity – including Morton – to seek as much support as possible from foreign leaders. That support was readily secured from Francis of Brittany and Charles of Charolais, but from elsewhere there was little enthusiasm or sympathy.

Indeed, Henry's Northumbrian stronghold was being systematically dismantled. On 25 April, Montagu defeated a band of 5,000 Lancastrians at Hedgeley Moor, Sir Ralph Percy losing his life. Then, on 15 May, Montagu fought a smaller army at Hexham, but with greater consequences. Over thirty Lancastrian leaders were killed or executed including Somerset, Hungerford, and Roos. Sir William Tailboys was caught hiding in an open-cast coal mine and executed, having fled with £2,000 of Henry's Treasury.

Montagu's successes were warmly greeted by Edward who rewarded him with the earldom of Northumberland on 27 May. This made John Neville one of the most powerful men in the country, and with his brother Warwick and the royal artillery he set out from York to complete the subjugation of the northern castles. Alnwick and Dunstanburgh yielded without a fight but Bamburgh, in which Sir Ralph Grey and Sir Humphrey Neville were ensconced, decided to hold out. Northumberland let loose the cannons causing serious damage and badly wounding Grey, so much so that he was thought dead. The garrison then surrendered. Neville was spared, but the injured Grey was publicly shamed and then executed. That ended the last of the major Lancastrian leaders in England.

Henry was finally caught 13 July 1465 in the woods near Waddington Hall, Lancashire, and taken to the Tower of London.

Morton found himself unsettled with time on his hands. The intense activity of the past few years had become addictive and, if he wasn't having to keep moving his body, then at least he needed to keep moving his mind. He therefore sought and obtained leave to enrol at the Flemish University of Louvain, from both Margaret and Philip of Burgundy. The university had attracted some of the brightest contemporary theologians. Professionally, it brought him into contact with key players in the future of the Church. Politically, it provided a point of contact for information from England and elsewhere, well away from Margaret's court. Louvain was just 80 miles from Bruges and most of the 140 miles to St Mihiel-en-Bar could be covered by boat on the Meuse.

The university at Louvain was not old, having been founded in 1425, but its reputation was already widespread. The town had a long-standing cloth manufacturing industry, which meant that foreign traders were common and accepted, providing good cover for a spy-master's post box. According to the Benedictine monk, Matthew Paris, 'all the nations of the world are kept warm by the wool of England woven into cloth by the men of Flanders'.

Conveying secret messages was a serious and dangerous venture, and there were failures and disappointments: none quite so disturbing as what became known as the Cornelius Plot. In June of 1468, a Kent shoemaker, John Cornelius, was caught carrying letters from the Lancastrian exiles to friends and sympathisers in England. The poor postman was sent to the Tower and put to torture to obtain the names of those to whom he was to deliver the letters. This is the only recorded example of someone being officially tortured before the reign of Henry VIII. Indeed, torture was wholly alien to the English judicial system and was decried by Fortescue in a treatise he wrote comparing the English and French approach to the use of the rack. The use of torture was permitted under canon law if not English common law but, despite urges from the Papacy, had been resisted.

The torture revealed several names. One was John Hawkins, a servant of John, Lord Wenlock. Wenlock himself, who was escorting Margaret of York to Burgundy for her marriage to Duke Charles, was never indicted, but he did switch to support Warwick for the restoration of Henry. Both Cornelius and Hawkins were executed. Others implicated were Sir Thomas Malory, author of *Le Morte d'Arthur*, and Sir Thomas Cook, a London merchant.

A key discussion which emerged from the talks at St Omer and Hesdin between Warwick and Louis was the question of Edward's marriage. Bona, daughter of the Duke of Savoy was one possibility, another was a niece of Burgundy. Yet another was Isabella of Castille (would that have been a match to introduce the Grand Inquisition into England?). These leaks of information were of great importance in strategy planning for the Lancastrians at Koeur-la-Petite but also of prurient amusement to the court. But it is news that filters through to Morton by the beginning of October 1464 that really makes the Lancastrians, and indeed the rest of Europe, sit up. Warwick has been discussing a possible marriage for Edward, with both himself and whoever he is talking to at the time believing he speaks for and with the knowledge of the King. But twenty-two-year-old Edward was already married and was forced to declare in Council on 14 September that he had secretly wed nearly five months previously. The reaction was shock and deep displeasure, particularly among his family and the magnates on whom he relied.

It was accepted custom that a king should marry a foreign princess for political and economic gain, and ideally his queen should be a virgin. His wife ticked none of those boxes. Elizabeth Woodville was a widow with two children by her late husband, Sir John Grey, who fought and died for the Lancastrians at the second battle of St Albans. She was of a good family – her mother was Jacquetta, widow of John, Duke of Bedford, brother of Henry V – and she was a maid of honour to Margaret of Anjou. But she was not of royal blood. She was also five years older than Edward.

While courtly love was highly regarded, love itself was not considered a sound and sensible reason for marriage among the nobility. Edward had gained a questionable but tolerated reputation as a philanderer and it was anticipated that he would play the marriage game by the rules and then continue hopping from bed to bed. He intended though to marry by his rules – and of course, still hop from bed to bed.

The other concern to the governing class – to Lancastrians as well as Yorkists – was that Elizabeth had five brothers and seven unmarried sisters. These would all be needing and expecting elevation in society to reflect their kinship to royalty. All of these threads and possibilities would be analysed by Morton and Fortescue: not least those who might be disaffected by Woodville promotions.

Edward's mother, Cecily, was apoplectic at his action; and not because she hadn't been invited to the wedding. In her wrath, she felt that Edward had betrayed her husband's values and the traditions and standards of their class. So much so that she intimated that she would declare him a bastard and, as such, with no right to call himself a king. His younger brother, George, Duke of Clarence was also openly critical of the marriage, saying that Edward should have married a virgin. Edward's other brother, Richard, is only fourteen years old at this time and is therefore silent: although his later actions suggest that he also is not overjoyed at the situation. But it was Warwick's nose that was furthest out of joint.

Edward tried to show that he still favoured the Neville family, and George was translated to the archbishopric of York. But already Warwick was supplied with evidence of what was to come when one of Elizabeth's sisters was betrothed to Lord Maltravers, heir to the Earl of Arundel. The Woodvilles were already infiltrating higher levels of society. Warwick's general displeasure was soon conveyed to Louis, who made it known that he would support whatever action Warwick might settle on.

Morton matriculated in theology in the summer of 1469, which was perfect timing to ease back into court life and conspiracies.

It was the difference in foreign policy rather than anything else which caused the irretrievable breakdown of the relationship between Warwick and Edward. Warwick put everything into directing Edward to an alliance with Louis, whereas Edward would not hear of breaking his friendship with Philip of Burgundy, notwithstanding the occasional fallout. In Louvain, Morton saw first-hand the reasons for and effects of a Flemish embargo on English cloth in 1464 to protect their own declining industry from competition.

The Lancastrian plotting began to develop into a plan. It was, in fact, the only plan with any realistic ambition of success, and that was to cultivate the collapse in the relationship of both Warwick and Louis towards Edward and use them to provide the fuel to get Henry restored to the throne. That was not an easy concept for many to swallow – particularly Margaret. But with so many years now in the wilderness, they had run out of options. So Fortescue had been quietly sounding out Louis since 1467.

Louis appeared particularly keen on developing the idea: his fear of an alliance between England and Burgundy was such that he offered Warwick the principality of Belgium if he would displace Edward. Louis and Warwick also greatly admired each other's philosophy and panache: a true bromance. Margaret, of course, had always favoured France over Burgundy.

But the three sides to this treacherous triangle were each totally untrustworthy. Louis had already proven many times that treaties were there for today but not necessarily for tomorrow. His joy was in the scheming, which often trumped the delivery. And could a steadfast relationship truly be built from the hatred between Margaret and Warwick? The only sure thing for both of them was that once the enterprise started, there would be no way back for either.

Events accelerated the appeal of the plot. Edward was leaning ever more to tying up an alliance with Burgundy and a possible marriage between Philip's son, the Count of Charolais, and Edward's sister, Margaret of York, was being given air. This was provided greater credence with the death of Philip the Good on 15 June when Charolais, Charles the Bold, succeeded him, and on 3 July 1468 Margaret became his third wife. Edward also made a formal alliance not only with Burgundy but also Brittany. This effectively shut the door on Warwick's favoured foreign policy.

George Neville, now Archbishop of York, was found to be promoting himself with Rome to be made a cardinal without first obtaining consent from Edward. More than that, he was quietly sounding out the possibility of a papal dispensation being granted for Warwick to wed his daughter Isabel to Clarence. As a result, his loyalty and suitability as Chancellor were questioned in Edward's mind and on 8 June 1467 he was sacked from the post and Robert Stillington, Bishop of Bath and Wells, appointed in his place.

The rise of the Woodvilles was unstoppable.[1] Elizabeth's father was created Earl Rivers and appointed Treasurer; her brother Anthony Woodville married the heiress to Lord Scales; Elizabeth had paid £4,000 to the Duchess of Exeter to rescind the betrothal of her daughter, Anne Holland, heiress to the Exeter estate, with Warwick's nephew in favour of her eldest son, Sir Thomas Grey. Lord Grey of Ruthin, Elizabeth's cousin by marriage, was created Earl of Kent; her brother Sir John Woodville married the dowager Duchess of Norfolk, old enough to be his grandmother; four of her sisters were betrothed to the most eligible of the young magnates in the country – Anne to Viscount Bourchier, Joan to Anthony Grey, Jacquetta to Lord Strange, and Mary to Lord Herbert; and Elizabeth had acquired the wardship of the Duke of Buckingham enabling her to marry him off – yet underage – to her sister Catherine.[2]

A further development was the birth of a daughter, Elizabeth, on 11 February 1466. It would seem that Cecily's rage against her son's marriage had already subsided as she was happy to stand as a godmother to the new princess, alongside Jacquetta, Duchess of Bedford. Warwick stood as godfather. The event proved the fertility of the royal couple, which put all opposition on notice, as the first job of a monarch is to produce an heir. However, the next two children of Edward and Elizabeth were also daughters: Mary in 1467, and Cecily in 1469. It was a son that was needed.

While options and compromises were being discussed within the walls of St Mihiel-en-Bar, Warwick decided to make a play of his own. Or rather with his new ally, Edward's brother, nineteen-year-old George

Duke of Clarence. With only daughters, and no legitimate claim on the throne himself, Warwick sees his only route to re-establishing himself as the leader of policy is to remove Edward and put Clarence in his place – married to his eldest daughter Isabel to ensure the throne for the Neville bloodline. This proposed marriage was forbidden by Edward when it was put to him for approval.

In April 1469, a mysterious character naming himself (or indeed themselves) Robin of Redesdale emerged raising a rebellion, only to be quickly dispersed by Warwick's brother, the Earl of Northumberland.[3] Then in May, another rising, this one by a Robin of Holderness calling for the restitution of Henry Percy to the earldom of Northumberland.[4] These disturbances provided Warwick and Clarence the opportunity to validate an assembly of sizeable forces in readiness for their next move.

So, in June 1469 Warwick, Clarence, and Isobel, together with George Neville, Archbishop of York, and Thomas Kemp, Bishop of London, meet up at Sandwich and set sail for Calais where George performs the wedding ceremony with a papal dispensation in his pocket.[5] Being without Edward's knowledge or consent, it is therefore a clear act of treason.

They then return to England and with a strong army behind them issue a petition, called 'a remonstrance', in the time-honoured way, calling for the removal of the King's evil advisers (otherwise known as Woodvilles but including Herbert and Stafford). This call signals another apparently spontaneous and independent uprising in the north, towards which Edward sets out, only to find the rebel forces are larger than he expected. News then arrives that Warwick and Clarence are heading towards him from London. Wisdom propels him to temporarily withdraw to the safety of Nottingham.

At Edward's beckoning, Pembroke and Devon set out from Raglan and Dorchester respectively to meet up and tackle the rebels. This they did but fell out and ended up setting their camps ten miles apart. On 24 July, the battle of Edgcote, otherwise known as the battle of Banbury, was fought. The rebel army was helped by a superiority in archers and, decisively, reinforcements from Warwick's troops which gave them the day. Pembroke was captured and executed later, as was his brother Sir Richard Herbert, and having escaped the battlefield, Devon received a similar fate the next month from the citizens of Bridgwater. During the battle, Sir Richard Vaughan was killed. On the rebels' side, Sir Henry Neville and Sir William Conyers – both candidates for identification as Robin of Redesdale – were cut down.

In the aftermath of the battle, Richard Woodville, Earl Rivers, and Sir John Woodville were both executed, but most alarmingly,

Edward, Gloucester and Hastings were temporarily taken prisoner by George, Archbishop of York. Edward put a brave face on the situation and seemingly agreed to the demands of Warwick and Clarence. On 29 September, he went to York to witness the execution of old adversaries Humphrey and Charles Neville. He then returned to Pontefract from where a large group of armed men led by Gloucester and Hastings escorted him back to London from where, unfettered, he resumed his throne.

Warwick and Clarence had secured the removal of those advisors declared 'evil', but for Richard Neville this was not enough. He was determined to force through a French alliance against a wall of opposition. The objective had become an obsession, to the extent that he and Clarence agitated for further risings in the country.

The most serious of these was in Lincolnshire. Ostensibly, it began as the result of a private feud between Richard, Lord Welles, supported by his brother-in-law Sir Thomas Dymmock, and Sir Thomas Burgh, Master of the King's Horse. Welles burnt Burgh's manor house to the ground and stole all his goods of value. Welles was a second cousin of Warwick, and he and Clarence used the situation to activate a general insurrection, which was particularly accelerated by Welles' son, Sir Robert Welles, leading to calls for the restoration of Henry.

Edward summoned Welles and Dymock to London where they sought sanctuary in Westminster Abbey but emerged with the King's pardon. However, they were not freed but kept close by Edward on his march north to quell the rioting.

Warwick already had an army on the move – under the pretence of suppressing revolt – and was soon joined by Clarence. The intention was to trap Edward between their army and that of Welles.

But Edward sent Robert Welles a message that if he did not surrender, then his father and Dymmock would be executed. In an attempt to save his father, Welles turned back to face the King at Empingham, Rutland. Welles and Dymmock were dragged out in front of both armies and duly beheaded, after which the army of Sir Robert was completely routed. There was no support from Warwick, who discovered that he could not muster even 5,000 soldiers: the idea of Clarence as the next King of England appealed to very few indeed.

The battle was fought a few miles outside Stamford on 12 March 1470 at what became known as Loosecoat Field: the fleeing rebels discarded their surcoats which bore the badges of Warwick and Clarence.

Sir Robert Welles was hunted down and before his execution on 19 March he confessed to the involvement of Warwick and Clarence. With the discovery that they were indeed behind this discontent they were summonsed to London by Edward. Knowing what would befall them if they answered that call, they took flight to France and their friend and ally Louis XI.

For others, not least Edward's youngest brother, these are yet more examples – if needed – of how fragile sanctuary in holy buildings and the promises and pardons of kings might be.

The End of the Line, 1470–1471

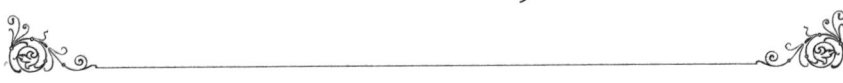

The principals of the parties met at the suitably named Angers from 15 July to 4 August 1470.[1] The experience of the last twelve months had taught Warwick that he could not rule England through Edward, nor did the people offer any hope for Clarence to take the throne. His one hope was to restore Henry. To put it bluntly, he was prepared to defect from York to Lancaster. Such was his immersion in his own ego and the French cause that other friendships and allegiances were of no consequence.

Similarly, Margaret's devotion to defending and enforcing the rights of her son to the crown overruled all other considerations. To obtain their desires, both parties would need to swallow a lot of pride and hatred. And they both needed Louis to bankroll them.

But Warwick wanted one big concession to bind the alliance: sixteen-year-old Prince Edward should marry his youngest daughter Anne, age fourteen. Both children were troubled. Edward had been brought up with violence and warfare as the norm and that was reflected in his thoughts, speech, and personality. Anne was, like her sister, delicate in health and reticent in company, strongly religious, and also given a childhood enveloped by violence. But Margaret's initial objections were not just that the marriage would provide a Neville incursion into the royal bloodline, she believed the best marriage for her son would be with royalty outside England. In the end though, she agreed.

The details of the tripartite agreement were drawn up with Fortescue and Morton leading the negotiations for the Lancastrian party. There was a thirty-year truce to be signed between England and France, Margaret signing on behalf of Henry. Louis would support the House of Lancaster against Edward. Warwick would head the government of England under the King. Prince Edward would marry Anne Neville. Louis would provide money, a fleet, and troops for the invasion.

The only point put forward by Warwick which Margaret flatly rejected was that Prince Edward should accompany him to England. Margaret insisted that her son would only make the journey with her, and they would only make the journey when they understood the country to be safe.

Having polished the script, it was now necessary to provide the performance for the benefit of the outside world.

Warwick arrived at Angers with the twenty-eight-year-old Lancastrian John de Vere, 13th Earl of Oxford, Clarence having been sent off to inspect and prepare the fleet at Valognes in Normandy. On the evening of 22 July, Warwick was ceremoniously brought into Margaret's presence, his hand held by King Louis. Playing his part, Warwick knelt before Margaret and admitted to all the wrongs he had done to her and her family, begging her forgiveness.

The forty-two-year-old is on his knees for some ten minutes and it is becoming evident that they and his patience are starting to wear thin. But Margaret is enjoying his discomfort and it is another five before she bids him rise.

Over the next three days the finer points of the consequences of the agreement are settled. Jasper Tudor and the Earl of Oxford will also accompany Warwick's expedition. Margaret, Edward, Anne, the Lancastrian ladies, and Morton will remain in France under Louis' protection until England is adjudged to be entirely safe. And Clarence – he will receive back all his lands, will be rewarded with the estates of the duchy of York, and if Edward and Anne produce no heirs then Clarence or his heirs will succeed to the throne. On 25 July, the engagement of Edward and Anne was solemnised in Angers cathedral, and all parties swore on a piece of the True Cross to uphold their agreement.

The marriage itself would have to wait a while. Unlike the marriage of Clarence and Isabel, there was no papal dispensation at hand, and this would need to be obtained. Morton gave some thought, but not too much, as to how Anne would be feeling, thrust into this arranged marriage to someone she did not know and who she has been brought up to see as an enemy. But such situations were not particularly rare among the nobility. It had to be seen as the price of privilege.

In the first week of August, Warwick joined Clarence at Valognes and began sending messages across the Channel to put the men of Kent on readiness. Messages of support from the Earl of Shrewsbury and Lord Stanley had been received. The Archbishop of York had been placed under guard at his home, The Manor of the More, Rickmansworth, in Hertfordshire. Warwick's other brother, John, to date a solid Yorkist supporter, was now entertaining a switch in allegiance to the Lancastrians.

Edward had a talent for making bad mistakes. John Neville, as Earl of Montagu, had been a dazzling success in subduing the north for Edward and well deserved his elevation to Duke of Northumberland. So it was astounding that Edward should release Henry Percy from the Tower and make *him* Duke of Northumberland instead. Edward had thought that making John the Marquis of Montagu sufficient compensation. He also made John's son the Duke of Bedford and betrothed him to his eldest daughter. But, no! Although marquis ranked above duke, there was an accompanying loss in land and consequently income. Not only that, but to accommodate a Percy – arch-rivals of the Nevilles – was unthinkable and insulting. Warwick played on this discontent with every card in his hand. At the same time, Edward was secretly trying to woo Clarence back into the family fold.

The invasion fleet was pinned down throughout August by Burgundian war ships with a spattering of English boats joining in. Nervous tension exacerbated by boredom ran through Warwick's men. Then in early September a storm scattered the blockade, allowing some 60 ships led by French Admiral of the Fleet, the Bastard of Bourbon, to leave the shore on the 9th with Warwick, Clarence, Pembroke (Jasper Tudor), and Oxford aboard.

Warwick's army landed on 13 September at Dartmouth and Plymouth without opposition, and the French fleet departed as soon as the landings were completed. There is no escape route, it will be success or oblivion.

Setting foot on English soil again, the first thing Warwick does is to issue yet another manifesto. This time, he calls on citizens everywhere to come together for the rescue and restitution of Henry. He then proceeds with Clarence and the army to Exeter where he is met by John Courtenay, Earl of Devon, from where they advance towards London. Jasper Tudor marches on to Wales.

When Warwick landed, Edward was in Yorkshire putting to flight a rebellion by Henry, Lord Fitzhugh, Warwick's brother-in-law, but struck south immediately, looking to reach London first and then engage with the Lancastrian force.[2] But at Doncaster he learned that Montagu had decided to switch sides and that his men were coming to seize him. Substantially outnumbered, there was no alternative but to flee. If caught, he would expect to be executed. With Gloucester, Hastings and Rivers he reached King's Lynn in Norfolk and survived a perilous crossing to the Burgundian Low Countries.

Warwick was sensitive to the ill-will caused by Margaret's Lancastrian troops, and foreign troops at that, in her march to the second battle of St Albans, and had issued a field order that anyone found pillaging or molesting women would be immediately executed. It was therefore of particular concern to him that, on having heard of his arrival back in the country, the men of Kent stampeded towards London, causing fear and chaos as they robbed foreign merchants and any ale houses in their way. The city gates were closed to them, and the pregnant Queen Elizabeth fled the Tower for sanctuary in Westminster. Similarly, Robert Stillington, Bishop of Bath and Lord Chancellor, together with William Grey, Bishop of Ely, took refuge in St Martins Le Grand.

Claiming to act as Warwick's advance representative, Sir Geoffrey Gates attempted to bring the mob under control and took surrender of the Tower on 3 October, allowing those inside to take themselves and their possessions to sanctuary at either Westminster or St Martins.[3] Then, along with William Waynflete, the Bishop of Winchester and Sir John Stockton, the Mayor of London and his aldermen, he began the search for King Henry. They found Henry in a distressing state: poorly dressed for his status and alarmingly dirty in body and clothing. Moved into the apartments recently vacated by Elizabeth, he was cleaned up and his care and that of the Tower handed over to George, Archbishop of York, who arrived on the 5th. The next day, Warwick and Clarence entered London.

Given a week to acclimatise to his newfound freedom, Henry is the centrepiece of a procession to St Paul's where he is crowned once more, signifying the 'Readeption' of his reign, Oxford bearing the Sword of State and Warwick carrying the King's train.

There is no question that Warwick is in charge of government. That said, the intent is to cause as little change to the old regime as possible. Warwick regained the Captaincy of Calais, and the positions of Great Chamberlain and High Admiral. Of significance was the limited power conferred on Clarence and such reinstatements of position as were made were slow in their confirmation. A resentment was brewing which would prove dangerous. Supporters such as Pembroke, Montagu, Oxford and Shrewsbury saw little gain other than restoration to their previous standing. Prominent Yorkists who submitted to the new regime such as Norfolk and Essex were treated well.

The one person who was not treated well was John Tiptoft, Earl of Worcester. Hated by all, he was tried for treason by John de Vere, Earl of Oxford, whose father and brother he had sent to their death eight years before. Tiptoft was well educated, an Oxford scholar in the early 1440s when Morton was there and studied in Italy for two years. He was brother-in-law to Warwick and that relationship underpinned his rise. It was his extermination of so many Lancastrian leaders, and the manner of their execution, which led to his reputation as a 'butcher'. At his own execution on 18 October, he famously asked the axeman to employ three strikes to his neck in honour of the Holy Trinity.

Over the winter, Warwick was concerned firstly with trying to piece together a proposal for a French alliance that might pass through parliament, but the opportunity did not arise. His other concern was persuading Margaret and Prince Edward that it was now safe to return to England.

In fact, what the general populace, and particularly the moneyed class of merchants and gentry, most wanted was a return to peace within the country and the justice of the common law, a lowering of taxation, recovery of lost possessions in France, and the restitution of reciprocal trade with Burgundy. None of these things were on Warwick's agenda or within his capability.

He therefore could not press the alliance directly. He did secure a thirty-year truce from parliament and also made incursions into Burgundy's territory from Calais. But there was no treaty forthcoming as promised at Angers and no open declaration of war on Charles of Burgundy.

Margaret had remained in France with Prince Edward and Anne in Louis' court; first at Amboise where Edward and Anne were formally wed on 13 December and then Paris. Henry sent word in February for them to join him, but the intelligence reports received did not provide assurance that the country was fully secure or that Edward and the Yorkists sufficiently suppressed. Indeed, the rumours and reports received suggested that Edward was about to make a return to England himself. It was not until 24 March that they felt safe to set sail from Honfleur, along with Warwick's wife and some other Lancastrians, including Morton and Fortescue. Bad weather delayed their crossing until 13 April, Margaret and those accompanying her landing at Weymouth the next day.[4]

From Weymouth, under advice and guidance from Morton, they travel due north for the sixteen miles to Cerne Abbey, which is to be their first resting place.[5] They are greeted by Abbot John Vanne; showing signs of illness, this will be the last year of his life of service. The Guest House at the Abbey was designed and built by him, and it is clear that he takes great pleasure in seeing his creation occupied by such distinguished visitors.

The following day they were joined by Edmund Beaufort, Duke of Somerset, and John Courtenay, Earl of Devon. They had been waiting in London for Margaret's arrival, and on learning that she was to land in the west country, had set out with their retinues to meet her. By the end of the day though, they were joined by other travellers seeking to team up with Jasper Tudor's forces in Wales, and who deliver the crushing news that Warwick is defeated and dead.

The impact on Margaret in particular, and on her close advisors generally, is one of devastation. Though she had no love for the man, her success depended on his success. Now her options were gone, just as the ships that brought her over from France were gone. Surrender was not something to consider: Prince Edward would certainly be put to death, making the way clear for Edward to rid himself of Henry also. For a moment she could neither breathe nor think.

The fleeing Lancastrians were able to provide some detail, which, as emotions receded, helped in deciding what to do next.

On reaching Holland, Edward and his small band had received hospitality from Louis of Bruges, Lord of Gruythuyse, who governed the area for Charles, Duke of Burgundy. In fact, the hospitality and assistance provided by Gruythuyse was so generous that Edward would make him Earl of Winchester in 1471. But what really tipped the scales in Edward's favour was a declaration of war on Burgundy by the Warwick regime, this being one of the conditions imposed by Louis for his sponsoring of the invasion to recover Henry. Charles's immediate response was to fund Edward's return to England with a small but useful Burgundian force, estimated to be about 2,000. Their ships had been spotted off the Norfolk coast as long ago as 14 March. Margaret interrupts: why had she not received this intelligence? She would not have set sail if she knew of it.

Edward landed further north, at Ravenspur at the mouth of the river Humber, avoiding the fleet patrolling the coast under the direction of Thomas Neville, the Bastard of Fauconberg.[6] Few came forward to join his army, but York opened its gates to him on 18 March. At this stage there was no reason for the Lancastrians to be concerned. John Neville, now Marquis of Montagu, was standing by at Pontefract. John de Vere, Earl of Oxford, along with Henry Holland, Duke of Exeter and William, Viscount Beaumont were marching towards Newark, Nottinghamshire. Warwick, based at Coventry, therefore anticipated catching Edward with a three-front attack. But Montagu allowed Edward to pass by Pontefract unchallenged. As Edward marched further south, so his army gathered in men. Nottingham was very supportive and then Sir William Stanley and Sir William Noreys substantially added to his host.

Neither Shrewsbury nor Stanley responded to Warwick's call to arms. Jasper Tudor would not move outside Wales but insisted on waiting for Margaret; as for Somerset and Devon – well, they had left London wide open. Their action can only be understood by a hope to gain political advantage from being the first to welcome Margaret and strengthen her army.

Oxford and Exeter panicked on seeing some of Edward's scouts, and Edward passed by Coventry with Warwick refusing to commit to battle. Then Clarence decided to return to the Yorkist fold and Edward marched on to London, which he entered on 11 April and re-captured Henry. He had gained the upper hand through being a better and more aggressive general, poor resolve on the part of his foes, and a lack of coordination and communication between the leaders of the opposition.

Warwick concluded that, even with absence of support, he had to take Edward on, and so he left Coventry, marching through St Albans to arrive at Barnet, Middlesex, on 13 April. He held the reserve and command of cannon, Montagu had the centre, Exeter the left wing, and Oxford the right wing. The battle was fought the next day, at first in fog, in which nineteen-year-old Richard of Gloucester had outflanked forty-four-year-old Exeter, and on the right, Hastings had been outflanked by Oxford – but in doing so Oxford lost contact with the battle. When he eventually tried to get back into the action, in the poor light his men were thought to be Edward's as their respective banners were similar, and they ended up being attacked by their own side. A renewed attack by Edward's men broke the Lancastrian centre. Montagu had already been killed and now Warwick was cut down trying to make his escape.

Henry had been brought along with Edward's army and during the fighting he had tried to escape. However, he was caught half-way to St Albans and returned to the Tower. He knew his days were now limited.

All this happened on the morning of Margaret's landing.

Morton, and even Fortescue, were now feeling out of their depth, unable to offer advice or comfort. Their own resolution is held together simply by their faith and sense of duty. This is now a military matter, and their absence of experience and training pushes them to the perimeter of discussions.

It is Somerset and Devon who provide optimism, reminding Margaret of the depth of support which she holds in the west country. They enthuse that the death of Warwick will cause even greater numbers to answer the call to arms, although this may in part be to deflect criticism of their error in leaving London before the battle and leaving it open to Edward's return.

While Margaret and her army move to Rougemont Castle at Exeter, they call for Sir John Arundel and Sir Hugh Courtenay to mobilise troops throughout the region to assemble there.[7] The plan is to move north and either meet up with Jasper Tudor's Welshmen or with faithful friends in Cheshire and Lancashire. So they progressed to Glastonbury and then Wells, where they sacked the Bishop's Palace and broke open the prison, in anger at Robert Stillington, Edward's Chancellor. Then on to Bath on

30 April, adding adherents from Somerset, Wiltshire and Dorset all the while. False moves attempt to deceive Edward that they are heading for London, but this is not something he falls for.

Reinforced and now equipped with artillery, Edward set out from Windsor on the 24th seeking Margaret's army, and by the 29th had reached Cirencester. Here he discovered that the Lancastrians had fallen back to Bristol, from where they were marching north hoping to cross the River Severn at Gloucester, which was the only crossing point. If they succeeded, then they would be able to join Jasper Tudor's force. But the city denied access to Margaret and her army had to move further on, to Tewkesbury. By now, Edward was marching a parallel line and with retreat cut off by the Severn and the Avon, Margaret's army, exhausted by the hard march, turned to fight.

The Lancastrian army took up a strong defensive position, but the Yorkists were better rested and fed. The Lancastrians were also outgunned and had fewer archers. So, early in the morning of 4 May, the battle commenced. The bombardment of shot and arrows was so devastating that it caused Somerset to lead his vanguard out of its defensive position in an attack which saw a chance of reaching Edward, but it was smashed by a flanking assault of light cavalry which put the Lancastrians to flight. Edward then went for the remaining Lancastrians who continued to hold their defensive position. They were soon broken. The Earl of Devon fell on the battlefield and no quarter was given to the common soldiers. In the rout that followed, Prince Edward was cut down. Others who died included John Beaufort, 'Earl of Dorset', Lord John Wenlock, Sir Edmund Hampden, and Sir Robert Whittingham.

Several fugitives were found ten miles away in the church at Didbrook and were dragged out and killed. Many, including Somerset, had sought sanctuary at Tewkesbury Abbey but were taken from there as prisoners when Edward refused to accept that an abbey could offer sanctuary, threatening to enter and kill them all there and then.

On the second day after the battle, Somerset, Sir John Langstrother, Sir Hugh Courtenay, Sir Humphrey Audley, Sir Thomas Tresham, Sir Gervaise Clifton, and others were brought to judgement in front of Richard of Gloucester (being Constable) and the Duke of Norfolk (as Marshal).[8] Needless to say they were all then taken out to the market square at Tewkesbury and beheaded.

Generally, though, Edward only demanded the execution of those who had previously sworn allegiance to him: that is, they were clearly traitors. For those who had not acknowledged him as their sovereign, he was prepared to issue a pardon.

Morton was a part of Margaret's retinue who had taken refuge away from the battlefield in Little Malvern Priory between Tewkesbury and Worcester along with Princess Anne, John Fortescue, Ralph Makerel, and Lady Katherine Vaux.[9] They were discovered by William Stanley and taken to Edward at Coventry. Margaret, now a completely broken woman, submitted meekly.

There were still discontented Lancastrian sympathisers in the country who demanded Edward's attention. The Kentishmen were, as seemingly always, stirred up, this time under the leadership of Thomas Neville, and in the north supporters of Henry were even greater in number, but the latter soon submitted to the Earl of Northumberland on learning of the outcome at Tewkesbury. Thomas Neville posed the more difficult problem, raising a large force from Kent, the Cinque ports, and Essex and Surrey, not to mention several hundred Calais soldiers. They mustered at Sittingbourne and sought access to London but were denied. On 12 May London was attacked: boats fired from the Thames, cannon shot from the South Bank and although some damage was inflicted, by the end of the week he and his followers had fled in the face of Edward's arrival, eventually surrendering.[10]

Edward's processional arrival in London was on 21 May and behind him in a chariot was Margaret as prisoner. She would be kept a prisoner in England for the next five years, but it would be a comfortable imprisonment befitting her status. Either she would be lodged (and 'lodged' is more accurate than incarcerated) in apartments at the Tower, or she would stay with Alice de la Pole, the Duchess of Suffolk, at Ewelme, Oxfordshire.[11] She was also waited on by Lady Katherine Vaux and two other ladies, Petronella and Mary.[12]

That same night, on Edward's order, the fifty-year-old Henry was probably poll-axed and stabbed to death in his prison within the Wakefield Tower.[13] With the eradication of the direct Lancastrian line, Edward would at last feel secure. Not only that, but Elizabeth had given birth to a son, also named Edward, on 2 November while in sanctuary at Westminster: the guarantee of safety for his heir was now of primary importance. The following morning Henry's body was paraded through London from the Tower to St Paul's[14] where it was embalmed and taken from there to be first buried at Chertsey Abbey on 23 May, but later to a tomb in St George's Chapel, Windsor Castle.

16

New Order

Thomas Bourchier pauses his conversation with a sigh, passing a slow gaze around Morton's cell within the Tower. This is a plague year, and he would very much like to conclude business and get out of the city. That said, Canterbury wasn't particularly safe for the moment either, but for political reasons rather than health. It is only a week since Edward's formal re-accession to the throne, during which time Morton has been subject to no interrogations and indeed has been treated well. He has gone beyond worry as to whether the absence of castigation means his fate is already determined, death. He projects an air of passive resolution.

But Morton's resolve to stand firm for the Lancastrian cause and his anticipation of death are to be lifted by the careful persuasion of the Archbishop, who has come with a full pardon if John will only submit to and acknowledge Edward as his king. He argues the wisdom of learning from one's predecessors, and recalls Morton's great-uncle Robert who fought at Agincourt. There was a time when he refused to acknowledge Henry IV as king, even though Richard II had been deposed and had died. In part, perhaps, because he was married to Ofka, lady-in-waiting to Richard's first wife. Perhaps also because of his affinity to the Duke of York, Richard's favourite. And, like Edward of York, he got himself linked to the Mortimer Plot to remove Henry. But they both received pardons – and moved on to greater things.

Morton has to do what is best for the times. What is pragmatic and realistic. Fortescue, Makerel, even Margaret have accepted the pardon offered and have acknowledged Edward as their true king.[1] The situation is simply that Henry and his son are both dead, and with them the Lancastrian line. There is nothing to be achieved by fighting for a cause which has died with them. Past oaths and fealties no longer bind anyone to them. Edward's right to the crown is sound by the rules of hereditary and legitimate in law. There is no one else who has anywhere near as valid a claim.

The new regime wants Morton to accept the pardon offered, pledge himself to serve Edward, and serve the country. England needs men of his abilities. Flatteries are served. The King himself has specifically cited the positive role which he sees John playing in government. Society's institutions change slowly but they do change, and there is a discernible shift now away from the barely controlled power of large families to a greater role for administrators, the church, and the new gentry, whose wealth and positions are determined more by industry and trade.

Morton is promised the restitution of lost appointments, but there are other, higher, placements which will be open to him. And very soon. There is a lot of work to be done. Would he accept the pardon and swear allegiance to Edward? The answer was inevitable.

He was immediately reinstated to the prebend of Dinder, Bath and Wells, prebend of Fordington and Writhlington, Sarum, and archdeaconry of Norwich, which provided a modest income, added to the following year with the rectorship of St Dunstan's-in-the-East (between London Bridge and the Tower), prebend of Isleden and canon of St Paul's (which he resigned the next year for the prebend of Chiswick).

But his astounding appointment in March 1472 – just one year after receiving the King's pardon to his attainder – was to Master of the Rolls. Below the King and the Lord Chancellor, this was the third most important administrative role in the country.

Master of the Rolls was a post created by Edward I in 1286 and was first held by the Bishop of Chichester. In fact, Morton was the first doctor of civil law to hold the position. The role was to oversee and collate all the writs and records issued by the Court of Chancery as they related to the common law of the land. Record keeping had been severely disrupted through the years of the civil war and a mammoth organisational challenge faced the incoming Master, one which Morton relished. Which was just as well, as the failure to enforce common rights and processes over arbitrary 'justice' and unwritten and unrecorded local custom were a major complaint during the years of strife. The gentry were particularly fearful of the way in which some of the more aggressive and greedier peers had been misusing the law to undermine and destabilise their rights. Similarly, debasement of the jury system through arbitrary decisions in the lower courts had been undermining faith in the capacity of the crown to deliver on its role as the defender of its citizens.

Morton's official residence was on Chancery Lane at the imaginatively named Rolls House.[2] Here was the office for himself, his staff and for the storage of legal archives. The building's past was not such a beacon of excellence for law and justice: its previous name was Domus Conversorum, or the House of Converted Jews. When Edward I expelled all Jews from England in 1290, residence in this building was the only legal way in which a Jew who had converted to Christianity could remain in the country.[3]

Further evidence of the growing trust in him came in the autumn of 1473 when he was given temporary custody of the Great Seal during a period of illness for Lord Chancellor Stillington.

As Master of the Rolls, Morton returned to the Privy Council where his position and experience as a lawyer of the highest calibre required some measure of input and advice in trying to resolve a fierce disagreement between the King's brothers. Edward was a giant of a man, standing six feet three inches, and with the big build to match his height. Just short of his thirtieth birthday, he had spent so much of his life on the edge of danger that it was easy to read in him, and easy to understand, a desire now for more relaxed, luxurious, and extravagant living. Projecting an outgoing, affable personality, he was easy for Morton to warm to.

George, Duke of Clarence, was twenty-two years old, and had the same outward countenance of Edward, albeit he was much shorter, about 5 foot 5 inches – akin to Morton's height. There was nothing else to endear him to Morton though. His history of avarice, duplicity, deception, and spinelessness was obvious to Morton. Here was a man completely untrustworthy, displaying all the unsavoury attributes of privilege and entitlement.

In complete contrast to his fair-haired, handsome brothers, nineteen-year-old Richard, Duke of Gloucester is dark-haired and has a pinched, sour face. At five feet eight inches, he is just above average height for the times but is showing signs of a stoop caused by scoliosis, or curvature of the spine, not that this causes him to project anything but authority and the confidence of one who has proven his courage and command of men on the battlefield.

The argument between Edward's brothers started when Richard declared his intention to marry Anne Neville, the widow of Prince Edward and sister to George's wife, Isabel. The real reason for the fall-out was, of course, the distribution of the assets of Warwick and of Montagu, following their deaths at the battle of Barnet. Morton had a lot of reading to do, and questions to ask, before voicing any opinions, as matters had developed well before he attained his place in the Privy Council and the politics demanded caution.

English law relating to inheritance had no written code or rules of succession which barred a woman from owning land, but married, her husband would assume title to ownership. In the specific case of the

Warwick estate and title, this had come to Richard Neville as a result of his marriage to Anne Beauchamp and on his death would normally revert to her as Countess of Warwick. Assuming that she did not marry again, her two daughters stood to inherit on her death, the title going to the eldest daughter or her husband.

The Neville lands within the inheritance were different. These were subject to a binding condition, an entailment, requiring inheritance by a male heir only. So with no son of his own, Richard Neville's heir of those lands would be John Neville, Lord Montagu. But he was also dead. The next in line would be Montagu's ten-year-old son George. Young George had been made Duke of Bedford in 1470 in anticipation of being wed to Edward's daughter Elizabeth. But with George's father and uncle rebelling that idea was no longer credible. In fact, their rebellion put all those hopes and expectations to one side.

Edward made the decision to seize possession of all the estates and titles of these two traitors and redistribute them according to his wish. This redistribution, perhaps unsurprisingly, favoured Richard. If he should marry Anne Neville, then it would prove likely that the evident disparity in wealth and favour enjoyed by Richard over George would become even more apparent.

Another spanner in the works was that after Tewkesbury, the fifteen-year-old Anne had been placed in the custody and care of her sister Isabel. George's interpretation of this was that, as Isabel's husband, he had that right and duty of custody. More than that, he saw himself as her guardian. This meant that he had control and command over her property, her right to marry and to whom, as well as her general well-being and upbringing.

Morton's next train of thought would be to consider what outcomes his 'clients' sought. Edward wants his brothers reconciled, he is content to see Richard marry Anne, he wants to show due reward to Richard for his loyalty and service in restoring his throne, and he wants to see Richard controlling the north of the country on his behalf. He doesn't trust George, but then no one trusts George. George wants what he regards as his rights and fair recognition of his standing as the older brother of Richard. Richard wants Anne as his wife and a palatinate in the north. He had forcefully removed her from George's house.

Each of the younger brothers wants to hold their lands of right, whether their own or through their wives, and not at the behest and whim of the King. For this reason, neither wishes to see Warwick and Montagu attainted.

A Council meeting had been held at Shene in February at which George and Richard presented their respective cases direct on the proposed marriage and Clarence's guardianship claim.[4] Nothing was agreed.

The answer seemed to be best presented in stages. That is, an answer which would, as much as it could, suit the three brothers – but neither the Countess of Warwick nor George Neville could or would be treated fairly.

First, since Edward did not wish to pass an Act of Attainder against the deceased Richard and John Neville, they were formally declared traitors in 1472. Second, there needs to be a general agreement on the division of the assets of the two traitors. This will be an accommodation, not out of brotherly love and understanding but to save George from losing everything. While the great minds of King and Council are struggling to find a way to resolution, the catalyst reveals himself as John de Vere, erstwhile Earl of Oxford. De Vere has been causing problems with his small fleet making raids on Calais and generally acting the pirate up and down the Channel with support from the French King. He has been keeping in touch with George Neville, Archbishop of York, who has himself been plotting with George of Clarence. Edward is aware of these shenanigans and has George Neville arrested and incarcerated in Hammes Castle.

On 30 September 1473, de Vere lands at and seizes St Michael's Mount in Cornwall. Unfortunately for him, neither the good men of Cornwall nor King Louis respond to his call for help. Under siege, he eventually surrenders on pardon for his life only, in February 1474.[5] However, Clarence has called his own followers to arms, publicly proclaiming that he will get his revenge on brother Richard. He then finds himself isolated and accommodating Richard, if only to please Edward, is his only route out of trouble.

This agreement will be ratified by Act of Parliament. Clarence will get all of Warwick's estate that came to him either by right of his wife or by right of his title as Earl of Salisbury, except for those parts which had already been transferred to Gloucester with Clarence's consent. Those will include Middleham, Sheriff Hatton, and Penrith: in effect, the most northern estates. Gloucester's share is basically the Montagu lands.

George's interests are to be subject to a parliamentary Act ensuring that these can never be taken from him or his heirs. As to the rights of the Countess of Warwick, in the spring of 1474, parliament passes an Act to partition her land between her two daughters – effectively giving her the status of someone who is legally dead.

For Richard, things are more complicated, and these complications will have repercussions in the future. The rights and titles of George Neville, the Montagu heir, were taken from him and from 1476 his wardship was passed to Richard. However, the 1475 Act of Parliament which decreed that the Neville inheritance in the north of England should pass to Richard, Duke of Gloucester and his heirs this was subject to George and his heirs' survival. It seems probable that it was Edward who insisted that this condition being put into the Act – not least because it would have required his signature and seal. Why would such an unusual stipulation be made – other than to afford the boy George the best chance of avoiding any fatal accident?

In fact, George Neville died on 4 May 1483, aged seventeen. He was unmarried and so had no heirs of the body. His sisters then became co-heiresses and Richard, who might reasonably have expected to bequeath the Montagu estates to his son Edward, suddenly found himself as a life tenant only. This would put him, and particularly his heirs, in a very weak position. But the 1475 Act would not be something which would engage Morton's time or mind.

Third, Clarence would be given the titles Earl of Warwick and Salisbury and will retain his title as Lieutenant of Ireland. Richard surrendered the Great Chamberlainship of England, but retained the titles of Constable and Admiral of England, together with the Western Marches along the Scottish border, was Warden of the Royal Forests beyond the Trent, and Steward of the Duchy of Lancaster beyond the Trent.

And fourth, Richard would marry Anne.[6] She had been hidden in the house of one of Clarence's associates but was seized by Richard and placed in sanctuary at St Martin le Grand. They married in July of 1472 and left London shortly afterwards for Middleham, from where Richard impressed his authority and character on his estates and the north generally.

Edward had also expressed his favour towards Richard by granting him the forfeited lands of the Earl of Oxford (mainly in Essex) in December 1471, which Richard then followed up by coercing Oxford's elderly mother into signing over her own inheritance to him.

Morton's contribution to these family arguments is minimal, in that he consciously avoids giving any strong steer, as to do so would inevitably create a black mark against his name with one or other brother, even the King. While he has no trepidation in giving advice or service to either, it is abundantly clear that this must never be for one of the three against the others.

There is one carefully constructed clause in the 1474 Act to which both Morton and Fortescue would have had input, if not authorship of. Should the marriage between Richard and Anne end in divorce or be annulled, then the Warwick estates which he held would remain with him and not go with her. This is not so much for Richard's protection but more to try to acknowledge George of Clarence. Putting to one side the Montagu estate, which Richard now held in his own name and not by right of his wife, the lands coming out of the Warwick inheritance had been recognised as Clarence's personal 'gift' to Richard, and if there was any danger of those lands or their value leaving the immediate family then that would be challenged by George: either in the courts or by other means. To save any further mess or embarrassment on this issue, Edward thought it easier to clarify the position now and the parties (or at least the men) seemed to agree.

17

The Last of the Beaufort Line

In the summer of 1473, Anne of Gloucester is pregnant and is anxious to have her mother by her side. The Countess of Warwick is still in sanctuary at Beaulieu Abbey, writing to anyone who will receive her letters for assistance in regaining her possessions and position. Her disposition towards her daughters and their husbands cannot be said to be warm. The rows over her property between Clarence and Gloucester are public fare and an embarrassment. However, she receives Anne's plea to come to Middleham and, delivered by Richard's close confidant Sir James Tyrell, it is a plea she cannot refuse.[1]

This will not be Richard's first child. He has two bastard sons and a daughter, hardly surprising bearing in mind the years of close companionship with brother Edward and William, Lord Hastings, whose example rubbed off on him in so many ways.[2]

Anne gives birth to a son, Edward of Middleham, at the beginning of December. Edward and Elizabeth have had a second son, Richard of Shrewsbury, Duke of York, on 17 August.

While Morton perceives both brothers as dangerous, and both able to go against the King if their ambitions dictate, his view of the other significant group on the council is more accommodating. Just as Edward grew to be independent of Warwick, so Clarence and Gloucester seek a freedom from him and to be recognised and feared in their own right. The Woodvilles, though displaying all the annoying arrogance of the *nouveau riche*, know full well that their ascendancy is wholly due to their relationship to Queen Elizabeth and the desire of Edward to elevate her family to a status appropriate to that relationship. Because of this, they are considered more reliable by Edward than most of the other peers who surround him. Just as important, they have a level of education, appreciation of the arts, and are more culturally refined than many.

Moreover, most started out as Lancastrians. In all, Morton finds them perhaps the easiest around the table to get along with. They are the ones it would be most agreeable to sit down with, open a bottle of Burgundy and philosophise on the meaning of life. The world is changing, and government needs educated rulers as much as war lords.

The leader of the Woodville clan was thirty-three-year-old Anthony, Earl Rivers, brother to the Queen. Wounded at Barnet, he had a widespread reputation as a champion in the jousting lists and was renowned for his intelligence and breadth of knowledge. So much so that in 1473 he was appointed Governor of the Prince of Wales's Household and his tutor. He struck up a friendship with William Caxton when exiled with Edward in Bruges and his translation of *The Dictes and Sayings of the Philosophers* was one of the first, if not the first, book printed in England. A poet and man of letters, he was also devout, known to wear a hairshirt under his robes.

Thomas Grey, Lord Harington and Bonville, (Marquis of Dorset from 1475), was Elizabeth's eldest son from her first marriage. Eighteen years old, he was engaged in a serious feud with Lord Hastings who opposed his marriage to Hasting's stepdaughter Cecily Bonville (by whom he gained his title and with whom he had fourteen children). He fought with Edward at Tewkesbury aged just sixteen.

Other Woodville family members were not at this time of particular prominence. Richard Grey, Elizabeth's youngest son had just turned sixteen. Catherine Woodville, fifteen in 1473, and the Queen's sister, was married to Henry Stafford, Duke of Buckingham, who deeply resented being wed to someone of 'inferior birth' and despised the Woodvilles profoundly.

Twenty-five-year-old Lionel Woodville, brother to the Queen, was also an obscure figure at this time, making his way as a cleric. He would become Dean of Exeter in 1478, and Chancellor of Oxford University 1479–1483 (and was the first person in the records to be awarded an honorary doctorate in civil law by Oxford). In 1482 he was elected as Bishop of Salisbury.

Edward Woodville, eighteen years old, was the Queen's youngest brother. Gaining a reputation as a soldier, he also had one as a 'promoter and companion of the King's vices' and as such did not endear himself to his royal sister. And there is William, Lord Hastings, forty-two years old and Edward's closest friend. He is Chamberlain to the Household, meaning anyone who wanted access to the King had to go through him. This made him powerful, influential, rich, and corrupt. But more than that, Hastings was the man who knew how to party. He was Edward's gofer and was a pimp for him. This generated a great hostility towards him from Elizabeth, increased by his disapproval of the marriage between her son and his step-daughter, and because he took the position of Captain of Calais supposed to have been promised to Lord Rivers.

The other major presences on the Council at this time included Henry Bourchier, Earl of Essex, who was Edward's uncle by marriage and his Treasurer. John, Lord Dynham, was one of the foremost members of the government, his lands being mainly in Devon and Cornwall. Another peer close to the centre was Walter Deveraux, Lord Ferrers, tutor and councillor to the Prince of Wales.

Most of the ecclesiastical members sitting on the Council or in the House of Lords Morton had known for a decade, but there were some new faces. Robert Stillington was Bishop of Bath and Wells, an astute and ambitious political animal. John Alcock, Bishop of Rochester, was of great intellect and a proficient architect, but also politically aware and capable. James Goldwell, Bishop of Norwich and Thomas Rotherham, Bishop of Lincoln, were both new to their sees in 1472. John Booth had been translated to Exeter on the elevation of George Neville to Archbishop of York, and Edward Story was Bishop of Carlisle, succeeding William Percy.

For now, in 1473, the government was functioning well, held together by strong leadership from the King. The priority was very much one of establishing routine and order with little desire for change. But it was clear that there were tensions which would likely manifest themselves soon. Not least was the constant sniping at and about the Woodvilles. The previous year had seen the death of fifty-six-year-old Jacquetta of Luxembourg, Countess Rivers and the Queen's mother. Not content with the execution of her husband and eldest son after the battle of Edgecote in 1469, Warwick had one of his retainers, Thomas Wake, accuse Jacquetta of witchcraft. (It was interesting to note that Thomas Wake was the widower of Margaret Lucy, one of Edward's conquests, and he went on to marry Elisabeth, Lady Latimer, the aunt of Eleanor Butler, another.) Jacquetta was exonerated by the King's Council in 1470 but the stress created by the charge, coming immediately after the death of her husband and son, hastened her death two years later. The witchcraft accusation would also be raised again by Richard III, suggesting that she and her daughter had procured the marriage to Edward by sorcery.

The other council of note was that of Prince Edward, though this Prince Edward did not benefit from having Dr Morton in attendance. Nonetheless, it's make-up, and how its influence was perceived, did have an impact on Morton's future. The council originally comprises the Queen, Clarence, Gloucester, Rivers, and Hastings. Thomas Milling, the Abbot of Westminster, is its Chancellor. He is held in special regard by

Edward and his family as he gave sanctuary to Elizabeth and her children while Edward was in exile. He is also godfather to the young prince and will later become Bishop of Hereford – a rare thing for an abbot.

Steward for the Prince is Richard Fiennes, Lord Dacre, and Chamberlain is sixty-one-year-old Thomas Vaughan.[3] The last place on this council is taken by John Alcock, the new Bishop of Rochester, who holds the title President of the Council, and it is he who holds the real power over decision making. Sir Richard Grey, Edward's half-brother, would later assume a significant role towards the Prince and indeed to Wales generally.

Prince Edward was educated and brought up at Ludlow castle for the next ten years. His council changed slightly over that time, but the main officers remained the same, attending to the Prince's development, administering his estates and law and order in Wales and along the Welsh Marches. Although based at Ludlow, the council and its administrators regularly moved around the province, holding meetings at Cardigan and Carmarthen, generating a measure of inclusion.

Whilst a prejudicial eye might see the Prince's Council as being Woodville-dominated, that would not be the view of the dispassionate. It would seem, and was, deeply misogynistic to resent or disparage a maternal influence over the upbringing of a child. Not least with the tribulations this mother and child had been through together. At the same time, it would have been irresponsible to place the youngster's development in the hands of his disturbed and disturbing paternal uncles. But this council was selected by King Edward and those sitting on it were first and foremost loyal to him and not a Woodville faction.

Edward's clearing of Lancastrian support from Wales pretty much boils down to the removal of Jasper Tudor, erstwhile Earl of Pembroke. Jasper was quite close to Tewkesbury as the two armies clashed, but not close enough and on the wrong side of the Severn to be of use. On hearing of the destruction of the Lancastrian army, forty-year-old Jasper retired with his army and fourteen-year-old nephew Henry to Chepstow. They were pursued on Edward's instruction by Roger Vaughan of Powys.

Roger's father and maternal grandfather both fought and died at Agincourt but notwithstanding such Lancastrian credentials, he was a sound Yorkist and half-brother to William Herbert, the Yorkist Earl of Pembroke. More pertinent, he had led out Owen Tudor, Jasper's father, to his execution after the battle of Mortimer's Cross. When he was trapped and captured by Jasper at Chepstow, he would have known what his fate would be.

Edward was particularly interested in getting his hands on Henry Tudor. The son of Edmund Tudor, his grandmother was Catherine

Valois, widow of Henry V. His mother was Margaret Beaufort, the sole heir of John Beaufort, Duke of Somerset and a legitimised descendant of John of Gaunt. In terms of wealth and pedigree she therefore had immense importance and in June 1472 marries her fourth husband, Thomas, Lord Stanley. Henry is her only child. Her first husband Edmund Tudor was twelve years her senior and she gave birth to her son when thirteen; the experience so bad that she had no further children. Edmund died of plague whilst a prisoner of the Yorkists and never saw his son. Her second husband's nephew is Henry Stafford, 2nd Duke of Buckingham.

The Tudors realise that in the long term there is no safe place for them, and Edward will take increasingly vigorous steps to eliminate them. Effectively, Tewkesbury has made Henry and his mother the last of the Beaufort line. They move on to Pembroke Castle where siege is laid by Morgan ap Thomas, Roger Vaughan's son-in-law. Luckily for them, the rest of the ap Thomas family are Lancastrian supporters and the siege is relieved by Morgan's own brother David, at the head of 2,000 men.

The Welsh, and the Scots come to that, have been receiving funds from Louis to keep Edward 'busy', too busy to be thinking about invading France or otherwise interfering in his sphere of activity. But word filters through that the Scots are discussing the possibility of coming to an accommodation with Edward, which will release more resources to root out the Tudors. So Jasper reckons on France as being the safest destination for Henry and himself and they sail from nearby Tenby. But they are sold short by their ship's captain and are landed at Brittany as 'guests' of Duke Francis II. They are in fact treated very well and are promised protection, but they are guests under surveillance, and it is clear that they are too politically valuable to be allowed to leave their host's domain. In fact, both Edward and Louis soon make overtures to have them handed over, but that level of interest only strengthens Francis's resolve to keep them close.

Foreign Affairs, 1473–1475

Morton was sitting in a private chamber at Westminster Palace attending William, Lord Hastings and in the company of Sir Thomas Montgomery and Sir William Hatclyf towards the end of 1473.[1] They were being briefed by Hastings for a fact-finding mission to Burgundy.

Edward intended to give Louis of France more than just a bloody nose in retribution for his succour and support of Margaret and Warwick, to press for the French throne itself. Regaining some of the territories lost by Henry VI would be sufficient to claim a victory, and war itself would satisfy the expectations arising from Edward's original manifesto, which would also help refocus magnates and citizens alike in nationalistic fervour on the Crown. That was the vision.

England could not achieve success on its own. The cost of raising an army to meet the French in open battle would be huge, and if sieges were required then it would be nearly impossible. To the outside world it would be a finance mission, seeking a new agreement with the Burgundians over rates of exchange. Their real instructions were to sound out the possibilities for an alliance against France incorporating Burgundy, Hungary, and the Holy Roman Empire. But it is Charles of Burgundy who is key to Edward's plans and his association with him, bearing in mind Charles is married to Edward's sister Margaret, is grounds for optimism. Edward's credibility as a military commander is also very high and he hopes this will give confidence of victory to prospective partners.

On a cold, unpleasant day in January 1474, the small ambassadorial team crossed the Channel on their journey to Utrecht in a small, flat-bottomed boat each gazing at the others' green countenance trying to predict who will next throw up and whether they will judge the wind direction correctly. After a while, no one cares.

Hatclyf had made this journey in the preceding summer with Dr John Russell but had elicited scant response from Charles, who had his eye on greater things; namely negotiating the marriage of his daughter Mary to Archduke Maximilian, son of Frederick III, Holy Roman Emperor, which he saw as the key to his own aggrandisement.[2] So while these earlier discussions had been going on for a potential alliance against the French, Charles had also been negotiating extending his truce with Louis to May 1475; later presenting the excuse that the winter months were not the season for warfare anyway. Not that Charles's plan came to much. When he and Frederick met in the autumn of 1473 at Trier, and Charles's ostentatious plans were revealed during weeks of non-stop feasting, Frederick slipped away in the night, leaving Charles to shut himself up in his room and completely wreck it in a fit of temper.

Now they would try again to see if Charles was serious in his resolve against the French king. While the mission would at least conclude with an understanding of the basis for a treaty with Burgundy, it accomplished nothing of positive value as far as building a wider alliance. King Matthias Corvinus of Hungary would make no commitment. Frederick had been so discouraged by his experience with Charles that there was little interest in a joint venture to be found there. Indeed, Charles showed a similar preoccupation with other matters as he exhibited during the earlier visit. This time, his attention was drawn to Cologne, which he decided to assimilate as a Burgundian protectorate in defence of his kinsman in a contest for the archbishopric, and he began his campaign by laying siege to the fortified town of Neuss, about twenty-four miles from the city of Cologne itself. The effect of this was to delay the return of Morton to report back until the first week of June.

The time spent in Flanders was well spent. Here Morton could see the development of capitalism in the migration of the cloth weaving industry from village and cottage into the towns. The burgeoning printing industry in Bruges was particularly noticeable, as was the city's function as a centre of finance. It was also a well organised centre for brothels and prostitution – something to report back on to Bishop Waynflete perhaps?

Back in England, Edward was not too displeased with the findings of the mission, though he let his feelings on Charles's lukewarm reception be known. As it was, a slight pause in proceedings was practically advantageous, if not necessary.

The first problem, as ever, was money. Parliament was both generous and patient in helping Edward to build up a war chest, but he needed more. The seed for achieving this was planted by Morton, who would improvise on the idea for Henry VII. Benevolences would be sought from wealthy individuals specifically for the forthcoming war. Essentially these would be forced loans with no prospect of repayment, sought by a direct approach from the King to a well-researched script, in which the target's capacity for payment was pre-calculated. In the event, so popular was the idea of a French war and, no less, a direct personal appeal from the King, that the anticipated return was exceeded. Edward gained some contributions by selling kisses to wealthy widows.

The second problem was to firm up on alliances and ensure that his back was covered while he and his army were abroad. The Tudors had been evicted from Wales, and Scotland pacified, for the time being at least, with the betrothal of their two-year-old Prince James to Edward's four-year-old daughter Cecily. The groundwork achieved with Burgundy was developed and concluded with his officials in England, while he continued to focus his attention on the siege of Neuss – and which would continue for ten months until he was forced to retreat by an advancing superior army of the Holy Roman Empire.

In July 1474, a declaration of friendship between Edward and Charles was published. Edward undertook to provide an army of 10,000 within twelve months, while Charles promised to support him with his own army until Edward retrieved the throne of France. Both sides promised not to undertake any further negotiation with Louis XI. Burgundy's share of the territorial spoils was then specified and agreed upon, and finally, the outstanding half of Margaret of York's dowry. This was Charles's third wife and not the happiest of marriages. He saw Margaret only infrequently, there were no children, and his physical and mental decline had set in as he pursued the creation of a kingdom from his ducal lands.

The year 1474 proved to be a good one for John Morton. His efforts in diplomacy and government were well rewarded. Having picked up the Prebend of Chiswick the previous year and St Paul's the year before that, he was now collated as Archdeacon of Chester and Rector of South Molton (which he resigned the following year). Another elevation was to Master of the Hospital of St Bartholomew in Bristol, and then to Dean of the Court of Arches.[3] The latter made him judge in the ecclesiastical court of the Archbishop of Canterbury, acting either as commissary to the Official or chief judge of the court, or increasingly in his own right. Being a metropolitan court, it sat in London and not in Canterbury. But it would be a while before he heard cases there: there was more work to do abroad.

In the spring of 1475, Edward makes a formal demand of Louis that he surrender Normandy and Guines. Knowing that he would not, the war begins. So large is the English force and its supplies that it takes three weeks using 500 ships to get all safely across the Channel from Sandwich to Calais. Edward has had the foresight to make peace with the Hanseatic League, so keeping the seas free of their potential intervention. Morton was in one of the last boats to make the crossing and although it was a balmy July, he still provided Neptune with lunch.

Two days after arriving at Calais, with the English army spread out for miles around the city, Duchess Margaret arrives to greet her brother, not having seen him for some years. It is a full week later that Charles arrives, but not with an army, only his personal bodyguard. Morton is one of the English team sitting in on discussions and it is clear that Charles has no intention of working side by side with Edward and it is doubtful whether he is sincere in taking on Louis at all. His plan is to move the Burgundian army into Lorraine for pillage and conquest as part of his personal ambition, suggesting that Edward takes Normandy with the assistance of the Duke of Brittany and the Count of St Pol, then to move on where both forces will meet up at Reims to crown Edward King of France. Edward was less than impressed but held his tongue and decided to at least give the plan credence.

Their march was slow, and two nights were spent camped on the site of the battle of Agincourt. This proved a morale booster to all the troops who had expressed disappointment and scepticism when Charles turned up at Calais without his army. Morton would feel a particular race of fire through his veins and recalling tales of the engagement from his boyhood he spent significant time tracing the lines where the men of both armies clashed, fought, and died. And he marvelled that, just sixty years on, you would never know unless someone told and showed you.

On 29 July, Charles rejoined them having spent a few days with his wife at St Omer, only to irritate Edward once more by spending the night with his bodyguard in the town of Peronne while Edward and the English camped in fields. The French army was now massing in large numbers and getting near; English foraging parties were being attacked. And when they reached St Quentin, they were fired on by cannon, signifying St Pol was going to side with France rather than Burgundy or England.

Charles left to join his army on 12 August and an enraged Edward called his Council together. Here was the largest army sent abroad and, if lost, England would be in severe peril. His so-called allies had all let him down. Supplies were limited and there were no funds for a prolonged war. The French outnumbered him and were not going to fall for the kind of tactics employed at Agincourt. The ground was baked hard for a start, which favoured their cavalry. Without the additional strength provided by allies, engagement was high risk indeed. While pride and valour called for a fight, prudence suggested otherwise.

Richard of Gloucester argued fiercely for the fight. There was some hesitancy and uncertainty among the peers. Were they about to witness another family fall-out with Gloucester on the one side and Clarence on the other? It seemed clear to Morton which way Edward wanted the debate to go, and it would have been equally clear that, as one of the diplomatic team of recent months but also because of his lengthy residence in Louis' France and his understanding of the policies and interests of the enemy, he would be required to add to the discussions.

Reviewing options, Louis is a serial schemer. He enjoys plotting and manipulation. But he is not a good general. He does not like high levels of risk but prefers others to take risks for him. He will be nervous and will avoid confrontation if possible.

If the object of an engagement on the battlefield is glory and valour, then that is achievable. But with the size of the French army it will be at a high cost. However, under King Edward's leadership the English army should be able to win the day and push the French into retreat. Normandy can be taken. But it will be taken behind a retreating French army who will ensure the desolation of the ground the English advance over. So keeping the army supplied and, indeed, in supporting the civilian population without whom there is no value in the territory, will be a logistical and financial nightmare.

Taking Normandy is not taking France. The real prize still awaits and needs allies to secure it. If they have shown themselves slow, or even false, up to now, why will they materialise later on? Could those sought-after allies turn later, when the stakes were higher?

Why is the war being fought? Eventually, it has to be that the end prize enriches and empowers the King and his people. The past shows Normandy and Guines both cost more to hold than the income they can generate for the Crown. There are, at present, no reserves in the royal treasury: to go forward will require heavy taxation in England and drain individual resources, particularly of those Lords with responsibilities for protecting the borders.

Louis is nervous of a fight. If he could be persuaded to negotiate, it should be possible to secure such a financial settlement to the advantage of England that in monetary terms – income against expenditure – exceeds the value of Normandy.

This is the reasoning adopted, but Morton, Hastings, and others advocating it score a black mark with Gloucester, judging by his glare around the table.

The mood is overwhelmingly in favour of exploring what might be achievable from a negotiated settlement. By chance, the English were holding a prisoner, Jacques de Grassay, who they released, but not before John Howard, Duke of Norfolk and Lord Thomas Stanley had impressed upon him that Edward, or at least many of his nobles, might listen to an approach for peace if the terms were good enough.

A positive response came by return that very evening and on 15 August Morton accompanied Howard, William Dudley, Dean of the Chapel Royal, and Sir Thomas St Leger to conduct negotiations with the French at a village near Amiens.

The terms agreed were good. A seven-year truce was concluded to run until 1482. Differences between the two kings, such as Edward's claim to the French throne, would be referred to arbitration, the arbitrators being the Archbishops of Canterbury and Lyons, the Duke of Clarence, and the Count of Dunois. Charges levied on trade between the two countries which had been in place since 1463 would be abolished. Englishmen going to France would no longer require safe-conduct passes. Louis would pay Edward 75,000 crowns immediately and a pension of 50,000 crowns a year thereafter for as long as they both lived. And Louis' son Charles would wed Edward's daughter Elizabeth when they reached marriageable age. Finally, Louis would agree two months later to ransom Queen Margaret for the sum of £50,000.

Richard had been in a thunderous mood even as the negotiators were agreed upon by Edward's council, and he leaked what was going on to both Charles of Burgundy and the Count of St Pol. Charles was back with Edward barely before the negotiating team could report on the package agreed. For two days he raged, cajoled, threatened and swore, but all to no avail. Similarly, the Count of St Pol begged Edward not to deal with Louis (but by letter rather than in person). He received the reply that if he had only kept his word then no treaty would have been made. Edward had clearly had enough of his fickle friends.

The two kings met on a specially constructed bridge at Picquigny to conclude the deal on 29 August. Prior to this, the French King had provided a feast of food and wine over four days for the English army at Amiens, where all became so uncontrollably drunk that they had to be evicted from the city. John Morton could only gaze on in frozen horror. If the French wanted to annihilate the English, this would have been the ideal moment.

As it was, the days of festivities provided the time for the bridge construction with a fence formed halfway across as a security measure, illustrating Louis' fear of assassination and, particularly, the fate of John the Fearless. In fact, so great was Louis' concern for his wellbeing that he had Philippe de Commines, the diplomat and author, dress as his double on the bridge. Only a dozen men were allowed to attend each king on the bridge: on the English side, the absence of Richard of Gloucester was notable.[4] But all went to plan, the treaty signed and sealed.

The English returned home in September, at least for the most part. Some 2,000 archers decided to try their luck for some heroics and loot with the Duke of Burgundy.

For Morton, he had begun a real friendship with the King and with Lord Hastings. He also developed a positive relationship with the old Lancastrians as represented by the Woodvilles. At the same time, he had found himself the other side of a widening gulf with Richard of Gloucester and several of those peers who regarded anyone who had switched from Lancaster to York with great suspicion.

He had also picked up a pension from Louis of 600 crowns a year. Of course, this did not match the rewards bestowed by the French king on those key players of rank: Chancellor Rotherham gained 1000 crowns, Lord Howard and Sir Thomas Montgomery received 1200 crowns a year each, and My Lord Hastings a tidy 2000-crown pension. Nor has Morton been forgotten by the Church, having received the appointments of Archdeacon of Winchester, Archdeacon of Huntingdon and Canon of Wells in the spring.

And Edward had picked up something: a tertian ague, or malaria, which would harass him for the rest of his life.

Departures, 1476–1478

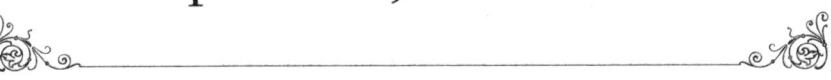

The English casualties in the French adventure were few, but one stood out from the rest. At the battle of Barnet, the Lancastrian Henry Holland, Duke of Exeter had been badly wounded and, it was thought, dead. Eventually found alive, he was imprisoned in the Tower and his wife Anne, sister to Edward, took the opportunity to divorce him for years of physical and mental cruelty. Exeter had no wish to linger and, in all probability, die incarcerated, and so he pleaded for the opportunity to go to France with Edward. On the return journey he was thrown overboard on Edward's orders to end an unpleasant life without the cost of an executioner.

Another unattractive figures to fall foul of the campaign was the Count of St Pol. After Edward completed the treaty, he received a bitter letter from St Pol berating him for being a coward and declaring that Louis would deceive him before too long. Rather than reply, Edward simply forwarded the letter to Louis. A fearful St Pol then fled his lands to seek protection from Charles of Burgundy, but to no avail. Charles handed him over to Louis who found him a traitor and had his head removed on 19 December. After all the shouting, Charles then went on to sign a peace treaty with Louis in the wake of Picquigny.

In January 1476, Margaret of Anjou finally returned to France having renounced any claim she may have had on the English throne and was delivered to the Seigneur de Genlis, captain of Rouen on the 29th of that month. Having been ransomed by Louis, he now expected her to defray his costs and she was required to give to him all rights she had inherited from her parents. For this, Louis awarded her an annual pension of 6,000 livres. She died 25 August 1482, aged fifty-two, at the Chateau de Dampierre near Saumur.

The previous year, George Neville, Archbishop of York, had received a pardon on 11 November and was returned to England from his prison cell in Hammes. However, two-and-a-half years under such a harsh regime had broken him physically and in spirit. He died on 8 June.

Edward had returned to some disquiet and disappointment over the outcome of his French adventure, but people were weary of internal strife and there was no outward manifestation of unrest. That was lucky, because he could not reveal all the details of the treaty he had entered into with Louis – not least the clause of 'amity' by which each undertook to help the other in the event of civil unrest. Peace, better foreign trade arrangements, and the remittance of part of the taxes which parliament had voted him all helped to placate the middle and merchant classes at least.

The necessity of dealing with law, order, and justice without further delay was made very clear though, and Edward's energies were put to administering the King's law across the country. However, this was no easy task as any thoughts of reform to the justice system had to be tempered by the dependency of the Crown on the magnates. who were very disinclined to surrender or moderate any of the judicial functions they had acquired over the years. Nonetheless, improvements were made over the lawlessness which accompanied the reign of Henry VI.

Although Edward's treasury was now healthy and holding the promise of a strong regular income, his court was expensive to run. Moreover, his extravagant designs for new places of worship and education were costly. One immediate project is the reinterment of Edward's father and brother. Since their death at the battle of Wakefield fifteen years earlier, the Duke of York and Earl of Rutland had been laying in a modest tomb in Pontefract. Edward and his brothers now wanted to rebury their father and older brother 100 miles to the south at the family home, Fotheringhay, in a mausoleum in the Church of St Mary and All Saints which had been especially refurbished for the purpose.

The bodies were exhumed on 24 July and laid in state with Duke Richard's remains under a model of his image, dressed in ermine-trimmed clothes under cloth of gold. The next morning, Richard of Gloucester led the sombre procession taking the corpses on their five-day journey to their final resting place. Lawrence Booth, Archbishop of York, kept ahead to ensure each of the resting churches along the way were properly dressed for the procession. Provision had also to be made for every person coming to honour the dead at these way-stations to receive one penny or, if a woman and child, twopence.

John Morton was waiting for the cortège at Fotheringhay, having ridden up from London where he was supervising his team of lawyers at Chancery, studying the rolls and registers seeking to find and fine anyone who had entered onto inheritances without observing due legal procedures – an exercise proving to be very lucrative for Edward. It was also proving to be another lucrative year for Morton. He had gathered in prebends at St Decuman, Bath and Wells, and at South Newbald in Yorkshire. Later in the year prebends at Horton, Sarum, and at Exeter would be added, together with the benefits of archdeacon of Berkshire and of Norfolk.

There is an impressive assembly of important individuals attending the ceremony. Edward, Clarence, Dorset, Rivers, Hastings, and other nobles, together with their wives. There are ambassadors from France, Denmark, and Portugal, and after the ceremony Morton receives the first instalment of his pension from the French.

Edward is feeling comfortable and secure on his throne, but there remains that irritation to his royal house who is Henry Tudor. In his discussions at Picquigny, Edward secured Louis' agreement not to attack Brittany. For this good turn, it seemed worthwhile making one more attempt to gain possession of and dispose of the young man. Henry and his uncle Jasper had been split up and were now housed in separate locations twenty miles apart, Henry in Elvan Towers, a castle not far from Vannes. Edward's concern for the well-being of Brittany certainly touches Francis and he agrees to hand Henry over. With English ships waiting off St Malo, Henry is brought to the harbour town for extradition. Knowing what his fate will be, something he has been well schooled on by his uncle and by experience, the stress overwhelms him, and he falls ill with fever. While he takes sanctuary in St Malo Cathedral to recuperate, Francis has a change of heart, and he is reunited with Jasper at Chateau de l'Hermine at Vannes.

On 21 December, Isabel, Duchess of Clarence died. She was twenty-five years old. She had gone into labour and gave birth to a son, Richard, on 6 October at Tewkesbury Abbey but had developed an infection leading to puerperal fever.[1] Her condition was probably not helped by being moved thirty miles to Warwick Castle on 12 November, where she passed away five weeks later. Her son followed her soon, dying on the first day of January 1477.

George's grief was real and deeply felt but, as in all things with George, the grief turned inwards and fuelled the twin beliefs that everyone was out to get him and that he deserved, indeed his greatness gave him the right to, a higher standing in society than he held. He was suffering from serious mental illness but its murderous expression forestalled any sympathy. Then twenty-seven years old, this would quickly result in increasing levels of instability and recklessness.

At the same time, events in Europe added to the chemistry that would cause Clarence's final collapse. On 5 January, Charles the Bold was killed outside the city of Nancy in his campaign to subjugate Lorraine. His exhausted troops, laying siege in the snow, were attacked by a combined relief army of Swiss, Alsatians, and Lorrainers, who smashed through the Burgundian ranks. Caught in flight, Charles's naked body was found some days later, his head frozen to the ice surface of a lake. An axe had split his skull and a lance had been thrust into his backside. The exposed cheek of his face had been eaten by wolves.

His death produced an immediate danger to Burgundy now open to a likely attack from France, and France does indeed start to pick up the cudgel. But Charles had left an heir, his twenty-year-old daughter Mary, known as Mary the Rich – because that is exactly what she was.

The first reaction in England was for Richard of Gloucester to seek authority to send troops into Burgundy to protect the Dowager Duchess, his sister, and her step-daughter. He is angered when his request is refused, not least because he sees money and other resources lavished on his sister-in-law's family rather than on blood relatives, but also because Edward has again shied away from the military option. However, Edward is determined not to do anything which maybe construed as a breach of his treaty with Louis.

Receiving money for *not* doing anything, as opposed to having to go out and wage war for it, is becoming a habit with Edward and this is not helping his image. It is also not helped by his creeping obesity, extra-marital dalliances, and generally ostentatious lifestyle. Some of his advisors and officials are following suit. That is not to say that Edward is not concerned for Burgundy's integrity. The commercial links between England and Burgundy are profound and, in addition, part of the duchy adjoins Calais. So the first move is to see Hastings strengthen the garrison at Calais and then on 16 February Morton and Sir John Donne are sent on an ambassadorial assignment to Louis.[2]

Their mission is mainly one seeking reassurances and, if possible, more money to buy off English aid to Burgundy; to make public the treaty of amity and extend the trade agreement from seven years to however long the two kings should live, possibly by signing a new, improved treaty to reflect this; to offer Edward as a mediator between France and Spain; to open up a meeting of the two kings and the Duke of Brittany to resolve tensions; and other details on finance and trade. They then pressed for assurances that the rights and wellbeing of Duchess Margaret of Burgundy would not be endangered and that the proposed marriage between the Dauphin and Edward's daughter still stood.

Returning with optimism and 10,000 crowns of overdue ransom money for Margaret of Anjou they were welcomed back home in March. Morton would have little time to ease himself in as Archdeacon of Norfolk which he had become just before leaving on this latest French undertaking.

The resolution of who Mary of Burgundy should marry was now a pressing matter. Behind everyone's back, Louis had suggested that Mary should wed the Dauphin. However, since he was only six years old that was scarcely likely to be seriously entertained. Nonetheless, it showed that Louis' word was not to be trusted, nor was his commitment to the treaty they had signed.

More worrying for Edward was the Duchess Margaret's suggestion that Clarence, her favourite brother, should marry Mary. Clarence went for this wholeheartedly, only to come up against a total prohibition by his brother. Edward had no wish to afford Clarence a base from which to work against him, a possibility which was reinforced by opinion from Louis received in early June. Clarence was completely crushed by Edward's rejection, and it marked, if not his unhingement, then certainly a final act of disassociation and disaffection.

As it was, Mary herself was not inclined to consider Clarence. Her need, and that of Burgundy, was for someone who could provide proper protection against France or anyone else who had designs on her lands. Her choice was that which her father had sought for her and in August she married Archduke Maximilian of Austria, heir to the Holy Roman Empire.[3] This did not come in time to fully forestall fragmentation of Charles the Bold's assembly, but it did prevent total collapse and integration by France.

Clarence received added injury following his failure to advance his suit for Mary when it was revealed that a particularly preposterous proposal had emerged for the Earl Rivers to be joined to her. This provided tinder to a growing fire of paranoia within Clarence that not only was he being marginalised at court, but that there was a tangible assault taking place on his life by the Queen and her family. And the first evidence of this was the death, nay the murder, of his wife.

George had convinced himself that a conspiracy had taken place which effected the poisoning of his wife and the baby Richard. By April (three months after Isabel's death and six months after giving birth – so no rush to judgement) he decided who was culpable. First was a seventy-two-year-old gentlewoman, Ankarette Twynho. She was the widow of William Twynho and was related to John Twynho, cloth merchant and Bristol MP in 1478 who become Attorney General for Edward, Prince of Wales. This same John Twynho received a gold and gilt goblet as a gift from Clarence. She and her late husband owned land in Shropshire.

At one time she had been in the service of Elizabeth Woodville, and then a lady-in-waiting to Isabel of Clarence. She was one of several people present and assisting at the birth. She was charged by George of purposefully administering a 'venomous' drink of ale and poison on – very specifically – 10 October, four days after the birth. Keeping in mind that Isabel returned to Warwick on 12 November, any poison would have had to be very slow working indeed.

Around midday on 12 April, a mob of some eighty men, led by Richard Hyde, a servant of Clarence from Warwick, and Roger Strugge of Beckhampton, Wiltshire, arrived at the Twynho residence, Keyford Manor, Frome, Somerset. The elderly lady was seized and taken to Warwick over the course of three days and then brought to the Guildhall, where Clarence himself was waiting to preside. Within three hours she was tried, found guilty, taken out, and hanged.

With Ankarette at the gallows was John Thoresby of Warwick, found guilty by George of poisoning the baby Richard. Of course, there was no evidence here either. After the trial, jurors begged forgiveness from the convicted, claiming that the verdict was forced from them under duress.

Lastly, George accuses and finds guilty of abetting these murders Sir Roger Tucotes of Bromham, Wiltshire.[4] Sir Roger fought on the Yorkist side at Towton and at Tewkesbury and would go on to be a leading local player in Buckingham's Rebellion and at Bosworth. Luckily, he wasn't at home when the posse called and soon had his conviction quashed.

There appears to be no attempted explanation of motive. If foul play had taken place, why? A conspiracy to kill Isabel and her baby seems pointless when Clarence himself and his two older children are ignored. Clarence's action is seen not only as an attack on the Queen and the Woodvilles but as a message to Edward that George believes his authority should be greater than that of Richard and he should be able to, and is capable of, dispensing 'the King's justice.' Unsurprisingly, Edward is not of the same mind. Believing that his own life is under threat from poisoning, Clarence avoids eating and drinking at Court.

Things get worse. In May, he interferes directly in a prosecution carried out by the Court of the King's Bench. John Stacey, a fellow of Merton College, Oxford, Thomas Blake, a chaplain also of Merton College, and

Thomas Burdet, a landowner of Arowe, Warwickshire, are found guilty of trying to predict the King's death by sorcery.[5] On 19 May, Burdet and Stacey are hanged, although Blake is pardoned. Stacey is known as 'the Astronomer'. Burdet is one of Clarence's liegemen. Two days after the execution an apoplectic George storms into a meeting of the Council with Dr William Goddard, a Franciscan friar, who he has read out a statement of innocence concerning the executed and he then storms out. This is viewed as seriously scandalous by those sitting in Council and they report all that has happened to Edward (then out of London, in Windsor). Clarence's actions have gone too far and are treasonable, since they seek to override the King's justice and, by defending convicted traitors, are themselves traitorous.

At this time, there is also an uprising in the counties of Cambridge and Huntingdon under an imposter posing as the Earl of Oxford with which Clarence's name was associated, just as it had been with Oxford's attempted invasion at St Michael's Mount. Whatever the truth there, Clarence was helping to spread, if not generating, stories that Edward and the Woodvilles were trying to kill him by poison and necromancy, that Edward was in fact a bastard (the heated exclamation of their mother at the time of the marriage to Elizabeth the basis of that claim), and that he, Clarence, was the person who should be sitting on the throne by virtue of his right and because Henry VI had put in writing that he should succeed him. He also directly attacks the Queen as the person responsible for murdering Isabel.

Edward had had enough. Clarence was now making direct threats and not only were these affecting him but his family. He could no longer ignore the situation: to do so was creating a dangerous precedent and an imminent threat as well. On 10 June, Clarence was summoned to an audience with Edward where he was berated in no uncertain terms, and in front of the Mayor and aldermen of London, accused of violating the laws of England and threatening the safety and integrity of judges and jurors. Clarence was then taken to the Tower.[6]

On 1 July, an ambassadorial delegation arrived from France to formalise the agreements made earlier in the year. Edward selected John Morton, Sir Thomas Montgomery, and Lord John Howard to treat with them and on 21 July a new treaty was signed prolonging the truce of Picquigny for as long as both kings should live and, after the death of the first, a further year beyond that. But that was all. The French ambassadors departed leaving the English with nothing more than disappointment and suspicion. These suspicions about Louis and his intentions increased as reports arrived in the English court of Louis' attack on St Omer, laying siege to the town and laying waste to the countryside. This was a direct attack on the assets of Duchess Margaret and Edward was on the verge of signing a pact with Maximilian and Mary, only then to hear that the duplicitous Louis had entered into a peace, for the time being, and reined in his armies.

Morton is standing in a packed St Stephen's Chapel in the Royal Palace of Westminster to witness a marriage.[7] It is mid-winter, 15 January 1478. This could only happen at a royal marriage: the bride is six-year-old Anne Mowbray and the groom four-year-old Richard, Duke of York.[8] Anne's father, John Mowbray, Duke of Norfolk had died on 9 January 1476, his vast estates being left to his child daughter. Negotiations for the marriage conducted by the Dowager Duchess of Norfolk together with the obtaining of a papal dispensation as the two were related by blood, meant two years from the inception of the idea to the wedding.[9] The celebrations were extensive and expensive, having been deliberately planned for the day before the state opening of parliament, which ensured as many members of the nobility as possible would attend.

The service was conducted by James Goldwell, Bishop of Norwich, and King Edward himself gave Anne away. Richard of Gloucester also played a prominent part in the ceremonials, throwing gold and silver coins to the spectators and then, in the company of the Duke of Buckingham, leading the bride to the wedding banquet. A few days later there would be a jousting tournament and the making of twenty-four new Knights of the Bath to mark the occasion. But beneath all the joy and festivities everyone was aware that one of the young groom's uncles was missing and that the following day he, the Duke of Clarence, was to be called to account in parliament.

On 16 January, Thomas Rotherham, Bishop of Lincoln and Chancellor, opens parliament with an address on the faithful obedience which all subjects owe their king, thus providing the setting for the main business to be conducted. It is the King alone who brings a Bill of Attainder against Clarence, and he sets out in detail all the unlawful and traitorous acts which George has carried out, and when forgiven then repeated. The construction of the Bill is the work of Morton as lead, with help from Fortescue, albeit ill and trying to enjoy a retirement, just as they had drafted the attainder of Edward himself years previously.

Morton recites in his head the charges brought against Clarence ahead of them being actually read out.

Having overcome so many attempts to remove him from the throne, says Edward, he now finds a new threat against not only himself but his wife and children. This threat is organised by Clarence with the aim of making himself King. The language employed to describe the depth of anger and loathing Edward now holds towards Clarence is such that all those present lower their eyes. He proclaims that not only has Clarence been elevated above all men, but past efforts by him to aid his enemies and force him to flee abroad have been forgiven. But now he has gone too far, shows no remorse, and can no longer be trusted. Towering, menacing, a vindictive victim, Edward is now in full majestic flow.

Item. That Clarence has maliciously and deliberately created discontent and sedition within the people.

Item. That he has publicly declared his servant Thomas Burdett to have been unlawfully put to death, notwithstanding his conviction of treason in the King's own court, and that he has, corruptly and with bribes sought to influence people to that conclusion.

Item. That he has accused the King of using witchcraft against his subjects and, in particular, had poisoned his subjects. [This is an accusation that Edward orchestrated the death of Isabel and son Richard; in a bid for the Crown, there is nothing to be gained by blaming the Woodvilles.]

Item. That he had claimed the Crown for himself, citing Edward as a bastard. [The story that Edward was illegitimate came from two main sources. First, Cecily, his mother, was so distraught at his marriage to Elizabeth Woodville that she threatened to declare him illegitimate for debasing his father's honour in marrying someone 'beneath' him. But she didn't. When she had calmed down, she accepted it and took her role as grandmother to the children of Edward and Elizabeth seriously. Not only that, but Richard of York fully acknowledged Edward as his son. And would Cecily declare herself unfaithful? Second, it was often the case that when important people were born abroad, they would be attacked by their enemies questioning their legitimacy. So it was that such a claim arose from France, citing a French archer named Blaybourne as the father. But there is no evidence, let alone proof, that it was true. In any event, Edward was King by conquest and acclaim. He was a usurper. Hereditary and illegitimacy were not relevant.]

Item. He had persuaded, cajoled, or bribed people to swear allegiance to him over and above the allegiance owed to the King.

Item. He had spread malicious lies that Edward had taken away his livelihood and intended to exterminate him. [This was a reference to the distribution of the Warwick and Montagu estates, which obviously still festered within him as an injustice and for which he still wanted to bring down Gloucester.]

Item. He had secretly preserved a document from the time of the Readeption that declared that if Henry VI and Edward of Westminster died without heirs [as, of course, they both subsequently had died], Clarence should become king.

Item. Clarence had sought the help of John Strensham, the Abbot of Tewkesbury, John Tapton and Roger Harewell to bring a child to Warwick Castle, to act as a doppelganger for his son the Earl of Warwick, while sending the real Earl of Warwick to Ireland to provide a focus for rebellion against Edward IV.[10] Clarence's servant John Taylor was sent to take the earl abroad, but Tapton and Harewell refused to hand the boy over and exposed the plot.

And so, with reluctance, Edward called upon parliament to find George guilty of treasonable offences and pass the attainder against him with the proviso that property held jointly with others should pass in whole to his co-owners.

There was no one to speak for Clarence. Even Gloucester, who had the opportunity, said nothing. Indeed, there was no defence. His only response was to deny each charge, his only offering of proof being a call for trial by combat.

With the bill of attainder being passed, Edward appointed cousin, Henry, Duke of Buckingham Seneschal of England to pass sentence, removing that duty from Gloucester. On 7 February, the sentence of death was duly passed.

In the early afternoon of 18 February, John Sutton, Baron Dudley and Constable of the Tower of London with three leather-jacketed executioners entered Clarence's apartment in the Bowyer Tower. Clarence is waiting for them by the fire, to the side of which is a cut-down wine butt used as a bath, now some two-thirds full of water. His hands and legs are bound. In the swiftest of movements, he is lifted and inserted headfirst and held until still.

One week later, on 25 February, he is laid to rest next to Isabel in a vault at Tewkesbury Abbey.

The consequences of Clarence's attainder and death are soon made clear. Most of the foregone estates are retained by Edward. The title Earl of Salisbury is given to Richard of Gloucester's son, Edward. The office of Great Chamberlain is passed to Gloucester himself. The lieutenancy of Ireland is given to Edward's eighth child, George, Duke of Bedford (only one year old, and with only one more year to live).

Clarence's son, the Earl of Warwick was allowed to retain his title and was at first placed in the care of Lady Agnes Stanley, wife of Sir William

Stanley at Stourton, Cheshire, only thirty-seven miles from Warwick castle. Thereafter his wardship and marriage are purchased in 1480 by Thomas Grey, Marquess of Dorset. The daughter, Margaret, remained in the care of the King at Shene with Edward's own children and they are later joined by young Edward of Warwick.

Further afield, on hearing of Clarence's execution, Oxford throws himself from the walls of Hammes Castle into the moat, but he is pulled out and survives, returned to his prison where he remains for six more years.

On 26 February, parliament was adjourned having repealed all Acts made during Henry's Readeption. The next day, 27 February, fifty-eight-year-old Robert Stillington, Bishop of Bath and Wells, was arrested and placed in the Tower where he resided until 20 June when payment of a fine secured his release. His crime was to 'violate his oath of fidelity by some utterance prejudicial to the King and his estate'.[11] No further details were publicly revealed.

After parliament had been adjourned, the bishops and other clergymen present had met up as an informal gathering to discuss outstanding clerical matters, not least the introduction and congratulation of Richard Bell, recently selected as Bishop of Carlisle.[12] Morton was present at this meeting and was deeply concerned to hear Stillington highly vocal in condemning the attainder and, particularly, the execution of Clarence. This was profoundly disturbing, as criticism of the King's Bench was a significant element of Clarence's indictment, and here was a bishop railing against the judgement and probity of an even higher court – namely parliament. Morton is drawn aside by Thomas Rotherham, Bishop of Lincoln and Lord Chancellor and they decide it is their duty to report this dissension to Edward to ensure such views are suppressed. Edward's response is swift, and the message is clear to all.

Stillington has had a long-standing friendship with Clarence. His diocese overlaps one of Clarence's main estates and he was a primary force in the reconciliation of Clarence and Edward in 1471. Stillington had been Archdeacon of Taunton 1450–1465, the year of Edward's marriage. Before that he had obtained a doctorate in civil and canon law at Oxford, was Principal of Deep Hall in 1442, in 1445 Canon of Wells, and in 1447 Chancellor of Wells. So, a bright and promising start to his career. After Edward regained the throne, Stillington became Keeper of the Privy Seal until 1467 and having been translated to Bishop of Bath and Wells in 1465 became Lord Chancellor until 1473, when Edward abruptly dismissed him.

The year 1473 was, of course, the time of the intrigue between Clarence and Oxford, with a little help from Louis of France, and Edward's loss of trust in Stillington politically is likely to have been precipitated by his involvement. It was suggested at the time that his resignation of the Chancellorship followed a bout of illness from October 1472, but this was more likely to have been a face-saving exercise. By 1475 he was being tested again, employed in an unsuccessful attempt to get Henry Tudor out of Brittany while the French adventure was progressing. At the very same time, he was summoned to Rome to answer 'grave charges', though what these were has never been uncovered. It is difficult to imagine papal charges other than some political interference which did not sit well with papal policy. He appears to have continued his ecclesiastical duties unscathed.

Stillington never forgave Edward for his political demotion or for his stint in prison which, given the times and Edward's wrath, must have been most uncomfortable and nerve-shredding.

Morton continues to receive tasks from the King, particularly as Edward sets in motion extra efforts to organise the public and his private purse. In particular, on 20 July, Morton and William Essex, Remembrancer of the Exchequer, are tasked and given powers to settle up any creditors of the Crown pre-dating December 1470.[13]

Then, on 4 August there is another significant departure. William Grey, the Bishop of Ely, dies. Within four days, at Edward's direct request, John Morton is elected as the new Bishop.

20

Bishop of Ely

Becoming a bishop or, rather, being translated to a bishopric, is no quick and easy thing: particularly if you are an important cog in the diplomatic and administrative wheel. That said, it was always the intention of both Edward and Morton that his political and diplomatic role would likely be increased. He would now sit with the Lords and his seat in the Privy Council would continue. But his administrative responsibilities would decline, and his vast array of more minor ecclesiastical positions would need to be surrendered. An active role in Archbishop Bourchier's Convocation as well as administering the office and estates of his new diocese would consume as much time, if not more, than he was gaining.

John was more than happy to secure for his nephew Robert the position of Master of the Rolls. Robert had been working diligently in several legal and administrative roles during the past few years and, although not making a perceptible public impact, had developed an impressive range of skills and contacts. A year was available to be sure of a smooth transfer of power, with forty-three-year-old Robert officially taking over the post half-way through that period in January 1479.

Of his outstanding ecclesiastical positions, these were resigned during 1478 and included Archdeacon of Berkshire, Archdeacon of Chester, Prebend of Exeter, Archdeacon of Norfolk, Archdeacon of Leicester, and Prebend of St Decuman, Bath and Wells. In addition, Archdeacon of Bournemouth, Prebend of Chiswick, and Prebend of Horton were assumed by Robert, providing him with income for his new role.

As soon as the vacancy at Ely occurred, the administration and profits of the secular assets of the see, known as the temporalities, transferred to the Crown. The spiritual administration and finances transferred to the Archbishop of Canterbury. This practice was very much an English one and it did not apply across Europe and some dioceses resented the interference by Canterbury in their affairs. The reason is not hard to find: a vacancy provided the opportunity for an episcopal visitation – an audit of finances, staff, and proficiency in executing the required tasks and services. In most cases, this visitation brought forward few, if any, irregularities requiring correction. But it took time.

An appointment also required papal approval. Like all other papal approvals, such as dispensations, this also took time. But approval was in hand by the end of December and temporalities were restored by the Crown to the diocese on 4 January 1479. On 31 January, sixty-two-year-old John was consecrated as Bishop of Ely at Lambeth Palace by Archbishop Bourchier.

His installation as bishop – his first visit to his new diocese – took place in late summer. It was good to be out of London. 1479 was a particularly bad plague year. Edward's youngest son, one-year-old George, died from the disease in March. But the weather is fine, and it is one of the quietest, most peaceful years of the reign, so an ideal time for ceremony and feasting. Accompanied by Robert, Morton arrived at Little Downham and the old Bishop's Palace on 28 August, where they spent the night fasting and in prayer.[1]

The next morning they set out on the three-mile walk to Ely Cathedral. Morton wears only a rochet, a white muslin tunic, with neither hat nor sandals, and he walks with Robert alongside, muttering prayers while counting beads. About a mile short of the cathedral, they stop at St Mary's Church, where Robert, who is carrying a small sack of coins, makes an offering of five shillings. They are met at the church by the parochial clergy who greet Morton and wash his feet. They then form a procession behind their new bishop and follow him to the cathedral.

Ely is on an island, and remains so until the Fens are drained, a geographical feature which helped it support the resistance fighter, Hereward the Wake, against the imposition of Norman rule four hundred years previously. The flat countryside emphasises the size and magnificence of the cathedral, its west tower standing 215 feet high. The central octagon tower with its suspended wooden lantern is one of the most breathtaking feats of medieval engineering.

He enters the cathedral by the west door to find it with a full congregation and richly decorated with carpeting, lighted tapers, and flowers arranged around the bishop's throne. Morton enjoys ceremony.

Within the cathedral the prior passes him the aspersorium containing holy water with which he crosses himself and then blesses the body of advisors who will be assisting his future work. The archdeacon steps forward with burning incense to perfume him. So cleansed, Morton is handed the archbishop's cross, which he kisses. The notary public for the diocese then reads out the royal mandate for John's installation and with the precentor, or leader of hymns and prayers, intoning the first of those prayers, *Preces summae Trinitatis,* they proceed slowly to the high altar.

At the altar, he kneels while the prior gives up a prayer and, rising, Morton makes an offering of five shillings. The precentor then begins his intonations again, this time *O Rex Christe,* the choir and then the whole congregation joining in, as Morton and the procession move on to the shrine of Saint Etheldreda where the usual five-shilling offering is placed.[2] While further prayers are being said, Morton then has the unenviable task of kissing Etheldreda's relics, after which yet another five-shilling offering is made.

This process is repeated at the several shrines within the cathedral, after which he enters the vestry. There his feet are washed once more and he is dressed in his full bishop's magnificence. With jewelled mitre, golden staff in gloved hand, he stands before the whole congregation as Lord Bishop of Ely.

With the congregation kneeling, the Archbishop of Canterbury's commission is read out and to the acclamation of all, John Morton is seated on his throne, the *Te Deum* being sung. He is then taken to his stall in the choir and thus 'installed', moves on again to the altar of St Peter where he greets the prior and the convent. Finally, high mass is celebrated.

Morton then took possession of the Bishop's Palace where a great feast took place with the doors open to rich and poor alike, although the rich and influential were segregated in the Great Hall. Among the leading guests were friends old and new, including John Fortescue, Sir William Brandon, Sir John Cheyne, and Sir John Dunne.

Though not on the scale of George Neville's installation banquet, this was still something to talk about. French chefs were brought in to prepare the food. There were three 'courses', each course having between eight and twelve dishes. These dishes would include meats such as venison, pheasant, boar, swan, and peacock; fish such as sturgeon, carp, and bream: and sweet dishes including apples, quinces, custards, and tarts. Between each course were 'subtleties': these would be a presentation or illustrative representation such as a model accompanied by verse to tell a story or reflect on some truth. So, one would be a thanksgiving to King Edward, another a remembrance of Saints Peter, Paul and Andrew.

The time that Morton spends within his diocese is both pleasurable and practical, free of political stress but still intellectually rewarding. It is also rewarding financially, and he begins accumulating a portfolio of private property interests. Travelling between the ten manors, castles, palaces and estates which form part of the see of Ely, he soon becomes aware of the flooding which so frequently occurs in the fenland. It isn't long before he is calling on his knowledge of the engineering of dykes in the Low Countries, absorbed during the years of exile, and applying this to a scheme to drain part of the Fens and extend navigation up the River Nene. Work begins in 1479 to cut a ditch forty feet wide and four feet deep from Wisbech to Peterborough, a distance of twelve miles. It will take until 1490 to complete and will be known as Morton's Leam.

Another major project was the restoration and refurbishment of the Old Bishop's Palace at Hatfield, which provided one of the finest examples of English mediaeval brickwork.[3] Morton also initiated the rebuilding of Wisbech Castle, severely damaged by flooding way back in 1236. In fact, the damage was so great that repair was out of the question and a complete rebuild was required. Completion was under Morton's successor, John Alcock.

Much of Morton's work still required attendance at court, in Privy Council, in parliament, at the Court of Arches, or in convocation with his brother bishops, and this was generally in or near London. For this reason, he had use of Ely House in Holborn. Referred to as a town residence, it was in fact a substantial mansion with nine cottages and occupied a site of twenty-three acres including vineyard, orchards, pastures, and a kitchen-garden famous, of course, for its strawberries, and where Morton would spend leisure time tending the plants and recalling his days at Cerne Abbey. John of Gaunt, grandfather of Henry V, lived here after his Savoy Palace had been burnt down during Wat Tyler's rebellion. It provided an invigorating winter walk over a mile or so down to Westminster.

A very uncomfortable Charles de Martigny, Bishop of Elne, sat opposite an aggressive panel of negotiators in one of Westminster's smaller halls, yet still large enough to be intimidating. The Bishop's nerves were not at their best: the English crowd had little difficulty in picking him out and picking on him when he travelled about the city. Constantly suffering verbal abuse, the intensity of feeling against him, and Frenchmen generally it seemed, had escalated so that he feared for his safety. And this was something which these so-called negotiators, led by a brother bishop of all people, were encouraging and exploiting with barely concealed threats.

Above: Cerne Abbey Guest House. John Morton spent several happy years at Cerne Abbey before going to Oxford University. In 1471 he brought Queen Margaret here with her retinue to stay in this Guest House while on her way to reclaim Henry VI's throne, only to learn of the defeat of his army at Barnet by Edward IV.

Right: Charles the Bold, Count of Charolais and then Duke of Burgundy was a friend to the House of York and took Margaret of York as his third wife. His preoccupation with creating a Burgundian state led to frustration with him by the English and, eventually, precipitated his downfall. (Attributed to Rogier van der Weyden. Kaiser-Friedrich Museum, Berlin. Wikimedia Commons. Public Domain)

Above left: Charles VII effectively destroyed the Treaty of Troyes and England's claim to the French throne, a major contribution to Henry VI's mental breakdown and 'The War of the Roses'. (Louvre Museum, Paris. Wikimedia Commons. Public Domain)

Above right: Somerset led the vanguard of Margaret's army at Tewkesbury. His strategy has been criticised as a major factor in the Lancastrian army's collapse and indeed the dynasty's. Late 15th century Ghent manuscript. (Wikimedia Commons. Public Domain)

Above left: Humphrey of Gloucester, younger brother of Henry V and a leading figure in government while Henry VI was a minor. Admired for his intellect and patronage of the arts, he was accused of treason and died in mysterious circumstances.

Above right: Henry Chichele was an ecclesiastical lawyer and diplomat who rose to be Archbishop of Canterbury. He was a fierce enemy of the Lollards but is best remembered for founding educational establishments. These included All Souls College, Oxford where Morton gained his Doctorate.

Right: Ely Cathedral Octagon. Morton spent probably the happiest years of his life as Bishop of Ely. The outstanding Ely Cathedral was a wonder of English mediaeval architecture, renowned for its octagonal tower, shown here.

Below right: Henry VII was particularly well-served by Morton. Henry had a hard and stressful life, most of it in exile and under threat of betrayal and death. This translated to his outlook as a king. (Wikimedia Commons. Public Domain)

Below left: Jasper Tudor coat of arms. Jasper Tudor was the step-brother of Henry VI and uncle and faithful protector of Henry VII. A skilful commander he became Duke of Bedford after Bosworth and married Catherine Woodville, the Duke of Buckingham's widow.

Above left: John Howard, painting of a stained glass image formerly at Tendring Hall or South Chapel, Stoke-by-Nayland church, now lost. John Howard's wealth and status were wholly aligned to the House of York and in particular to Richard III, with whom he died at Bosworth. He was present and participated in the arrest of Hastings, Morton, Rochester and Stanley at the Tower of London.

Above right: Lambert Simnel was promoted by several political interests, including Richard III's nominated successor the Earl of Lincoln, as a claimant to the throne of Henry VII. First as Edward, Duke of Warwick then as Richard, Duke of York. It all came to an end at the battle of Stoke Field. (Wikimedia Commons. Public Domain)

Henry VI's wife Margaret of Anjou put all her energy into keeping her family together and safe. The battle of Tewkesbury resulted in the death of her son and her husband, breaking her spirit and eventually resulting in her return to France and death in poverty. (Wikimedia Commons. Public Domain)

Above left: Margaret Beaufort was Henry VII's mother, ferociously plotting and advancing her son's cause. She and Morton became close friends in the wake of Richard of Gloucester's ascendancy.

Above right: Margaret, Duchess of Burgundy was the sister of Edward IV, though her favourite brother was George of Clarence. She was a constant thorn in the side of Henry VII and supported anyone seeking to bring down the Tudors.

Above left: Perkin Warbeck probably posed the greatest threat of the pretenders to Henry VII's throne. This is thought to be a portrait of portrait of him.

Above right: Morton never took to Richard III or his cause and was highly involved in his downfall.

Left: Robert Willoughby de Broke became a High Sheriff of Cornwall, and Lord of the Manor at Callington. He was one of the chief commanders of royal troops against the Cornish Rising of 1497. Effigy at Callington church. (Creative Commons Zero. Public Domain)

Below left: Thomas Bourchier was Morton's predecessor as Archbishop of Canterbury and, although always one looking to influence from the inside, he was a life-long mentor and supporter to Morton.

Below right: William Catesby. 1450-1485. Memorial brass at Ashby St Ledger. William Catesby was a lawyer who rose quickly through service to Hastings, who he informed on to Richard of Gloucester. He became one of Richard's most valued advisors, fought with him at Bosworth, and was executed after the battle. (Wikimedia Commons. Public Domain)

'Parson of Bloxham' – Morton's first ecclesiastical appointment and his title/description in his Attainder. The tower is 14th century but the church was substantially modified and improved in the 17th and 19th centuries. (Author)

Brecon Castle, home of Henry, Duke of Buckingham and where Morton was sent from the Tower of London for questioning but where 'Buckingham's Rebellion was hatched. (Wikimedia Commons – Public licence by WelshDave under Creative Commons Attribution-Share Alike 4.0 International license.)

Cock Beck from the bridge near the Crooked Billet Inn on the B1217, North Yorkshire. Part of the Battle of Towton battlefield 1461 from which Morton fled under arms. The stream is notorious for the lives it claimed of the routed Lancastrians. (Wikimedia Commons. Public Domain)

Top left: Denbigh was the destination of Morton and the royal party fleeing from the victorious Yorkists of the battle of Northampton. (Wikimedia Commons – Public licence by Llywelyn2000 under Creative Commons Attribution-Share Alike 4.0 International license)

Left: Kenilworth Castle. Morton was at Kenilworth Castle with Queen Margaret and the Duke of Exeter when they heard the news of the Lancastrian defeat at Northampton and were compelled to flee into Wales.

Below left: Knole House, Morton's favourite residence and the place of his death. The archbishop's palace was remodelled by the Sackville family into a stately home and is now owned by the National Trust.

Below: Richard, Duke of York rode out from the safety of his castle at Sandal on this highly defendable position, to lose his life in battle. Also killed, following the folly, were Edmund, Earl of Rutland and the Earl of Salisbury. (Wikimedia Commons – Public licence by Tim Green of Bradford under Creative Commons Attribution 2.0 license)

Edward, and his Council for that matter, were near the end of their tether with Louis' procrastinations. Morton was leading Robert Stillington, working his way back into favour, Henry Bourchier, Earl of Essex, Earl Rivers, William Dudley, Bishop of Durham, and Lord John Howard. And it was Morton, confident and comfortable now in his power and wealth, who is the King's enforcer.

The Bishop of Elne is given no room for manoeuvre. Morton demands that he signs and recommends the draft agreements before him with the threat that he will not leave England until he does. It is put to the Frenchman that Maximilian of Austria wants a treaty with England and he has offered to help Edward conquer France and take the throne that he claims of right. Further, Maximilian is prepared to pay to England not 50,000 crowns a year but 60,000.

The agreements call for the existing truce to last for 101 years after the death of either Edward or Louis and for the current arbitration system to remain in force. The Dukes of Burgundy and Brittany are to be named as among Edward's allies, and there should be free passage for merchants of Venice, Florence, and Genoa. Then (unsurprisingly) France should continue to pay the King of England 50,000 crowns a year for as long as the truce exists. And the 'amity' between the two kings should last as long as the truce.

The Bishop of Elne is given three days to consider the detail of the agreements. On the third day, Morton himself goes to de Martigny's lodgings and takes the miserable Bishop by the arm to the council chamber where he is forced to sign and then, on 27 February, sign again before Walter Bedlow, apostolic and imperial notary.

The Bishop knows he should not have signed, of course, and he hastily sends word to Louis of the duress he has been put under, stressing that he has reserved the right for Louis to deny the agreement. At the same time, Edward sends his emissary, Oliver King, to present his side of events. Louis will continue masterfully to delay, distract, and defer. Not only that, but the put-upon Bishop of Elne's return to France saw him rewarded with a six-week trial in the Paris Parliament for alleged malfeasance. Luckily, he survived with reputation and head intact.

Louis continues a multi-fronted policy of aggression towards Flanders and Burgundy. French law is Salic law. It does not recognise the rights of inheritance of women, only through the male line. Therefore, Louis considers Burgundy to be reabsorbed by the French Crown since the death of Charles the Bold. Beyond that, he also has eyes taking Flanders from Mary and Maximilian. To achieve success he has to ensure that there is no treaty or alliance between England and Flanders, and his method is by use of intrigue and bribery. He is not known as 'the Universal Spider' for nothing.

Part of his strategy to appease Edward is, of course, the payment of the 50,000 crowns a year which will only happen while there is greater benefit flowing to France. As the benefits dilute, so do the payments. Because it is money on which Edward has come to rely, delays in payments infuriate him. Louis knows how to play on this addiction by creating withdrawal symptoms and then providing release.

Another part of the strategy is to keep promising, with varying provisos, respect for the rights, estates, and income of Edward's sister, the Duchess Margaret of Burgundy. Of course, he doesn't mean a word of it and continues to nibble away at her position and reputation. That said, it is well known that Clarence was her favourite brother and that she has a conspiratorial inclination in her character.

The constant belligerence of Louis towards herself, but also to Mary and Maximilian, leads Margaret to leave her Burgundian home for a three-month visit to England specifically to press the case for an alliance between England, Flanders, and Burgundy. The Flemish embassy in Edward's court were making almost daily representations for aid against Louis, particularly for archers. Margaret's intention was to turn those pleas into a reality.

The first thing that struck Morton was her height. Edward was majestically taller than his two brothers, but not so with Margaret, who was a full six feet; and whereas Edward was now somewhat rotund, his sister's height was accentuated by her being particularly thin. She was without doubt her brother's sister. Margaret's negotiating skills, coupled with increasing annoyance with cheap talk and cheaper actions from France, led to Edward confirming the renewal of the treaty of perpetual friendship he had made with Charles back in 1474, with Mary and Maximilian. In addition, on 1 August, Mary's two-year-old son Philip was betrothed to Edward's five-year-old daughter Anne. Needless to say, this was all intended to benefit Edward financially, but he did promise to send archers to Flanders, though only 1500 rather than the 2000 originally promised.

Each side was playing with the other and Margaret's good work was substantially dented by Maximilian and Louis secretly agreeing a seven-month truce, but then Louis continually found excuses not to take that forward to peace treaty negotiations. Edward annoyed Louis by negotiating the betrothal of the Prince of Wales to the Duke of Brittany's daughter.

The third part of Louis' strategy towards England was to keep Edward's eye fixed on Scotland and his purse emptied thereby. Louis' efforts to encourage aggression from the Scots increased, such efforts often neither subtle nor secretive.

Intermittent border raiding into the marches was stepping up in 1480 culminating in a large-scale raid by the Earl of Angus on Northumberland, which saw Bamburgh burned. Since these acts violated the truce between Scotland and England, on 12 May a new role was created for Richard of Gloucester as Lieutenant-General of the North. This provided him with palatine powers over the whole of the border marches and the ability to call up men from both the marches and their adjoining counties. The immediate result was a summer counter-raid by Richard and the Earl of Northumberland, after which they fell back to build defence works against future attacks.

As with other matters in which Louis was involved, Edward and his Council were losing patience and in November decided to lay plans for a full-scale invasion of Scotland to bring them to heel once and for all. Moreover, it was to be Edward in person who was to lead the army. But Edward did not go north.

To a degree Edward found the potential cost too great for his immediate funds. 1479 had been a bad plague year and the 1481/82 harvest proved to be the worst for many years, creating food shortages across Europe as well as England. Consequently, there was unrest in the south and in the midlands to such an extent that raising taxes or making another play for 'benevolences' was not going to be popular or successful, and the manifestation of that unrest kept Edward in the south to maintain the safety of his throne. But there were also signs that Edward's physical ailments were increasing as his excesses took their toll on his body.

Richard was not a man with the temperament to do nothing and he decided to take steps to secure at least one objective on the English agenda: the re-taking of Berwick-on-Tweed, surrendered to the Scots by Henry and Margaret. Siege was laid to the town and castle, which stretched on into 1482.

Then, there was a development in the political play. James III's brother, Alexander Stewart, Duke of Albany, who had been exiled for his disloyalty, decided to lay claim to the Scottish throne, and Edward decided to back him. He travelled north as far as Nottingham to meet Richard during October 1481, introducing him to Albany and making plans for invasion. Edward then returned to London leaving Richard to prosecute the war against Scotland as supreme commander with an army of 20,000, and generals including Northumberland, Thomas

Stanley, Dorset, and Edward Woodville. The combination of freedom and responsibility sat well with him.

Leaving the siege of Berwick under Stanley's command, Richard then struck hard at Scotland, burning and laying waste all in his path until he reached Edinburgh, which meekly opened its gates to him at the end of July. He then marched to Haddington, about eighteen miles outside the city, to confront the Scottish army, who also surprisingly gave way without a fight. Here Richard shows, from one viewpoint, the clearest example of his readiness to disobey his brother's commands when he disagrees with them, and from another point of view, his ability to respond quickly and decisively to changing circumstances.

Scotland was at his mercy. James III had been seized and locked up in Edinburgh Castle by his lords on his way to confront Richard, and his four favourites hung from the bridge into the city. But Richard did not depose James in favour of Albany as Edward had directed. It was made evident that the Scots had even less desire to be ruled by Albany than they were James, so the latter was restored to his throne.[4] Albany came to an agreement to behave and his estates were returned to him.[5] Richard also demanded the return of all money paid towards the dowry for Edward's daughter Cecily and James's eldest son. But what Richard really wanted, and what he got, was the surrender of Berwick back to the English.

Richard then returned to London for Christmas and public acclaim. Although Edward was less than happy that his orders had not been carried out and the opportunity to install English rule over Scotland foregone, yet his brother's success drained away criticism from the populace and put the forthcoming January parliament in a better mood than it would otherwise have been.

The importance of Richard of Gloucester on the national scene warrants further examination of his character and motivation. As a younger son, he had no great inheritance of his own to support his status. There were ironic similarities between his situation and that of the Woodvilles. His wealth came from rights of marriage and grants or rewards from the King. But he also had the urge within him to carve out his own destiny, and the border marches provided an ideal opportunity to create his own demi-kingdom away from the restraints of Edward and his court.

The acquisition and consolidation of his estates was indeed his job, and it was his commitment to and enjoyment of that task that caused him to spend so much time in the north rather than at court. That was the primary instruction with which he was tasked. There appears to be no evidence that he was at daggers drawn with the Queen or her family, although his devotion to Edward seems to have waned from the time of Picquigny in 1475. He was away from court just as much before Clarence's execution as afterwards and, equally, he was away from the north when his many national responsibilities required. His name appears on every royal charter issued between February 1478 and January 1483, so he remained close to court and government.

Perhaps he withdrew from Scotland because his army faced a long northern winter with immediate supplies limited and a long logistical lifeline at risk physically and financially. The immediate opportunity to secure Berwick and absorb it into his empire was in his mind: Scotland had shown itself weak and for the taking on another day. Richard petitioned for, rather than was simply given, Cumberland as a palatinate, for hereditary wardenship of the marches, and a free hand to take as much Scottish land as he could conquer. Scotland would be his future business venture: for himself and his family rather than his king or his king's puppet ruler. Such a future would have kept him happy. Unfortunately, circumstances were soon to put all these gains and dreams at risk.

Richard has lived his life under constant threat. Self-preservation is his first lesson learned. He is a fighter, aggressive, impatient, and ruthless. These are traits seen in most, if not all, of his peers to some degree. But violence, high-handedness, and self-publicity are to the front. His relationship with others is cordial if his interests are not crossed. He has no running enmity with the Woodvilles, unlike Hastings. Nor does he shrink from advancing those he can trust, even if they are not of the highest blood in the land.

His successes were based on his ruthlessness towards opposition and reward for submission. Claims that he was accepted in the north as 'the heir of Neville' are difficult to square with his role as a leading player in the destruction of Neville. His successes were due more to his ability to bully, cajole, and flatter the Percies and the Stanleys and bend them to his will, while they thought they were acting in their own self-interest. The strength of the bonds he has created with these northern magnates will be tested soon enough at Bosworth.

Important in establishing Richard in the north was Sir John Conyers of Hornby, Richmond. He was head of one of the wealthiest gentry families in the north-east and became steward of Middleham, Richard's favourite northern home, in the early 1460s. Conyers delivered the northern Neville affinity to Richard's service, which became the core of his following. Others attracted to Richard were Lords Fitzhugh, Greystoke, Scrope of Bolton, and Scrope of Masham. Lower ranking followers were Robert Brackenbury and Richard Ratcliffe.

But Richard was not welcomed by Henry Percy, Earl of Northumberland, Lawrence Booth, Bishop of Durham or Thomas,

Lord Stanley, all of whom lost out to him in land disputes. Rather, the relationship was one of resigned acceptance from a fear of, or sense of duty towards, Edward. Their interests were always there own first and after that they were Edwardian Yorkists rather than Ricardian Yorkists.

Richard presents himself as a great general and a great administrator. While he showed competence, greatness would be going too far. In both, it was his opponents' fear of crossing him that covered up chance and weaknesses. Richard is regarded as a religious person, but so are all people within society. Church services are attended as required and the Church itself supported financially according to an individual's wealth and standing. This is duty performed instinctively and without questioning, as a rule. But among the elite the purchase of indulgences, payment for prayers and intercedence for oneself or forebears, and the enrichment or even creation of places of worship, offset rather than forestall killing, murder, theft and treachery. Oaths given are oaths which can be broken. As with his peers, Richard is skilled in utilising religious ceremony and benevolence to support and project his persona. Heretics continue to burn while conformists get away with murder.

The Setting of the Sun, 1482–1483

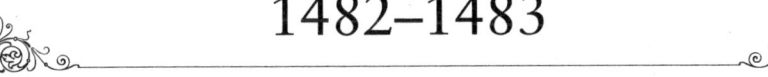

Since his enthronement, Bishop Morton had made a point of administering Easter service at Ely and he had no intention of 1483 being any different – particularly as Easter Sunday would fall early, on 30 March. It had been a hectic eighteen months given over primarily to diplomatic missions running to and fro across the Channel or organising revenue to pay for the Scottish war. Church work had drifted into second place and immersion into the life of his diocese would, he knew, be restorative.

Not that he hasn't made time for activities outside of government and church. Some of his old connections at Oxford have been re-established and this has enabled him to keep up to date with contemporary theological thought. Moreover, he has begun to create his own property portfolio with some fortuitous purchases which, if he is honest with himself, have come at a financial discount for services and support rendered, with manors and tenements in the Home Counties, not least at Mote, near Maidstone, Kent, from Earl Rivers and the Marquis of Dorset. Is this corruption, or a necessity to support your social and political status, your authority? Probably both.

He was quite willing to engage in commercial risks, taking a lease of the New Inn at Westcheap, in the City with Sir John Donne and others.[1] Perhaps his largest acquisition is the manor of Milborne Deverell, otherwise known as Milborne Cary, from Sir Robert Willoughby. This substantial holding comprised six messuages, one watermill, 800 acres of arable land, 200 acres of pasture and 20 acres of meadow in Milborne St Andrew.[2]

He also holds the manor of Milborne Churchstone, purchased from the Dorset MP Thomas Hussey in 1481 for the sum of 220 marks 13 shillings and 4 pence.[3] This estate was made up of twelve messuages,

300 acres of arable land, 20 acres of meadow, 300 acres of pasture, 20 acres of wood, 10 acres of heath, and other lands in Somerset and Dorset. Praise be to Louis XI.

On 3 February 1489, he will lease the farms to his brothers and nephews who are still farming at Milborne St Andrew and will leave his freehold interest in his will to Edith Coker, the widow of his brother Richard, to hold for his nephew John Morton.

He's missed out on some family milestones. Robert was awarded an honorary doctorate in law by Oxford. His position as Master of the Rolls deserves no less. But John could not get to the ceremony. Robert now holds the sixth stall in St George's Chapel, Windsor; the honours on the family accumulate. But brother William died in 1482 and John had to miss the funeral. National events will also prevent him from honouring his brother Richard who will pass away this year, not quite eighteen months after being elected High Sheriff of Somerset and Dorset. These are all moments that can never be revisited.

The Easter services go well, the choir is in fine voice, the new year has begun. And then, the next day, arrives an urgent summons to Westminster: the King has been taken seriously ill and is not expected to last.

Edward's health had been worsening over the past six months. In part this was physical due to immoderate living with excess food and drink, giving rise to suggestions of bulimia, insufficient sleep, and an increasing level of debauchery (alienating him from Elizabeth). But his mental health has been suffering through stress and the failure of so many of his political ambitions.

The cost of the Scottish war was coupled with likely future drains on the treasury for who knows how long. Much as Edward needed Richard to divert popular attention from other, failing policies, the costs were soon going to come home to roost. It didn't take much reflection to conclude that the January parliament had conferred far too much power in Richard's hands and, sooner or later, some reckoning and power adjustment would be needed.[4] Alongside Richard's apparent success in regaining Berwick, the past year had shown disturbances in Northumberland, Yorkshire, and Lancaster, which reflected poorly on Richard's administration of justice there. When the time came, would Edward's anger, or his love for his brother, come to the fore?

His handling of the relationship with France and with Burgundy had failed due to his weakness for ready money. Louis had beaten him in the diplomatic game hands down. When the secret renewal of their truce had been published by Louis in September, Maximilian saw that the rug had been pulled away from under his feet and an accommodation with the French was the only way that Flanders would survive. And so the Christmas present that arrived for Edward from Europe was a copy of the Treaty of Arras, whereby Maximilian's daughter was to marry the Dauphin, ending Edward's understanding that it was to be his daughter, Elizabeth, who would be the next French Queen. Moreover, Maximilian provided the counties of Burgundy and Artois as his daughter's dowry.

1482 had also seen the death of Edward's fifteen-year-old daughter Mary, who was the prospective bride of the King of Denmark, and any ideas of daughter Cecily marrying the son of James of Scotland were also cancelled. Edward's plan for securing his family's dynastic future through marriage into the crown families of Europe had folded.

Weighed down by these troubles and the ill health that had been wearing away his strength and vitality over the past couple of years, he moved from Windsor on 25 March to Westminster, where he planned to celebrate Easter. Having spent some leisure time on the river in the company of fishermen, he fell ill on Easter Sunday with chest pains and breathing difficulties.

It was apparent that this was a terminal illness, possibly typhoid fever developing into pneumonia, but it was more than a week before he succumbed.[5] That would not prevent news of his death being announced prematurely and in York the bells tolled three days before he actually died.[6] In the time left to him it was said he added codicils to his will. With the succession to the forefront of his mind, he brought together Hastings and the Marquess of Dorset, Lionel Bishop of Salisbury, and Sir Edward Woodville, representing the Woodville family, whom he had promise to bury their differences for the good of twelve-year-old Prince Edward. Dorset and Sir Richard Grey in particular are regarded as promoters and companions of Edward in his vices, but so is Hastings, who is said to be particularly despised by the Queen.[7] Hastings and Dorset have each been competing for the favours of Edward's mistress Elizabeth 'Jane' Shore and have become enemies as a result. There is also resentment of the preferment of Hastings over Rivers for the Captaincy of Calais. The Woodvilles are not the kind of people to admit that, with the threat on Calais posed by Louis, Hastings was the safer pair of hands.

Morton, and indeed most of the bishops, have now arrived at Westminster and he takes his turns in praying for the King's body and soul. On 9 April, three weeks short of his forty-first birthday, Edward dies, his Queen by his side.

The news of Edward's death caused shock and consternation. Shock because of his age and the suddenness of the event, consternation because here was another under-age king and an orderly transition of government was far from guaranteed.

In line with tradition and to scotch any thoughts of foul play, the body was laid out naked, save for a loin cloth, for twelve hours, so that it might be viewed by the lords and senior clergy who were already In London and by the City's Mayor and Aldermen. During the night, the body is wrapped in a waxed cloth and in the morning is moved to St Stephen's Chapel where it lies in state for eight days. On each day, a mass is sung by the Bishop of Chichester, Edward Story. Queen Elizabeth's offerings are made on her behalf by her chamberlain, Richard Fiennes, Baron Dacre.

On 18 April, the King is borne to Westminster Abbey, led by ten bishops and two abbots. A final service is led by the Archbishop of York after which the corpse is placed in a chariot, an effigy or 'personage' of Edward placed on top of his casket, and a slow procession towards Windsor begins. There is a night's stop-over at Sion nunnery, where Edward's niece Anne de la Pole held orders.

The following day there was another halt at Eton where John Morton and John Russell, Bishop of Lincoln, took the body and perfumed it by the burning of incense, silently swinging censers according to the required ritual. At the gates of Windsor Castle, the cortège is met by the Archbishop of York, and the Bishops of Winchester, Norwich, Durham, and Rochester. An overnight vigil is conducted by Lord Howard, Sir John Savage (nephew of Lord Thomas Stanley), Sir John Cheyne, Master of the Horse, and William Collingbourne, an officer in Queen Elizabeth's household.[8] The next day, the final rites and requiems are performed and Edward laid to rest.

22

Betrayals, 1483

The priority is the continuance of government and establishing the basis for a smooth transition to the new regime. For this, an emergency Council meeting has been called for 10 April, while the late king lies in state. John Morton arrives early, only to find that most other members have done the same. Few have found it easy to sleep.

There are some notable absences. Archbishop Bourchier remains in Canterbury: he is approaching his eightieth birthday and has been infirm for a few years now. In fact, from 1480, William Westkarre, titular Bishop of Zeitun, had been appointed Auxiliary to help in the performance of his duties.[1] Most of the northern lords are not present, nor those from the west and south-west. There are other absentees due to advanced age. Important voices such as Gloucester, Northumberland, Rivers and Lord Grey are not present. Most of these do not yet even know of the King's death.

The tone of the Council is conservative. It seeks calm and continuity. In doing so, it is proposed that the twelve-year-old Prince of Wales should be crowned Edward V as soon as possible, and a date of 4 May is settled on. Henry VI had been crowned when only seven and took up full powers when he was sixteen. Until the new king's administration takes up the reins of government (although there is little, on the face of it, to anticipate a radical change of personnel) royal authority devolves on the late King's Council. There is an immediate need to renew the appointment of judges, and this is done.

There is then the need to consider any present external threats to the country. Here the 'Universal Spider' Louis XI was threatening English boats in the Channel through his piratical Admiral Philippe de Crevecoeur, whose activities could be anticipated to increase once knowledge of Edward's death spreads beyond England. For this reason,

Sir Edward Woodville is given command of twenty ships to protect the English coast and its trading vessels. There was logic in this, as Sir Edward had received the king's commission earlier in the year to prepare an expeditionary force against France, so he had some logistical planning well in hand. For fear of what the French might be up to, 300 Derbyshire men are sent to reinforce Calais.

There was also seen to be a need to afford better protection to the royal treasure kept at the Tower. The eighty-three-year-old Constable of the Tower, Baron Dudley, was therefore relieved of his duty and his place was taken by twenty-eight-year-old Thomas Grey, Marquess of Dorset.

Things then start to get heated as the discussion turns to the structure of governance until the young King comes of age. There are two competing views. The first is pressed by William, Lord Hastings which is that Richard of Gloucester should be proclaimed Protector of the realm and the King until he reaches his majority. His claim is that precedent provides authority for such a solution, and that it was King Edward's wish as given on his death bed. This argument is not accepted by the lawyers on the council, among whom Morton takes a lead.

The precedent they need to follow, he argues, is that it is the Council that assumes government until the King is able to take on his full responsibilities. Council *may* decide to elect a Protector of either the King or the realm or both, and may determine the extent of any powers to be conferred upon said Protector. But neither the law nor precedent say there *has* to be a Protector.

Council may decide, particularly given the age of the new King, that a Protector of the realm is not needed. Council can perform the function of government adequately itself, but perhaps with the leading member of the nobility – the Duke of Gloucester – assuming the role of principal councillor or chairman of the council.

But any decision ultimately rests with parliament and requires its approval. Lord Hastings says it was King Edward's declaration that the Duke of Gloucester should be Protector, but the Marquess of Dorset says that he misconstrued what was said by the dying King. Be that as it may, however much the late King is loved and respected, the monarch has no legal power to direct on this issue.

As things stand, the King's Will of 1475 is in force (even though three of the named executors therein have since died). No codicils have been produced for Council to view. No later will has been produced for Council to view. In addition, wills have to be proved by the Church, through the Prerogative Court of Canterbury. Any new will or codicils to the old one will need to be presented to John Morton for proving. None has been.

There is also the need for Council to consider the practicalities of the situation the country is in. There are immediate and impending wars with France and Scotland. Sir Edward Woodville is alert to the French threat. The Duke of Gloucester is on the verge of launching an attack on Scotland. What will be the situation if he is diverted from commanding the English army in the field by being burdened with the role of Protector?

As for the protection and development of the new King, the late King had shown great confidence in the Council of the Prince of Wales, particularly the Earl Rivers, and all accounts say the result is that Edward exceeds the knowledge and confidence of someone his age. What would be achieved by altering the protection and guidance now given, which has proved to be so productive? Gloucester has a seat on the Prince of Wales's Council but has not used it. Young Edward has been under the tutelage and guidance of Rivers for ten years: what would be achieved by transferring that responsibility to someone who he doesn't know very well and who is likely to be engaged in military actions far away during his last few years before reaching his majority? Being brought up by the family of one's mother is not unusual: was this not the case for Richard of Gloucester himself?

This proves to be the majority view of the Council, that is, a regency council with Gloucester as chief member. Of course, there are things unsaid. Everyone knew that Hastings was putting a case for his own well-being as much as anything else. Fifty-two-year-old William Hastings is the grandson of Lord Comoys who commanded the left 'battle' at Agincourt. Whilst he represents the 'traditional' or 'old blood' of the nobility to some, he is in fact only very distantly related to the house of York and has been elevated by successes on the battlefield, financial acumen, and his service and loyalty to Edward IV. He is not 'old blood'. He and the Woodville family are bonded by hatred: it is that strong. Unless he can retain a guiding influence in Council, he is likely to lose the cash cows which his present roles provide. Moreover, a Woodville-dominated Council might see him indicted for syphoning off the fortune he has amassed from being Master of the Mint, Chamberlain of the Exchequer, and Lord Chamberlain. And, of course, it is Hasting's licentiousness which is seen by the Queen's party as being responsible for leading Edward to an early grave rather than something inherent in Edward himself.

The Woodville family and allies also stand to lose wealth if they lose control of the Council. The Queen, of course, has no power in her own right and her wealth is limited to what has been bestowed on her in Edward's will. Like Hastings, several of the Queen's relatives hold lucrative positions which could be lost, should family representation on Council be reduced. But they find reassurance in the fact that they 'control' the King's person, which provides the means for controlling Council.

There is a rumour later that Richard holds some or all of the Woodvilles responsible for the death of Clarence and that he will be seeking revenge now that he is no longer controlled by his brother. There seems little to sustain such speculation. Relationships have always been cordial and Clarence's fate was clearly of his own doing, pressed home by Edward and supported by Richard even to the extent of ensuring the vote in parliament. Moreover, public sentiment for Clarence had been shown to be notably weak and 'revenge' for his loss was not an issue likely to invoke any sympathy or support among the populace.

It would be left in Hastings' hands, as Chamberlain, to write with the news of Edward's death and the coronation date to all those lords absent from London, including the Prince of Wales, Earl Rivers and the Duke of Gloucester, and the cities and major towns.[2]

Before he did so, agreement was reached to request the Earl Rivers not to come to London with an escort for the new King in excess of 2,000 men. London had always been on edge with the arrival of large forces and it was accepted, on Hastings' argument, that the escort should be of a moderate size.

Immediately after the Council meeting, Hastings ensures that letters are issued in accordance with the instructions of Council. The news reaches Henry, Duke of Buckingham 177 miles from London at Brecon Castle, Wales on 14 April.[3] A similar notification reaches Richard of Gloucester on 16 April, 248 miles from London at Middleham Castle.

To Richard's letter, Hastings has added further information. He gives a summary of the Council meeting and, having successfully argued for Rivers to bring only a moderate size retinue to protect the new king, urges Richard to come to London with a 'strong' force, secure the person of the King, and assert his 'right' as Protector. Hastings is both awakening fears in Gloucester which may be dormant and is acting against the wishes of a Council of which he forms a leading part. He is actively promoting factionalism.

Richard has already been alerted to the imminent death of Edward. When the city of York was tolling its bells for the King's soul, they did not fail to send a message of condolence and support to Middleham, which was only 45 miles away, a comfortable day-and-a-half's ride. So Richard was making preliminary plans well before he received the official notification from Hastings. Immediately concerned about his political and financial prospects if he did not receive the Protectorate, he had a suitably sized army assembled and camped outside York by 18 April. Here he begins his campaign of self-preservation, securing his base.

He starts by demonstrating his regret for the passing of his brother with a funeral service and makes public vows to support and serve Edward V. More troops are raised for his procession to London. Most important, he writes to Elizabeth with condolences and again giving assurances of his goodwill and support for young Edward. A similar letter is sent to the Council, but in which he demands the Protectorate by right of law and his brother's will. This last comment rather gave away Hastings as the conveyor of Council's deliberations as there was no other way he could know that Edward was being said to have amended his 1475 will, let alone what might be in it.

He also sends letters to Northumberland and to Buckingham putting them clearly in the picture and clearly asserting that he will revenge for the insult done to him by the family of the Queen; meaning the attempt by the Woodvilles to block his path to the Protectorate. This letter reaches Buckingham 240 miles from York on 21 April after five days' hard riding.

The last letter he dispatches is to Earl Rivers at Ludlow. Again, pledging his fealty to Edward and his goodwill towards Rivers, Richard suggests that they all meet up at Northampton, as he is progressing down the Great North Road, for an impressive and harmonious joint entrance into London with the King. Rivers immediately responds positively to this idea.

Henry Stafford, Duke of Buckingham, is one of the richest and highest placed peers in the country, a descendant of Edward III's youngest son, Thomas of Woodstock. Both of his grandfathers, and his father, had died fighting against the House of York. The twenty-seven-year-old Henry aspired to be a person of significance, a master of his own destiny and the destiny of others. His role though, was one common to minor royalty, being wheeled out to perform ceremonial functions but never let loose as an administrator or as a military commander. Pride in his heritage marked him out to Edward IV as someone not to trust, especially when, without consent, he adopted the arms of Thomas of Woodstock. Of course, Buckingham didn't see that his own actions and demeanour sidelined him in government and instead he chose to hate and despise the Woodvilles as the source of his difficulties. In particular, at the age of 10, his wardship was bought by Elizabeth Woodville and she married him to her eight-year-old sister Catherine. Despite the fact that they produced five children, this forced marriage was a permanent dark cloud, as he believed his royal blood demanded a wife of far greater standing.

When Henry receives Richard's letter he immediately sends a reply with Humphrey Percival, one of his most trusted men, promising his complete loyalty and 'a thousand good fellows if needed'. A move against the Woodvilles will always find his support. Percival finds that he has missed Richard at York but catches up with him at Nottingham on 26 April. Richard suggests that Buckingham joins him at Northampton, where he will be meeting Rivers and the King. Leaving Nottingham at once, Percival meets Buckingham already on the road, having left Brecon on the 24th with 300 men anticipating an intersection with Richard on the road from York to London.

Just as Richard seems to be taking his time in getting to London, so does Earl Rivers. The news of Edward's demise is, of course, a shock to all at Ludlow, but surprisingly Prince Edward takes it very badly and so needs some time for grieving and composure. The strength and duration of his reaction is surprising because he hasn't had a close relationship with his father, nor has he spent that much time in his company. Perhaps, thinks Rivers, he is simply overwhelmed by the situation he now finds himself in and the responsibilities which will change his life completely. Time is spent assembling their escort and letters are also sent out in his own name and that of Edward to various towns to which he has an affinity bringing them up to date and sending assurances. He also decides that they will wait at Ludlow to celebrate St George's Day on 23 April. To allow travel to Northampton in proper time it will be best for the 2,000-strong escort to travel as light as possible within the boundaries of safety and so, knowing that armaments are already gathered along the Great North Road with a new Scottish campaign in mind, he writes asking for sufficient halberds, swords, and spears, but particularly chain and plate armour and other items of soldiers' harness to be picked up near St Albans by his hastily gathered army.

The royal column leaves Ludlow on 24 April, headed by Edward V, Anthony, Earl Rivers, and seventy-three-year-old Sir Thomas Vaughan. Also with them are Edward's tutor, John Alcock, Bishop of Worcester, and Sir Richard Haute, Controller of the Prince of Wales's Household. The weather is good, the ground firm, and they travel faster than anticipated. The west-east journey along Watling Street cuts the Great North Road some miles south of Northampton and they make their camp at Stony Stratford on 29 April. The troops are billeted in the villages and hamlets around Stony Stratford, with the leaders and Edward lodging at the Rose and Crown Inn within the town. Rivers is relaxed and is thinking about spending some time, if not the night, at the Woodville family home of Grafton Manor, which is only about five miles back towards Northampton, when his twenty-six-year-old nephew Lord Richard Grey arrives having ridden up in haste from London. Elizabeth is worried that they are not going to reach London in time for Edward's coronation. The King will need to be reassured and rehearsed for the day and the 1st of May is the latest from a practical and still comfortable point of view. She, and elements of the Council, is also concerned about the aims and integrity of Gloucester. London is still fifty miles from where they are, and they need to press on as quickly as possible.

At the time the King's escort is setting up camp, Richard is arriving in Northampton and learns that Edward has passed by the town earlier in the day. Incoming riders also tell him that Buckingham is close and will arrive before sunset, so Richard takes up occupation of one of the inns available and his three-hundred-man troop also settle into accommodation.

Gloucester is just settling in having satisfied himself as to his guards' disposition when Rivers arrives with a small bodyguard. The Earl has left his nephew back in Stony Stratford to recuperate after his long, hard ride. Made conscious of Richard's proximity and concerned at Grey's calls for urgency, he has come to ensure that Gloucester is still wanting to project unity and enter London together, with the coronation due for 4 May. That said, he has left Stony Stratford with orders that they should all proceed to London first thing in the morning even if he has not returned to them.

Rivers finds Richard overtly friendly in his reception and over a tankard of ale he explains that the King and his entourage are seventeen miles down the road because that is where their respective routes bisect, and it was felt that a host of 2,000 was too great a number to wheel north only to have to retrace their steps in the morning. It seemed easier for Richard to join them and then journey the last fifty miles together. This is received with an understanding demeanour. It is, of course, for the subject to go to the King rather than King to subject, and there is a limit to the miles that a twelve-year-old can ride in a day and still retain stamina for a couple more in the saddle.

Northampton is far from being a one-inn town and Rivers is found suitable accommodation, allowing him to freshen up before re-joining Richard for supper, during which Buckingham arrives.[4] The sun is now low in the sky and his men are camped outside the town, it being too late to consider securing lodgings for three hundred, with Richard's men mainly accommodated within the castle. If Rivers is surprised to see Buckingham, he does not show it but buys into the story that he is on his way to the coronation and this meeting is a fortuitous coincidence.

Over a convivial supper with reminiscing, gossip, and bragging, Rivers re-emphasises the need to get to London within two days. To underline this, he shares the information that most of his Welsh force is unarmed, it being hastily put together with only limited weapons held at Ludlow. The lightness of load also helped to ensure their march was of good pace. Hence, they would be meeting up with several carts of arms near St Albans to suitably fit out his soldiers for their entrance into the capital.

After Rivers retires to his quarters, Gloucester calls in Sir Richard Ratcliffe, a close confidant and henchman, and with Buckingham they discuss plans into the small hours.[5] What they know tells them that the Woodvilles, through Council, have organised an agenda where a Protector or Regent will not be required. With Edward crowned, government will be through Council until he reaches his majority at fourteen, and he will no doubt be led for a few years beyond that. The Woodvilles, with the support of the bishops, are likely to control Council and direct policy. The outcome for the position and livelihood, let alone the ambitions, of Gloucester, Hastings, and Buckingham is not one to be confident about. The more they talk, the more they fear for their lives. The immediate task is therefore to ensure that the coronation is put off. The preference would be for it to be delayed until Edward reaches the age of his majority. But it must be deferred to enable Gloucester to take up the Protectorate and advance policies sufficient to secure and advance their standing.

To achieve this first aim, they have to control the King, which means securing possession of him from the Woodvilles. The necessity to hold the King comes from experience gathered with regard to Henry VI, but also Edward IV: let him slip away and your ability to control minds and events is lost. However they look at the problem facing them, it can only be resolved by removing the Woodvilles from power, both locally and in London. Confrontation and conflict are inevitable and need to be faced sooner rather than later. A pre-emptive strike is necessary for their survival, for they will be close to treading on the quicksand of treachery. A believable argument has to be constructed that the King is being rescued from unscrupulous and immoral influences. But most important, if Rivers' 2,000 men are mostly unarmed, then the nominal 3-1 odds are no longer a worry. The opportunity to secure these immediate goals with little or no bloodshed is too good to resist.

And so, as the morning sun rises the lodgings of Earl Rivers and his men are quietly surrounded. Rivers is arrested and locked in his room and his retinue marched into the castle under the watchful eye of Sir Thomas Gower, Constable of Sheriff Hutton castle.[6] Guards are posted on the roads into the town to prevent news of what has happened being spread abroad, while Gloucester and Buckingham with a strong troop of men-at-arms gallop south to Stony Stratford.

They arrive just as Thomas Vaughan is helping Edward into his saddle. Richard and Buckingham dismount and drop to their knees, paying homage. Keeping up the appearance of amiability and servility, the new arrivals seek a private audience with Edward, Vaughan, Grey, Alcock, and Haute. With the company of a few men-at-arms, they retire to the lodgings from which Edward has just left. Here the mood swiftly changes. Gloucester holds forth. Certain ministers, he imparts staring into Edward's eyes, have been the cause of the late King's death by encouraging him in his excesses. (Neither Gloucester nor Buckingham have knowledge of what in fact Edward died from, other than it was a sudden death. Moreover, if there is a heart-felt need for revenge on those who have helped Edward indulge in his 'excesses', then expectations for Hastings do not look promising). They must be removed from Edward's presence to prevent their corruption of him. Feeling the boy quake in his gaze, he turns to Grey. These men have conspired to deprive Richard of his rightful role of Protector of the King and the Realm. Not only this, but they have laid a trap for his life. (This is working well. He must use the same routine again.) These evil men are led by Lord Richard Grey, the Marquess of Dorset, and the Earl Rivers.[7] As Constable of England, Gloucester already has Rivers under arrest and now these others shall be dealt with in the same way.

Edward keeps some composure and bravely pleads his mentors' innocence, but it is no use. When he argues that he has full faith in the peers and the Queen as to the best form of government he is cut short by Buckingham, who tells him not to mention the Queen as government is not for women, only men.

The 2,000 guards brought from Ludlow, mainly Welshmen, are dismissed and told to return home. There are some murmurings but eventually they do disperse and those arrested return to Northampton as prisoners: it is the last day of freedom which Edward will enjoy. Alcock and Haute will be quickly released, but Rivers is sent to Sheriff Hutton castle in North Yorkshire, Grey to Middleham and Vaughan to Pontefract.

In Northampton, Richard writes to the Council and to Edmund Shaa, the Lord Mayor of London, informing them of what has happened and that he has 'saved' Edward.[8] He and Buckingham now wait on the response, in particular news from Hastings as to how safe it is to progress.

There is an urgent commotion outside Ely House rousing Morton from his bed well before his steward appears to announce a midnight messenger from Archbishop Rotherham. Wrapping himself in a heavy woollen robe he descends to the reception hall to learn of the coup, or at least as much as can be gleaned at this moment. But even the stark outline of events is shocking enough. There appears little that can be done for now and it is agreed that he will meet with Rotherham at mid-morning the next day,1 May, when perhaps more will be revealed.

What is revealed is greater chaos. The whole city is in a state of fearfulness. The Woodvilles have not found armed men rushing to their support: citizens are too busy squirreling away their riches against potential looting. This mirrors the Woodvilles' own actions. A sizeable part of the assets of the Treasury has been divided between Elizabeth, Dorset, and Sir Edward, the latter taking to his fleet, sailing down the Thames to anchor off The Downs.[9] Learning of the arrest of her relatives, and the effective arrest of her son, Elizabeth swiftly concludes that the liberty and possibly the life of all Woodvilles is now at risk and takes sanctuary at Westminster Abbey, where she is duly received and registered by Abbot John Esteney along with her youngest son, Richard, Duke of York, her five daughters, the Marquis of Dorset, and Lionel, Bishop of Salisbury.[10] There are already rumours circulating that Richard has his eye on the throne, and these will grow.

Archbishop Bourchier is now in London having come up from Canterbury and he receives a letter signed by Edward, but obviously written by Richard, calling on him to safeguard the Tower and, in particular, the treasure stored inside. Thomas Rotherham, Archbishop of York, is appraised of this and being already suspicious of Richard's aims and motives, he rides with Morton to Westminster to pass the Great Seal of England to Queen Elizabeth. They are confident that what they are doing is within the law as there is no Protector confirmed – indeed, Council has rejected that idea – and placing it safely in royal hands within sanctuary gives the Great Seal maximum security. The precincts of the abbey are in turmoil with furniture, crockery and cutlery, food supplies, and treasure being carried from the royal apartments. What confidence they still have is deflated by the sight of the distressed Queen sitting on the straw-covered floor in a state of complete distraction. Providing what assurances they can for the safety of herself and her family, they agree between themselves that they will keep closely in touch and work for as speedy a coronation as possible.

Edward enters London on 4 May, the day on which he was supposed to be crowned. With him are the two Dukes and the Lord Mayor and Aldermen of the City, together with five hundred citizens who greeted him outside the city perimeter. They enter with 500 men-at-arms – over the coming month or so the armed presence in the city will increase to 20,000. Such is the measure of Richard's feeling of insecurity. The throng is also accompanied by four wagon loads of soldiers' harness marked with Woodville badges and some weaponry. The propaganda that these were all for the purpose of exterminating Gloucester and Buckingham is immediately put about: but only a few credulous souls will believe this.

Hastings, of course, is jubilant, as are many others whose only interest is seeing the fall of the Woodvilles and he, and all high-ranking persons present, swear fealty to their new King as he rides through the city gates. Edward is then taken to temporary lodgings in the Bishop of London's Palace until 9 May, after which he is taken to cleaned and refurbished apartments in the Tower. The next day Richard is confirmed as Protector of the Realm by Council.

As commercial life in the city settles back to normality over the course of the next few days, Archbishop Bourchier, who has responsibility for ensuring that Edward IV's will is properly applied, calls for a meeting of the executors on 7 May at Baynard's Castle, the London home of Dowager Duchess Cecily and informal headquarters of the House of York. The executors are hesitant to take any action, however. The claims that there is a more recent will than that of 1475, or that codicils to that will were made on Edward's death bed, were unsettling. None of the executors claimed to have seen such a will except Hastings. The Woodvilles who had been present when the late King died denied one existed. None of the churchmen who were present at Westminster when Edward died had seen it either.[11] In an unusually decisive move, the Archbishop sequesters the assets within the Will and orders sufficient of them be sold to settle the bills for Edward's funeral, which amount to a staggering £1496.[12]

Within a fortnight the political scene has changed quite markedly as several positions in government and administration change hands. In a mix of hope and fear the Council has approved appointing Richard Protector and Defender of the Realm, giving him full powers as if he were a king. He has also been given full guardianship responsibilities over Edward. This is a far different role than that granted to the previous Protector back in 1422.

The next most noticeable and significant change is the rise of the Duke of Buckingham. Now effectively a viceroy operating in Wales, he is Chief Justice and Chamberlain of the province, Constable of all the Welsh and West Country castles, and has the right to muster armies. He also has supervisory powers over Shropshire, Hereford, Somerset, Dorset, and Wiltshire. Buckingham has the promise of the disputed Bohun estate and the marriage of his daughter to Gloucester's son.[13] He is Richard's 'gofer' – there everywhere you turn; organising, networking, nothing gets past him, making up for years of being overlooked and only wheeled out when someone was needed to look good in a procession.

John, Lord Howard is a particular rising star and supporter of Richard. The 38-year-old is created Chief Steward of the duchy of Lancaster south of the Trent. But it is the title Duke of Norfolk that he yearns for, and there is an understanding that he will soon get it.

Having been chastised by Gloucester, Archbishop Rotherham has retrieved the Great Seal from Elizabeth, but has nevertheless lost the Chancellorship to John Russell, Bishop of Lincoln. Lincoln's role as Keeper of the Privy Seal has been transferred to John Gunthorpe, a long-standing diplomat and administrator for Edward IV, Clerk of the Parliaments and also a monk who was Dean of the King's Household Chapel and, a strange item on his cv, a secretary to Queen Elizabeth.[14] Sir John Wood, having stood down as Speaker of the Commons, is the new Treasurer of the Exchequer. This is the culmination of a career within the Treasury, although not an honour to be enjoyed long as he will die the following year.

John Alcock, Bishop of Rochester, arrested at Stony Stratford, has been released and is back on the Council. Hastings' deputy at Calais is made Steward of the Duchy of Cornwall, a county in which he owns some land.

For Hastings himself, there are no new appointments.

Perhaps feeling pushed to the perimeter of things, or because the direction of government is not how he envisaged, Hastings calls a clandestine meeting of known conservatives at his residence.

Morton is received at Hasting's abode by William Catesby, a lawyer who has worked in Hasting's household for some years and who has just been elevated to the Council. Also present are William Rotherham and Thomas, Lord Stanley. With the exception of Catesby, the group are representative of 'older and wiser' heads on the Council. Morton is sixty-five, Rotherham is sixty, Hastings fifty-two, and Stanley fifty. They are traditionalists in outlook but resolute of purpose, that purpose being to ensure Edward is crowned and a functional Council operating as quickly as possible. Hastings has to eat some humble pie as his initial support of Richard is well known, but he now shares the fears of his new friends.

The coronation has been put off until 22 June. There are intimations that the Protector will be seeking an extension of his powers beyond that date, until the King reaches his majority. That could prove to be anywhere between two and five years and would have a profoundly negative impact on the effectiveness of Council, and the importance of individual councillors.

Some in the city say that it might be no bad thing if the Protector took it upon himself to rule rather than endure the catastrophes of a child on the throne. But without the continuity provided by heredity there is seemingly no point in monarchy. The alternative is some form of elected leadership or a dictatorship. If they believe in hereditary monarchy, then they must support it. To acquiesce in the undermining of it through factionalism or family feuds would eventually, they fear, undermine their own hereditary rights.

Richard is in a difficult position. His actions towards Edward come close to treason. In any event, he may have gone too far. Can he release Lord Rivers and Richard Grey? Having terrified the Queen, can he expect forgiveness? He is in peril, if not of his life, then for his future in government. He is also not a person to be content with limitations to his power or to bow to criticism and controls.

Richard is now dividing Council into groups. Hastings, Rotherham, and Morton, joined by Richard's closest allies Buckingham and Howard, will continue to meet at the Tower but will be focussed on administration and another, under Rotherham, will oversee preparations for the coronation from Westminster. Although it is said that a full council will meet from time to time in the Star Chamber, real policy is to be discussed and determined by another group meeting at Richard's home at Crosby Place and on which Catesby will sit.[15]

There is a latent 'Woodville majority' on the Council which they by no means support, but it is worrying that Richard will seek to break it by breaking the powers of Council itself. They are all well aware of his anger when Council refused to accept that Rivers, Richard Grey, and Vaughan should be tried as traitors, and they anticipate he will attempt to attaint them again when parliament assembles on June 25.

The previous day, Rochester had to go with an increasingly arthritic Archbishop Bourchier, Richard, and Henry of Buckingham to see Queen Elizabeth. They were trying all they could to persuade her to release the young Duke of York into their custody, but she bravely stood her ground, and they came away empty-handed. There is fear a more aggressive attempt will be made very soon; the idea of breaking holy sanctuary does not instil fear in them, only the opprobrium of the people if they do.

The cabal determines to provide the Queen with as much intelligence and support as they can. Elizabeth Shore, the late King's and now Hastings' mistress, is volunteered to feed through messages to Thomas Grey (another of her conquests), as is Hasting's servant John Forster.

There is much coming and going at the Abbey and indeed visitors are being encouraged, to give the Queen and those in sanctuary less cause to fear the world outside. Lord Dorset had escaped the Abbey precinct and is in hiding somewhere in the country, and Sir Edward Woodville is now in Brittany, keeping company with Jasper and Henry Tudor.

Sir Thomas Fulford and Sir Edward Brampton had managed to spread word through Woodville's fleet that they would all be pardoned if they abandoned him, and all but two ships surrendered themselves. But he and his closest followers escaped, and he is now declared an enemy of the state with a handsome price on his head.

Another tidbit of news. Archbishop Bourchier summoned a convocation for May 16. The bidding-prayer called for intercession for King Edward and for his mother, but there was no mention of the Duke of Gloucester. This information got back to the Protector, who then summoned poor Bourchier before him the next day for a severe dressing down. It seems Duke Richard finds himself needing to be in everyone's prayers continually. Further, Bourchier was made to understand in no uncertain terms that he had to translate Thomas Langton to the see of St Davids – which he did on 21 May.[16]

For now, these self-appointed leaders of the opposition agree that once the coronation takes place their aim is to ensure that government becomes rooted in Council. It is accepted that Gloucester may need to be seen as chief minister but not as Protector. The big problem will be if the Woodvilles seek some sort of revenge or compensation. As it is, some of their estates are already being unlawfully redistributed by Richard.

As the council committee on which Morton sits meets at the Tower there is an opportunity to meet and converse with the young King in the royal apartments. The boy is certainly as bright as his reputation promises, but there is a wariness and uncertainty in his demeanour which pulls his councillors back from saying too much. It is best to present an optimistic vision. His most pressing questions are on the fate and fortune of his uncle, step-brother, mother, and siblings. He is clearly lonely and stressed.

It is the arrest of Rivers, Grey and Vaughan that worms away in Morton's appraisal of the explosive events of the last six or seven weeks. There are many obvious and prudent reasons why Richard would want to isolate the Woodvilles but they are, when it comes down to it, selfish reasons rather than being motivated by an urge to protect and serve the King. If it was truly believed that they had committed crimes against the state, then why not bring them to London for trial by their peers?

After all, that would have been less than 70 miles distant rather than the 170 miles to Middleham. They need to be kept out of the way as there is no evidence to support the charges against them.

There is no Woodville plot. The Woodvilles do not even have the capacity for a counter-strike. Events have demonstrated that very well, which is why the Queen is in sanctuary and the remaining two – Edward Woodville and Lord Dorset – have fled. They do not have their own base. They may be able to talk well but they do not have muscle. They relied on Edward IV, no one relied on them. The general population simply want peace and prosperity. They will support Edward V because he is the son of Edward IV, not because he is the son of a Woodville.

So removing the Woodvilles is no less a personal thing for Richard than it has been for Hastings. And they have been effectively broken as a political force. But their arrest, and moving them away from the centre of justice, suggests that Richard wants more than simply to keep them away from the coronation. He wants them exterminated. Richard's reaction to losing the vote in Council to have the captives from Stony Stratford declared traitors is a key moment in Morton's mind. Unlike Council, Richard has no respect for legalities when they get in the way of the safety of his ambitions.

There have seemed to be moves to redress the balance on the Council in the Protector's favour. Francis, Viscount Lovell, completely Richard's man, has been made Chief Butler: a title taken from Rivers. Bishop Stillington of Bath and Wells has shown himself to have a similar affinity along with Thomas Langton, the newly nominated Bishop of St Davids. At the same time, Hastings in particular but also others who might be considered staunchly supportive of King Edward are finding their influence on and their proximity to decision making diluted almost by the day.

Morton shares Rotherham's concern at the pressure being put on Elizabeth to surrender the Duke of York to Richard. Few are now prepared to accompany Buckingham to the Abbey to keep up this unpleasant attempt to break her will and sanctuary. There is distaste at the lack of dignity and respect afforded her, not least because it is still so soon after her husband's death. But more than that. Just as Henry VI was safe as long as Prince Edward was alive and free so Edward V is safe as long as Richard of York is alive and free. If they are together in custody then neither is safe and any attempt to usurp the throne is made so much easier.

The four of them, Morton, Hastings, Rotherham, and Stanley, continue to meet at each other's house prior to their committee meetings so that they can respond constructively and with unity to the agenda. Catesby is no longer joining them. He is on a completely different committee, and they have all begun to feel unsure about where his loyalties lay.

Finances are a problem, as usual, for government. It goes without saying that there are no more payments coming from France. Moreover, with Edward's death, the right of the Crown to levy customs ended and cannot be resumed until parliament sits and restores it. London ceased collection of customs as of June 3. Edward left no surplus within the Treasury, the accounts just about balancing – though that in itself is no mean feat for a monarchy. The Woodvilles did remove an array of assets, some going with Edward Woodville and most into Westminster Abbey to maintain the Queen, but the bulk of this was 'personal' wealth, which featured in Edward's will, bequeathed to various members of his family. As it is, even the King's jewels stand surety against loans.

They would discuss options. If push comes to shove they could seize Edward just like Richard did and get him into sanctuary with his mother while steps are taken to remove Richard from power. But the practicalities of that are so insurmountable that the idea is fleeting and then gone. Their only feasible course of action is to ensure the coronation goes through speedily and smoothly, after which the battle for the release and rehabilitation of the Woodvilles, together with the supremacy of Council during the King's minority, will be fought out in parliament.

So their sense of unease remains palpable, fearing that the lion that is Richard of Gloucester will soon be leaping from his cage. What they do not realise is that this lion has been prowling free for some time and is now about to pounce.

Contest for the Crown, 1483

It is Friday the thirteenth, and a bright June sun ascends over London. After morning service at six o'clock in his chapel, Morton strolls to the Tower for the Council committee meeting, arriving at his seat at eight. Present are Hastings, Rochester, Stanley, Buckingham, and Lord John Howard, plus a few scribes and servants. They chat amicably as they wait for the Protector. Though the agenda for this meeting is light, they all have a lot of business to conduct elsewhere.

Richard arrives around nine, apologising with good humour for his lateness. He has overslept: yes, contrary to rumour, he does sleep. There is some banter and Richard gently pricks Morton's pride in his garden, requesting a mess of John's renowned strawberries for Council's table. Morton's vanity misses the symbolism: crushed strawberries representative of crushed virtue. He sends one of the attendants to High Holborn for the fruit.

The meeting is just starting when a messenger enters and whispers something to Gloucester, who gives his apologies for having to step outside and asks that the meeting progress. Buckingham takes over the Chair. Almost an hour has gone by when Richard returns, taking his seat. But the earlier levity is gone: his brow is furrowed, eyes dark, and he bites at his thin lips. All present sense something is seriously wrong.

Richard breaks the silence. 'Having in mind that I am of royal blood, of the nearest royal blood to the King, and am elected Protector of the King's person and this realm, what should be the fate of those who consider and plot my death?'

Everyone is uncomfortable, shifting in his seat, avoiding eye contact. Assuming responsibility for Council, Hastings responds. 'Such people should be punished as traitors.' The others murmur agreement.

Richard is now warming up to a reprise of his performance at Stony Stratford. He leans across the table. 'And those traitors are my brother's wife and his mistress Jane Shore who have been counselling each other to destroy me by witchcraft and sorcery.'

Those present are shocked. It is evident that Elizabeth Shore's movements taking and fetching messages to the Abbey have been spied upon, but the accusations of witchcraft are an overtly absurd confection in Richard's pursuit of the destruction of Queen Elizabeth.

Hastings is obliged to respond again, even though he knows whatever he says will lead him into a trap. Reason was left outside the door the moment Richard stepped into the room. 'Certainly my Lord, if they have done anything so heinous then they deserve to be severely punished.'

Gloucester's rage explodes. 'You give me your "ifs"? I'm telling you that this is what they have done, traitor. You're in this with them. By St Paul, I swear I will not dine tonight until I have had your head brought to me.'

With that Richard smashed his clenched fist down onto the table. In response to this pre-arranged signal guards secreted in an ante-chamber rushed in, led by Thomas Howard with Sir Charles Pilkington and Sir Robert Harrington crying 'Treason!'[1] In the chaos, Hastings is arrested and force-marched out of the room. Stanley gets the flat face of a poll axe across his head from Robert Harrington as a salutation from his brother James, and he collapses to the floor with blood flowing from around his ringing ears. Rotherham and Morton are also seized and taken away under protest to separate cells, as is Dr Oliver King.[2]

A bewildered William Hastings is taken out onto Tower Green. Here he is afforded a short confession and then brought to kneel, an axe removing his head on a log. There has been no trial. A written indictment has been pre-prepared for public proclamation. Richard's coup d'état is now in full swing.

Morton was convinced that he and Rotherham are alive only because they were churchmen. He was mortified to learn of Hasting's fate, not only for the man and his family but also for the confirmation of a tyranny which now gripped government.[3] If there was any good news to be had, it was that Stanley was not too badly injured and in fact had been released. But he also learned that John Forster, treasurer and receiver-general for Edward as Prince of Wales was arrested on 12 June. Anyone with Woodville connections or affiliation to Edward appeared to be at risk.

He was allowed some vetted visitors to his cell in the Tower and was able to be fed updates on what was happening outside, none of these reports conveying any comfort. Writing materials had also been provided, which eased his mind as their presence suggested that he wasn't seen as an immediate danger – or that he was in immediate danger. Nonetheless, anything written would need to be either bland or coded.

News of the coup spreads slowly in some quarters but fast in others. So, on 15 June the Mercers' Company of London had no knowledge of Morton's arrest as they were planning to petition him as Master of the Rolls. At the same time, George Cely, a wool merchant active in the city, thought Morton was dead.

As news of Hasting's murder and the seizure of the prelates spread around the city, fears of a revolt grew within the establishment. That this did not materialise was in good part due to the efforts of Mayor Edmund Shaa in stifling discontent, but also by reports of thousands of northerners marching on London in support of Richard. As Queen Margaret discovered, Londoners had a particular fear of the rough ways of northerners.

Gloucester had also remembered that a bit of street theatre, charged with public punishment, would help placate the populace and embellish his image as a man of moral rectitude. So, on Sunday 15 June, under instruction from the Protector, the Bishop of London compelled Elizabeth Shore to do public penance in her kirtle or chemise holding a lighted taper, after which she was sent to Ludgate prison.[4] John Forster, the other messenger between Hastings and Dorset, was also arrested, jailed, was half-starved in prison, and had to meet stiff bond conditions for his release 10 March 1484.

There was hardly time to catch breath: certainly not for Richard, who was now driving his campaign hard and fast. By a combination of fear, favours, and absences, the Protector's justification for his actions was accepted by Council and, in addition, approval was given to fetch the young Duke of York, by force if necessary.

In the end, force is not required: only the threat of it. On the morning of 16 June, members of the Council under the leadership of Gloucester and Buckingham and accompanied by a substantial retinue of well-armed guards assemble at the Tower. With them, protesting against the action but accompanying nonetheless, is Archbishop Bourchier. With one of the realm's two archbishops in custody, there comes a point where argument gives way to compliance. Boarding boats, they are rowed up the Thames to Westminster. The Abbey is surrounded by this fearsome band, who make sure those inside know of their presence.

The Archbishop and Lord Howard, heading up about half of the councillors, enter the Abbey to meet the Queen. They argue that the King is melancholy and pines for his brother's companionship; that a refusal to release Prince Richard will make it look that he is held by force, and by force he will be released; that if sanctuary is thus broken once, then there is no safety for Elizabeth or her daughters. Bourchier then guarantees the safety of the Prince and that all will be well after the coronation. Elizabeth cannot see a way out of the situation. She concedes. Outwardly calm and amiable, internally confounded and distressed.

Richard also holds the custody of Clarence's son, ten-year-old Edward, Duke of Warwick, who is residing with Anne, the Protector's wife. Although Warwick possesses no real claim to the throne, his father having been attainted, it is wise to hold as many cards as possible.

The next phase of Richard's plan can take place.

With both princes now under his control, all the King's attendants, including his physician Dr John Argentine, were removed and replaced by Gloucester's own men so that there was no risk of an assisted escape. They are provided with four attendants in all, one of whom is Miles Forest, Keeper of the Wardrobe for Richard at Barnard's Castle. The boys are moved from the royal apartments, which Richard takes over for his own use, into the inner apartments of the Tower, to be seen less and less frequently as the days go by. Dr Argentine relates how depressed and anxious Edward is: he knows his history lessons well enough to conjecture his fate and that of his brother.

At the same time, June 17, Richard unilaterally postpones the coronation and the Parliament of the 25th for an indefinite period. No reason is given but the work in readiness for the coronation – a coronation – goes on regardless. The lords continue to be summonsed to London but with a request that they leave their retinues behind. The murmurings that Richard intends to take the throne for himself get louder.

Confirming these whispers, the next day, June 18, warrants are sent out in the King's name to the sheriffs ordering them to fine those refusing to accept a knighthood. Back in May, the sheriffs were told to submit the names of anyone who had been receiving an income of £40 a year from land over the past three years. These lucky people were to be elevated to knighthood at the coronation. The catch was that receiving a knighthood was a costly business and it left you exposed to receiving requests for money in the future which you could not say no to. To be chasing so hard immediately after postponing the coronation suggests that another coronation is about to happen.

Exactly one week after Elizabeth Shaw was publicly humiliated at St Paul's Cross, a large crowd has gathered in the cathedral precincts to listen to a well-known orator on the day when Edward V was due to be crowned. St Paul's Cross is the most important open-air pulpit within the City and it has recently been rebuilt by Thomas Kempe, Bishop of London. It is no 'Speaker's Corner' but the podium for official, invited lecturers. Dr Ralph Shaa, brother of the Mayor of London, stands behind an oak lectern on the raised stone platform shielded from the risen sun by the structure's lead roof. He reads clearly and carefully from a prepared script with the mannered intonation of a well-practised theologian. Shaa had been a chaplain to Edward IV, which provides a measure of credibility to his story.

Edward's marriage to Elizabeth Woodville was bigamous, declared Shaa, and their children were consequently bastards and none should stand in line to inherit the throne. Because of this only the Protector had a rightful claim to the crown.

The crowd gasped at this. It was not just the shock of what was said, but that it had been said at all, for attending the sermon were the Dukes of Gloucester and Buckingham. Anyone who spoke such treason could expect to be dragged away for a traitor's execution: but nothing happened. It was clear that the two dukes were present to hear what was said, that they knew what was going to be said, and they showed no disagreement. The initial murmurings were of disbelief of the story itself, rather than that such a thing had actually happened. The crowd then displayed its verdict with silence.

The tale told was that on or about 8 June 1461, Edward promised to marry Lady Eleanor Butler, a widow, and that the contract had been consummated so that, according to church law, they were married.[5] Thus Edward's later marriage to Elizabeth in 1464 was unlawful.

Eleanor was the daughter of John Talbot, Earl of Shrewsbury, and in 1449 she married Sir Thomas Butler, heir of Ralph Butler, Lord Sudeley. Thomas died in 1461 leaving Eleanor a widow with no children. Lord Sudeley had given them manors in Fenny Compton and Burton Dassett in Warwickshire. Lord Sudeley himself lived at Sudeley Castle, near Winchcombe in Gloucestershire. Unfortunately for him, he had crenelated it without royal consent and Edward, crowned in 1461, decided to confiscate it. The story is that 25-year-old Eleanor pleaded with Edward to restore the castle to Lord Sudeley and slept with him to secure the favour. The castle was indeed restored to Sudeley later that year, but he was forced to sell it to Edward in 1469 as punishment for supporting Henry IV's Readeption. Edward then gave it to his brother Richard.

Most people would find credibility in tales of Edward taking advantage of his position to entice a woman into his bed. Indeed, probably any woman. But why would he offer marriage? Especially if the lady in question wanted something, namely a castle. If a pre-contract for marriage had been entered into, why would Eleanor not have sought to enforce it, particularly when she heard of the marriage of Edward to Elizabeth? She had nothing to lose and a crown to gain.

A pre-contract was a promise before witnesses followed by intercourse. As it was, there were no witnesses to this alleged pre-contract, and Eleanor died in 1468 – 15 years earlier, with nothing said in the meantime. If it had happened, would Eleanor have said something to Ralph Butler, Lord Sudeley who would have been at liberty to use that information to keep hold of his castle on which he had spent a fortune in restoring?

Determining all this would normally have fallen on the ecclesiastical courts. It was a church matter, possibly even requiring papal intervention. The chief legal voice for the church was, of course, locked up. As it is, Shaa finds himself shunned and his reputation severely shattered as a result of his sermon. Within twelve months he is dead.

Similar speeches have been orchestrated to be read out from pulpits in churches across London. With several thousand more soldiers from the north arriving at the city gates the day before, no one questions or displays doubts. Some of these other versions of Dr Shaa's story are embellished with the equally loose tale that Edward IV and also Clarence were bastards and that only Richard is the true son of Richard of York, for he is the only son that looks like the great man. Again, there is no challenge to such claims. Duchess Cecily is enraged when news of such talk gets back to her.

Although disappointed that the crowd had not acclaimed Richard there and then, there had been no vocal or physical reaction to what was a declaration of intent. Accordingly, on 24 June, Buckingham tested the water once more, delivering a half-hour speech at the Guildhall before the most prominent citizens of the capital. Further challenges to the validity of the marriage between Edward and Elizabeth are raised. Buckingham claims the agreement of an assembly of the lords would have been required for the marriage to be lawful. This was not true. Not even Warwick or Clarence raised such an objection, or indeed anyone else in the eighteen years of the marriage. The assertion would have applied to the marriage to Eleanor Butler, which would have been equally void of consent by the lords. As it was, all the lords – including Gloucester – recognised Elizabeth as Edward's wife and queen at her coronation and swore fealty to that effect.

Buckingham went on to claim that Edward was compelled to marry Elizabeth by sorcery practised by not only herself but by her mother, Jacquetta of Luxembourg. Not even those who seriously believed in witchcraft were buying into that. And thirdly, it was claimed that the marriage was invalid because it was made secretly without banns being read. Except that the reading of banns was not necessary for a lawful marriage in the eyes of the Church and there were witnesses to this event, unlike the alleged pre-contract marriage to Eleanor for which there were no witnesses.

Again, the response to this declamation is underwhelming but, lessons learnt, a number of those present have been planted or bribed to shout 'Yea, yea,' to a call for Richard to be king.

By now, a sizeable number of peers of the realm had gathered in the city and were well aware that they were effectively surrounded by troops wearing the badges of Gloucester or Buckingham. In this atmosphere they were called to an assembly – most certainly not a parliament – under Buckingham's orchestration the purpose of which was to draw up (and support) a petition calling on Richard to accept the crown by common acclaim. This petition was presented to Richard on 26 June at Baynard's Castle by a delegation including the Mayor, aldermen, and other leading Londoners, which, in a most Caesar-like manner, he humbly accepted: riding on to Westminster to sit in the marble King's Bench, demonstrating his formal assumption of the throne.[6] The coronation date was fixed for Sunday 6 July.

The news that spreads around London on 29 June causes great anxiety in Morton, not least for the implication that he may find himself without a head once the coronation is done. Rivers, Grey, and Vaughan have been executed.

On 11 June, Richard Ratcliffe rode out of London with letters in his saddlebags to the city of York and to major towns and lords in the north. He also carried the death sentences on Earl Rivers, Sir Richard Grey, and Sir Thomas Vaughan.

It's a hard ride, and he reaches Leconfield Castle, the residence of Henry Percy, Earl of Northumberland, on 14 June. He is fortuitous in finding Percy at home as he only arrived at Leconfield the day before from York – they could have crossed paths. The messages from Richard are clear: he should take a good number of men to Pontefract to meet others there on the 18th. And he should make preparations for carrying out the Protector's sentence on the three traitors when Ratcliffe brings them to him.

Ratcliffe's next stop is York, where Richard's letter pleading for men and assistance is read out to the Council. He desperately needs their help as 'the Queen, her blood, adherents and affinity … intend to murder and utterly destroy' himself and Buckingham. They are asked to meet with Henry Percy at Pontefract on the 18th. Being so far from London, the good councillors of York do not know that, as well as Rivers and Grey being detained at the Protector's pleasure, the Queen is isolated in sanctuary, and Edward Grey and the Marquess of Dorset have fled the country. Any other enemies – presumably Hastings, Rotherham and Morton – will be lured and trapped well before this missive arrives. It is difficult to see where the Woodville threat is to be launched from or indeed by whom. This is a fine piece of political craftwork and obfuscation. At worst, there is no plot to depose Richard, but there is definitely a party intent on seeing Edward V crowned as king. On the 16th, York sends 300 of its sons to Pontefract under the command of past Lord Mayor Thomas Wrangwysh (who will get another term in the following year) while Ratcliffe proceeds to complete his task as postman, collecting up the three prisoners who are executed, or ritually murdered, at Pontefract Castle on 25 June.[7]

Morton's mind and stomach turn over. The Constable of England can only dispense justice on traitors if there is a state of martial law in the country. The law courts and judges have all been fully fit and capable of considering any of these cases where Gloucester has seen fit to deliver execution, imprisonment, or any other sentence. By no stretch of the imagination could Rivers, Grey and Vaughan be said to have been instigating a threat to the King or to the safety of the realm; which is more than can be said for Richard's actions.

Just a few months after the death of the brother to whom he owed everything and all supposed he had unqualified loyalty, Richard had accused Edward of being a bastard and bigamist, had disinherited his children, and had violently suppressed opposition to his own personal interests and ambitions.

So he stands a tyrant and murderer, with no one seemingly willing or able to stop him.

On 28 June, Buckingham was made Great Chamberlain of England – Hasting's most prominent role – and it was as such that he stage-managed Richard's coronation at Westminster Abbey on 6 July (with Queen Elizabeth, her family and entourage tucked away in the sanctuary of the grounds). The ceremony might have been organised by Buckingham but it was noticeable that his wife, Katherine Woodville, was absent, as were others such as Sir Robert Willoughby, Sir Roger Tucotes, Sir William Haute, and John Fogge.[8]

Richard was anointed and crowned, as was Anne, by a revitalised Bourchier, although he absented himself from the post-coronation banquet. It was noteworthy that the new Queen's train was borne by the wife of Lord Thomas Stanley, the Lady Margaret Beaufort, mother of Henry Tudor.[9]

Revulsion and Rebellion

Sitting in the window of his apartment at the Chateau de l'Hermine in Vannes, Henry Tudor could catch the smell of the sea on the southern July breeze. For half of his twenty-six years he had been an exile from England living with his uncle Jasper in Brittany, partly the guests, partly the prisoners, of their host Duke Francis II. In that time they had been in constant fear that Francis would succumb to pressure from England or France to surrender them, an act which would have resulted in their death. But while they lived under the largesse of the Duke and the several lords and captains who oversaw their daily concerns, ensuring of course that they did not travel too far for their own safety, they enjoyed a standard of living well in keeping with their status.

The thirteen-year-old boy had become a tall, fair-haired, slender young man: educated, fluent in French, fully attuned to court life, proficient in hunting, archery and other sports. Jasper, Earl of Pembroke before their flight from Wales, was now fifty-two, his life devoted to protecting and advising his nephew who had become an increasingly important person in English politics, as those with a far better claim to the throne were struck down in civil war.

Henry's claim to the throne was weak, going back to John of Gaunt but through the Beaufort line: that is, the offspring of Gaunt and Kathryn Swynford produced before their marriage and barred from the throne by Act of Parliament. Really, no claim at all. Except that a growing number of Englishmen fleeing attainder at home were attaching themselves to him, gathering on the coast about fifteen miles away in or around the Chateau de Suscinio.

Henry's desire had been permission to return to England to take up his position and property as Earl of Richmond, and for Jasper to reassume his role in society. Henry's mother, Margaret Beaufort, only seen infrequently during his childhood, had made all efforts to help achieve this by pleading with Edward IV. There was hope that reintegration might be achieved, although Edward's sincerity was open to question: certainly, Jasper was doubtful. In February 1482, Edward offered to support Francis against threats from Louis of France with 4,000 archers to be provided on a month's notice, if only he would surrender Jasper and Henry. Then, just four months later, he was offering to welcome them back into the fold holding out the prospect of marriage to his daughter Elizabeth and a guarantee of the inheritance of his mother's Beaufort estate. Edward's death made the ambiguity academic.

The prospect of Edward V's accession provided a small window of optimism for a safe return, only to be closed with the usurpation of the throne by Richard. With this, the fears and sense of hopelessness had returned, added to which the reports coming in from disillusioned Yorkists and closet Lancastrians caused the feelings of depression and negativity towards the future to deepen. However, the steady inflow of dissidents to the Ricardian regime is engendering invasion plans.

Edward IV's death has freed Francis from his promise to keep Jasper and Henry under close custody and they have been keenly aware of the increase in their freedoms, but not so much as to take them for granted. They are also aware of the declining health of 60-year-old Louis XI and have been pondering how that may also affect their fortunes.

Of particular interest has been a letter delivered to Francis by a Dr Thomas Hutton on behalf of Richard, which he composed on 13 July, just a week after his coronation.[1] It was a strange letter, suggesting a meeting between England and Brittany and enquiring about the status and activities of Edward Woodville. On the subject of Henry Tudor, 'the only imp now left', the letter was mysteriously silent. Intrigued, and feeling impish himself, Francis leaves replying for a couple of weeks before sending Hutton back to England, where he would land on 26 August, the letter from Brittany to reach Richard in the first week of September.

The reply will not please him. There is no mention at all of Woodville. What the letter mischievously says is that Francis is being pressed by Louis of France for custody of Henry and is threatening war to secure him. Will Richard reaffirm Edward's promise of 4,000 archers to withstand Louis' demand? Knowing of course that he will not.

In any event, by the time Richard reads the letter Louis is dead, his heir Charles VIII is only thirteen, and France is now in the hands of a regency led by Charles' twenty-three-year-old sister Anne and her husband Peter of Bourbon.

Everything has changed again.

A different July vista, this one from a window in the Welsh castle of Brecon, home of the Duke of Buckingham; though Buckingham is not at home. The contemplative face looking out over the river Usk and toward the Brecon Beacons is that of John Morton, who finds this a more amenable place of imprisonment than the Tower – but it is still a prison and his fate remains in the balance. Morton had been kept in touch with the progress of events through various visitors and correspondence at the Tower, and even more liberally at Brecon. No doubt written communications were read but there was a generosity in the privacy allowed in conversations.

After the terror of 13 June, there were inevitable replacements among those holding office to suit the Protector's politics, and of servants too, although this was gradual. If incumbents demonstrated their allegiance to the new regime, then change was not necessarily introduced.

The double-agent William Catesby had found particular favour with Richard and was elevated to Chancellor of the Exchequer on 26 June. Francis Lovell became Lord Chamberlain, John Russell, Bishop of Lincoln, was made Lord Chancellor, and John Kendal King's Secretary. John Gunthorpe was rewarded as Keeper of the Privy Seal, and Sir Robert Percy of Scotton as Comptroller of the Household.

Two days later, more rewards were bestowed. As well as being elevated to Duke of Norfolk, John Howard was appointed Earl Marshal, and his son Thomas is made Earl of Surrey.[2] Viscount William de Berkeley was elevated to Earl of Nottingham.[3] But the action of Richard which caused deep concern to Morton, as it should have done for any jurist, was the distribution of the Mowbray estates between Howard and his cousin Berkeley. This property was owned by Prince Richard and had been settled on him by Act of Parliament, so the distribution was illegal. The underlying significance was that it raised fearful questions as to the planned fate of the child: if indeed he was still alive.

Just before the coronation, Archbishop Rotherham is released from the Tower on 4 July, having been overseen in custody by Sir James Tyrell, who now had an intimate knowledge of the geography and security there. Rotherham carries a distaste and disgust for Richard and his regime which he will neither hide nor suppress. He quickly retires to his diocese in York and does not attend the coronation.

Keen to show apologies and try to get back some good will, Richard makes Thomas Stanley Steward of the Household, and also confers on him the status of Knight of the Garter, but alongside the Stanley family tradition for self-preservation and self-interest there now sits an inherent distrust of Richard's motives and morals. Stanley also suspects that the only reason he did not suffer Hasting's fate was the threat to

Richard of a potential rebellion in the north-west by his son, George, Lord Strange.

There is no release yet for John Morton, notwithstanding pleas on his behalf from Oxford University. Richard is in need of a civil service experienced in administration, finance, and the law. While he is ready to break the law to establish what he considers to be in the best interests of good government, he also wishes to establish a society which is safe under the law: as long as it conforms to his will. He therefore wants Morton brought onside if possible. Because Richard is a man who believes that if something works once, then it will work twice, he is confident that just as Morton accepted political reality in 1471 with the end of the Lancastrian line, so he would accept the political reality that the line of Edward IV has no future. To this end, Morton is sent under escort to Brecon Castle where Buckingham will attend on him later and attempt the conversion. What he fails to appreciate is just how deeply and dearly Morton holds the principles of heredity and legitimacy in law.

After the coronation, Richard retired to Greenwich and spent a week finalising details for a Royal Progress to the west, the midlands, and then to the north to confer largesse and project a regal impression on his subjects. During this period of preparation Buckingham receives his longed-for confirmation that he has the second half of the Bohun estate and that he is Constable of England. Norfolk is confirmed as Admiral of England and Northumberland is appointed to the Wardenship of the whole length of the Scottish border, albeit for just one year. Lovell adds Chief Butler to his *curriculum vitae*. And for Robert Brackenbury there are the roles of Master of the King's Monies, Keeper of the Exchange (Master of the Mint), and Constable of the Tower, lucrative positions which enable him to enjoy an income greater than most barons. Also in this week, Richard's son, Edward, is made Lieutenant of Ireland.

On 21 July, Richard set out on his Progression leaving John Russell, Bishop of Lincoln and Lord Chancellor to lead the government in his absence. Now enthroned, Richard seems to have embraced fine clothing and jewellery befitting his status. And it is Richard's protégé, Bishop Thomas Langton, no less, who reports 'sensual pleasures hold sway to an increasing extent' on the royal progress post-coronation.

Buckingham and Norfolk both remained in London to acquaint themselves with some of the outstanding matters pertaining to their new responsibilities and issue appropriate instructions. For Norfolk, continual interruption of trade in the Channel by French privateers was the subject of persistent lobbying by London merchants. After attending to such matters, he could then remove to his East Anglian bailiwick. Similarly, for Buckingham there were briefings to be taken and orders given for the many areas of state over which he now exercised authority. He would then take a leisurely route back to Brecon after meeting up with Richard at Gloucester. This plan provided him with the ideal excuse of not having to attend Richard's meeting with Katherine Neville, Lady Hastings. Richard will shamelessly present Lady Hastings – who happens to be Richard's first cousin – with a 'pardon' so that her late husband would not be attainted and her estate and possessions secured for herself and her children. He was also far from displeased at missing Richard's stay in Oxford, where the entertainment was listening to philosophical discourses in Latin.

While Richard was sitting in Magdalen College as the guest of William Waynflete listening to learned disputations, an attempt was being made to rescue the princes from the Tower. About fifty Londoners had tried to distract the guards at the Tower by lighting fires nearby, but they were unsuccessful and soon dispersed and the leaders placed in custody. John Smith, groom of the stirrup for Edward IV, Stephen Ireland, wardrobe of the Tower, Robert Rush, sergeant, and William Davy, pardoner, were held for more than six months – presumably questioned under torture – and executed on Tower Green on 26 February 1484.[4]

Of greater concern perhaps, with Bishop Lionel Woodville emulating the Marquess of Dorset in slipping away from sanctuary, came the contemporaneous revelation of a plot for the princesses to break out of Westminster Abbey and flee abroad. This reflects the beginning of rumours that the princes may either be dead or, if not, that their lives are in great peril. If the princesses could find suitable husbands in Europe, then there would still be the possibility of providing a future monarch of Edward IV's bloodline. Aware of such risks, a cordon was immediately placed around the Abbey precincts under the supervision of John Nesfield.

Content that all was as well as could be, Buckingham decided to set out for home via Gloucester. Such is the information filtering through to Morton through letters and visitors. Obviously, the laxity of his confinement still means he is monitored, but seriously secret communications are possible.

Buckingham arrives at Brecon Castle at the beginning of August but does not visit Morton until mid-morning the following day. They establish a rapport. Morton is circumspect, half-suspecting a trap, trying to determine the line of interrogation and the possible outcomes he faces. But as they talk, it dawns on him that Buckingham is anxious and troubled when he should be confident and dominant. Truth begins to emerge.

Buckingham confesses that, like Hastings, his earlier actions were fuelled by a detestation of the Woodvilles – even including a deep dislike for his wife. But now circumstances have so changed that he has to apologise to her for past behaviour.

When he arrived at Gloucester to advise Richard of the insurrection in London and the plot for the daughters of King Edward to flee from sanctuary, he found that Richard already had word of these and had written to Bishop Russell from Minster Lovell, Oxford, the day before, calling on him to take matters in hand. The impression was that his concern was more for the latter than the former. And the reason for this was that steps were already being taken to ensure that the princesses were the last of Edward IV's blood alive. All deposed kings have been disposed of kings – Edward II, Richard II, Henry VI. This deposition would be no different.

Richard's man on his way to London was Sir James Tyrell, riding with one of his henchmen, John Dighton.[5] They arrive at the Tower after dark and are admitted through the main gates by Robert Brackenbury, the Constable, who then, at their request, passes them into the hands of Miles Forrest who will lead them to the Princes' chambers. They all know each other well enough: Brackenbury's family own the manor of Saleby, close to Barnard Castle (one of the towers there is named Brackenbury's Tower) and he had worked from there as Treasurer of Richard's estate, coming into contact with Forrest, the Keeper of the Wardrobe then, and now in his role as a guard-cum-servant to the Princes. Tyrell is also known to him from working for Richard, accompanying him on his journey from the north to London after Edward's death.

Once in the Princes' apartment they tread quietly, Forrest and Dighton gathering up a spare feather mattress kept ready for the deed and then pressing it onto the sleeping boys until their struggles and muffled cries cease. Tyrell checks that they are indeed dead and the bodies are buried within the building, but Richard later has Brackenbury raise them up and have them buried with proper rites, but in a secret location away from the Tower. Nothing more will be said of this murder or indeed of them.

Back in Brecon, Buckingham's remorse continues, it never having been his intent to have any responsibility in the death of two children, his own nephews. He and Richard had their first serious disagreement but it was not an argument he could win. The deed was being done as they spoke.

It must be said of course that there is no more hotly debated event in English history than the fate of the Princes in the Tower. Perhaps the position is best put by Annette Carson, author of *Richard III: The Maligned King*:

> Generally speaking it's uncontested that there is no tangible evidence that Richard was guilty of the various crimes (particularly the murders) laid at his door. Nevertheless, he was a human being who wielded enormous power, made mistakes, sometimes acted rashly and ill-advisedly, and inevitably made enemies. Whether some of his actions were 'illegal' is a difficult question, and one that arises in relation to any medieval king.

Tempers eased somewhat and the atmosphere cleared. Seemingly to change the subject, Richard began to engage Buckingham in a letter he was constructing to James Fitzgerald, Earl of Desmond, to accompany some frankly over-the-top gifts he was sending. Key in his thoughts was to emphasise their common tie – namely that those persons behind the murder of Desmond's father were the same as those who were behind the murder of Clarence, by which he meant Queen Elizabeth Woodville.

It was twenty years ago, and an oft-repeated tale. Thomas Fitzgerald, Earl of Desmond, was Deputy Lieutenant of Ireland, and came over to England to attend Queen Elizabeth's coronation. It was put about that when out hunting with Edward, Desmond was asked by the King what he thought of his wife. Ever one to speak plainly, Desmond replied that it was obvious that Edward had married for love and not for political gain as she was not the daughter of a duke or earl. When this got back to Elizabeth it was spun as if it were a slur on her and her family and so – it is said – she decided to have him killed should the opportunity arise. In fact, opportunity did arise when Desmond was displaced in his role by John Tiptoft, Earl of Worcester, 'the Butcher of England'. Tiptoft had him executed on dubious charges and also brought about the murder of two of Desmond's children. It was said at the time that Desmond may have been plotting the murder of Tiptoft or indeed assuming the crown of Ireland. He also had a viperish enemy in the Bishop of Meath, a man reputedly as vicious as Tiptoft himself. For his deeds, Tiptoft continued to find favour with Edward.

Richard's letter promised Desmond that he would take every opportunity to prosecute the guilty parties for both crimes. It was evident that Clarence still weighed heavily on Richard's mind and that, as it was Buckingham who passed sentence on him, his final intentions towards Duke Henry seemed frighteningly clear.

Morton could see an opening to turn Buckingham to revolt. They hypothesised. If Richard was not on the throne, who could be? Who was there who could command sufficient support to see Richard removed?

There is Edward, Earl of Warwick. He is, of course, barred from the throne by his father's attainder – although that could be reversed. But he is only eight years old and is reputed to be somewhat slow-witted. It would seem unlikely that men would rally to his cause. There is then Buckingham's own claim to the throne. On his paternal side he is in direct line from Thomas of Woodstock, youngest son of Edward III, but it is through his daughter Anne. On the maternal side, his lineage is from John of Gaunt's Beaufort line. So the claim is strong, but – being already married – it cannot become any stronger than it is. And would he have sufficient military support within the country to succeed? But it appears essential that he does act. There are already stirrings in the country against Richard. Should he no longer be king, for whatever reason, Buckingham would be at risk by his association with him. If he does nothing and Richard eventually turns against him, then it will be too late.

There is another option. One by which Buckingham would retain his present status but in safety. This other option is Henry Tudor, who is attracting attention from the dissenting and dispossessed. The real claim though is with the Princess Elizabeth, Edward's eldest surviving child. If she was to be wed to the Earl of Richmond then that would prove a highly attractive focal point for winnable insurrection, and unite Yorkists, Lancastrians, and the Woodvilles. Would such a situation leave Buckingham comfortable?

Another plot is revealed around 13 August at Maxey, Northamptonshire, only sixty-five miles and forty-five miles from Richard's next halts on his Progression, Coventry and Leicester respectively. The leader is John Welles, half-brother to Margaret Beaufort and uncle to Henry Tudor. He swiftly flees to Brittany and Henry's growing assembly.

Morton senses Buckingham is a man who takes pleasure in intrigue, and he draws him in to a series of possible planned scenarios. The outcome is that since it is the restoration of Edward V which will motivate most dissidents, they will keep the knowledge of the princes' fate to themselves for as long as possible in order to maximise the movement. As that news becomes more widespread, then Buckingham will declare as captain of the *putsch* against Richard in favour of Henry and Elizabeth.

On Morton's advice, Buckingham writes to his aunt, 50-year-old Margaret Beaufort, who is at Lathom House, Lancashire asking her to send her receiver-general Reginald Bray for talks.[6] It will take at least a week for any response from Margaret or Bray, so Morton uses the time to brief his host on the state of unrest in the southern and midland counties. While they discuss such things, the need for secrecy is reinforced by receipt of an order issued by Richard on the 17th for Buckingham to head a Commission into treasons in London, Surrey, Sussex, Kent and the Home Counties generally. It is clear that Richard's spies and his personal political antennae sense an attempt at a counter-coup is brewing, and it goes without saying that Richard's order is not one that is going to be obeyed. Buckingham receives more than a couple of commands to attend Richard with progress on this, but he pleads illness each time.

Key among the plotters is, of course Margaret Beaufort; motivated first by the restitution of her son's standing in England and then by a drive to see him on the throne. There are few who know Henry Tudor and any hope he has rests with the arrangement of a marriage to Princess Elizabeth. There is a line of communication on this between Margaret, from the Stanley's London home, and Queen Elizabeth: they are both served by the physician Lewis Caerleon who John Nesfield allows to pass and repass through the cordon surrounding Westminster Abbey.[7] The two mothers come to an agreement on the plan, indicating Elizabeth's acceptance that her sons are no longer alive.

The chain linking these rebels together is, more often than not, their former associations with the household and service of Edward IV. Some indeed are Lancastrians, but it is their ties to Edward and his son and their reaction to the murder of Hastings and the Woodvilles which drive them. They also tend to be of the gentry class and have little support within the nobility.

In the south-east, leaders such as Sir George Brown of Betchworth in Surrey are found. Brown's father was a Lancastrian who had been executed by Warwick for his role in defending the Tower. His mother remarried to Sir Thomas Vaughan, which swung the young George to a Yorkist position. He was a Sheriff of Kent, MP, and carried the banner of St George at King Edward's funeral, and then his stepfather was executed, or murdered depending on your point of view, by Richard. Other major influencers in the south-east were Sir John Fogge of Ashford, Kent; Nicholas Gaynesford of Carshalton, Surrey; Sir Thomas Bourchier of Barnes; Thomas Fiennes and Sir William Haute.[8]

In Wiltshire, John Cheyne, a giant of a man at 6 foot 8 inches, is a leading dissident living on his estate outside Salisbury. Onetime Esquire of the Body to Queen Elizabeth, he had been promoted to Master of the Horse only to lose that position in June 1483 to Sir James Tyrell. No less influential among the active opposition was Lionel, Bishop of Salisbury, who was agitating from his diocese alongside his brother Sir Richard Woodville and his nephew Thomas Grey, the Marquess of Dorset. With them stood Sir Roger Tocotes; Sir William Norreys; Sir William Berkeley of Beverstone, Gloucester; Sir Giles Daubeney of Barrington Court, Somerset; Sir Walter Hungerford of Wiltshire and Sir William Stonor.[9]

Further west, unrest orbited around Sir Thomas St Leger; Sir Robert Willoughby: Sir Thomas Arundell and Richard Nanfan.[10] And there were the Courtenays: Sir Edward of Boconnoc, and Peter, Bishop of Exeter. Most of the rest of the Courteney family supported Richard, though.

And so, as the conspirators are knitted together by Morton, Bray, and others, a date of 18 October, St Luke's Day, is set for a united uprising. Details are finalised with a meeting at Buckingham's Thornbury Castle on September 22 at which Lionel Woodville attends, ostensibly to call on his sister, Buckingham's wife. But the plot starts to unravel.

The likelihood of counter-coup was front and centre of Richard's mind. Cementing his role as sovereign was a prime reason for his speedy start to his Royal Progress, and the news which followed his departure from London was a disappointment but did not come as a complete surprise. Reports began to filter in from his spy network of wider discontent. He decided to continue with his Progress giving as relaxed an appearance as possible in the hope of drawing out all opposition, rather than send it deep underground. If there was a misstep in the planning of the Progress it was that he made no attempt at projecting his desired image and generosity in the south and south-west counties but directed his efforts to consolidating his northern power base. From Gloucester, he had visited Clarence's tomb at Tewkesbury, then moved north to Warwick where he was joined by Queen Anne on 8 August, progressing through Coventry, Leicester, Nottingham, and Doncaster, to reach Pontefract on 27 August.

Richard and Anne were joined by their 9-year-old son Edward at Pontefract from where they would go on to York for Edward's investiture as Prince of Wales. The boy had a history of illness and was too sickly to ride the thirty-mile journey, having to be conveyed in a cart. They arrived in York on the 29th to a great welcome under the direction of Richard's principal secretary John Kendal, especially lavish to impress the southern contingent in the travelling court. Some 13,000 White Boar badges were distributed for the population to show support for their king and champion. The only fly in the ointment was Archbishop Rotherham, who refused to indulge in the spectacle, but that did not deter Richard from spending three weeks in the city, eventually starting out on a leisurely return to London on 20 September.

Across the Channel, the Tudors are anxiously awaiting the assembly of their force which will participate in the rising, landing on the south coast. Henry's mother had sent him substantial cash, raised in part by loans from the City, strongly advising him to make his return via Wales and seize the throne together with Princess Elizabeth for his wife. Cash and messages were forwarded by two different routes to Brittany using her servants Hugh Conway and Sir John Rame, who surprised each other by arriving on exactly the same day.[11] Buoyed up by this, Henry approached Duke Francis for support and, with Louis of France having died at the very end of August, he found him in a benevolent mood. So benevolent that fifteen ships were being fitted out to take a 5,000-strong invasion force. The final seal on the enterprise comes in the first week of October with a letter from the Duke of Buckingham dated 29 September formally calling on Henry to take up the crown and pledging support from himself and his army.

Richard's spies are well placed and well informed. They have spotted the movements of Lionel Woodville and have recorded meetings between him and Robert Morton. They have not only monitored the meeting of Lionel and Buckingham but have intercepted a letter from the Bishop to the Abbot of Hyde directly implicating Buckingham as part of the conspiracy. The reaction is swift. Robert Morton is removed from his position as Master of the Rolls on 22 September. Although there is no direct proof against him he is guilty by association and his access to the mechanics of government is denied. On September 23 all of the Bishop's temporal assets are confiscated. Then, on the 29th, Buckingham formally declares and throws his hat into the ring. Although half-expecting this, it is still an event which shocks Richard deeply when he learns of it on 11 October. Jolted into realising the seriousness of the situation, he sends immediately to Chancellor Russell for the Great Seal, which is delivered to him on the 18th at Grantham. As he reaches Lincoln on his journey south, a call to muster arms is issued, his supporters to meet him at Leicester. But this is a revolt which will be resolved without major battles.

The rising begins in Kent, where else, on 10 October, a week before the appointed day and the start is delayed the further west travelled due to unprecedented torrential rainstorms which cause huge areas of flooding. This makes it incredibly difficult for the rebel troops to muster, draw in sufficient supplies, and then march and manoeuvre. So hampered, Wiltshire doesn't fire up until the 23rd, and for the south-west it is the beginning of November.

Morton is seriously worried. The revolt in the south-east has ground to a halt and is collapsing. The Duke of Norfolk has efficiently fortified

London and has also secured Gravesend to prevent passage across the Thames.

Buckingham's position is dissolving by the day, his army and supplies sodden and his planned route to join the Courtenays from the west made impossible by the impassable rivers Severn and Wye. But the problems are more fundamental than that. Buckingham is not liked in Wales and has a hard time in raising the insufficient number of troops that he has, and they are deserting in droves as the hardships of the campaign increase.

Moreover, Buckingham and their cause have failed to attract any of the nobility who, at best, are hanging back to see what happens, as their primary concern is the safety and integrity of their lands and standing. Richard has been particularly clever in keeping Lord Stanley within his Progress, thus tying his hands. Stanley's son, Lord Strange, raises an army of some 10,000 men but does not commit to one side or the other.

Buckingham's men are harassed by guerrilla bands of the Vaughan affinity who have no time for Henry's cause, Jasper Tudor being the man who executed Thomas Vaughan's father back in 1471. Once they are sure Brecon Castle has been left, they fall back and sack it. Meanwhile, Sir Humphrey Stafford of Grafton Manor (no relation to the Buckingham Staffords) was destroying bridges and ferries from Wales into England.

The march strikes through the Forest of Dean seeking a way across the Severn and out of the flood zones, then looking to turn north-east into the western midlands. Much depleted, they reach Woebley in Herefordshire. Still it rains.

News arrived at their camp. Richard had made a proclamation accusing the rebels of sedition and making an extraordinary attack on the immorality and lewdness of many of the leaders of the uprising. In particular, rewards were offered for the capture of Buckingham, Bishop Lionel Woodville, and Bishop John Morton. Each commanded a price of 1,000 marks and land producing £100. There would be no joining of forces with the Courtenays and the west country men, nor, it would seem, with troops under Henry Tudor. The game was up.

25

Recovery and Revenge

A leather flagon of mulled cider kept Morton company as he read again through a sheaf of letters and reports sent to him from England. The winter daylight offered limited hours for comfortable reading and, now in his mid-sixties, he avoided reading by candlelight as much as possible for fear of straining his weakening eyesight further. He had fled to Flanders when it was clear there was no hope for the revolt, riding hard and fast across the width of the country, avoiding towns and the larger villages, until he reached Ely. With him in his escape were John Halwell, Edward Poynings, and Christopher Urswick. To have stayed would have meant execution: his holy orders would not have saved him this time. At Ely he had gathered some clothing, books and other comforts, and friends had provided him with funds to pay for his passage across the water and establish himself, if frugally, at Louvain. Here he intended to continue studying philosophy, and to help his thin resources by providing some tuition – but also to conspire and coordinate dissent in Richard's England.

Piecing things together produces a handbook on how not to run a revolution. The multiple gathering points were just that: gathering points. They had no immediate objective, nor did they form up into a formidable army or front. Richard moved his force down from Leicester to Salisbury where he expected to take on the Woodvilles, except that they and their Wiltshire colleagues had fled. Meanwhile, the offer of a reward had produced success in triggering the capture of Buckingham, who had been delivered up from his Shropshire hiding place in Wem by Ralph Bannaster, one of his own men. Brought down to Salisbury, Buckingham was refused an audience with Richard, tried for treason by Sir Ralph Ashton on November 1, and beheaded in the Market Square outside the Blue Boar Inn the next day.[1] His right arm was also sawn off, further symbolising his treachery.

For the west country, the Courtenays proclaimed Henry as king at Exeter, but in the face of Richard's march on the city, which he reached on 8 November, they fled into Cornwall where they again proclaimed Henry at Bodmin. Richard's brother-in-law Sir Thomas St Leger was captured and executed at Exeter, despite offering substantial sums for a pardon. Those who had fled into Cornwall had gone to Brittany by Christmas.

Morton quickly heard of Henry's failure. The Tudors had attempted to put to sea to make landfall by 18 October, but the storms which devastated the Severn and Wye were equally ruthless in the Channel and their fleet could not emerge from harbour. At the very end of the month, they were finally able to emerge from Paimpol's harbour, but only Henry's ship and one other would sight the Dorset coast, the rest were scattered up the Channel and had to fight their way back to Brittany or Normandy. The cliffs and shores of Poole were well guarded, Richard having posted troops on his route to Exeter via Bridport and tacking down to Plymouth they discovered they were too late and that Buckingham was dead. It was a difficult and miserable return to Brittany. When they eventually got back to Nantes, an understanding Francis provided a 10,000-crown loan to keep them and a now rapidly expanding community of exiles in some degree of comfort.

Although the battle had been lost (or not even joined), the cause was far from buried. The English coast was anything but secure. Few rebel leaders were caught and executed, some sought and received pardons. Of 104 who were attainted by parliament, about a third received a pardon. None of those pardoned were restored to their administrative roles in their own communities however, which left many still uncertain in their loyalty. Most secured passage across the Channel to congregate in Brittany around Henry Tudor. In general, it was clear that while many did not rise for Buckingham, neither did they rise for Richard far outside his close circle.

Despite the apparent victory, Richard was palpably feeling insecure. He was back in London by 25 November, cheering himself and his supporters by planning magnificent celebrations for Christmas and also planning his first parliament, how to replace the collapse in the administration of southern and western counties, and how to build Fortress England.

When parliament assembles in January 1484, great care is taken to stage-manage the event so that there is no dissent and Richard's business agenda is dealt with promptly and efficiently. This is not a forum for debate but a legislature dictated to by fear. The Speaker of the Commons is declared to be Sir William Catesby rather than chosen by the House.

Richard's title and right to the throne is set out by Act of Parliament, *Titulus Regius*, which broadly mirrors – with a few extra details – the speech of Dr Shaa and the plea from the ad-hoc assembly of Lords and commoners made requesting Richard take up the throne the previous June. That final declaration destroys the myth of Richard's love and respect for his brother.

Parliament also makes lawful all the unlawful distributions by Richard of property owned by the rebels, and then passes Acts of Attainder against them. To ensure that all understand the fundamentals to Richard's regime, these Acts of Parliament become the first to be published in English.

One exception to the usual punishment handed out to traitors is Margaret Beaufort. Her life is not forfeited but her property is passed to her husband, Thomas, Lord Stanley. However, it is a life interest only, so in theory it would revert to the Crown rather than be inherited. This action reflects how much Richard needs stability and support from the peers of the realm. The military strength of Stanley and his son, Lord Strange, together with their capacity for sitting on the fence, means he cannot risk offending them. That said, Richard should know from his own experience with the Westmoreland estates that life interests do not cement loyalty.

Richard now sets about rewarding his supporters, placing them in the offices vacated by the rebel leaders. But it isn't just about rewards, necessity also requiring the replacement of over forty per cent of principal officials in the south. The effect is a plantation of northerners into southern communities, taking over roles such as sheriffs or constables, and leading to local resentment.

In Wales, Sir William Herbert, who had been forced to surrender his title of Earl of Pembroke to Edward, Prince of Wales in 1479 for the lesser Earl of Huntingdon, was able to regain it, becoming Chief Justice of South Wales. He also took Richard's illegitimate daughter Katherine as his second wife.

The Duke of Buckingham had wielded extraordinary and concentrated power in Wales, including custody of all the royal castles. Now, this power would be distributed to several key men. Sir Richard Huddleston was created Constable of Beaumaris Castle on Anglesey, and Thomas Tunstall became Constable of Conway Castle.[2]

Another key player in Wales was Rhys ap Thomas, to whom Richard gave an annuity of 400 marks for life. This was not for anything that Rhys had actually done but was reward for not joining Buckingham's revolt. Rhys had not shunned the revolt out of any admiration or affinity to Richard but simply because he had an unrelenting hatred of Buckingham. As it was, Rhys was more a likely supporter of Henry Tudor, as he also held a deep-seated grudge against Sir William Herbert, whose men had killed his father Thomas ap Gruffydd.

Thornbury in Gloucester, an estate particularly favoured by Buckingham, was given to Sir William Stanley, and the lands of Sir John Fogge and Sir George Brown were passed to Sir Ralph Ashton.

The greatest rewards went to Sir Richard Ratcliffe, in particular the Courtenays' Devon estates.[3] Sir Robert Brackenbury also gained substantially from the manors in Kent, Surrey, and Sussex of Earl Rivers, the Cheyne family, and Walter Roberts, together with Buckingham's property in Essex and Kent.[4]

Across the Channel, Morton was delighted to be joined by his nephew, Robert, who had decided the risks to his freedom were too great to remain in England since losing his position of Master of the Rolls to Thomas Barowe.[5] Robert is able to impart that despite, or because of, Richard's overt display of patronage and opulence exceeding that of Edward, coupled by a reluctance to increase taxation or accept gifts at this time, his Treasury was actually under great stress. His necessity to increase defences would soon be adding to that stress. For the moment he is selling off some of the treasure accumulated by Edward together with some of the chattels raided from those under attainder. Although it was planned for his parliament to outlaw 'benevolences', it would only be a matter of time before he had to reintroduce them by another name.

Morton's position at home is no different to other absconders. In December 1483, receivers and bailiffs are appointed in respect of all his estates and receipts are being distributed already. Being prior to the sitting of parliament, this action is illegal. In January 1484, the temporalities of Ely are seized. This prompts the start of legal action by Henry Edyall (chaplain of Ely), William Timperley (the Bishop's receiver), and Ralph Green for an injunction to halt these proceedings, which is, surprisingly, granted at the King's Bench on 29 May.

In Brittany, Henry Tudor finds he is now at the centre of an even larger community of exiles who are looking to him for leadership and purpose. Some 500 have fled from England, one of whom is Richard Morton who took a stand with the men of Dorset and, previously on the bench and a controller of customs at Poole, is now a named rebel. But most of them hardly know Henry at all: the majority are Yorkists – that is, Edwardian Yorkists versus Ricardian Yorkists – and even those from Lancastrian families or affinities have little or no first-hand knowledge of his character or intellect. His claim on the throne is very weak and is only going to find acceptance if he bonds himself to the Yorkist family by wedding Elizabeth of York, who, after all, is the person with the best lineage to Edward IV. There were many reasons why 'Buckingham's Rebellion' had failed, but it had to be recognised that apathy was one of them and a re-focus on the potential of new leadership needed to be communicated. And so, at Rennes cathedral Henry gathers all his co-rebels around him on Christmas Day, 1483, and swears an oath that he will marry Elizabeth and take the English throne from Richard, holding out the hope of unity, justice, and prosperity. In response, all those present swear an oath of allegiance promising to uphold his claim against all others. There is nothing new in politics, then or now.

Negotiation, cajoling, bullying, whatever you want to call it, has been going on relentlessly with Queen Elizabeth – or Dame Elizabeth Grey as the government would have her named – to get her to leave sanctuary. It is an embarrassment to Richard's standing, and he is aware of the disdain in which he is held both at home and, more especially, abroad. The French will not even reply to his letters seeking a rapprochement, regarding him as 'inhuman'. He senses a mounting need to turn real and potential enemies into friends and, if he is to get the die-hards to die, then a better image and better bonding is needed within Europe.

From Elizabeth's perspective, the failure of the 1483 uprising has crushed any optimism for a change in regime within the foreseeable future. The psychological pressures as well as the economic ones on her daughters' welfare and that of her staff and supporters is becoming unbearable, and the decimation of her family tells her that the Woodville cause is lost. Her present does not indicate a tolerable or fair future.

And so these Westminster talks start to take on a mutual seriousness. For Richard, if he can isolate and exterminate Henry Tudor then there will be no figurehead around which the exiles and dissenters can gather, and if he achieves this he is willing to be unprecedently forgiving. For Elizabeth, her concern is the safety and well-being of her daughters.

On 1 March, Elizabeth and her five daughters emerged from the sanctuary of Westminster Abbey after a ten-month residence. Richard, before the lords spiritual and temporal and the Mayor and aldermen of London, took a public oath guaranteeing the safety of Elizabeth's daughters, undertaking to support them, place them in good homes, and arrange good marriages for them. He then swears to pay 700 marks a year for life for the upkeep of Elizabeth, who is to be protected and served by John Nesfield, the same knight who had been supervising the security cordon around the Abbey during her occupation. The stipend awarded to Elizabeth was certainly generous, just as was Richard's treatment of Lady Katherine Hastings. His level of generosity seemed to mirror his level of guilt: the displaced Duchess of Buckingham received an income of only 200 marks (after the Duke of York's attainder, Richard's mother Cecily was awarded 1,000 marks a year by Henry VI). Nor was he particularly generous in compensating the widow of the 12th Earl of Oxford (the sister of Hasting's widow), who was compelled to surrender her property to him in 1475.

The promises, the commitment, and the reasons for Richard's new politics were something that Elizabeth could buy into. So much so that she urged the Marquess of Dorset to return to England with the hope of regaining his lands and title. It was a convincing plea; a homesick Dorset took flight from Henry's court in Brittany. Henry was well aware that if Dorset did return to enjoy reinstatement (whether temporary or not) his example would seriously undermine the resolve of his supporters. So a speedy squad is sent to bring him back to Brittany. Luckily, he is intercepted at Compiègne, between Paris and the French coast and 'persuaded' to abandon his trip.

With spring weather came the likelihood of another attempt at invasion, and for a base central to all likely landing points Richard moved his court to Nottingham. But in mid-April came news from Middleham that Edward, his son, had died. The grief of the parents was inconsolable and likely aggravated the tuberculosis from which Anne would die within the year.

Through the mists of that grief it is clear that actions are necessary. Without an heir apparent, Richard's position is made so much more precarious. Pending the creation of another son, after all he is only thirty-two years old and Anne twenty-eight, the candidate with the strongest claim on paper is probably Edward, Earl of Warwick, son of Clarence. But that claim is not helped by the attainder against his father, which bars him from the crown, the fact that he is only ten years old, and that he is apparently of impaired intelligence. The preferred candidate is seen as twenty-year-old John de la Pole, Earl of Lincoln, the son of Richard's sister Anne. Appointing Lincoln as Lieutenant of Ireland on 21 August is an affirmation of his expectations.

But the threat of invasion required practical actions. Richard reintroduced, but on a grand scale, a network of relay posts such as Edward had devised during the Scottish campaign, such that messages could be transported 200 miles in two days. Reacting swiftly to danger was his Plan A.

Keeping the Channel free was the next concern and he took action to ensure that any privateers or potentially hostile ships were swiftly dealt with, whether French, Breton, Scots, or West Country pirates. Success was not easy. In one action against French ships off Scarborough, John Nesfield and Sir Thomas Everingham were lost. Generally, offensive action at sea could not be maintained for long, particularly against Brittany, which risked interrupting trade and therefore the support of London and its money. Moreover, Richard required a rapport with Brittany if there was to be any hope of extraditing Henry. On land, commissions of array were issued to ensure archers and men-at-arms were ready if called upon and the arsenal of artillery was enlarged at the Tower.

England was on a war footing.

The key for Richard was of course to get hold of Henry Tudor, and the late spring of 1484 provided an opportunity. France just would not have any truck with Richard, not least because the English Crown refused to give up the pretence of a claim to the French Crown. Of course, in his precarious political position it was impossible for Richard to even think of accepting what would have been a national humiliation. But one way to get France to the negotiating table could be by forgiving Brittany for its support of the Buckingham Plot and succouring Henry Tudor and entering into an alliance with Duke Francis. The opening arose when Francis suffered a temporary mental breakdown requiring a period of rest and recuperation. This prompted the Breton chief minister, Pierre Landois, to seek an understanding with the Ricardian regime.[6] Negotiations for an alliance were conducted on both sides of the Channel and eventually a year-long truce was agreed, with the promise of military support from English archers if France should attack Brittany. In fact, this alliance with Brittany further entrenched the French position.

Behind the scenes additional talks were being conducted, with the offer of considerable funds if Landois would deliver up Henry. In September, William Catesby had travelled to Vannes, the home of the Tudor exiles, getting ready to take Henry into custody while a Breton embassy under the Bishop of St Pol de Leon was in London finalising the agreement. Word of what was happening leaked out to Morton's network and details of the plot reached him in Flanders. With him at the time was Christopher Urswick, who was immediately despatched to Vannes to warn Henry.[7] They had been anticipating danger and sent Urswick to the court of Charles VIII with a request for asylum – rapidly confirmed, such was the eagerness to cause Richard displeasure.

The Tudors put into action their escape. With permission, Jasper and a small band of nobles left Vannes for Rennes where Francis was recuperating, ostensibly to wish him well and pay their respects to their friend and benefactor, leaving Henry behind to allay suspicion. When they neared the border with Anjou, they whipped their horses to a gallop and crossed into France. A few nights later, disguised as a groom, Henry with half a dozen companions made a straight run for the border, crossing into France barely an hour ahead of Landois's men who were in pursuit.

The five hundred or so rebels back in Brittany were not left leaderless for too long. Duke Francis soon recovered enough to give Landois a stern lecture and, to emphasise his sense of valour as well as his sympathy towards Henry, he advanced sufficient funds for all the exiled Englishmen to join Henry, also providing them a guard to the border. In truth, he was annoyed as he had lost his one bargaining tool for English support against France: on the other hand, he was now free of a huge and growing number of English exiles whose maintenance he had to pay for.

In France, Henry had been well received by Charles VIII and his court at Langeais on the Loire and where they were soon joined by the French Council. Charles was only fourteen years old and the government was run under the regency of his sister Anne and her husband Peter, Duke of Bourbon.[8] So well did they all get on or, looked at another way, so much was Richard a common enemy, that the French agreed to underwrite the cost of invading England and on 17 November provided Henry with 3,000 livres to help assemble troops.[9]

The escape of the Tudors was a great blow to Richard and politically he felt a need to give public demonstration of his strength and intent. He decided to use forty-two-year-old John de Vere, Earl of Oxford, as an example and deterrent. De Vere had been languishing for ten years in Hammes Castle since his failure to incite revolt which had culminated in his capture of St Michael's Mount collapsing under siege. Now, yeoman of the guard William Bolton arrived in Calais with orders from Richard to bring him back to England. Sir James Blount, Lieutenant of Hammes and Oxford's jailer, had become disillusioned, however, following Richard's usurpation of the throne and – with a little nudge from Thomas, Lord Stanley – following news of Henry's reception in France, fled Hammes with Oxford to Paris. Alongside them, and aiding the escape, was the Porter of Hammes, a nephew of Morton's old colleague and mentor Sir John Fortescue. This was not only a blow to Richard's immediate plans but would have a significant effect on the outcome of his showdown with Henry the following year.

Although Oxford's noble pedigree made him a fine addition to Henry's cause, his reputation as a military commander was not particularly commanding. His courage was undoubted, but his competence was in the balance. His next step tipped the scales very much in his favour. Hammes had been left under the command of James Blount's wife and was now under siege by the men of Calais. Oxford immediately returned to Hammes and after his harassment of the besiegers an agreement was reached allowing the whole garrison to leave unharmed. They marched to Paris to join Henry with Oxford at their head, who received a hero's welcome.

That is not so say that Richard was having no successes at all. With much pomp and ceremony, negotiations with Scotland for a three-year truce were concluded at Nottingham in September. It is difficult to see much sincerity behind these negotiations though. If he didn't have so many other concerns, Richard would likely have favoured a military campaign against an enemy over which he had had some tangible victories. And the Scots looked to continue the development of a relationship with France and, via France, supplied a contingent of soldiers under the command of Sir Alexander Bruce of Earlshall to Henry Tudor for his invasion.

There were intermittent local insurgencies, malicious rumours circulated, and an increasing level of espionage, all of which served to deepen the gloom engulfing Richard since his son's death. He was constantly trying to raise his standing in the eyes of the people by his endowments and foundations in religion and education, but the impact tended to be localised. Aware of a rising and widespread cult of the 'saintly' Henry VI, Richard decided to align himself with the slain monarch. Doing this says a lot about his state of mind and his political misjudgement, as he was thereby reinforcing his distance from Edward and any claim of brotherly love or respect. Regardless, in August Richard staged, with all the publicity he could create, the reburial of Henry, his remains moved from Chertsey Abbey to St George's Chapel, Windsor. This was a desperate, hypocritical show, which, with his several high moralistic, virtue-expounding pronouncements through the course of the year, showed up starkly against the realities of his court with its richness and extensive, exuberant entertainments.

Morton's role in handling agents and relaying messages between England and Henry's court was facilitated by his location in Flanders, which was physically easier and safer to access than Brittany or France. There had been further unrest in Kent led by men who were all at Morton's table celebrating his consecration as Bishop of Ely. In November, seditious talk is reported to the authorities in Colchester featuring men known to Morton, who quickly take a boat to Flanders without a second thought. These include Sir John Risley, Sir William Brandon, Sir William Stonor, and Brandon's sons, William and Thomas. Earlier the Sussex gentry demonstrated their discontent at Winchelsea but with the same result: a distraction, failure, and more competent and skilled fighters spilling across the Channel to Henry.

As invasion plans were developed, so secret communications increased. Contact was made, and political messages and promises conveyed, to Rhys ap Thomas in west Wales, Sir Walter Herbert in south Wales, and of course to the Stanleys. Even Henry Percy received an approach and understanding.

But the role of the spy is never secure or safe. Landowner William Collingbourne of Wiltshire had been an employee of Cecily, Duchess of York, but joined Buckingham's Revolt having lost his position to Viscount Lovell at the behest of Richard. John Turberville of Bere Regis (thereby linked to Morton's family) had introduced Collingbourne to Thomas Yate in London seeking to get messages to Henry to make good his invasion and land at Poole. Yate was apprehended in France but spared punishment and allowed to continue. Collingbourne then composed his famous verse 'The Cat, the Rat, and Lovell our Dog, who rule all England under a Hog', fixing this to the doors of St Paul's. Tracked down in the summer of 1484, Richard decided to make an example of him. Tried for treason under a notable commission of the Duke of Norfolk, the Duke of Suffolk, Earl of Nottingham, Earl of Surrey, Viscount Lovell, Viscount Lisle, Lord Stanley, and six others, Collingbourne was unsurprisingly found guilty and then hung, cut down alive, and his bowels and heart ripped from his body. The viciousness of this execution had the opposite effect to that desired and turned many away from Richard rather than generating awe and fear. Turberville was sentenced to imprisonment, managed to escape, and fought at Bosworth where he was knighted in the field.

Richard is well aware of John Morton's role in stirring and steering discontent. Not only is he a persistent thorn in his side but he is a living data file of unrest in England and the degree to which any person may be swayed from their allegiance to the Crown. Assassination might be one way of removing the problem, but better if Morton could be persuaded to switch allegiance and return home. After all, he had proven to be an unbendable servant to Edward once it was demonstrated to his satisfaction that Henry's line had run its course. And so, on 11 December, without any solicitation, Morton receives a royal pardon. Before he can assemble his thoughts on this radical turn of events, Morton learns that, as if to prepare for his homecoming, William Timperley, the bishop's receiver at Ely, has been reinstated to his original post with the authority to remove any or all of the officers previously put in place by Richard following Morton's attainder.

To make sure John fully understands what is on offer, Richard sends a special commission to Flanders, loaded with delegates known to Morton, in the hope of finally enticing him into the fold. The team include Richard Arnold and Thomas Maddys, both of Peterhouse, Cambridge. Morton had installed Arnold as Rector of Bluntisham in Hertfordshire in 1481, the parish being within the ownership of the Bishop of Ely. Maddys would become a close associate of Morton and would leave him a gold cup in his will. Others included Edward de Bolney from Sussex, and John White from Hatfield, who after the battle of Bosworth became resident at Morton's manor of East Dereham. But Morton would not be swayed by any of their arguments and succeeded in sending them home with doubts as to where they stood and messages for old colleagues. That this is no exaggeration was evidenced by the fact that on 2 August 1485 Richard issued each of these emissaries with a pardon for offences committed before 26 July.

Morton was feeling uncomfortable in Flanders, now that it was clear that Richard knew exactly where he was and, in all probability, had him under surveillance. He also had business to attend to which would be best served by visiting Rome. He set out just after Christmas with Robert Morton and Oliver King as companions. It was good timing, as Richard's men Sir James Tyrell and Sir Philip Chesnalle arrived in Flanders in January, by which time Morton had gone. The trio called first on Richard Fox, who was based in Paris. Fox, like Morton, was an ecclesiastic and lawyer, though a Cambridge man, and John was keen to make sure that he was standing with Henry. And indeed he was. He would become Henry's Keeper of the Privy Seal, Bishop of Exeter, and then Bishop of Winchester. He would become extremely important to Henry and lead all foreign negotiations, also working closely with Morton in government finance.

From Paris they travelled on to Rome where they obtained papal authority for reforms to Peterhouse, delivering on some of the things discussed with Arnold and Maddys, and also secured permission to sell some indulgences to raise money for the repair of the dykes at Ely. Morton displays a fairly consistent approach to money, in that if it is needed for a 'good' cause then it doesn't much matter how it is raised. The group's main task though, was to pave the way and satisfy all requirements and questions for a speedy papal dispensation for the marriage of Henry and Elizabeth once England had been gained. With the necessary assurances in hand that the pre-enquiries had been satisfied, Robert Morton and Oliver King departed to join Henry and the invasion force in France.

John Morton stayed on in Rome for a few months longer. He was now 68 years old and felt he was physically unable to help the invasion and did not have the stamina to flee if things went wrong. It would be a high-risk enterprise. His extended time in Rome was taken up in study and discussion, but his skills as a lawyer were also applied in the Apostolic Chancery, reviewing petitions and suits and providing reports and advice to Innocent VIII. By the beginning of September, news was getting through of Henry's invasion – though not its result – and so Morton left the Papal City, reaching Dunes and its Cistercian monastery, less than twenty miles from Calais, on 5 October.

In England, nothing now seemed to be going right for Richard. The threat of invasion receded with the approach of winter and although the pain of losing their son had not departed, it had diminished enough that on returning to London in November 1484, Richard and Anne decided to raise their spirits at Christmas and pushed the boat out with lavish displays and entertainments. Whether it was the uncertainties of the times or simply that Richard had reached a point where it was inevitable that his moral carping of the past eighteen months had come back to bite him, the jollities and japes of the celebrations attracted criticism puritanical and prurient. This was heightened when Anne and Elizabeth swapped dresses between dances, causing censorial comment that Richard intended to substitute one of them for the other.

This was possibly the last episode of gaiety in Anne's life. Already showing signs of failing health, she was avoided by Richard and in mid-March she succumbed to tuberculosis. There were rumours being spread that, anxious to secure a new heir with a new wife, Richard had helped Anne on her way with the use of poison, or by simple neglect. These rumours were not helped by the further, and more widely believed, story that Richard intended to take Elizabeth of York as his wife. She certainly had desirable and seductive attributes. Similar in looks to her mother but with red-gold hair, the 18-year-old was of medium height, and displayed and impressive decolletage according to the Portuguese ambassador. She was also intelligent, literate, and artistic. There were further rumours spreading that Richard and Elizabeth had had an incestuous, adulterous, relationship while Anne was still alive. An absence of proof would not dampen a good story and it was so widely circulated that it reached Henry's court in France. He was quite convinced of its truth and began to consult for a possible alternative Yorkist bride should the marriage take place, one prospective candidate being the sister of Sir Walter Herbert.

The emotional impact of the story on Henry was not helped by further tales that Elizabeth was actually encouraging the relationship. The stress and misgivings generated would be seen in difficulties Henry and Elizabeth would have to manage in their marriage.

No wedding with Richard took place. So alarming and widely believed was the tale that Catesby and Ratcliffe sternly informed Richard that he had to forget any thoughts or ambitions he might have in that direction, unless he wanted to bring his reign and government down. Although papal dispensations for marriage between an uncle and niece had been granted on occasion, the degree of consanguinity was so close that it was deeply frowned upon and not only by the Church but by the community at large. More important, Richard had declared Elizabeth a bastard: to rescind that would be to rescind the bastardisation of the two princes and acknowledge the legitimacy of the marriage between Edward IV and Elizabeth Woodville. That would effectively pull the rug from under the claim of Richard to be king as of right. To try to make good, Richard was compelled to attend the Hospital of St John and there publicly read a denial that he had any intention of marrying his brother's eldest daughter. Elizabeth was sent away to Sheriff Hutton. Was this to be the low point of his reign?

News of Richard's public declaration feeds back to Henry, allowing him to breathe a sigh of relief. Nonetheless, the incident spurs on the need for action. Richard is well capable of forcing marriage on Elizabeth to someone else, simply to stop Henry delivering on his promise. The attempted defection by Dorset also presses him on. If one head can be turned, then so can others.

It is now late spring. Richard knows an invasion is coming and has returned to Nottingham. He has reports of the assembly of a fleet at Harfleur and Honfleur together with the build-up of troops. But where will they land? What support will they attract? He hears Henry is now signing himself with an H or HR, signifying his claim to kingship. Richard's nervousness increases: he does not find waiting, or any inactivity, easy. His habit of biting his lower lip becomes more frequent and he is often pacing fiddling with the dagger in his belt. Totally oblivious to his own hypocrisy, he spews out ever more viperous proclamations as to the illegitimacy, lewdness, and felonious behaviour of all those who oppose him.

He takes what precautions he can. Sir George Neville takes a fleet of ships into the Channel to mount watch. Viscount Lovell supervises the muster of men on the south coast and strengthens its defences. The Duke of Norfolk guards the approaches to London as he did successfully during Buckingham's Revolt. That is not to say possible landing points other than the south coast are unconsidered, the waters of Milford Haven certainly being on the list of possibilities. However, Richard had unnecessarily antagonised Rhys ap Thomas by not only requiring a special oath from his Welsh commander but called on him to deliver his four-year-old son as a hostage. This Rhys refused to do. Although Richard took no action from the refusal, the fact that he had made the demand was enough to tip Rhys to Henry's side. Plus, of course, the promise of Lieutenancy of South Wales.

Henry receives word from Welsh lawyer Trahaearn ap Morgan reaffirming support from Rhys and from Sir John Savage with a recommendation that he lands in Wales.[10] This time he will follow the advice his mother previously gave him. With the help of Phillipe de Commines, Henry and Jasper were able to secure a loan of 40,000 livres to fund the invasion. Dorset and John Bourchier are left behind as sureties for the loan.

With about 3,000 men, 2,000 of whom are hired from Frenchmen demobbed from the Franco-Burgundian war, in a fleet of fifteen ships commanded by Philippe de Shaunde, they set sail on the first day of August.

26

Renewal

Morton spent a nervous but restful couple of weeks in the monastery of Dunes. He is well aware of Henry's triumph over Richard and he has been asked to wait for the arrival of the papal legate, Giacomo Passarella, to check his credentials, and then cross with him back to England.[1] In the meantime, there has been a preponderance of unsettling rumours, including one that Henry had died in London from the plague. However, the true nature of events was revealed in correspondence he had received from nephew Robert.

Robert is a good letter writer, once he gets past the usual introductory flourishes and flatteries: 'Beloved uncle and eminence', 'I commend myself to your eminence.' That sort of thing. He paints a wide and literate landscape with just enough personal detail.

It was fine summer weather with just a light southerly breeze for the journey to Milford Haven. Landfall was made just before dusk on 7 August and all were disembarked and in camp with guards suitably posted before nightfall. Robert Morton is pleased to note that on landing, Henry kisses the ground and recites from Psalm 43, 'Judge me, O Lord, and plead my cause.'

From Milford, Henry's army advances to Haverfordwest, the county town of Pembrokeshire, under the flags of Cadwallader's red dragon, the Cross of St George, and the dun cow of the Beauforts.[2] The ships have all departed, which commits the mercenaries to the fight. No resistance is met, but men are not exactly clamouring to join the throng. To display themselves to more potential recruits Henry therefore turns his army north towards Machynlleth. Sir Walter Herbert deliberately keeps out of the way, indicating he does not wish to come down on one side or the other.[3] But two of his captains, Richard Griffith and Evan Morgan, together with their troops, join the train.[4] Rhys ap Thomas takes a more northerly route into England to spare the countryside having to support one large army, and also to ensure no quarrelling between Welsh and French.

The two forces join up at Shrewsbury where Henry is well received, in contrast to the reception given to Buckingham less than two years ago. Sometimes it is the singer, not the song. Henry sends messages to his mother, the Stanleys, the Talbots and others but cannot wait on their replies, he has to keep moving. On the way to Stafford he is met by Sir Gilbert Talbot who joins him with about 500 men and then, on reaching the town, he finds Sir William Stanley.[5] Henry takes up an invitation to a private meeting with Thomas, Lord Stanley, his stepfather, at Atherstone about five miles away. The result is unsatisfactory.

Henry learns that Richard first heard of his landing on 11 August when he would have been somewhere between Aberystwyth and Shrewsbury. Richard was concerned that neither Rhys ap Thomas nor Herbert had kept him alerted nor had they evidently stood in Henry's way. In fact, it seemed that an enemy could move within his kingdom quite unopposed. Richard sent messages to Stanley, Norfolk, Surrey and Northumberland calling on them to meet him at Leicester. But when he left Nottingham for the rendezvous, only twenty-eight peers had answered his call: fewer than half of those available. And of these, fewer than half actually turn up to fight at Bosworth.

For a monarch who has invested so much time and energy in the north, and who seemingly regards himself as a man of the north, Richard has a foreboding of indifference if not treachery among his northern peers. Thomas, Lord Stanley is one who gives cause for concern. Ever since Hasting's execution, Richard has kept him close by appointing him Steward of the Royal Household. Eventually, Thomas obtained permission to visit home but was required to leave his son, George, Lord Strange, with Richard as hostage to his good behaviour and his return. Richard already had doubts about Thomas's brother, Sir William. As Chamberlain of North Wales should he not have intercepted Henry's progress? The situation for the Stanley family had deteriorated since that point. George had tried to escape but had been caught and under pressure confessed that he, Sir William, and Sir John Savage had been in communication with Henry. William and Savage were immediately declared traitors. Savage had escaped captivity and would prove that he was indeed a traitor by joining Henry in the next day or two.

Meanwhile, Thomas Stanley could only promise Tudor for now to stand back from any engagement between Richard's and Henry's forces. He has to consider the fate of his son and of his younger brother. Thomas had avoided returning to Richard by pleading illness with the 'sweating sickness' but is now hoping that if he and William join Richard, they will both regain favour. Henry adds to Thomas's worries by stating the obvious that his mother, Thomas's wife Margaret, is likely to lose her head if Richard wins, as this will be the second time she has supported her son. Not only that, but since Thomas undertook to keep his wife under control, failure to do so has put his head at risk, too. One way or another, the whole Stanley family's future is on a knife edge.

After the battle, Robert learns that Northumberland is under suspicion. On 16 August, Richard received a deputation under Sir John Spooner from the city of York asking for instructions on whether to raise men, as they had heard of an invasion but had had no official word to commission troops.[6] This was worrying, as Henry Percy was Commissioner of Array for the East Riding. How many others had he failed to call on? On whose side would he stand? The York delegates went home to raise eighty men, but they were too late to get to the fight.

After the disappointing meeting with the Stanleys, spirits are raised somewhat by Henry's army being joined by Sir Walter Hungerford and Sir Thomas Bourchier, who had escaped from Sir Robert Brackenbury after being arrested by him and were being conveyed to join Richard's forces.[7] They are soon followed by Sir John Savage, Sir Brian Sanford, and Sir Simon Digby.[8] Henry's army camps for the night at White Moors, near Market Bosworth. Richard's army, joined by Norfolk, Surrey, and Northumberland, have moved to Sutton Cheney, just three miles away.

Robert Morton expressed particular pleasure in reporting that on the morning of 22 August he and Bishop Peter Courtenay led the traditional pre-battle Mass for Henry's men in the field. The other principal clerics, Richard Fox and Christopher Urswick, decided not to join them on the battlefield. Robert later learned that the enemy were denied a Mass, and the opportunity to confess their sins, before the fight, Richard declaring that if God was on their side they needed no last supplications. If he was not, such prayers would be simply an idle blasphemy. For an allegedly pious king, this was a blasphemy in itself, thought Morton.

Henry moves his men forward, the sun at their backs. Robert reports that Richard's men are on elevated ground known as Ambien Hill.[9] Henry protects his position with a large area of marsh on his right. His vanguard is led by Oxford with most of the archers. To Oxford's right, providing protection for the archers, are mounted men under the command of Gilbert Talbot. The left wing is led by Sir John Savage. Henry is with a small reserve, which includes Thomas Stanley, Sir William Brandon, and Sir John Chaney.

Overlooking them, Richard is moving along his army, which he has spread out along the ridge of Ambien Hill. This makes it look even greater than its 2:1 advantage suggests. Astride a pure white charger, and with gold crown glistening in the morning sun, he appears in complete command. Except that he isn't.

Northumberland has protested that his men are not battle-ready having just arrived after a particularly long, forced march. And so his army is posted at the rear as reserve. What it means, of course, is that he does not have to commit to the fight and can sit back and watch.

The Stanleys have posted themselves apart from Richard's army where they can observe and intervene should circumstances require. Sir William Stanley's presence suggests that there have been discussions with Richard and an agreement reached for the removal of his attainder. But they remain seemingly uncommitted. Not only that, but the topography of the battle site prevents Richard from deploying his forces to best advantage, particularly on the flanks.

There is an exchange of cannon fire and handguns, and the opposing ranks of archers let fly their arrows, after which the two vanguards collide. Cleverly, Oxford orders his men to stay at all times within ten feet of their standards. This gives them extra strength in resisting superior numbers and also causes Norfolk's men to pause their pressing, suspecting trickery. They are right. Talbot and Savage close in as a wedge formation and Norfolk is killed early in this engagement and his son, the Earl of Surrey, wounded and captured.

Seeing his vanguard losing ground, Richard sends a furious message to Lord Stanley calling on him to charge Henry's forces or he will execute his son, George, Lord Strange. Stanley considers the situation for only the shortest while. Given that George has already confessed to treason and that he is married to a Woodville, it is unlikely that Richard will spare him the block if he is victorious. In fact, none of the Stanleys look secure no matter what they do. Richard's 'pep talk' before the battle was simply stressing that retribution would descend on anyone who wasn't fully committed to him after Henry is defeated. Thomas Stanley's response is that he has more than one son.

Without Stanley or Northumberland participating, the odds between the two fighting sides are nearing evens. Spitting fire, Richard orders Lord Strange's execution. Luckily for George Stanley, no one complies.

Outmanoeuvred and frustrated now, Richard decides to risk everything on killing Henry himself. Spotting Henry's position, he charges across the battlefield at him with a detachment of heavy cavalry. Robert is there in Henry's group and sees all. Sir William Brandon is slain by Richard's battle axe and he even knocks the giant John Cheney from his horse. But that is as far as he gets. Sir William Stanley has at last committed his men to the fight and they charge down on Richard's small contingent.

Richard's fine horse is taken from under him, he loses his helmet and succumbs under a torrent of blows to the head. The final blow comes from Rhys ap Thomas. Well, that is what the Welsh poets will proclaim.

The action lasted about two hours. Richard's men were chased from the field as far as Stoke Golding, some five miles to the south, and then the victors regrouped.

Of Henry's army, Sir William Brandon is the only member of the nobility to lose his life. Of Richard's force, as well as the king himself, Norfolk, and Sir Robert Brackenbury; also killed are Walter Deveraux, Lord Ferrers, Sir Richard Ratcliffe, and John Kendall. William Catesby is captured and executed two days later at Leicester. Hanged with him are father and son, William and Robert Bracher, who seem to have advanced well in Somerset under Richard's patronage and are suspected of betraying west country rebels during Buckingham's Revolt.

Few though are hounded and cut down, as it soon becomes apparent that many were pressed into fighting for Richard through fear rather than volition. The Duke of Northumberland is taken into temporary custody partly as a preventative measure and partly for his own protection, as many of his men would have preferred to fight. Henry Percy was a childhood friend of Henry Tudor and the new king does not wish to see him harmed by others, or possibly by his own foolishness. Lord Lovell, Sir Humphrey Stafford and Thomas Stafford have fled to sanctuary at Culham in Oxfordshire.

A *Te Deum* was sung on the battlefield and the dead stripped of weapons, armour, and anything else of value, and the contents of Richard's tent were awarded to William Stanley for his vital role in winning the day. Henry at once issued a proclamation forbidding robbery and violence and called for peace in the wake of his victory. The French were paid off and dispersed as quickly as possible. Robert Willoughby was sent to Sheriff Hutton to fetch Elizabeth and Edward of Warwick.

It is notable that on the very day of his success, Henry issues a warrant for the arrest of Bishop Stillington and he is housed in York's prison inside a week, 'for heinous offences imagined and done'. Without doubt this is to ensure that Stillington knows where he stands if he continues to denigrate the King's bride. Stillington is deprived of the deanery of St Martins, but his standing as a bishop is left alone. On 22 October, he is granted a pardon 'because of his great age'. He is sixty-five.

Richard's naked body was slung over the back of a horse and returned to Leicester where, after two days on display in St Mary de Castro church, it was buried in the grounds of the city's Franciscan monastery without ceremony.

27

New Foundations

It was a close call for Morton to get back to Westminster in time for the coronation. Bishop Passarella of Imola eventually arrived at Dunes monastery. During the wait, Morton sounded out the garrison at Calais to gain assurances that they could leave from there to Dover. Captain of Calais, and in residence, was Richard's bastard son, John of Gloucester, and the Lieutenant, based at Guines, was Sir James Tyrell.[1] But it seems there was nothing to fear as both commanders and their troops were keen to surrender to Henry's general pardon and allowing and aiding the departure of Morton and the papal legate would provide active proof of their acquiescence.

Of Henry, after a short rest at Leicester he slowly journeys south to London. The journey is deliberately slow as Henry is well aware that few people know him or of him, and it is important that as many as possible see their new king as soon as possible. Advance riders ensure he will receive the best of welcomes and on 3 September he is warmly greeted by the Mayor and aldermen at Shoreditch, from where they move on to St Paul's, their progress being celebrated with sixty-five 'mysteries' or tableaux, culminating in the award of a gift of 1,000 marks. Henry then accepts accommodation at the Bishop of London's palace for a few days before moving on to Westminster.

Henry's arrival in the City is marked by an outbreak of 'sweating sickness', so virulent that the Mayor, his successor, and six aldermen all fall victim to it and die.[2] The disease sweeps swiftly through the community and the coronation is put off until 30 October. It is an ill wind that blows nobody any good, and this tragedy allows Morton a few days to reacquaint himself with Holborn and engage in a dress rehearsal for Henry's big day.

For the coronation, Henry would proceed from the Tower to Westminster so that all in the City could see him in his magnificence, and his peers in their finery. No expense had been spared in creating their robes of state. On arrival at Westminster, the short walk from Palace to Abbey was taken under a canopy of cloth of gold. On his left side was Morton as Bishop of Ely, and on his right, Peter Courtenay, Bishop of Exeter. Their task is to physically support the King during the long ceremony, which is overseen by Archbishop Bourchier. This physical support includes holding the weighty crown.

The new King's Council has already been selected, its core comprising the relatively small group of people proven in Henry's eyes to be trustworthy. Trust and competence will be a theme threading throughout his administration, and a consequence will be a slow but perceptible decline in the influence of the nobility in favour of the gentry and mercantile classes. And so, on the Council with Morton we find Thomas, Lord Stanley, who is now Earl of Derby; Richard Fox is Principal Secretary; Jasper Tudor, who has now become the Duke of Bedford; John de Vere, reinstated as Earl of Oxford and now High Admiral of England and Constable of the Tower; Edward Courtenay, now Earl of Devon; George, Lord Strange; Sir William Stanley is Lord Chamberlain; Giles Daubeney; Lord Dynham; Sir Richard Edgecombe; Sir Edward Poyntings and Reginald Bray.[3]

To be honest, the choices are limited, thanks to the civil wars. There are three dukes, one marquess, and fifteen earls within the nobility. Only one of these is within Henry's immediate family: the Duke of Bedford. Of the higher peers, four are children, two had better claims to the throne, and one (Surrey) was technically not a peer and was imprisoned in the Tower. Many were time-servers or political lightweights. Derby and Northumberland possessed established political power bases and only four – Bedford, Oxford, Devon, and Shrewsbury – seemed to possess the ability to create something similar.

What Henry did have though, was possession of more extensive Crown lands in his hands than had been enjoyed by any previous English monarch. This supplied him with the means to promote lesser peers and competent members of the gentry whose loyalty he could rely upon.

The principal administration posts have also been filled. John Alcock, Bishop of Worcester is Lord Chancellor.[4] Thomas Lovell is appointed Chancellor of the Exchequer; John Fitzherbert, King's Remembrancer; Richard Edgecumbe is Comptroller of the King's Household; and not least, Robert Morton is reinstated as Master of the Rolls.

In less than a fortnight of entering London, Henry calls for a parliament, to be held on 7 November.[5] In the meantime, as well as sorting out who will be on his Council, he rewards numerous supporters with grants of lands and the custodianship of royal castles. A notable innovation is the establishment of the first permanent army on English soil (outside of Calais). Fewer than fifty strong at inception, these soldiers were the Yeoman of the Guard, later to be internationally renowned as the Beefeaters.

The young Edward Plantagenet, Earl of Warwick is confined to an apartment in the Tower, but the immediate future is brighter for other survivors of the Yorkist lineage. John de la Pole, Earl of Lincoln, who was Richard's designated heir, is respectfully treated and is invited to the coronation. Clarence's daughter, Margaret, is created Countess of Salisbury.

And he has not forgotten to redeem Thomas Grey and John Bourchier from France! The Marquess of Dorset is then restored to his lands and title, as are Sir Edward and Richard Woodville.[6]

There are other family matters to indulge in. Aged fifty-four, Uncle Jasper finally decides to get married and on 7 November, the same day as the opening of parliament, he weds twenty-eight-year-old Catherine Woodville, the widow of Henry, Duke of Buckingham. She brings to the marriage four children (they had no children from the marriage) and also the estate of her executed husband, restored to her by Henry. Henry has to give consideration to the matriarchs of the new dynasty.

Margaret Beaufort is revered by her son, as she is devoted to him. Although she has no formal role in the business of state, he will seek out her advice or approval whenever he feels in want of it. But he makes it clear that she should not seek to interfere or intervene in policy on her own initiative. This is conveyed gently over time to present an outward appearance of balance in his relationship with his mother-in-law, which is somewhat different. Margaret is raised to Countess Richmond as well as Countess Derby and all her lands will be returned to her in her own right being declared *femme sole*, making her a legal person in her own right, not merged with the legal identity of her husband. Along with her mansion at Woking, she is given a London mansion at Coldharbour by the Thames and her manor at Collyweston in Northamptonshire is refurbished.

Elizabeth Woodville is another matter. Though her estate and status are returned to her, and she is provided the income for life from seventy manors by separate grant from the King. But being naturally opinionated and ever with an eye to the advancement of the interests of her family, she will become an irritation and more to Henry. She is not entirely trusted, nor does she go out of her way to show trustworthiness and her surrender from sanctuary and of her daughters to Richard remains a question which Henry has not resolved. What are her loyalties and values?

The parliament is opened by Chancellor Alcock and the Commons elect Sir Thomas Lovell, Henry's Chancellor of the Exchequer, as their Speaker. Henry has made it more than clear that he does not want to be seen as his wife's 'gentleman usher' but as King in his own right and for this reason his marriage, let alone Elizabeth's coronation as Queen, must come after parliament's recognition. A notably short Act of Parliament is thus passed pronouncing Henry King by law. It's as simple as that. There is no discussion or debate about any defects in his title. He's King. Move on. However, this does not prevent Henry later commissioning an investigation into his pedigree which, needless to say, provides a direct line to Brutus, the founder of Britain.

Parliament is then asked to enact that Henry's kingship commenced on the day before Bosworth. This creates a sense of unease among jurists within the assembly, as it means anyone who fought against him is a traitor and can be attainted. However, in the knowledge that Henry will issue a general pardon in the New Year to all who swear allegiance, the resistance is short-lived.[7] But Richard himself, for his many crimes including the 'shedding of infants' blood', and twenty-eight of his principal supporters are named in a Bill of Attainder. But many, such as the Earl of Surrey, will be soon pardoned.

Titulus Regius is repealed, as are all past attainders under Richard including Henry VI and his family and Queen Elizabeth and hers. No longer is Henry's bride-to-be illegitimate. Nor are Edward IV's sons. This seems proof, if further proof be needed, that all knew the two princes were dead. It would be ideal for Henry if he could produce the bodies of the princes, as without them he knew there were risks of pretenders coming forward. But a thorough search of the Tower and its apartments comes up with nothing.

Parliament also grants the usual subsidies of tunnage and poundage for keeping the seas safe, and the wool subsidy for the defence of the realm. For now, no other taxes are sought. For now.

Then there are other laws to be debated and passed which provide a framework to Henry's intent. Private armies, providing their maintenance and their liveries, are outlawed. Also outlawed is interference with the due process of justice, bribing jurors, and unlawful assemblies. These all seek to curtail the excesses of the old order.

An Act of Resumption puts him in possession of all Crown lands held by Henry VI on 2 October 1455. This provides him with a steady income stream and rescinds most of the favours bestowed from the Crown by Yorkist regimes unless reviewed and bestowed again by the Tudor King. Henry will also take immediate steps to bring the expenses of the royal household under control: though inevitably that will become a losing battle. Finally, he expresses great pleasure in receiving a petition from his parliament requesting him to marry Elizabeth of York, to which he confirms that it is his earnest intention.

That intention is realised on 18 January 1486. The formal request for the Pope's dispensation to permit the marriage is not dispatched to Rome until after the November parliament, but the preliminaries having been attended to and found satisfactory. Papal Legate Giacomo Passarella is able to provide a dispensation himself. Innocent VIII issues a confirmatory papal bull on 27 March, which also gives full recognition of Henry's right to the throne and, particularly heartening, threatens excommunication for any who might oppose him.

Perhaps Morton is getting cynical in his advancing years but he is well attuned to Henry's fears and foibles. With the foundation work he had laid down in Rome prior to Bosworth and having ensured Bishop Passarella's presence in the country well before the coronation, the wedding could have been carried out much earlier. Whilst it was politically desirable to engage with parliament in the marriage process, it was well known that this was to happen and that Henry had sworn an oath at Rennes to take Elizabeth as his wife. In the face of so many rumours, was he delaying to ensure that she was not carrying Richard's child?

What the royal wedding will be particularly remembered for, though, is the debut of the symbolic Tudor rose, merging white with red.

Morton was resuming where he had left off prior to Richard's coup, and with some speed. After the November parliament he, along with Peter Courtenay and Thomas Langton, received formal reinstatement to their respective sees, which meant regaining possession of all temporalities.

As the new year progressed so new circumstances and new opportunities precipitated change. In February, Morton's friend Richard Fox was given custody of the Privy Seal and then on 6 March it was John who received the Great Seal, being appointed Lord Chancellor in place of John Alcock, providing another continuity from Edward IV's administration to Henry's.

On March 30, Cardinal Thomas Bourchier died at Knole House at the age of eighty-two. Officiating the marriage of Henry and Elizabeth had been the last state duty of this monolith of the mediaeval English church. Morton is designated to administer the vacant see and is put in possession of the temporalities. At the same time, Henry communicates his wish that Morton should be elected as the new Archbishop. and John Alcock is to be translated to Ely; in his place as Bishop of Worcester is to be none other than Robert Morton.[8] Proceedings now wait on the drafting and collation of papers to be sent to Rome for the Bull of Translation, which will not arrive until later in the year.

Morton has reached the apex of the power pyramid within the English Church, but the range and depth of work he now has to engage with alongside the challenges in the judiciary facing him as Lord Chancellor limit celebrations to a quiet evening meal with Alcock and Robert.

Morton always undertakes his tasks conscientiously and energetically. He feels that he has no need to stress to his companions the urgency of their role in re-establishing a stable society whose citizens have safety and certainty, and he will fulfil his role in this, if only to ensure that they are with him. He is conservative and does not wish to get involved in theological controversy, believing that most people, like him, obtain comfort from the conventional, the old ways.

At the same time, he, like his bishops, is aware of the old ways coming under increasing questioning and attack. The emerging Humanism, Machiavellian politics, the challenges of science and exploration, are all requiring the Church to re-examine itself and justify its position of leadership in society. He looks at how the Inquisition in Spain has been bringing to light subversions within the Roman Church. His aim is to maintain the status of the Church in England by reforming the clergy and this he intends to do either with or, should it prove necessary, over the heads of his bishops. The Pope, through the Church, will have authority in all things spiritual and the King will have authority in all things temporal. What is left unsaid is that Morton will be the conduit to both authorities.

The slackness and indulgent lifestyles associated with the later years of Thomas Bourchier's incumbency and the example of George Neville had to be reined in. And so he called his first synod, even though not yet enthroned, at St Paul's to regulate the discipline and customs of the clergy. The clergy of London in particular were severely rebuked for effeminately wearing open coats and for frequenting taverns. The opportunity was also taken to raise £20,000 for Henry to support Francis, Duke of Brittany against aggression from France.

The reform of the clergy would be continued by visitations to the dioceses under Canterbury's supervision, although Morton never carried out inquiring visitations personally, always through commissaries.

Henry is well aware that he has enemies with an eye on his throne and decides to make a Spring Procession to acquaint as many as possible with himself and how life will be under his rule.

What kind of king will Henry's subjects discover? He is certainly God-fearing and pious. He has attended three Masses a day throughout his life. He also believes that God has ordained that he shall be king. On the other hand, he is continually fearful of treachery and conspiracies against him, keeping memoranda of his suspicions, emerging factions, financial and familial dependencies close to hand. He mops up the minutiae of gossip and smulls over them.

Physically, he is slender but muscular, is of good height, and of cheerful appearance. He ages fast during a life of stress: his eyes are small, hair thin, complexion pale, and his teeth rotting away to black stumps.

His court has several jesters: 'the foolish Duke of Lancaster' and Thomas Blackall are two favourites. His dogs are usually to hand, spaniels and greyhounds, and he may often be seen stroking his pet monkey. Sports and games are eagerly engaged in, archery and tennis being notably popular, but it is hunting with hounds and hawks that provides the greatest pleasure. He buys and reads books, most often in French.

First and foremost, they will see a monarch who wants to bring stability, peace and justice to the country. One of his principal weapons for creating safety within the realm is his insistence that anyone whose fidelity is not cast iron should sign a bond in which they swear to remain loyal or pay a hefty fine, which is itself underwritten by two others standing surety. In this way he creates a triple financial lock on good behaviour. He is a businessman taking England out of the mediaeval world, and his business is being King.

Stability is also enhanced by having few changes in his councillors. Edward IV tended to shuffle them around from one portfolio to another, rarely letting them bed into their responsibilities. For example, after the first few months when his regime was settling in, Henry had only two Lord High Treasurers throughout his reign.

He sets out north with his court. A pregnant Elizabeth is left behind. Also pleased to be left behind is Morton who needs to immerse himself in his new duties. Henry's Progress is well received in the east and it is at Lincoln that he celebrates Easter. His pleasure and leisure are soon disrupted with news that rebellion is being stirred by those who fled Bosworth. Around Worcester, the ringleaders are Humphrey and Thomas Stafford and in the north of the country Viscount Lovell is raising his standard. Henry's reaction is to put together a small army and set off north with Jasper Tudor in command of the troops. They are joined by

Henry Percy, recently released from his confinement and, more by waving pardons than swords, the rebels are dissipated by the time they reach York, with Lovell going into hiding and eventually reaching Flanders and safety at the court of Margaret, Dowager Duchess of Burgundy, the sister of Richard III.

The Stafford brothers fared no better, in fact worse. They found the people of Worcestershire were not interested in rebellion and so fled to the sanctuary of Culham Abbey in Oxfordshire. This did not protect them from Sir John Savage though, who dragged them out two days later on 13 May. They were put on trial and it was ruled that the Pope's support of Henry meant that sanctuary could not be applied to traitors, as he had ordained that they should be under excommunication immediately at the point of their treachery. So it was that in July Humphrey Stafford was beheaded at Tyburn, although his younger brother Thomas was pardoned and thereafter remained true.

The city of York went out of its way to prove itself loyal, not least because of its reputation in serving Richard III. From York, Henry moved on to Birmingham, then to Worcester cathedral where John Alcock – still Bishop of Worcester – read out the papal bulls against rebels, together with the confirmation of Henry's title and marriage.

The Progress then moved on to Gloucester, Bristol, then Richmond, arriving there by June. It had been a success. Henry had seen parts of the country which were totally unknown to him, had spoken to many people to understand their problems and aspirations, particularly economic, and had established his presence and outlook with those he met.

But Henry's travels were not yet finished. He first spent some time with Morton at Westminster discussing future policies and consolidating his thoughts and experiences from the Progress. The most urgent matter they have to discuss is the coronation of Queen Elizabeth, delayed while she is pregnant. There are reports beginning to emerge through Morton's network of informants that Margaret of Burgundy is playing host to a pretender to the throne, and this could erupt into something serious in the spring of next year. For safety's sake alone, it would seem wise to hold off on the coronation until the danger has passed, so planning for a date towards the end of 1487 is preferred. Henry will discuss this plan with Elizabeth and with his mother. Morton agrees to inform the King's mother-in-law on Henry's behalf.

Henry is spending more and more time at Shene (now being named Richmond reflecting his old earldom) and at Windsor, in preference to Westminster or the Tower. He tells Morton that he has noticed an increasing number of pilgrims visiting the tomb of Henry VI, convinced that miracles can occur there. Seeing mileage in getting behind this as a drain on Yorkist nostalgia, Henry asks Morton to begin a campaign for Henry VI's canonisation by compiling a book of miracles attributable to him, planning a new tomb for him in Westminster Abbey, and drafting a petition to the Pope.[9]

Like most nobles of the time, Henry took great enjoyment from hunting with hound and hawk, so he went with Elizabeth to Winchester for her confinement in the Cathedral Priory and spent his time having fun in the New Forest with courtiers such as Thomas, the Marquess of Dorset and Giles Daubeney, Master of the Harthounds, whilst she did her duty for England, presenting Prince Arthur to the world on 20 September.[10] The association of Winchester with Camelot, the Round Table, and the Briton King's legendary status was as renowned as this show of linking the Tudors to the Arthurian tradition was contrived.

Although a month premature, Arthur was strong and healthy and he was christened four days later with Queen Elizabeth Woodville godmother, and Dorset, Cecily – Elizabeth's sister – and John de la Pole, Earl of Lincoln assisting at the font.

John Argentine, the physician who attended the Princes in the Tower, was appointed to serve the child. After Christmas, Arthur would be handed to the care of Peter Courtenay for his first two years. Courtenay was translated from Exeter to the see of Winchester on 29 January following the death of William Waynflete in the preceding July. When the Prince attains his seventh year he will then be sent to Ludlow as Prince of Wales with his own Council and household. The building blocks for the new dynasty begin to be laid.

On 5 December, papal authorisation from Innocent VIII for Morton's translation to Canterbury arrives in London. It is dated 6 October: the journey of the papal bull has taken two months. On the very same day that it arrives with Morton, he is off to Westminster to swear the oath of fealty to the Crown before Henry – we don't want any excuse for confused loyalties – and the temporalities of the see are formally released by the King. This is, indeed, very much a formality as Morton has been administering them on behalf of the Crown since Thomas Bourchier's demise.

As swiftly as 9 December, William Celling, the Prior of Canterbury Cathedral arrived at Ely Place and delivered the Cross of Canterbury, or archbishop's crozier, in the chapel there.[11] December is spent almost exclusively in Westminster overseeing and performing the necessary religious ceremonies celebrating Christmas. Where time allows, it is put to contemplation over what he has achieved and the cost of that achievement, but such time is scarce as there are so many matters of State and reviews of court proceedings on which to deliberate and to diarise.

On 16 January 1487, Morton sets out on a deliberately slow procession to Canterbury for his enthronement. Not only does this allow the opportunity to visit properties within the Church's temporalities but it allows him to focus on and absorb the spiritual significance of this climax to his life's work. So, gathering up an increasing following, he stops over at Croydon Palace, Knole Park, the Archbishop's Palaces at Maidstone and Charing, and finally to Chartham from where he walked the last four miles to the cathedral precinct barefoot.

To the sound of bells he is met at Christ Church gate by a procession of monks who cense him to provide a ritual cleansing before leading him through the cathedral's west door. On entering the building the event overtakes his emotions and he kneels and weeps before receiving assistance to the High Altar. He recovers his normal, controlled demeanour whilst the *Te Deum* is being sung ready for being dressed in his pontificate robes, over which the woollen scarf-like pallium sent by the Pope is set in place.

Robert then steps forward to read out the papal bull confirming the appointment, after which Morton is consecrated and installed in the marble Chair of St Augustine where his bishops and the other clergy approach and kiss his hand, to swear fealty. He then leads a procession to the vestry where Mass is celebrated. Thomas Langton, Bishop of Salisbury, is cantor for the Mass, John Alcock reads from the Gospel, and Edmund Audley, Bishop of Rochester, who carries the Cross, reads the Epistle. With the ceremonies completed, all move on to a great feast which, as one observer put it, 'was the best ordered and served feast that I ever saw or that might be compared to'.

Hopefully they did not deplete the kitchens completely as the next day Henry arrived to celebrate Mass as a mark of respect to his new Archbishop and to further mark the occasion the King waived payment of a recent tax levied on the clergy within Canterbury.

Problem Solving

The year 1487 had started well for Henry. Morton had his promised conversation with his mother-in-law and she had agreed, without any great objections, to retire from public life. Of course, the Archbishop had always got on well with her, notwithstanding they had so little in common in their characters unless it was a fierce loyalty to family. But she had confided that her thoughts had turned to a life more contemplative and private ever since the previous spring. It was quite common for widows of noble birth to retire to a religious foundation, and so on 12 February she went to Bermondsey Abbey where, because of her status, she was provided with free hospitality in apartments once reserved for the earls of Gloucester. Standing on the south bank of the Thames, opposite the Tower, the Abbey was described as being a beautiful peaceful place with notably elegant gardens.

She was certainly not banished or forced to the Abbey. For example, in 1489 she was back with Queen Elizabeth helping with the birth of her daughter Margaret, the future Queen of Scotland and, in 1491, at the birth of the future Henry VIII. She also came to court on special occasions and continued to be referred to by Henry as 'right dear mother'. Because she no longer had to provide for her daughters, Henry transferred her property to his wife and as compensation provided her with an annuity of 400 marks. This was far from mean, being equivalent, more or less, to the whole of the income of the Abbey, and in 1490 he increased that annuity to 400 pounds. That would be similar in 2024 to an income of about £380,000 a year. In essence, without her husband she no longer had a public role and could now enjoy – if that's the word – a trouble-free retirement.

Henry being Henry, he did make one attempt to get some or all of that money back by arranging a marriage for her with James III of Scotland.

Much to Elizabeth's relief, James was killed in battle in 1488 and so nothing came of the idea.

In law and administration, progress is being made with Morton revising and reviving the functioning of the Court of Star Chamber. This is a court, overseen by a small panel of Privy Councillors, designed to apply impartially the royal prerogative in deciding serious cases involving the abuse of powers held by lords and peers of the realm, or to abuses of law likely to threaten royal authority. Established as a check to local abuses by the magnates, it tends, however, to develop into an avenue for justice in civil cases and will soon become detested by many for its own arbitrary judgements.

Secular law dominates Morton's time notwithstanding his ecclesiastical supremacy. Nonetheless, it is in Convocation with the Bishops of Ely, Exeter, Lincoln, Norwich, Rochester and Salisbury that the big story of the year formally breaks.

There have been rumblings since autumn 1486 that a conspiracy to revolt is brewing. Now, on 17 February, William Symonds, a twenty-eight-year-old friar and Oxford scholar, stands before them about to reveal the details of that incredible conspiracy.[1]

Symonds had been providing some tutoring to a ten-year-old Oxford grammar school boy called Lambert Simnel, named after the martyred Bishop of Maastricht. His father, Thomas Simnel, was a carpenter and joiner who specialised in making the housing for organs in the city's colleges and churches and was able to secure a scholarship for his bright and well-mannered son. So bright and well-mannered that in mid-1486 Symonds made mention of the boy to John de la Pole, Earl of Lincoln, whose family home was at Ewelme, about fifteen miles south-east of the city. Further discussions were held with Lord Francis Lovell who was in hiding near his home at Minster Lovell, also fifteen miles from Oxford but to the north-west. A plan was hatched whereby Symonds would educate Lambert as if he was Edward, Earl of Warwick, the son of George of Clarence. With him as a figurehead, a revolt would be launched against Henry. Although not spelled out at this stage, the plan would, if successful, put Lincoln on the throne as the designated heir to Richard III. Simnel would quietly disappear, as the sons of Edward IV had.

Symonds took the boy to Ireland, which always held a strong affection for the Yorkist cause. Presumably with his confidence bolstered by the endorsement of Lincoln, Lieutenant of Ireland, and of Lovell, Gerald Fitzgerald, Earl of Kildare, who was officially Lord Deputy of Ireland, unofficially 'the uncrowned King of Ireland', took Simnel under his wing. Many, though not all, of the Irish lords are happy to join in with a blow against the English, even though few (if any) actually believe in the deception. Lovell, soon to be followed by Lincoln, was in the Low Countries, bringing Margaret dowager Duchess of Burgundy – an implacable enemy of Henry following the death of her brother Richard – into the conspiracy.

Margaret agreed to sponsor the invasion by paying for 2,000 German mercenaries under the command of an unpleasant Swiss commander, but of some renown, Martin Schwartz.[2] While Lincoln puts the final touches to their preparations, Lovell passes through Scotland to the Lake District to scout the Furness islands for good landing points. This was an area which had strong Ricardian ties and was the home of Sir Thomas Broughton who had given Lovell refuge the previous year. Here he is joined by a small group of Irish captains who have sailed across for the same purpose, accompanied by William Symonds.

After conferring with Lovell and Broughton, Symonds decides to work his way across the Pennines to York and then southward to contact those who they can be assured will prove sympathetic to the cause. Lovell returns to Ireland and Broughton stays to coordinate their welcome in a few months' time.

Symonds is almost immediately betrayed though by a lay brother at Furness Abbey, who is none other than the father of Morton's long-time friend and colleague Christopher Urswick. He is arrested and, being a priest, is brought before Morton and his court of bishops where he quickly confesses.

They're not quite sure what to make of it to begin with. Who is Lambert Simnel? An anagram? Embalmers lint? But no, it's not a joke, as they know: there is an associate of Symonds also under arrest in the last of the ecclesiastical cells available at Lambeth, and so the Mayor of London is requested to take Symonds to the Tower.

In fact, the cell at Lambeth Palace Morton mentioned to the Mayor is not yet occupied, but reserved for the co-conspirator Robert Stillington, Bishop of Bath and Wells. Symonds had been dropping Stillington's name to ecclesiastical contacts from Furness Abbey and beyond. Though this only provided circumstantial evidence against Stillington, it was certainly sufficient to seek his arrest. There was a problem, in that Stillington had taken refuge in Oxford and the University refused to surrender him. This news produced a chilling reply from Henry: 'If you obstinately refuse to obey our commandment, we shall not only send force to carry out our demand but also to provide for the punishment off your disobedience in such a sharp way as shall be a fearful example of any so presuming hereafter.' But the University held its ground and it was not until March, when Morton seemingly extracted a sworn promise from Henry that the Bishop would not be harmed, that he was released into the King's custody. This 'good cop-bad cop' partnership would be an oft repeated strategy between them. Stillington was then taken to Windsor Castle where he was kept, without charge, in what amounted to house arrest until his death in March 1491.

Henry had Lambert Simnel formally named as an imposter on 17 February and the real Warwick was brought out of his accommodation in the Tower on the last day of February and paraded to St Paul's Cathedral for Mass, where he was allowed to speak to several people who knew him. Held to be slightly slow-witted, something not helped by the fact that he was receiving little or no education other than learning religious chants and catechisms, few people had ever seen him so the value of the exercise was limited, other than to flag up the lie to some of standing who might have been wavering in their loyalty.

With that in mind, the Marquess of Dorset – never to be fully trusted – was placed into what might be termed voluntary arrest in the Tower apartments for the duration of the coming hostilities, Henry suggesting that as a true friend he would surely not mind a short period of restriction on his movements. Once the Simnel problem was resolved, Dorset would be released without any abiding suspicion or stain upon his character. But alongside his experience of being surety to Henry's loan from Charles VIII of France, the penny finally drops that he will not be trusted anywhere near command of an army.

Henry tours East Anglia having heard that there is a fleet assembling along the coast of Holland, with Morton in attendance as the judicial courts in London shut down for April while the plague stalks the city streets. But by early May Henry has reports that this foreign fleet is in the Channel and the risk of a landing being made in eastern England dissipates. The likelihood now is that the invasion will come on the western shores. Henry locates his headquarters at Kenilworth and begins assembling an army at Coventry. With Henry at Kenilworth are Elizabeth, Prince Arthur, Margaret Beaufort, and Morton, who cannot help but reflect on his time there over a quarter of a century ago with that other Henry, Queen Margaret and Prince Edward, on the eve of the battle of Northampton.

Morton issues a proclamation that anyone spreading false rumours about the developing situation will find themselves pilloried.[3] On 6 June, Henry, with Morton in attendance, leaves Kenilworth and joining the assembled army at Coventry they march on to arrive at Leicester on the 10th, where Morton is so offended by the number of vagabonds and loose women present that he orders them all outside of the city until the army has passed through, in order to keep the troops focused on the task before them. Robert Morton assumes responsibility for the men-at-arms his uncle has brought, and they incorporate themselves within Oxford's force. Now seventy years of age, Morton has nothing to contribute by his presence on the battlefield, so as the army moves out of Leicester he returns to Kenilworth.

In Ireland, Kildare and Lovell have been promoting the claim of the new Warwick and with the German troops along with Lincoln and Schwartz now landed, on 24 May he is crowned King Edward VI (acknowledging the demise of Edward V) in Christchurch Cathedral, Dublin. When the celebrations have finished and the sobering-up is complete, the invasion force sets out to make landfall at Foulney, Furness, on 4 June.

The force had a few Englishmen accompanying them such as Richard Harliston, Governor of Jersey, and Sir Henry Bodrugan, with his son John Beaumont who had fled Cornwall in February in the face of an arrest warrant.[4] In the main though, they were a mix of Germans and Irishmen with little ability to communicate between each other, let alone their English-speaking reception committee. All in all, 'King Edward VI' and his invading force gathered few supporters, nor did they have any advantage of surprise as their enterprise and much of its detail had been known about for months.

The rebel army swells slowly as it crosses the Pennines, making its way down the Fosse Way to reach about 8,000 in number, and on 16 June they confront the royal army at the village of Stoke, about four miles from Newark, Nottinghamshire. Unfortunately for them, Henry's army numbers at least 12,000 and probably nearer to 15,000. Oxford commands the King's vanguard taking the opening salvo of German crossbow fire and a charge from men who know they are unlikely to live out the day. The response from the English longbows cuts into the rebels, particularly the unarmoured Irish who fall looking like hedgehogs. The impetus is now all with Oxford, who smashes through the enemy leaving some 4,000 dead. The men-at-arms on the wings and in the reserve have had no need to participate.

Lincoln, Schwartz, and Sir Thomas Fitzgerald were all killed in the battle. Henry regretted this as he would rather they, and particularly Lincoln, had lived so that he could understand why they had embarked on such an unfathomable adventure. Indeed, few high-ranking Englishmen were executed after the fight, although many hefty fines were levied. Any Germans who survived were allowed to return home, although the Irish and some Englishmen were hanged.

The body of Henry Bodrugan was not recovered. Some say he died at the battle but others claim he escaped and made it back to estates he held in Ireland, only to succumb to his wounds a year or two later.

Similarly, there was no trace found of Francis Lovell. He may have drowned in the River Trent fleeing the battle. A more exciting story is that 200 years on, workmen at Minster Lovell found a skeleton sitting at a desk in a walled-up secret room: was this him?

As for Lambert, he was taken prisoner at the battle but it was clear that he was neither an instigator nor a threat and he received a pardon, together with a job in the royal kitchens. From this lowly beginning he rose to be a falconer, and it would seem married to father a son, Richard Simnel, a canon of St Osyth's Priory in Essex, about twelve miles from Colchester. Lambert died sometime after 1534.

Gerald FitzGerald made a tentative peace with Henry: neither had the strength nor will to fight the other.[5]

The resolution of the Simnel affair means that work can now proceed on calling a parliament for 9 November and the coronation of the Queen on the 20th. Although the weather may be poor for both events, the proximity of dates will ensure that each gets a good attendance.

Meanwhile the life administrative has been no less busy than the life military. Trade in wool and cloth were the mainstay of the English economy and therefore the English exchequer. An important import in sustaining that industry was alum, used as a fixative for dyeing fabrics. With the fall of Constantinople to the Turks in 1453, they had gained control over its supply. However, a substantial find of alum rock at Tolfa, twenty-five miles outside Rome and within the Papal States, provided the opportunity for huge profits to flow into the Vatican coffers, which would serve to fund resistance to any planned offensive westward by the Turks, if not a Crusade. In 1464, Pope Pius II sought to enforce a monopoly of alum supply over Europe with the threat of excommunication to anyone thwarting that happy state of affairs.

The English wool and cloth merchants, Merchant Staplers, were not philosophically attached to the idea of monopolies unless they were their own. So Henry decided to break the Papal monopoly and enrich himself and his exchequer by doing so. With the help of, of course, Italian bankers Ludovico Della Fava and the House of Frescobaldi, he licensed ships to obtain more cheaply priced 'black market' alum from the Ottoman Empire and then sell it on in England and the Low Countries to undercut the Vatican.

Needless to say, this did not go down well with the Pope, now Innocent VIII, and antagonism extended well into the reign of Elizabeth I. It was Morton who endured the wrath of the Pope and had to politely justify English policy. For a while he was able to plead that Henry needed time to establish his reign before making dramatic changes to English laws and customs. Within a year or two the excuses wore off. The ill-will created would have no small impact on requests for Morton to be raised to Cardinal and on requests for Henry VI to be canonised.

There more successful dealings with the Vatican in August, when Pope Innocent issued a bull confirming that those carrying out treasonous offences a second time had no right to sanctuary. It was also confirmed to Morton that he could absolve from excommunication anyone causing disturbances against the King. This provided flexibility to a bull which previously did not allow for any.

Immediately after the battle of Stoke, Henry moved back to Leicester where Morton arrived to greet him and they returned together to Kenilworth, staying there a month to plan out their agenda, though also enjoying some recreational hunting. But Henry's instinct was to keep moving around the country getting to know his realm and the people in it, and creating his own propaganda. After all, neither still knew much about the other. Morton would accompany the royal family for another month, visiting Nottingham, Pontefract, York and Durham, finally departing on 28 August to arrive at Mortlake on the Thames, where he stayed a week with Margaret Beaufort updating her with every scrap of information she had missed. By mid-September he is back in London, which, as he is both Lord Chancellor and Archbishop of Canterbury, is his home. Whereas he is only outside the capital for a week during the next six months, Henry is only inside it for six weeks.

Morton's near-continuous presence in London makes him the face of government, particularly unpopular government, and he offers an ideal foil to deflect criticism against the person of the King. His ubiquity can be measured by his attendance at fifty of the fifty-nine legal terms running between his appointment as Lord Chancellor and his death, and his attendance at more Council meetings in that time than any other councillor.

The touring Tudors return to London and notably elaborate victory celebrations on 3 November, being greeted by Morton at St Paul's. Within the week, Morton opens and presides over his first parliament. Not that he is nervous. His messages are fully rehearsed. Moreover, he knows the important players so well that confidence and clarity come with ease.

His opening speech, which is to set the tone of the parliament, breaks the long-standing tradition of being based on a text from the Scriptures. He comes to the point quickly. The first business needing their advice concerns the fate of Brittany, which is under attack from France. How should England respond? Next, with the recent invasion in mind, Morton stresses the evil of disloyalty and the need for the proper administration of justice. Finally, he promotes the idea of protection of English industries and the minimisation of imports.

In foreign affairs, Henry is granted a subsidy to aid Brittany, the results of which will be seen in the following year. On the home front, measures are passed to suppress riots, the role of the Court of Star Chamber is extended and, subject to obtaining certification from the Court of Common Pleas, a person's title to property was to be held unimpeachable if unchallenged within five years. This particular law was introduced because of the absence of, and defects in, title for so much property as a result of the Wars of the Roses, not least the attainders and forfeitures and their administration during that period.

Towards the end of the parliament there was a riot at Westminster on December 15 while the King was sitting in the Parliament Chamber involving some eighty persons. An Act was immediately passed through parliament making it a capital offence for any of the King's household servants to conspire to cause the death of any lord of the realm or member of the King's council, offences to be tried in the Court of the Steward of the Household. Six of the ringleaders of this riot were declared felons, attainted by Parliament and executed without delay and without benefit of clergy. This all reflects the continuing fear and uncertainty which hangs over Henry and his government. Overall, from the point of view of the government, this was a successful parliament, although for liberal jurists and hard-pressed tax payers from the middle orders it set the tone for a sense of repression and discontent.

Henry and Morton were as one in their aim to unify the country under strong central government. One example of this occurred on Henry's tour. Richard had created the Council of the North seeking to unify the interests of the Nevilles and the Percies and also to provide coordination in the protection of the border with Scotland. The reduction of the Nevilles and dilution of the power of the Percies now suggested the relevance of the Council was at best exhausted or, at worse, a platform for contention. So he did away with it, with himself and his national Council as the only channel for the debate of policy. Similarly, Morton sought to enforce and increase the central rights and powers of the church of Canterbury. This would provoke considerable resistance in the next decade.

On 23 November, Queen Elizabeth steps onto the royal barge at Greenwich accompanied by her mother-in-law, her sister Cecily, and the ladies-in-waiting who will care for her needs at her coronation. The

seventy-foot long barge, with eighteen oarsmen, joins a flotilla on the river all decked out in silk banners and streamers, among whom are the Mayor and Alderman of the city in full livery. This was the most elaborate procession the Thames had ever seen, but among all the music and gaiety, the star of the show is the 'Bachelor Boys' barge, which sports a red dragon breathing out fire. When they reach the Tower, Elizabeth is greeted by Henry and they stay in the royal apartments overnight.

The next day there is an extensive dinner commencing around 11:00. Henry is absent from this, as is tradition. He has gone on to Westminster. After the dinner, Elizabeth is dressed in white cloth of gold with a mantle of the same, edged with ermine. Her fair hair hangs loose and she wears a gold circle on her head studded with precious stones. Elizabeth is then borne by four knights on a litter with a canopy of gold through the London streets to Westminster Hall where she will spend the night.

Finally, it is coronation day. She walks from the Hall to the Abbey but is subjected to some distress as such is the adulation of the crowd that they try to cut pieces of the carpet even as she is walking over it. Recomposing herself at the Abbey, the coronation then proceeds. Watched with satisfaction and pride by Henry from behind a latticed screen, it will be the first and only coronation performed by Morton.

Royal watchers note with interest that Catherine Woodville is present as the wife of the Duke of Bedford, and nineteen-year-old Princess Cecily is there, carrying her sister's train (she will marry Viscount John Welles, eighteen years her senior, half-brother to Margaret Beaufort) but these Woodvilles are there because they have a Tudor connection, not because they are Woodvilles. So Elizabeth's mother and Dorset are both absent. The coronation is a political act and it makes a political statement.

At the same time, the coronation provides the opportunity for those same royal watchers to share Henry's celebration of pride in his wife. Some criticise Henry – a long way behind his back – for not providing a more overt demonstration of his feelings towards Elizabeth in public, regarding him as reserved and distant. Other than when demonstrating anger, projecting a degree of reservation and distance is an essential characteristic for a king. He was never less than respectful and companionable towards her. It is unlikely that either would be in love with the other, considering that they both had emotionally scarred upbringings and were brought together in what was essentially an arranged marriage. But it was a relationship which provided them both with what they were looking for within society and was happy enough in its foundation to produce eight children.

Regrouping from 1488

Henry is once again touring extensively; entertaining, hunting, and assessing the mood and wealth of the country. For Morton, this is a time to devote perhaps a little more time to his responsibilities as Archbishop, although his role as Lord Chancellor is never out of mind. They are responsibilities which he takes very seriously. He is not a radical or reforming archbishop, rather one who is focussed on supporting the Pope (where this doesn't clash with supporting his King), on efficiency in administration, and solid finances.

The Archbishop of Canterbury has a diocesan role much as any bishop has. In this respect, like all bishops giving service to the King, he is more often than not an absentee and so relies heavily on his Archdeacon, John Bourchier. He also has a role as a metropolitan bishop, that is to say he has responsibilities and powers in overseeing the administration of all English sees other than those north of the Trent which come under the Archbishop of York. That meant Morton was responsible for thirteen dioceses in England and four in Wales. Of particular importance is the administration of vacant sees and periodic visitations to ensure the proper and efficient functioning of dioceses. He also performs a judicial role. Consequently, as an archbishop he has a workforce of considerable size, not only to execute his religious and administrative functions but also to serve and maintain his cathedral and several palaces and manors. He is therefore able to patronise and develop the careers of many, both clerical and non-clerical.[1] The Archbishop exercises his judicial role through four Courts.

First was the Court of Audience. This was held at Lambeth Palace, the official London residence of the archbishop. In fact, the front of the Palace is a brick gatehouse commissioned by Morton and completed in 1495. The Court of Audience is where the archbishop exercised his authority as representative of the Pope and it therefore dealt with ecclesiastical matters such as the election and confirmation of bishops, consecrations and the like. It had a surprisingly large staff: a president, registrar, sixteen advocates, and ten proctors.

Second was the Provincial Court, or Court of Arches. This is the court in which Morton especially made his name decades previously and consisted of the Official or his deputy, a registrar, ten advocates, and sixteen proctors. It could also be convened by one of two examiner-generals. It was primarily a court of appeal from any lower ecclesiastical court. This made it a court which, from its earliest existence, created resentment among bishops, who did not appreciate their decisions being subject to scrutiny and possible censure. Much of the Court's work involved wills, probate, and even admiralty matters, which had financial implications.

Third was the Prerogative Court, which proved wills where the testator held goods in more than one diocese. This court was run by a Commissary General assisted by several auditors and an apparator general, or summoner.

Fourthly, there was the Consistory Court which dealt with matters arising within the jurisdiction of the diocese of Canterbury. This court was also presided over by a commissary-general.

And, just as you might think 'enough', the Archbishop also has a supervisory role, usually exercised through the commissary general, over 'peculiar' or 'exempt' jurisdictions. These are churches outside the province of a bishop or his archdeacon. Being jurisdictions, they are not confined to places or buildings. So, for example, the deanery of Bocking comprised four parishes in Essex and three in Suffolk, the jurisdiction being exercised on behalf of the Archbishop by the dean or co-deans. There are eight such peculiars and also Calais, which is similarly attended to by a commissary of the Archbishop.

Most of the caseload is routine and requires only an orderly, precise, and legally competent mind to resolve. Some cases though are less ordinary, and some have overtly political overtones. Some examples of the variety of work handled will illuminate.

In 1489, Rochester bridge is in a state of collapse, with some masonry falling onto a boat passing under it and causing it to sink and its two owners to drown. Morton allows indulgences to be sold to the penitent of Canterbury over a forty-day period to raise money for reconstruction of the bridge.

Another case from 1489, this from the Prerogative Court, concerned righting some abuse of power by Thomas de Feld, the Abbot of Burton-on-Trent. Most of the abbeys were outside of the Archbishop's jurisdiction, but Morton was particularly keen to clear up abuses and misdemeanours which were evident and outside any administrative control. Pope Innocent VIII agreed with him and provided him with authority to visit and reform these houses. In this case, Henry Punt, of Littleover, Derbyshire, died leaving a will, his wife, son, and a friend being executors. Because his property was held in several dioceses, the Archbishop had legitimately sequestered this property pending inspection of the will and the granting of probate. However, the Abbot, who held a 'peculiar' jurisdiction over Burton, secured the will and attempted to administer probate himself, and threatening to excommunicate the executors if they obstructed him. The Abbot was called on to cease his involvement with the will and submit himself to the Prerogative Court at its next sitting. If all the property had been within his 'peculiar' jurisdiction, he would probably not have had a problem.

In the Court of Audience another abbot is pulled up, here providing a more salacious case. William Wallingford, the Abbot of St Albans, received a public admonition from Morton for the 'defects' in St Albans Abbey. It was to the point. 'The Abbot is notorious for his simony, usury, and for the dilapidation of the possessions of his house, and for his laxity and negligence in administration,' begins the warm-up to the censure. Wallingford is accused of admitting a married woman, Helen Germyn, who had left her husband for a lover, into the St Albans Priory of St Mary de Pre as a nun, and then promoted her to prioress. A monk named as Thomas Sudbury begins a sexual relationship with her and soon the monks and nuns are indulging, 'as to a brothel'. The Abbot is called to get his house fully in order within thirty days. Lo and behold! the answer is to give the prioress the sack. Wallingford himself is dead within eighteen months.

There is a strange postscript to this tale. The monk Thomas Sudbury seems to have been singled out for no particular reason or purpose. However, in 1488, two years before Morton's censure of the Abbot of St Albans, the priory of St Andrew's in Northampton (forty-four miles from St Albans) was claimed by two clerics: William Brecknock, who had been elected Prior in 1480, and Thomas Sudbury. They were both ordered to present their case before the Archbishop at the Court of Audience, but there is no record of their compliance until 1491 when Sudbury appears at Lambeth to read Brecknock's letter of resignation from the post, whereupon 'the office of prior, so far as the said Thomas was concerned', is declared vacant. A new prior, Thomas Roche, is elected.

Sexual misbehaviour was not, of course, only found in the orders residing in abbeys. Morton remembered his visit to William Waynflete, Bishop of Winchester, which had to be negotiated past the Southwark stews, the brothels, and the fact that those houses were licensed by the Bishop always sat uneasily with him.

In 1492, Peter Courtenay, then Bishop of Winchester, died and Morton quickly stepped in requiring an investigation into the 'gross sins daily committed by clergy and people: brothels exist openly and in these prostitution, fornication, adultery, debauchery, incest and other manifest sins are each day damnably and impiously committed'. This was to be his only visitation in person to a diocese. The investigations and visitation lasted over a year, during which time a concerted effort was made to generate a spiritual renewal, but the stews remained open until finally closed by Henry VIII in 1546 following a rise in syphilis cases in London. Thomas Langton was eventually translated to the bishopric of Winchester from Salisbury.

Although visitations were profitable and necessary for the Archbishop, being a full audit of financial and spiritual performance they were not popular with those under scrutiny. They could also be used to attempt to discredit colleagues. As an example, the see of Exeter was reviewed by two commissaries of Morton in 1492/93 following the translation of Richard Fox to Bath and Wells and before the provision of Oliver King. As well as the cathedral, all the parish churches within the diocese were visited over a period of five weeks with an itinerary of meals and lodgings being pre-planned. In general, all those interviewed confirmed that everything satisfactory and well-run. But there were exceptions and qualifications. The cathedral organ player complained that the instrument was exceedingly difficult to play. The Prior of St Nicholas complained about his monks, who ignored his instructions for them to have a decent tonsure, in particular one disturbed monk who broke down doors and threatened the others. The Prior of St John the Baptist reported all well, except one brother had run off with stolen goods. At Holy Cross, Crediton, it was said that 'vicars wandered about the town in a suspicious manner at night'. At Launceston Priory it was claimed that the sub-prior had sold off goods to outsiders and squandered the money. One of the monks of Tavistock Abbey could not appear as he resided in the Isles of Scilly and the perils of the sea were too great. Otherwise, complaints were of minor debts unpaid or withheld and of irregularities in the performance of services. Where there were complaints or irregularities, they were more often than not in the abbeys and priories.

Without doubt, the most ferocious challenge to Morton's construction of a more centralist approach to ecclesiastical authority came from Richard Hill, the Bishop of London. The fall-out began in 1491 when Bishop Hill investigated Thomas Percy, the Prior of Holy Trinity, Aldgate, who had not only been 'associating' with a married woman but had so mismanaged the priory that it was heavily in debt. If the charges proved true, then Prior Percy would be removed. However, Bishop Hill had acted outside of his authority, as the priory was within the jurisdiction of the Archbishop of Canterbury.

In full knowledge of this contempt of the Archbishop's authority, Bishop Hill went in person to Holy Trinity to remove Prior Percy forcibly but found the gates to the priory bolted and admittance refused. The furious bishop, seeking a means of retaliation, excommunicated the Prior and all those who might advise him. This had the effect of excommunicating his Archbishop.

The excommunications were published by fixing notices to church doors throughout the city. One of Morton's officers began removing these notices and was arrested. Bishop Hill then returned to Aldgate and the priory with a group of armed men who forced entry and then arrested the Prior, one of the Bishop's protégés being installed in his place. The Bishop had now escalated the matter to a very public challenge to the limits of the Archbishop's authority. The Pope backed Morton and in October 1484, Bishop Hill was forced to submit to correction.

Morton's persistent pressure to secure conformity and control throughout the English ecclesiastical world required him to maintain two full-time commissaries in Rome and throughout the 1490s he would be challenged, particularly by abbeys. But the 1487 papal bull *Quanta in Del Ecclesia*, which enabled his policy of reform and centralisation, meant the Pope would always be onside.

From a personal perspective, 1488 sees moves to raise Morton's status even higher, as Henry makes the first of several pleas to the Pope to elevate the Archbishop to Cardinal. Second only to the Pope in the ranking of the Church's officials, it is the College of Cardinals that elects each Pope. The request for the scarlet hat of a cardinal is rebuffed by Innocent more out of irritation with Henry's foreign policies than any concerns about the fitness of Morton for the position. Following the death of Pope Innocent, however, the new Pope Alexander VI grants the request in September 1493, and Morton is made Cardinal of Saint Anastasia.

His higher status is followed by an increase in wealth and in October 1488 Morton buys The Mote, a one-hundred-acre manor outside Maidstone, Kent, from Richard Woodville, 3rd Earl Rivers, and an adjacent mill from Thomas Grey, Marquess of Dorset. This transaction further reflects his amicable interaction with the Woodville family.

Foreign policy is also being reassessed. Henry's aims are essentially defensive rather than expansionist, not least because the Wars of the Roses have drained the country of fighting men to the point where any aggression would necessitate hiring mercenaries. Henry realises only too well that as an island nation it is the sea that provides the best defence, and he quickly develops a passion for creating an effective modern navy. He is also inspired by, or fearful of, the naval advances of Portugal and Spain, who are looking to create a New World empire, Christopher Columbus making his first landing in the Bahamas on behalf of Spain in 1492.

Defences of the Cinq Ports – Sandwich, Romney, Dover, Hythe, and Hastings – are improved and in 1495 the first dry dock in England is commissioned at Plymouth for building warships. In 1488, work began on building *The Great Harry, Regent, and Sovereign,* three great battleships.[2] *The Great Harry* is a three-masted ship, 240 feet long and 36 feet wide, having eight heavy guns each side. There are two decks but no portholes. It is known as the first ship of the Royal Navy.

The English position regarding France and Brittany is under review. Notwithstanding a truce being entered into with France in 1485 and a treaty of commerce with Brittany in 1486, France was once again looking to absorb the duchy and Duke Francis appealed to Henry for help. Henry dithers because he owes gratitude to both Brittany and France for his throne, but such an expansion of France would pose a real threat to English interests, not least to Calais. Sir Edward Woodville pressed the Breton's case. Ever keen for battle, he was looking for some action following on from his useful role in the defeat of Lincoln at Stoke Field. His presence in court was certainly remarkable and his warlike past was there for all to see. In 1486, to fulfil a promise to join a crusade, he had journeyed to Spain where he fought the Moors at the siege of Loja. While he was leading an attack one of the defenders hurled a rock into his face causing severe damage, including a broken nose and the loss of all his front teeth. Whilst beard and moustache hid some scarring, the rest of his disfigurement was worn with pride.

Henry decides to try to diffuse the situation by diplomacy. Although he does review border defences including Calais, he will not give Sir Edward permission to take English troops to Brittany. But the Woodville warrior believes that what Henry really wants is for him to take a small army of support for Francis, and so he recruits some three hundred men from the Isle of Wight, of which he holds the Captaincy. On 27 July 1488, at the battle of St Aubin-du-Cormier, Woodville led the vanguard, boosted with Bretons wearing badges of St George, but succumbed to a counter-attack in which every one of the Englishmen was slaughtered. Five weeks later, on 31 August, Francis signed a peace treaty with France at Sable. Three weeks beyond that, aged fifty-three, Duke Francis died having fallen from his horse.

By the peace treaty, Francis had declared himself a vassal of the King of France and assigned to him St Malo, Dinan, Fougères, and St Aubin-du-Cornier. In addition, he had undertaken to remove all foreign troops from Brittany thereby excluding the option of calling on English support at a later date. But perhaps of greater importance, Francis undertook to obtain Charles VIII's consent to any marriage of his twelve-year-old daughter and sole heir, Anne.

The Treaty of Redon, February 1489, sought to reaffirm solidarity between England and Brittany following the death of Francis. The Breton nobility were seeking to protect the Duchess Anne and Brittany's independence and in March Henry sends 6,000 men under Sir Robert Willoughby to aid their cause. Butt it is too late.[3] However, the French managed to seize Anne and she was forced to marry the eighteen-year-old Charles, placing the whole of Brittany under his control.[4] After fruitless campaigning, the English expedition returned home for Christmas.

Protection by securing alliances was still the favoured course of action by Henry, and he sent out ambassadors to Maximilian, controller of northern Burgundy and soon to be Holy Roman emperor, to John II of Portugal, and to Ferdinand and Isabella of Spain. It was particularly Spain on which he set his ambitions, proposing a marriage between Prince Arthur and the Spanish Princess Catherine of Aragon. Though the suit was not rejected, nonetheless there was a need for the Spanish to be comfortably sure that the Tudor throne was secure and for the English to negotiate a suitable dowry. With Arthur being only three years old and his prospective bride six months older, there was no rush on the Spanish side. But a general agreement was reached in the Treaty of Medina del Campo that neither party would support the other's rebels (once again, Henry displayed his fear of pretenders and insurrection), and one would help the other against its enemies.

It was evident that despite peace overtures, war with France was looming. So much so that the parliament of January 1489 voted an unprecedented subsidy to fund war, assessed on wealth and income and which would be automatically renewed for as long as war continued. A further sum of £100,000 was voted specifically for the support of Brittany. But these taxes had yet to be collected and they caused much resentment, especially in the north, which already carried the burden of defending the border with Scotland. It was Henry Percy, Earl of Northumberland, who tried to put the case for reducing this extra burden on those who could least afford it, particularly as those outside of the northern marches contributed little if anything to maintaining security against Scottish raids. Losing the argument, he returned north but was murdered at Topcliffe near Thirsk, while trying to explain the King's need to an army of rebels. Some 5,000 then marched south under the leadership of Sir John Egremont and a yeoman named John Chamber.

There were suggestions that the assassination was as much about local feelings towards Percy as towards the King. Many people in Yorkshire and Northumberland had respect for Richard III and resented the fact that Northumberland would not engage in battle for him at Bosworth, and it was reported that the Earl's bodyguard melted away when he became surrounded by the mob. However, for most it would certainly have been about perceived unfairness and an inability to pay more following the dreadful harvest of the previous year.

The rising was quickly put down by Thomas Howard, Earl of Surrey, as much by the issue of pardons as military force, although where executions were carried out they were done so as to have maximum visual effect on the community.[5] This involved the infamous construction of a two-tier scaffold for group hangings.

As the Percy heir was a minor, Surrey was promoted to Lieutenant in the North with the duty of reconciling the population to Tudor rule; something he performed with success. The region subscribed little or nothing to the Brittany subsidy which, nationally, only raised about a quarter of the prescribed sum.

Wars, Warbeck, and Warwick

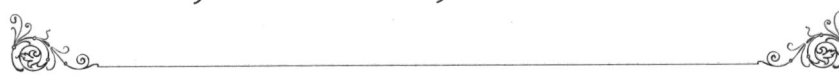

French belligerence continued, now expressed in support of a rebellion in Flanders where Maximilian of Austria's troops were being besieged at Diksmuide, about sixty miles from Calais. Its strategic position on the corridor between Calais and the Netherlands caused Henry to send a thousand archers across the Channel under the command of Henry Lovel, 8th Baron Morley. Morley and his men joined Giles, Lord Daubeny leading men from the Calais garrison and James Tyrell from Guines. In all, more than 3,000 men with 16 cannon marched overnight to Diksmuide, picking up 600 German troops on the way. In the ensuing battle, Henry Lovel – an exposed target on his horse – was killed by gunshot, and Tyrell was wounded by a crossbow bolt. But it was an Anglo-Habsburg victory. Possibly as a reaction to the fate of the men of the Isle of Wight at St Aubin-du-Cormier, but without justifiable cause, the English massacred all prisoners. Nonetheless, as soon as 22 July 1489 Maximilian and Charles signed a peace treaty: another blow to Henry's plan for a unified European front against French expansion.

It didn't take long before Maximilian and the French fell out again, and a treaty was signed with England on 11 September 1490 for a joint attack on France. There was also a treaty with the Duke of Milan, who was anticipating an aggressive move by the French. That summer, Willoughby had been elevated to Admiral of the Fleet to carry out a further expedition to Brittany, and the pot of belligerence was kept simmering by an exchange of raids on the coasts of France and of Dorset.

On the home front, Queen Elizabeth gave birth to a daughter, Princess Margaret, at the end of November 1489. She had been in quarantine for some time due to an outbreak of measles in London. At the same time, three-year-old Arthur was invested as Prince of Wales. The royal family continued to grow and on 28 June 1491, Elizabeth presented Henry with his second son, the future Henry VIII.

Just as the royal family grew, so did the number of plots to remove them. In August 1490 a Norfolk man, Richard White, was arrested for plotting against the King but released to infiltrate the confidence of sixty-year-old Sir Robert Chamberlain, a committed Yorkist currently under house arrest.[1] Chamberlain was indeed continuing his plotting, this time to see the Earl of Warwick on the throne. Either fearing he was being betrayed or simply believing that he could achieve more from anywhere but inside his own house, he attempted to flee abroad with his two sons, some friends, and the undercover spy Richard White. Their plan was to secure a boat at Hartlepool, but it quickly came to the notice of the authorities who dispatched a hundred men under Sir Edward Pickering to intercept them. The rebels ended up taking sanctuary at Durham Cathedral, from where they were forcibly removed on 26 January 1491, this being their second treasonable offence, which removed their right to sanctuary. Found to be financed by the French, Chamberlain was beheaded, but White received a pardon, as did Chamberlain's sons. The use of infiltrators and *agents provocateurs* by the Tudors and their spy-masters would increase.

The most serious threat to Henry's security, and the longest-lasting, was to emerge in 1491 in the form of a new pretender to the throne, claiming to be Prince Richard, Duke of York, brother of Edward V, and the youngest of the 'Princes in the Tower'. His name was Perkin Warbeck.

Warbeck was the son of John and Katherine Warbeck of Tournai, Hainault, in what is now Belgium.[2] Aged about ten, he was sent to Antwerp to learn Dutch and went into service with various merchants there, learning about the cloth industry. Eventually he entered the household of Sir Edward Brampton, the converted Jew from Portugal for whom Edward IV had stood as godfather.[3] Now in his mid-teens, Warbeck escorted Sir Edward's wife to Portugal, remaining there for a year and where he entered the employment of a Breton merchant, Pregent Meno. Warbeck had grown into an attractive young man of commanding stature and pleasant manner, such that Meno employed him to good effect in modelling the cloth and clothes which he was trading. They sailed from Lisbon to Cork where Warbeck caught the attention of John Atwater, a former mayor, who introduced him to the small colony of die-hard Yorkists in the city and with whom the conspiracy was hatched.

Establishing himself as Richard, Duke of York, Warbeck was then presented to the murderous Maurice Fitzgerald, Earl of Desmond, after which it was decided to tour Perkin around those European states who did not favour the current English regime and from whom support, particularly financial and military support, might be forthcoming.[4]

In France, Warbeck was welcomed to the French court as if he was indeed visiting royalty, and this was fed back to Henry with relish. It is most unlikely that they truly believed Perkin was indeed the son of Edward IV, but they were happy to simulate belief if it caused discomfort in England. The reaction was not quite what the French expected though. For Henry, pandering so overtly to an enemy was no less than a declaration of war. He was in funds to go to war and even though it was late summer he was minded to assert himself. He set sail to Calais with about 15,000 troops and from there began a siege of Boulogne. This unexpected aggression caused Charles to capitulate and compromise was reached in the treaty of Etaples, by which the French paid Henry's war costs together with an annual pension of £5,000 for fifteen years and arrears from the Picquigny treaty being paid off. In return, Henry undertook to withdraw from Brittany while Charles agreed not to give succour to any more pretenders to the English throne. The abandonment of Brittany to its merger with France was a bitter, and expensive, lesson learned though. Henry had spent almost half of the income of his first five years on supporting Breton resistance and, when it came down to it, it was money wasted.

With France no longer welcoming, Warbeck and his backers hastily moved to the Netherlands and the court of Margaret, Duchess of Burgundy, who not only opened her doors to them but publicly acknowledged Perkin as her nephew. She then set about schooling him in the family's history and in court manners, but equally importantly introduced him – as Richard IV – to significant figures such as Maximilian, crowned Holy Roman Emperor in 1493 at a ceremony to which Warbeck was invited. Margaret then set about rekindling contacts with known dissidents in England in preparation for an uprising.

At first, Henry had no way of proving that the challenge to his throne was not coming from the true Richard, Duke of York, since the body of neither 'Prince in the Tower' had been discovered. But by the middle of 1493, what he had discovered was Warbeck's real identity and he had also identified a number of Englishmen believed to be in contact with him, either directly or through Margaret. Among the foremost of those names were Sir Robert Clifford; Sir Simon Mountford; John Radcliffe, the 9th Baron Fitzwalter; Sir Thomas Thwaites and William Worsley, Dean of St Paul's.[5]

As with Charles, Henry sought retribution against Margaret, this time imposing an embargo on trade with the Low Countries but, as so often with trade sanctions, it was an action which equally affected English merchants. In London, warehouses became piled high with wool and cloth gathering dust and mites. There are riots, with violent attacks particularly affecting foreign merchants and their ships that are not subject to embargo. The economic turmoil throws up plots to assassinate Henry and threats of sedition.

In an attempt to disorientate dissenters, the three-year-old Prince Henry rides –unaided – to Westminster Hall on 29 October 1494, to be knighted by his father and on 1 November, created Duke of York. This is followed by a Mass being celebrated in St Stephen's Chapel, which is taken by John Morton surrounded by eight bishops.

Shortly after this it was discovered that within the Warbeck conspiracy is Sir William Stanley, hero of Bosworth, step-uncle and Chamberlain to the King. All Warbeck's known chief supporters are rounded up and dealt with. Much to Henry's regret, at the end of January 1495, William Stanley is found guilty of treason and is beheaded on 16 February. But there is now confidence that Warbeck has no cohesive or coherent support in England. Not that this proves sufficiently calming for Henry's nerves.

From March 1495 it had become clear that Maximilian was becoming tired of Warbeck's presence: the time for action had arrived. Henry and Morton shared responsibility for getting the coastal defences in place for southern England and when the King moved out of the city in June, it was left to Morton to continue organising the country's watchfulness. His placements and strategy were sound and when an attempt was made to land at Deal, Warbeck's expeditionary force of 200 men was quickly captured or killed. Sailing on to Ireland, Warbeck found that his support has faded away, not least because Sir Edward Poynings had been posted there from October 1494. He chased him off to seek refuge in Scotland.

There Perkin is once again well received and not only is he afforded status, money, and men, but also a wife, Lady Katherine Gordon.[6] Backing Warbeck gave cause for the Scots to set about raiding England once again, but they received no support south of the border and soon returned home after burning and pillaging a few villages. Henry's reaction was immediate and strong, securing from the parliament of January 1497 the right to more taxation to fund an invasion of England's northern neighbour. But that summer the invasion never happened.

The total amount granted was over £80,000, the largest to be awarded in any year of Henry's reign. Frankly, there were many parts of the country where the economy could not stand such a financial burden and that was the case in Cornwall. It was not only the amount of taxation called for; the Cornish did not comprehend why they should be paying for a solution to a problem so far away.

Much of parliament's grant was as two 'fifteenths and tenths'. This was a long-standing and accepted tax on property. In the towns it was a tenth and, in the countryside, a fifteenth.

In addition, a further £40,000 would be raised by seeking (or levying) loans based on an assessment of individual wealth. These loans were raised through local commissions and although regarded as 'forced' loans, pressure for payment was moral rather than physical. Assessing and collecting the subsidy was effected through the application of what became known as 'Morton's Fork', a *Catch-22* device developed by Morton and then Fox from past experiences of impositions of benevolences or forced loans. If the prospective taxpayer was found to live frugally, then it must be that they had savings stashed away. If the taxpayer displayed a lavish lifestyle then obviously, they were rich enough to meet what was expected of them. The 'loans' raised slightly more than the target, £42,146, a quarter of this coming from the clergy.

It was the argument of the Cornishmen that the border counties should be paying most if not all of the cost of defence against Scotland by the application of scutage – a payment made in lieu of feudal military service dating back to the reign of Henry I. They had a point – up to a point. But the centralisation of state and church, enclosure of common land, the rise of the gentry and the beginnings of the Reformation, Renaissance, and capitalism and industrialisation – these were not common currency in Cornwall.

Equally damning, and something for which Morton as Lord Chancellor has to carry the can, was the decision in 1496 to suspend the Cornish Stannary Parliament. The Stannary Parliament covered the tin mines of Devon as well as Cornwall and was created by Edward III alongside the Duchy of Cornwall. Its courts encompassed all civil lawsuits within its jurisdiction.

Led by the reasoning and eloquence of Thomas Flamank, a Bodmin lawyer, and Michael An Gof, a blacksmith from St Keverne, some 15,000 set out for London to protest the tax.[7] Among their demands was the removal of Morton along with the Chancellor of the Duchy of Lancaster Sir Reginald Bray, whose role and influence has been since compared to that of a Prime Minister.[8] Bray was only Treasurer for six months in 1496, but his grip on the financial affairs of state extended well before and after that time.

When they reached Taunton, a subsidy commissioner, Provost Perrin, was unlucky enough to fall into their hands and was lynched. From Taunton the rebels moved on to Wells, where they were joined by James Tuchet, 7th Baron Audley, who was acknowledged as their chief by virtue of his title but little else, but it was An Gof whose orders ruled the day.[9]

The rebellion had caught the authorities unaware and with their numbers swelling they reached Guildford in Surrey by 13 June. The army being assembled by Giles, Lord Daubeney in preparation for marching on Scotland had to be rapidly diverted. An advance of some 500 of his 9,000 men had an encounter with the rebels outside of Guildford, but this had little effect and the Cornish army moved on to Blackheath. The rebellion had certainly caused panic and the Queen and royal children moved into the Tower, joined by Morton on 15 June. Being an archbishop was no protection against the mob, as had been demonstrated a hundred years before during the Peasants' Revolt of 1381.

By advancing beyond the borders of Cornwall and Devon this had become not simply a protest against taxation but a *political* uprising. But there had been no general uprising joining them from the men of Kent or elsewhere, and Henry had brought more troops to join Daubeney's command. Many of the rebels lost heart and fled or surrendered. Michael An Gof argued strongly they should fight, but outnumbered, encircled, poorly led and equipped, it was more of a massacre than a fight, though remembered as the Battle of Deptford Bridge. Flamank and An Gof were captured and hung, drawn, and quartered, although Henry had sufficient sense not to send their dismembered bodies back to Cornwall for display. Audley was beheaded. Those Cornishmen who surrendered or fled were allowed to return home but fines of almost £15,000 were extracted from the county later that year: far more than the imposition of the approved taxes would have yielded.

Warbeck's support and options were diminishing fast. Maximilian withdrew his support in February of 1496 by the treaty of Magnus Intercursus, thereby restoring trade between England and the Germanic states. Warbeck had also lost the favour of the Scots, not least by a display of squeamishness over their border raids on England. Anticipating possible extradition, Warbeck left Scotland for Ireland once more, landing in Cork. The plan was then to utilise the aggrieved Cornishmen returning home from their humbling defeat at Blackheath. On 7 September, he and his shrinking band of only 120 men in two ships landed at Whitesand Bay in Cornwall and marched on Exeter, which they reached on the 17th. Morton tried to avoid further bloodshed by declaring a pardon for Warbeck and his retinue if they would yield: but it was a pointless gesture as those holding the puppet's strings were not going to allow compliance. The rebels lay siege to Exeter. It lasts just one day and then Edward Courtenay, Earl of Devon puts them to flight, Warbeck making it as far as Beaulieu Abbey before he is captured.

Brought before Henry in person, Warbeck fully admitted the fraud, after which he was first sent to the Tower but then kept at court, though always with a guard present. His wife was placed in the service of Queen Elizabeth. Particularly pleasing for Henry was the subsequent submission of Margaret of Burgundy, pleading for forgiveness for her actions. Stupidly, Warbeck attempted escape from the royal court in June 1498 and was easily recaptured at Shene, to be sent permanently to the Tower and kept in solitary confinement for a year.

At the same time Spain was prevaricating over when the Princess Catherine would be sent to England to marry Prince Arthur. The bottom line is that Ferdinand is not inclined to go further unless he is satisfied of the stability of the English crown. That means Warwick and Warbeck, by request of the King of Spain, need to be eliminated as potential magnets for insurgency.

Orchestrating the self-destruction of these two tragic and ultimately pathetic people required authorisation from the highest level. Henry was undoubtedly the instigator for the removal of these thorns in his flesh, which now threatened the international standing of his dynasty. It is difficult to believe that Morton was not also involved alongside Fox, Bray, and John de Vere, Earl of Oxford as Constable of the Tower.

Using guards as *agents provocateurs*, conversations were encouraged between the two prisoners inspiring them to plot their escape with a view to placing Edward on the throne. One of the jailers was Thomas Astwood, a convicted follower of Warbeck who received a pardon in 1495, and the other, Robert Cleymond: no action was taken against either of them. Sufficient evidence was put to the Privy Council on 12 November leading to a trial, which was presided over by Oxford himself, albeit wearing another hat, this one being Lord High Steward, a post to which he had been elevated just a day after Warwick's indictment. De Vere ensured that justice was seen to be done for the two witless young men before they were executed. In November 1499, Warbeck was hanged at Tyburn alongside John Atwater, the former mayor of Cork, who had initially sponsored Warbeck in Ireland. For Edward of Warwick, it was the axe on Tower Green.

The execution of Edward Plantagenet caused particular approbation and was probably the lowest point in Henry's reign: even he looked back on it with regret, if not shame, as it illustrated all his internal insecurities. The Queen was deeply distressed by the death of her cousin, in a decade which had her grieving for her mother, grandmother, and a daughter. Similarly, Catherine of Aragon would look back in later years, reflecting that her marriage had been bought with the shedding of innocent blood.

31

Closing Down

By 1499, well past his eightieth year, Morton was of course beginning to tire – and not simply because of his age and the the stresses of earlier years. A decade ago, the Cornish dead on the battlefield of Blackheath, or even the manipulated deaths of Warwick and Warbeck, would not have bothered him. Dispensing harsh justice on traitors for the stability and continuance of good government would not have disturbed his sleep: but not so now. Although he would continue good service to the King right up until his last breath, his time and mind were more focused on matters of the Church and less on those of State. Fox and the others were fully briefed in all matters and held the King's confidence.

Mortality was pressing in on him now. The loss of his brother Thomas, Archdeacon of Ely, in 1496 had caused immense sadness and then the following year he had lost Robert, which was an unfillable void.

For Henry, though little more than half Morton's age, 1499 also accentuates fears of mortality. He remained profoundly shaken that men so close to him as William Stanley and John Radcliffe could prove to be false. There seemed no one he could trust, particularly as Jasper Tudor had died in 1495. Not only was he seen to increase his time at prayer, but he had taken to consulting Italian astrologer and priest Guglielmo Parron, who prophesied that this would be a year when his life would be in great danger. This caused a collapse in Henry's mental wellbeing; so much so that it was reported that he aged twenty years in two weeks. The astrologer went on to say that there were two parties of very different creeds in the kingdom who were the source of this danger. This proved one trigger for constructing the demise of Warwick and Warbeck.

His focus and demeanour were jolted by the appearance of yet another pretender. This time it was a nineteen-year-old Londoner, Ralph Wilford, who in February declared himself to be the imprisoned Earl of Warwick. His arrest and execution came within days.

This was an era where the rich invested heavily in buildings and Morton, wealthy in his own right as well as by virtue of his ecclesiastical rank, spent widely both for good and to elevate his personal and professional standing. He appreciated the need for maintaining standards in physical presentation as well as administrative competence. Display was as important a messenger as any other medium, communicating authority, wealth, power, and propaganda. Buildings were an exciting motivator for Morton throughout the decade.

Lambeth Palace was the main London residence of the Archbishop of Canterbury. An administrative and social centre of the first rank, it was nonetheless in serious disrepair. Morton set to work at once commissioning the Great Gateway to be completely rebuilt with two five-storey towers on either side, which would afford lodgings for eight senior members of staff. He also provided a painted glass ceiling for the chapel. The other archiepiscopal houses and palaces at Allington, Croydon, Knole, Ford, Maidstone, and of course Canterbury, where he instigated the building of the cathedral's central tower, were all extensively refurbished or extended. His interest in engineering and the commercial world, which had seen expression while Bishop of Ely, developed further as he funded the iron foundry of Buxted, East Sussex which operated the first blast furnace in England revolutionising production.

This building work encompassed places of learning. He repaired the Canon Law School and helped fund work at the Divinity School and St Mary's Church Oxford (the site of the Oxford Martyrs). The academic world reciprocally conferred honours on him. In 1495 he was elected Chancellor of Oxford University for life and in 1499 was elected Chancellor of Cambridge University.

The arts were also patronised and promoted. Henry Medwall premiered his play *Fulgens and Lucres* at Lambeth Palace.[1] Sponsored by Morton, it was the first English vernacular drama, the first play to be printed in English, and the first with a woman as its central character. Medwall's second play, *Nature*, was also performed before Morton at Lambeth.

Books were another investment and in particular Morton funded the printing of a Sarum Missal (known as the Morton Missal), effectively the national liturgy, and with a ready market as it was an essential for every priest. It was described by the Cambridge Bibliographical Society (Vol.

XIV, Part 2 (2009) as 'the finest incunable made in England'. Its official publication date was 10 January 1500. Produced by Richard Pynson with a print run of about 600, it contains the country's first printed music.[2]

These last few years of the decade have not been uneventful. Foreign policy is becoming a mess once more. In the summer of 1496, Henry was persuaded to answer the Pope's call for a Holy League of states against French ambitions towards Milan and northern Italy, and the formal treaty confirming this was announced at Windsor on 23 September. So pleased was the Pope to procure this new ally that he presented a splendid Sword of State and a Cap of Maintenance to Henry, which Morton blessed and celebrated with a High Mass at St Paul's on 2 November.[3] With the Sword came the designation 'Protector and Defender of the Church of Christ' and the event was dovetailed into national celebrations of ten years of Tudor rule. But France should not be underestimated. Little by little, Louis XII entices the others of the Holy League into treaties of friendship and trade, so that in September 1499 France invades northern Italy for the beginning of what will be a five-year war.[4]

Closer to home, things were looking brighter. The formal betrothal of 12-year-old Arthur and 14-year-old Catherine by proxy took place at Bewdley in Worcester on 19 May. A very satisfied Spanish envoy, Don Pedro de Ayala declared to his master that 'there does not remain a drop of doubtful royal blood' in England. Good news – but not entirely true. While it was indeed true that by the death of Edward of Warwick, Clarence's male line was extinguished, his daughter Margaret, Countess of Salisbury, had five children with Sir Richard Pole and would be a source of anxiety in later decades. More immediately, Edward IV's eldest sister Elizabeth had six children with John de la Pole, Duke of Suffolk, the eldest of which, John, Earl of Lincoln, had already made a play for the throne and died at the battle of Stoke. His brother Edmund, Earl of Suffolk, was also making a nuisance of himself.

Suffolk was reputed to have a foul temper and, although attending Oxford, had a low level of literacy. When his father died in 1492, his lands had become forfeit to the Crown. Edmund was allowed to inherit them but only on payment in instalments of a £5,000 fine. Because he couldn't keep up the payments, the title was reduced from Duke to Earl.

Out on the town in London in 1499, he murdered a commoner, Thomas Crue, and fled to Guines where he first stayed with Sir James Tyrell. He then moved on to St Omer from where he was persuaded to return home.

Granted a pardon for a fine of £1,000 he would remain both a potential and actual cause of trouble, being executed by Henry VIII in 1513.

Scotland also stirs, as it regularly does, and raids Norham near Berwick in Northumberland. The attack is promptly repelled by Thomas Howard, Earl of Surrey, who slipped across the river Tweed for a retaliatory attack on Coldstream, 'throwing down' the Scottish castle. The Scots then came to the negotiating table to sign the Treaty of Ayton, which secured a peace for seven years. This was Howard's last action as Lieutenant of the North. For his good service he was called back to court, where his influence in East Anglia grew again, much to the jealousy of Edmund de la Pole.

Henry continued to indulge his interest in shipping and exploration and emulation of the Spanish and Portuguese he sponsored the Venetian John Cabot and his sons in their exploration of the Canadian coast. That interest continued in the exploratory voyage of William Weston, the first Englishman to lead an expedition to the 'new found land'. So much so that Henry wrote to Morton, in his role as Chancellor, requiring him to adjourn an injunction issued by the Court of Chancery against the explorer until his return. Henry VIII would show little interest in westward expansion.

John Morton had been continuing his assembly of a property portfolio, purchasing land and manors across the southern and eastern counties. The manor of Goosehays, Romford in Essex was one estate he picked up from the lands of Richard of Gloucester which Henry had absorbed after Bosworth, occupied by Avery Cornburgh up to his death in 1487.[5]

Atherstone Manor in Warwickshire was another tenanted holding which Morton bought. This was the house reputed to have been the location for the meeting between Henry and the Stanleys before Bosworth. Located near Bridport, the lordship and manor of Swyre in Dorset was also acquired, this from Henry's friend, the Irish peer Thomas Butler, Earl of Ormond.

With the turn of the century it was clear to all, including Morton, that the end of his time was near. He was at Canterbury all the time now, not least because of the Great Plague descending on London where it wiped out 25,000 over the winter 1499-1500 and into the spring. Henry and Elizabeth left England for Calais on 8 May to avoid the disease, returning to Dover on 16 June to call in at Canterbury and visit Morton. He was able to greet his King supported by his crozier, but it was a struggle and they knew it might be their last meeting. Which it was.

The intensity of the visit ensured that Morton completed the writing of his will that very same day. News arrived that Henry's third son, Edmund, Duke of Bedford, had died on June 19 at Hatfield House, messages also having been received of the demise of Michael Deacon, Bishop of St Asaph and of the passing of Morton's long-standing colleague Thomas Rotherham, Archbishop of York, on May 20 from plague.

He desperately desired to go to Knole, while he could still travel – albeit in a horse-drawn litter – and enjoy the rest of the summer months viewing its deer and wooded parkland. That he would set about organising in the morning.

32

Postscript

Morton's body was taken by horse-drawn hearse to Canterbury, arriving there on 26 September. After a sermon preached by Richard FitzJames, Bishop of Rochester, his remains were laid to rest beneath a marble slab in front of the altar of the Virgin in the Undercroft, the burial location originally chosen by and for the Black Prince. Unlike some of his contemporaries, Morton did not want to spend much money on his funeral, preferring to see as much of his wealth as possible distributed to family, friends, church and charity. Near his resting place is a cenotaph to his memory. Though evidently damaged – probably during the Reformation – and with no clear inscription, it was clearly erected to his memory as his rebus, or ornamental device, of a bird, or mor, upon a barrel or tun, remains visible.

By the seventeenth century the marble slab under which Morton lay had badly cracked and parts of his shrouded body had been taken by pilgrims seeking souvenirs. In 1670, Gilbert Sheldon, Archbishop of Canterbury (founder of the Sheldonian Theatre in Oxford), had his brother Ralph preserve the head in a lead-lined box. The skull was passed down through the Sheldon family at Beoly, Worcestershire, and now resides at the Catholic Stonyhurst College, Clitheroe, Lancashire.

John Morton was a man of his times and helped to form those times. In many ways he was a traditionalist and conservative rather than an idealist or reformer. But he was true and an anchor in turbulent times. He sought stability, order, efficiency, and certainty. With those values he believed justice, faith, equity, moderation and prosperity were all achievable.

Few of his achievements stood the test of time. If he had been able to return to Earth fifty years after his death he would have been horrified. The State was a tyranny, justice arbitrary, the nobility still feuding and conspiring. His Church had crumbled, the Pope ejected from England, men of faith killed solely for their beliefs, the abbeys sold off to anyone rich enough to buy them.

The death of Mediaeval England was imminent before Morton passed away, and it was buried with him. John Morton was a man of his times, but he would have been found out of step with the future.

Endnotes

Chapter 1

1. Some sources, such as the *Chronicle of London*, record Morton's death as October. The *Register of Canterbury* gives 15 September. Let us put our faith on this occasion in Canterbury.
2. Henry Edyall was a Chancery clerk in 1473 who continued in royal service under Richard III and was one of those sent to entice Morton back to England with a pardon. He transferred to Archbishop Bourchier's staff and became a close associate and protégé of Morton, supervising extension work at Knole. He was also an executor of Morton's will. John Fyneux will be knighted in 1503. The others in waiting are Clement Broune, Morton's chaplain; Robert Boure, another chaplain of Morton; Robert Rede, King's Sergeant; Ralph St Leger, lawyer; and Edward Ferrers, later knighted as a Member of Parliament.

Chapter 2

1. Morton's birth date is unknown as the parish registers of Bere Regis were burnt in 1788. He is generally believed to have been born around 1420. Information on his siblings suggests that the date was a little earlier, possibly around 1417–1418.
2. Robert Morton of Harworth held many official posts including Master of the Royal Falcons and Master of the Ordnance, the latter his position on Henry V's last campaign. A Sheriff of Nottingham and Derbyshire, he sat on numerous commissions of inquiry: which, as a man of the times, doesn't mean to say that he was always on the right side of the law.

3. Harfleur was the main port of north-west France in the Middle Ages. Being part of Normandy, it was governed by the King of England for several centuries, having received its charter as a town from King John in 1202.

4. The notion of 'affinity' is of increasing importance through the fifteenth century as the classic feudal system declined in the wake of the Great Plague and severe labour shortages. A bastardised feudal system emerged based increasingly on monetary or wage service and less on manorial obligations. Men were tied by family connections and aspirations and friendships, or local economic interdependence. These affinities could take on an importance of their own in competition with the classic pyramid structure of society, where ultimate authority and the right to allegiance was held by the Crown.

5. It is as though Henry, unlike the French, recalls his history lessons and the Battle of the Golden Spurs in 1302 between the men of Bruges and French cavalry. The town's ad-hoc militia were charged by the French horsemen who became bogged down in the peatlands between the two forces and were consequently massacred by their Flemish enemy, the 'golden spurs' of the French nobility taken as trophies.

6. Sir Thomas Erpingham (1357–1428) was the classic staunch supporter of the Lancastrian kings. The custodian of Richard II, he openly sought the death of the King and his supporters and succeeded in many cases. A renowned soldier and administrator he not a person to cross.

7. Michael de la Pole, Earl of Suffolk (1394–1415). His father died at the siege of Harfleur, so he had only just assumed the title. Sir Richard Kyghley or Keighley (1370–1415) of Inskip, Lancashire, was commander of the Lancastrian archers.

8. Sir Gilbert Umphraville (1390–1421) (unofficially known as Earl of Kyme). Died at the battle of Bauge, in which Henry's brother Thomas, Duke of Clarence also perished. Sir John Cornwaille (or Cornwall), later Baron Fanhope and Milbroke. (1364–1443) was born on board a ship in Mounts Bay, Cornwall. Renowned for his combative skills and for collecting ransomable prisoners, he was stood next to his son who had his head blown off by stone shot at the siege of Meaux in 1421, the horror of which caused him to reject warfare.

9. In 1403, when he was sixteen years old, Henry fought alongside his father at Shrewsbury to suppress the rebellion by Henry 'Hotspur' Percy and Thomas Percy, the Earl of Worcester. The arrowhead was extracted from his face by the Physician General, John Bradmore,

using a specially crafted tool – there were no anaesthetics of course – and the open wound was packed with honey as an antiseptic, then flushed with alcohol.

10. Isabelle (1389–1409) was only 6 years old at the time of her marriage to Richard II. He was 29. It was unlawful for a marriage to be consummated with a girl under twelve and Isabelle was eleven when Richard died. She was allowed to return to France in 1401 and in 1406 married Charles, Duke of Orleans. She died aged nineteen giving birth to a daughter. Charles' father, Louis of Orleans, had been murdered by John the Fearless, Duke of Burgundy, and Henry V's ally. Charles, Duke of Orleans, (1394–1465), was twenty-one years old when wounded and captured at Agincourt and was held prisoner for twenty-five years. As mentioned above, Charles was the son of Louis, murdered by John of Burgundy and had sworn an oath of vengeance on his father's killer. He was the natural head of the Armagnac faction in France in the struggle against the Burgundians. Henry had a strong alliance with Burgundy and so insisted that Charles was not released. Only when there appeared to be reconciliation between the Armagnacs and Burgundians, and Charles specifically renounced his oath for vengeance, was he released in 1440. That said, his 'imprisonment' in England was more akin to a never-ending royal tour as he moved from castle to castle, enjoying as good a standard of living as he had been used to before. When he did return to France, it is said he spoke better English than French.

11. Philip Morgan was a Welsh Doctor of civil and canon law who eventually became Bishop of Worcester and a Privy Councillor (1419) and Bishop of Ely (1426). He died in 1435. John the Fearless, Duke of Burgundy (1371–1419) is one of the more unlikeable French characters. His fearless side was more than matched by recklessness. In his efforts to gain control of the French regency over Charles VI, he had the king's brother Louis, Duke of Orleans, murdered and openly admitted to this. The consequence was the Armagnac-Burgundian civil war, which greatly aided Henry V's campaign. Burgundy was, in turn, murdered by the Dauphin with an axe in his skull while attending a set-up meeting to discuss reconciliation.

12. John Hovyngham, Archdeacon of Durham. An Oxford graduate in law. A favourite diplomat of Henry V he died 1417. Simon Flete was a London merchant, one time Master or Keeper of the King's Jewels for Henry IV.

13. Thomas Morton signed up for the campaign with William Balne (Clerk of the King's Kitchen), Walter Burton (Clerk of

the Comptrolership), Robert Castel (Clerk to the Marshalcy, a court to resolve disputes in the royal household – he survived the battle, apparently dying in 1436 following an attempted eviction of a tenant), John Feriby (also a Clerk of the Wardrobe), John Langville (Clerk of the King's Spicery), and Stephen Payne (King's Almoner and named in Henry's will), each also providing three archers.

14. At Caen in 1417, Henry orders 1800 to be slaughtered in cold blood. At the siege of Rouen 1418–19, Henry is responsible for thousands of non-combatants dying from starvation and cold.

Chapter 3

1. Also known as Cecilia or Cecily, Celia is, from her first marriage, an ancestor of Jane Seymour, third wife of Henry VIII. The Turberville family is the basis for Thomas Hardy's fictional D'Urbervilles.

2. Many sources say there are five brothers, but this seems a very weak claim. The fifth brother is said to be Sir Rowland Morton, born sometime around 1430. Rowland lived at Bosbury, Hertfordshire and it is known that he founded Bosbury Grammar School in 1540 (which would have made him about 110 years old). Neither he nor his offspring receive any mention in John Morton's will. All of which suggests Sir Rowland is from another branch of the Morton diaspora.

3. His symptoms persisted long enough for Catherine to visit him from England which suggests dysentery was not the principal or sole cause of death. It was also reported that he had 'St Fiacre's Ill', St Fiacre being the patron saint of haemorrhoid sufferers.

4. The Great Western Schism (1378–1417) followed the election of the Italian Pope Urban VI who was considered too regulatory and overbearing by a sizeable number of Cardinals who professed to being bullied into voting for him. So they elected a French Pope, Clement VII, who ran a separate church based in Avignon. The Avignon Popes were followed by France, Spain, Naples, and Scotland. The Roman Popes led the rest of the western Catholic world including England. The Schism was resolved at a general council in Constance, Germany with the election of Martin V as Pontiff.

5. The Black Death was not named as such until 1755.

6. In 1420, sown crops on demesne land were 10.8%, a half of what they were forty years previously. By 1450, they were 6.4% of production and by the end of the century had disappeared.

7. There is no extant information about William's bride, so her age is an estimation based on William's age. The details of the marriage ceremony reflect common practice in the south-west.

8. It is said that a third of brides at that time gave birth less than eight months after their wedding.

9. Abbot Godmanston was elected in 1436 and remained in charge of the abbey until his death in 1451. The local roots of the abbey community are shown by 6 of the 8 surnames of the 15th-century abbots being Dorset locations.

10. Wycliffe was declared a heretic in 1415 (although he had died in 1384) and his writings should be burned. His remains were dug up in 1428, burned, and the ashes cast into the River Swift at Lutterworth.

Chapter 4

1. Margaret, eldest daughter of Scottish king James I, is married to the Dauphin Louis in 1437, notwithstanding great effort on the part of the English to kidnap her in her sea crossing. It was an unhappy marriage and she died childless in 1445 aged twenty.

2. Calais is put under siege by Burgundy, who is seen of by Devon and Gloucester. Berwick is besieged by the Scots who are also sent packing, this time by Northumberland and Westmorland. The Scottish threat was diminished by the assassination of James I in 1437 and the accession of his son James II, a twelve-year-old boy, which threw the country into civil wars. James II (known as 'Fiery Face' from a birthmark) would die in 1460 at the siege of Roxburgh Castle when a cannon exploded next to him.

3. Edmund (1430–1456), created Earl of Richmond, would father the future Henry VII. However, he supported Richard, Duke of York against his half-brother Henry VI. He was captured and died, imprisoned, of bubonic plague. Jasper (1431–1495), created Duke of Bedford and Earl of Pembroke, supported Henry VI. He was subject to attainder by Edward IV and became a principal architect in getting Henry VII onto the throne.

4. Dervorguilla's youngest son, John Balliol, was supported to the Scottish throne by Edward I, only to be crushed when he tried to exert independence. After imprisonment, he was exiled to France.

5. William Grey (1412–1478) becomes Chancellor of Oxford University in 1440 and for part of 1442. He travels extensively in Europe absorbing Renaissance art and culture. He is Bishop of Ely from 1454 until his death, taking the position from Bishop Bourchier on his translation to Canterbury. He is succeeded at Ely

by John Morton. For a time, he was Lord High Treasurer, a post he held during a time of sharp economic misfortune. He also attempted to pacify the ambitions of the Yorkist leaders but failed here, too. His passion was for Italian Renaissance humanism and, on his death, his collection of manuscripts went to Balliol, reputed to be the finest and largest collection in England from the Middle Ages.

Richard Bole became chaplain to Cardinal Kemp, when Archbishop of York, and after several ecclesiastical appointments Archdeacon of Ely, a position he held until his death in 1477. Nicholas Saxton, a Yorkshireman, studied theology in Florence and developed friendships with the leading book publishers of the time. He became vicar of All Saint's, Malden in Essex and rector of Danbury.

Chapter 5

1. William Vowell is from Wells, Somerset. He goes on to become a notary public and a leading man in the town. Edmund Martyn is from Dorset.
2. Margery had also prophesied that Somerset's son, Edmund, would not die in battle if he avoided castles. He died in the first Battle of St Albans 1455 in the Castle Inn.
3. Adam de Moleynes was Dean of St Buryan's College, Cornwall, before being elected Dean of Salisbury. He provided evidence against Eleanor Cobham, was appointed to the Privy Council and carried out numerous diplomatic missions. He becomes Keeper of the Privy Seal in 1444 and Bishop of Chichester in 1445. Charles VII of France (1403–1461), known as Charles the Victorious, was disinherited by his father in favour of Henry V. He overcomes early indecisiveness from the example of Joan of Arc and eventually drives the English from France, with the exception of Calais, during his reign.

Chapter 6

1. To be merged into the site of Christ Church College during the reign of Henry VIII.
2. It is unclear which college Morton did move to. Merton is often suggested, possibly because of its proximity to and links with Balliol. On the other hand, All Souls is the only Oxford college referenced in Morton's will.
3. Also known as Domus Dei, or the Garrison Church after the Reformation.

4. It is often thought that the murder was carried out by servicemen in the town who were dissatisfied with the payments they had received from Moleynes towards their unmet wages. However, at the time of his death Moleynes was no longer acting as an agent of the state, so it is unlikely that he would have been distributing cash.
5. Richard of York was a Mortimer through his mother's side.
6. Cromer's widow marries Sir Alexander Iden, who captures and kills the mysterious Jack Cade. The rebels have a spy in their camp, John Payne, who smuggles out a list of their targets and demands to Sir John Fastolf (who is himself on the list). Others include Thomas Daniel, MP for Cornwall and later for Buckingham. Daniel is a turncoat and bribe taker, though at heart a Lancastrian. Always sailing close to the wind, he was attainted for treason in 1461 but recovered his lands in 1472 and died in Ireland. Another corrupt MP and member of the royal household was John Trevelyan, a Cornishman who first represented Huntingdon and later his home county. A staunch Lancastrian, he was evidently useful. Close to being attainted he regained favour in 1452 to become Armourer of the Tower and went on to be granted three separate pardons by Edward IV.
7. Tresham was murdered at Thorpland Close, Northamptonshire, about 14 miles from his manor at Sywell. He had been run through with a spear. His widow, Isabel, sought to impeach Lord Gray of Ruthin whose two named Welsh servants did the deed, and also Simon Norwich, a local landowner who had discovered Tresham's proposed route. The murderers were never tried and used threats to push the coroner's jury to return a verdict of suicide and later to persuade Tresham's widow not to pursue her petition to impeach.
8. Thomas Young (1405–1476) was an experienced lawyer and administrator with strong Yorkist leanings. It is unlikely that his petition was made without York's knowledge and consent. Young eventually returned to parliament as an MP for Gloucester and would become a judge on the King's Bench.
9. George Neville, (1432–1476) became Bishop of Exeter at the age of 25 in 1458. He would become Archbishop of York and a Chancellor of Oxford university. The extravagance of his enthronement at York is a mediaeval legend. 4000 pigeons and 4000 crays, 2000 chickens, 204 cranes, 104 peacocks, 100 dozen quails, 400 swans and 400 herons, 113 oxen, six wild bulls, 608 pike and bream, 12 porpoises and seals, 1000 sheep, 300 tuns of ale and 100 tuns of wine; the list goes on. He would make an art of switching sides to suit his purpose.
10. Thomas Bourchier (1404–1486) is a leading figure in this story. He was a great grandson of Edward III through Thomas of Woodstock.

Chapter 7

1. The rector was the official incumbent of a parish or church and received all tithes (by custom, 10% of income from all within its bounds). Often, particularly with plural benefices, the rector would appoint a salaried vicar to carry out his local duties.
2. John Talbot (1387–1453) was the most renowned and aggressive military commander in the later part of the wars with France. He died leading a charge against enemy cannon, wrongly believing the French were in retreat. The death of father and son is immortalised in Shakespeare's *Henry VI, Part I*, Act IV, Scene VI.
3. John Mowbray (1415–1461), Duke of Norfolk, was married to Eleanor Bourchier and vigorously applied himself against the family enemy William de la Pole, Duke of Suffolk. Described as a 'disreputable thug' he was constantly in trouble with the crown and imprisoned twice in the Tower. His violent and disruptive nature seemed to serve him well on military campaigns, but he believed he had the right to act in like manner when back in England. In 1460, he sided with York and played an important part in Edward IV's victory at Towton.

Chapter 8

1. Sadly, the 15th century records of the Court were destroyed in the Great Fire of London in 1666 along with the original church. Some copies of documents were held at Canterbury, though very incomplete, otherwise only glimpses of its proceedings are seen in in the records of some churches affected by its decisions.
2. Henry Beaufort, third Duke of Somerset (1436–1464) was by his father's side when the latter was killed at the first battle of St Albans. His life was dominated by the thirst for revenge over the killing, directed at York and Warwick.

Chapter 9

1. Robert Whittingham, later knighted, was a staunch Lancastrian and fought at both battles of St Albans, Wakefield and Towton. He was killed at the battle of Tewksbury, 1471.
2. John Treffrey will become an active supporter of Henry VII, against Richard III.
3. A prebend is a benefice drawn from specific sources within the estate of the diocese. For receipt of the prebend, the prebendary will

perform an administrative service such as auditing the accounts of the church or cathedral.

4. The commission was appointed 24 October 1457 to 'make inquisition in the county of Norfolk touching any treasons, misprisions, insolences or slanders committed by John Wode of Estbarsham (East Barsham), gentleman, against the king's person or majesty and royalty and against the persons and honour of Queen Margaret and Prince Edward.' Of the eight commissioners appointed, four meet violent ends and a fifth is attainted (and possibly flees). Lord Roos, who commands Henry's right flank at the battle of Wakefield, is beheaded after Hexham by the Yorkists, as is Sir Philip Wentworth (great grandfather of Jane Seymour) in 1464. Sir Thomas Tudenham is beheaded in 1462 and Sir Thomas de Scales, who held the Tower against the Yorkists, is murdered fleeing by boat to the sanctuary of Westminster Abbey in 1460. Giles St Lo, sheriff of Norfolk, is attainted in 1461. Only William Yelverton (a Norfolk judge and twice MP for Great Yarmouth), John Fyncham, and Thomas Danyell (widely described as 'a rogue') appear to have had a more peaceful end.

5. Lady Day is the first day of the New Year and remains so until the calendar changes in 1752.

6. The Hanseatic League was a confederation of trading guilds and towns in northern Europe which had a near monopoly of routes in the North Sea and the Baltic Sea. It began with some German towns and grew to include parts of the Netherlands, Poland, Estonia, and Russia. It was being challenged by the 14th century but remained strong until the 17th, and still had some recognition and meaning in the 19th century.

Chapter 10

1. Audley is killed by Roger Kynaston who, to celebrate his victory in combat, incorporates elements of the Audley coat of arms into his own. Kynaston was knighted by Edward IV after the battle of Tewkesbury in 1471. His first wife died in childbirth and his second wife, Elizabeth Grey, was a granddaughter of Humphrey, Duke of Gloucester, and the grandniece of his first wife. Of their six children, 'Wild' Humphrey Kynaston was the most noteworthy. A highwayman convicted of murder in 1491, he fled to a remote cave to live a Robin Hood lifestyle, eventually earning a pardon from Henry VIII.

2. Fortescue will go into exile with Henry VI and will be attainted himself by Edward IV in 1461. Henry makes him nominal

Chancellor of England during the exile, and he is with Margaret and her court from 1463 to 1471. Following Henry's murder, his attainder is reversed by Edward in 1471 and he returns to England. As with Morton, good legal and administrative minds seem hard to come by and they welcomed back into the fold by all parties.

3. Sadly for Thomas Thorpe, his revenge on York, while fully realised, was not to be enjoyed for long. He held out in the Tower to the 1460 invasion, was caught, escaped twice but was then summarily beheaded by the mob in 1461.

4. Those named in the bill of attainder are the Duke of York; his sons the Earl of Rutland and the Earl of March; the Earl of Salisbury, his wife and his three sons, the Earl of Warwick, Sir Thomas Neville, and Sir John Neville; Lord John Clinton; Sir John Wenlock; Sir Thomas Harrington; Sir John Conyers; Sir Thomas Parr; Sir James Pickering; William Stanley (Lord Stanley's brother). John and Edward Bourchier; Thomas Colt; John Clay; Sir William Oldhall and Thomas Vaughan. Richard Grey, Lord Powys, Sir Walter Devcraux and Sir Harry Radford were also named but having been given a life pardon by Henry after Ludford were now also formally given general pardons. In fact, Henry only gave a full pardon to five and three of those slipped back into their Yorkist ways: Harry Radford who was killed at Wakefield the following year; Lord Powys who switched in 1461 and was at the siege of Alnwick castle with Warwick; and John Wenlock, who hopped back and forth finally joining the Lancastrians at Tewkesbury in 1471, to be killed by his own side for failing to engage the enemy. Of the twenty-four named in the bill, fourteen met a violent end.

5. 'Tunnage and poundage' are the equivalents of customs duties granted to the crown. Tunnage relates to a duty payable on each tun, or cask of wine imported, and poundage was a tax on all imports and exports proportionate to value.

Chapter 11

1. There is disagreement between historians as to where Margaret and Prince Edward are while the battle of Northampton rages. Many, including Scofield and Kendall, say that Henry left them at Coventry. *Hall's Chronicle* is explicit in placing Margaret at Northampton. Dan Jones maintains Henry and Margaret travelled together, at least for part if not the whole of the journey to Northampton, but he is not specific. Stuart Bradley, in his life of John Morton, says that Margaret and Edward remained behind at Kenilworth. Even if

Endnotes

they did receive news of Warwick's advance at Cheylesmore House, Coventry, it would be natural for them to take the short journey to Kenilworth to fall in with and oversee the transportation of artillery and other weaponry. The threat was an urgent one (there was no time to wait for the northern lords to join them). For Henry to leave his wife and his heir in the substantial fortifications of Kenilworth seems the sensible option.

2. Exeter (1430–1475) is a faithful adherent to the Lancastrian cause but has a well-deserved reputation as a cruel, temperamental bully. While he was Constable of the Tower, the rack became known as 'the Duke of Exeter's Daughter'. On inheriting his title at seventeen, he was married to York's eldest daughter Anne, aged eight. Relations between him and his father-in-law are poisonous: to the extent that in 1455, York dragged him out of sanctuary in Westminster and put him into the Tower for a year. It would seem that Anne was physically and psychologically abused (not the best way to treat Edward IV's sister) and Exeter also played a leading part in her father's defeat and death. They became separated in 1464 and divorced 1472, when she married Sir Thomas St Leger, to die of complications in childbirth in 1476. Although Exeter was apparently rehabilitated with Edward IV, poor results in an incursion into France saw him 'slip and fall' from his ship on the return journey; just as likely a murder as an accident. Anne's daughter from her marriage with Exeter (also named Anne) predeceased her, but brother Edward allowed Exeter's estate (more or less intact) to be remaindered (passed on) to her daughter from St Leger (another Anne).

3. Francesco Coppini (1415–1464) was an Italian lawyer and priest. Ambitious, he rose to bishop but failed to obtain the cardinal's hat, which was his ultimate goal. His pro-York activities led to complaints to the Pope from England and from France. But more than that, he had been sponsored for elevation to cardinal by Warwick on the understanding that he would excommunicate Margaret's followers and absolve his own men. This he failed to do, knowing it was beyond his authority, and fled England just before the second battle of St Albans. An apoplectic Warwick withdrew support and became his enemy. In 1462 he was dismissed from his bishopric, tried for simony (such as selling pardons to anyone who fought for York against Henry VI), embezzlement, and using the church to incite civil war. Banished to a Roman abbey, he died soon after.

4. This Audley is John Tuchet (1423–1490), 6th Baron Audley, who assumed the title in 1459.

5. Harlech Castle is held by Dafydd ap Ievan against the Yorkists until 1468. The last major Lancastrian stronghold, it eventually falls to William Herbert.

6. Robert Hungerford, Lord Moleyns and Hungerford (1431–1464) was infamous for his violent quarrel with John and Margaret Paston of Gresham, Norfolk. He fled to Scotland with Henry after the battle of Towton and was captured at the battle of Hexham and executed at Newcastle. Sir Edmund Hampden fought at Towton and fled to exile in Scotland with Margaret. He became Chamberlain to Prince Edward and died at the battle of Tewkesbury in 1471.

7. The Earl of Kendal (1415–1485) was John de Foix, a Gascon noble. After the surrender of the Tower, he accompanied Warwick to France where he entered the service of Louis XI. John Lovell (d. 1465) appears to have found favour with the Yorkists and at his death held several manors acquired during Edward IV's reign. He was father of Francis, Viscount Lovell, Richard III's Lord Chamberlain. Sir Richard West, 7th Baron de la Warr (1430–1476) was the son-in-law of Robert, Lord Hungerford. He seems to have made his peace with the Yorkists and received a full formal pardon from Edward IV in 1471. In the meantime, he went on a three-year European tour with a retinue of servants, possibly to visit religious centres. Of his nine children, two sons and two daughters entered the Church. Henry Bromflete, Baron de Vesey, died in 1469 and the barony became extinct with him. Gervase Clifton (1438–1491) was Sherriff of Nottingham and later Treasurer of Calais. He fought with Richard III at the battle of Bosworth.

Chapter 12

1. This was the same Thomas Neville who was captured at the battle of Blore Heath just fifteen months previously.

2. It is claimed that Sir Henry Lovelace had revealed Warwick's position to Queen Margaret, as he had been spared after capture at Wakefield. Lovelace was steward of Warwick's household. He was never attainted but, according to the French chronicler Jean de Waurin, was executed in London just before Edward IV set out for Towton.

3. Thomas Hoo (1435–1516) of St Paul's Walden in Hertfordshire was half-brother to Baron Hoo and Hastings, great-great grandfather of Anne Boleyn.

4. Baron Tuchet (1423–1490) was originally a Lancastrian but after his capture in 1460 at Calais by Warwick and on meeting Edward,

he switched sides. He fought for Edward at all the subsequent major battles in the War of the Roses and was also Lord High Treasurer for Richard III. John Wenlock is another fence sitter who changed sides from Lancaster to York, York to Lancaster, finally falling at the battle of Tewkesbury in 1471. Walter Deveraux will be knighted after the battle of Towton and then made Baron Ferrers. He becomes a Knight of the Garter and a tutor to Edward's son. He will die at Bosworth fighting for Richard. William Herbert (1423–1469) known as 'Black William', was another protégé of Edward, made a Knight of the Garter after Towton and created Baron Herbert of Raglan, after which he was elevated to Earl of Pembroke in place of Jasper Tudor. He was executed with his brother Richard after the battle of Edgecote Moor. William Hastings (1431–1483) was a leading figure in the reigns of Edward IV of Richard III. Another close friend of Edward IV, he was knighted at Towton and created Baron Hastings. Humphrey Stafford (1439–1469). Earl of Devon and Baron Stafford of Southwick, like Tuchet, switched sides at Calais from Lancaster to York. Knighted at Towton and created a Baron, he eventually took over most of the Courtney estate and was created Earl of Devon in 1469. He fell out with William Herbert at the battle of Edgecote Moor. He escaped Herbert's fate, but only for a while. He was executed in Bridgwater soon after.

5. A notable event at this battle in the early morning was the apparent appearance of three suns: a meteorological phenomenon known as a parhelion caused by the refraction of light through ice crystals. Edward proclaimed it as a good omen and later adopted the Sun in Splendour as his emblem.

6. Baldwin Fulford (1415–1461), Sheriff of Devon, fought in the 1443 crusade against the Turks. Under-admiral of the fleet, he fought at Towton. He was executed at Bristol. His wife was the exotically named Jennet Bosom. Alexander Hody (1428–1461), MP for Somerset, died at Towton.

7. Edmund Hampden (1398–1471). Privy Councillor and Joint-Treasurer of Ireland died at the battle of Tewkesbury. John Heron (1418–1461) of Ford Castle, Northumberland died at Towton. Robert Whittingham (1429–1471), Mayor of the Merchant Staplers, died at Tewkesbury.

8. There is no clear evidence that this happened. However, it is commonly cited that Morton was appointed to this benefit in 1460 but did not take it up until 1461. This seems to be his only opportunity for doing that. Walter Hart aka Walter Lyhert was a former provost of Oriel College, Oxford (1435–1446). He was bishop from 1446–1472, dying in office.

9. To recap, this is the same Lord Clifford who slayed the seventeen-year-old Earl of Rutland at Wakefield.

10. Sir William Plumpton (1404–1480) fought against France under the Duke of Bedford, and then became Constable of Knaresborough castle from 1439. Appointed seneschal of the estates of the Earl of Northumberland, he oversaw some violent local conflicts with some success and was made Sheriff for Yorkshire and then for Nottinghamshire and Derbyshire. He had seven daughters and two sons by his first marriage, both sons predeceasing him – one at Towton. He then had two more sons, by a secret marriage, later legitimised before the ecclesiastical court at York. Like Morton, Makerel is an Oxford lawyer who will eventually retire as Parson of St. Giles church, Risby, Suffolk.

11. Sir Richard Salkeld (1425–1500). In the summer of 1461, he captained Carlisle against a siege by Lancastrian-Scottish forces.

12. Sir William Hastings (1431–1483) later to become Baron Hastings, King's Chamberlain (controlling access to the king), was one of the richest and most powerful men in the kingdom. His future and Morton's will become entwined.

13. Bourchier is replaced as Constable of the Tower by John Tiptoft, Earl of Worcester, in December 1461.

Chapter 13

1. Sir John Scudamore was a consistent supporter of the Lancastrian cause in Wales. He fought at Mortimer's Cross and though he managed to escape to Pembroke Castle, several close relatives, including his eldest son Henry, were among those beheaded after the battle. He was one of those who were excluded from the general pardon offered by Edward IV, and though he had been promised that he would not be deprived of his property when he surrendered Pembroke, his estates were eventually forfeited, although his 'life, goods and chattels' were spared. With the surrender of Pembroke Castle, Herbert was given custody of one of its occupants – the four-year-old Henry Tudor, son of Margaret Beaufort, Countess of Richmond and stepson of Sir Henry Stafford.

2. Margaret's faithful friend, Pierre de Breze, went on to be reconciled with Louis and died fighting for him against Charolais, the Duke of Berry, and the Duke of Brittany (under the flag of the League of the Public Weal) at the battle of Montlhéry on 16 July 1465. Perversely, it was Margaret's uncle, the Count du Maine, who proved treacherous to Louis on the battlefield, not Breze.

Chapter 14

1. Perhaps it is fair to say that the rise of the Woodvilles was also inevitable and, to a degree, necessary. Elizabeth was widely regarded by conservative society as too low-born for the role of queen. It would be necessary to see her family elevated to raise her own 'qualifications' for the job. It would be equally necessary to project a seriously regal image – which would readily feed claims by her enemies that she was arrogant, vain, ambitious and greedy. But she lived within her means, was not unduly extravagant (in the context of her husband's flamboyance), did her duty, and did not get involved in politics – unlike Margaret.

2. Anne Woodville (1438–1489) married William, Viscount Bourchier and, secondly, Sir George Grey, 2nd Earl of Kent and 5th Baron Grey de Ruthin. Joan Woodville (1452–1512) married Sir Anthony Grey who was made Constable of Harlech Castle. He was the eldest son of the Earl of Kent but died before he could inherit, the title going to his younger brother George.
   Jacquetta Woodville (1444–1509) married John, 8th Baron Strange. Mary Woodville (1456–1481) married William Herbert, Lord Dunster, who became Earl of Pembroke on the execution of his father, after which Mary assumed the title Countess.

3. Robin of Redesdale has been variously identified as Sir John Conyers, Steward of Warwick's castle at Middleham (probably the best possible suspect), his son, also a John Conyers, Sir William Conyers, Sir Richard Welles, or Sir Henry Neville. The Earl of Northumberland, John Neville, seems to have made only the feeblest attempt to catch 'Robin', suggesting that he may have known or guessed his brother, Warwick, was behind it.

4. This uprising is directly against the personal interests of John Neville, so he thoroughly crushes it and seizes and executes its leader, Robert Hillyard, a Percy tenant. It has been suggested though that this rising, and the execution of its alleged leader, was a fabrication of the Neville brothers to put John in a good light following his failure to nail Robin of Redesdale.

5. Attending Sandwich for the purpose of seeing her son George of Clarence was Cecily, Dowager Duchess of York. It has been speculated that she had caught wind of the conspiracy and sought to dissuade Clarence from going through with it. On the other hand, she may have been giving it her seal of approval. If she did disapprove, she doesn't seem to have warned Edward and if she did approve, she would have known or suspected that her insinuation five years previously that Edward was a bastard would be put about again.

Chapter 15

1. Angers is the principal city of Anjou, chosen by Louis for this meeting so that Margaret's father, Rene, would be on hand to add weight to the arguments should she prove difficult.

2. Henry, Lord Fitzhugh (1429–1472) married Lady Alice Neville with whom he had eleven children. Daughter Elizabeth was the mother of Catherine Parr, fifth wife of Henry VIII, and daughter Anne was the wife of Francis Lovell, Richard III's Lord Chamberlain.

3. Sir Geoffrey Gates, alternatively Gate (1402–1477) was sometime Marshal of Calais and Captain of the Isle of Wight.

4. The Countess of Warwick had chosen to land at Plymouth from where she went to Southampton. On hearing of her husband's fate, she took sanctuary in Beaulieu Abbey.

5. On 10 August 1471, Edward IV issued a general pardon to the Abbot of Cerne Abbey for all offences committed by him before 6 August and for all alienations and acquisitions of land made without the King's licence. There is a tradition that this pardon confirms Margaret of Anjou was entertained at the abbey and held a council there before the battle of Tewkesbury.

6. Thomas Neville (1429–1471), known as the Bastard of Fauconberg, was the son of William Neville, Lord Fauconberg. He was renowned as a sailor, fighting pirates in the Channel and North Sea.

7. Sir John Arundel (1421–1473) of Lanherne, Cornwall, was Sheriff and Admiral of Cornwall. Anne, the daughter from his first wife, married Sir James Tyrell (himself appointed High Sheriff of Cornwall in 1484), the self-confessed murderer of Edward V and his brother in the Tower. Sir Hugh Courtenay (1427–1471) He was twice MP for Cornwall.

8. Sir John Langstrother was Prior of the Knights Hospitaller in England, a previous councillor of Edward who defected to the Lancastrians to become their Lord High Treasurer.

9. There is no reference to the men accompanying the ladies in sanctuary, but it seems highly unlikely that they would have been without some male protection and the presence of these non-combatants makes it a reasonable assumption.

10. Fauconberg could have escaped with his Calais men but chose to seek pardon from Edward, which he received on 6 June along with letters of protection. He then went north accompanying Richard of Gloucester to put down disturbances there. The next official note is that he fled Gloucester's service, was apprehended by him, and beheaded at Middleham. It seems strange that he should flee only

a couple of months after spurning the opportunity to do so. Was it Gloucester's intention to get rid of him, being a Neville, once away from his supporters in Kent and the south-east, irrespective of Edward's pardon?

11. Alice de la Pole (1404–1475) was a granddaughter of Geoffrey Chaucer. She became Duchess of Suffolk on her third marriage to William de la Pole, who was murdered on his way into exile in 1450. A long-standing friend of Queen Margaret, Alice was a patron of the arts, a fierce protector of her son John de la Pole – who married Edward IV's sister Elizabeth, a wealthy and ruthless landowner, and one of the few Ladies of the Order of the Garter.

12. Katherine Vaux (1440–1509) was born in Piemonte, Italy, the wife of Sir William Vaux killed at the battle of Tewkesbury. Katherine was captured with Margaret at Tewkesbury and stayed with her both in England and when she was released into exile. Her steadfastness was acknowledged and rewarded by both Henry VII and Henry VIII.

13. Edward, Richard, and others were lodged at the Tower that night: no doubt celebrating their victories but also preparing to journey out the next day to deal with Fauconberg and the Kentish mob. There is also no doubt that Henry was killed on Edward's order and did not die of 'displeasure and melancholy' as one chronicler put it. When his body was exhumed in 1910, damage to the skull and bloodmatted hair were recorded. It is possible, though unlikely, that Richard would have been present or would have participated in the murder. More likely it would have been under the supervision of the Constable of the Tower, John Sutton, the Baron Dudley. Originally a Lancastrian, he later sided with the Yorkists and fought for them at Towton, for which he was rewarded. Prior to 1461, he had been a favourite of Henry VI. However, it seems unrealistic to suppose that Richard did not understand or was not complicit in what was going on.

14. It was said that blood was seen to drip from the body while resting on 'the pavement'. Cuts can leak blood or fluid from the muscle ten hours after death, so this is quite possible and ties in with reports by the chroniclers that Henry was murdered just before midnight.

Chapter 16

1. Fortescue re-joined the Privy Council in 1474 but Makerel decided on the less stressful life of a country parson.

2. It later became the Public Records Office and is now the site of the Maughan Library of Kings College, London.

3. That said, the house rarely had more than three Jews in residence at any one time. Was England (and, indeed, Europe) antisemitic? In practice, most definitely, but subject to the qualification that there was no toleration for anyone who was not of the Catholic Christian faith. Perhaps one of the most famous converted Jews was Sir Edward Brampton, for whom Edward IV stood as godfather at his conversion, and who became a successful merchant and landowner, commanded a squadron of ships against the Earl of Oxford, and became Captain and Governor of Guernsey. He also has a role in the Perkin Warbeck story.

4. In 1500, the name Shene was changed to Richmond, both for the royal palace which was then about to be rebuilt and for the town which surrounded it. Modern-day Sheen is a village attached to Richmond.

5. De Vere is sent to Hammes Castle and imprisonment, from which he eventually escapes to command Lancastrian forces at the battle of Bosworth.

6. There has been a lot of debate in more recent times as to whether the marriage between Richard and Anne was lawful – although seemingly no such debate at the time. In that respect the matter is only of academic interest since all the relevant parties were deceased by the time Henry VII came to the throne. To be lawfully married, the wedded couple must – as prescribed by the fourth Lateran Council of 1215 – have more than four degrees of consanguinity separating them (that is, be at least fourth cousins). Essentially, a 'degree of consanguinity' is a generation. If that condition is not met, then a papal dispensation is needed to permit the marriage. Because it was very difficult for royalty to find partners where there wasn't some degree of consanguinity, then dispensations in the fourth degree were not unheard of. Dispensations for a blood link in the first degree would be. So, obviously, brother-sister or son-mother marriages would not be permitted. A dispensation would be required here for exactly the same reason as one was required for George, Duke of Clarence and Isobel, Anne's sister. There is no extant or discovered dispensation for this granted to Richard and Anne. However, that doesn't mean one wasn't granted and there would be no impediment to the issuing of such a dispensation. The absence of appropriate dispensation(s) would have given Clarence immediate grounds to stop the wedding which he so violently opposed – let alone the legal and ecclesiastical experts sitting around the council table. Nor was it unusual for a marriage to take place prior to the receipt of a dispensation where one was confidently expected. For example,

William Bourchier married Isabel Plantagenet, Edward IV's aunt, sometime before 25 April 1426 by a dispensation dated 5 June – at least six weeks after the event.

There was also a need for a similar distance in the 'degree of affinity' between the two people. Affinity is an impediment to marriage due to the relationship which either party has as a result of a kinship relationship created by another marriage, or as a result of extramarital intercourse. Richard and Anne did require a dispensation with regard to the 'affinity' created by Anne being the widow of Prince Edward. This affinity was in the third and fourth degree and a dispensation was duly granted on 22 April 1472.

The other alleged defect in their marriage is from a claim that they were related in the first degree of affinity. The proscribed list of people a man and woman cannot marry was set out quite clearly. A man could not marry his sister, but neither could he marry his sister-in-law. There is no bar to a man marrying the sister of his sister-in-law. There is no 'affinity', which arises from a valid marriage, whether consummated or not, and is an impediment to subsequent marriages between a man and blood relations of his wife and vice versa. Thus George could not marry Anne, nor Richard marry Isabel; but there is no impediment to Richard marrying Anne.

Chapter 17

1. Anne Beauchamp did enjoy a reasonable level of maintenance and freedom while at Middleham. She outlived both her daughters and sons-in-law and eventually returned to Beaulieu where she died in 1492.

2. John of Gloucester (aka John of Pontefract), whose possible mother was Alice Burgh, was acknowledged by Richard, knighted in 1483, and made Captain of Calais in 1485. Henry VII removed him from Calais but provided him with a pension. Katherine Plantagenet was also acknowledged by Richard. Her mother may have been Katherine Haute. She was married to William Herbert, the Earl of Huntingdon in 1484 but had died by 1487. Richard Plantagenet (aka Richard of Eastwell) was a bricklayer and gardener who died in 1550 age eighty-one. He allegedly visited Richard on the eve of Bosworth and was promised recognition if the day went Richard's way.

3. Thomas Vaughan was originally a Lancastrian (as had been the Woodvilles) but converted to the Yorkist cause. Along with Philip Malpas and William Hatclyf, he sailed for Ireland with Henry's treasury after the Yorkist defeat at the Battle of St Albans, with

Margaret threatening to enter London. But they were captured by French pirates. Edward IV ransomed Vaughan and his colleagues, for which Vaughan was forever thankful.

Chapter 18

1. Sir Thomas Montgomery (1430–1495) was a future Knight of the Garter. Sir William Hatclyf (1417–1480) is the William Hatclyf who fled London with Thomas Vaughan seeking to save part of Edward's treasury from Lancastrian plunder, only to fall into the hands of French pirates. A doctor of medicine, he had been on several diplomatic missions to Brittany, Burgundy, and the Hanseatic League.
2. John Russell, Archdeacon of Berkshire, acted for some years as a diplomat for Edward IV. He was made Lord Privy Seal in 1474, then Bishop of Rochester in 1476, and Bishop of Lincoln in 1480 until his death in 1493. He was, reluctantly, Lord Chancellor under Richard III until July 1485. He was appointed Chancellor of Oxford University in 1484.
3. The Hospital housed a priest and twelve poor mariners, who remembered in their daily prayers all 'merchants and mariners passing and labouring on the sea' to the port of Bristol.
4. Richard was given a dressing down by Edward for being so lacking in good manners and showing dissent to outsiders. So he did avail himself of Louis' hospitality and came away with gifts of plate and horses. But his attitude had planted the idea in Louis' head that Richard was no friend of France, an impression also held by by his successor.

Chapter 19

1. Richard was Isabel's fourth child. Only two survived into childhood, both to suffer execution as adults.
2. Sir John Donne (c1420–1503) was a Welsh supporter of the House of York, serving them most notably in Calais and Burgundy.
3. It was a lively and happy marriage but short-lived. Mary's great passion was to ride horses, preferably hunting with a hawk (she kept falcons and hunting dogs in her bedroom). In 1482, while on a hunt her horse threw her and landed on her back, breaking it. She died from the resulting internal injuries a few weeks later.
4. Beckhampton, the home of Roger Strugge, is just eleven miles from Sir Roger Tucotes' home and the latter eight miles from Chippenham,

which was the second night's stop-over for taking Ankarette to Warwick. Could it have been intended to arrest Tucotes at his home on the way from Frome to Warwick, and could there have been some local issues between Strugge and Tucotes? Both possibilities are highly speculative. Tucotes was a three-times sheriff of Wiltshire and an apparently loyal supporter of Clarence, being comptroller of his household. He sided with Clarence when he joined Warwick's revolt and was indicted for treason alongside him, was pardoned, and was a commissioner of array in Wiltshire.

5. Edward had apparently once hunted in woods on the land of Thomas Burdet, or Burdett (1423–1477) and had killed a white buck, for which he was angrily cursed behind his back. His dislike of Edward went deep, and he wrote and published pamphlets in March and May which were deemed treasonable. The thrust of them was that Clarence was the proper heir to Edward's throne.

6. This was, reputedly, to the Bowyer Tower, midway on the north curtain wall surrounding the main White Tower.

7. After 1547, the Chapel became the debating chamber for the House of Commons until it was destroyed by fire in 1834.

8. Anne dies on 19 November 1481, aged eight.

9. Anne's great-grandmother was a sister to Richard's grandmother.

10. John Strensham (Abbot of Tewkesbury 1468–1481) was, with Edward IV, godfather to Clarence's son in 1475. He was saying Mass in the Abbey after the battle of Tewkesbury 1471 when Edward burst in with his men seeking to remove Lancastrians from sanctuary. And he was in charge of the Abbey when Isabel gave birth to Clarence's son Richard. John Tapton was Dean of St Asaph Cathedral 1480–1487 and would become Master of St Catherine's College, Cambridge. Sir Roger Harewell (1445–1501) was a Worcester man through and through, being born there and dying there.

11. It has been speculated that Stillington may have been jailed for suggesting that Edward's marriage was bigamous and that he had given Clarence information to that effect, or even Richard at that time. This is based on events which will be considered further on, but there is no evidence to back up such stories. If it were true, it is difficult to see why Clarence – or even Gloucester – did not raise it at, or before, the trial, or indeed at Edward's wedding.

12. Richard Bell's selection was on 11 February 1478 and his ordination was on 26 April.

13. The Remembrancer is, as the title suggests, responsible for keeping a record of business pending, and prompting or setting the agenda, for those Lords who oversee the Exchequer. He is the chief clerk within the Exchequer.

Chapter 20

1. Little Downham village stands on a raised escarpment in an area of fenland which was often flooded throughout the year. It had been known as Duneham, acknowledging this. It is not to be confused with Downham Market, which is much further from Ely.
2. Saint Etheldreda (modern Anglicised equivalent Audrey) was the founder of Ely Cathedral. The daughter of a seventh-century king of East Anglia, she married twice but remained a virgin and, when her husband kept on insisting on consummation, she left him to found a nunnery at Ely. She died of plague *c.*680.
3. The Palace was bought from the diocese of Ely in 1538 by Henry VIII for bringing up his children. It is most closely associated with Elizabeth I when, as sister to Queen Mary, she was kept under 'house arrest' until Mary's death.
4. Nonetheless, James III was deeply despised by his people, not least his wife and eldest son. Eventually, it was his 15-year-old son, the future James IV, who nominally led the rebelling Scottish nobles in 1488 when he was slain at the Battle of Sauchieburn.
5. This would not last long: Albany had to flee Scotland again the very next year. He crossed the border to England from where he launched another assault, but without English backing he had no chance. Fleeing again to France, he died from a jousting injury in an encounter with the future Louis XII.

Chapter 21

1. Sir John Donne (1420–1503) was a distinguished courtier, married to Lord Hastings' sister, and was knighted at Tewkesbury. He was ambassador to the French court with Morton in 1477 and commissioned 'The Donne Triptych' by Hans Memling, which today hangs in the National Gallery, London, and two illuminated manuscripts in the British Museum.
2. A messuage is a house or cottage with land and outbuildings.
3. This has the equivalent monetary value of about £118,000 in 2022, or 16 years of income for a skilled labourer of the time. Today's 'real estate value' would, of course, be exponentially greater than that.
4. The parliament had elected a strong supporter of Richard, John Wode, as Speaker of the Commons and having praised Gloucester for his Scottish campaign, parliament was only too pleased to back a 'good news' story. Consequently, with Gloucester's direct and indirect lobbying, Richard's wardship of the western marches was

made a hereditary title, Carlisle became his, as did all the royal lands in Cumberland. He was given the right to appoint sheriffs and escheators (escheators handle – for a fee – the property of people who die without heirs, which then reverts to the Crown), and palatine rights over any land taken from the Scots.

5. It is also possible that Edward died from a series of strokes, although the effort required to accomplish what the Chroniclers suggested he did on his death bed make that questionable.

6. This has to mean that either the Archbishop of York, Thomas Rotherham, was in residence and received a summons to London which the leaders of the city interpreted as notice of Edward's death, or that Rotherham sent an early note to his diocese from London the best part of a week before the event. Rotherham was a strong supporter of the Queen and the Prince and was arrested along with Hastings and Morton by Richard. Since the report of Edward's death took at least four days to reach Ludlow (150 miles), it seems reasonable to assume it would take five to six days to reach York (220 miles), the city of York responding to a message sent out on the day or the day after the King fell ill.

7. There is no surviving copy of this will. In the original will, which does survive, there is no mention of a Protector. Since the King secures a promise of goodwill between Hastings and the Woodvilles, it is difficult to see a reason why he should want now to recommend a Protector rather than rely on a Council.

8. Of the four, Savage and Cheyne will fight for Henry Tudor against Richard III, and Collingbourne will be executed for his support of Henry and for pinning the famous lampoon to the door of St Paul's. 'The Catte, the Ratte and Lovell our dogge rulyth all Englande under a hogge': the cat being Catesby, the Rat being Ratcliff, and the hog Richard.

Chapter 22

1. A titular bishop is one without a particular diocese: a 'Bishop without portfolio'. Zeitun is a district of Cairo famed for apparitions of the Virgin Mary.

2. While the formal notices of Edward's demise may have left London a few days after the event, it is difficult to believe that Gloucester and/ or Rivers did not have their personal agents in the capital to dispatch the news almost immediately, as it is to think that the city of York did not send their condolences on to Richard, who was only fifty miles away.

3. Brecon is sometimes referred to as Brecknock.

4. Although Northampton is far from prosperous at this time. The following year the mayor of the town will decry its state of 'desolation and ruin'.

5. Ratcliffe came from a well-established family of Cumbrian gentry and was knighted after the battle of Tewkesbury. He became steward of Barnard Castle, fought alongside Richard in the Scottish wars and was married to Agnes, daughter of Henry, Baron Scrope.

6. Sir Thomas Gower (1445–1485) was knighted by Richard of Gloucester on the Scotland campaign in 1482.

7. Gloucester has no difficulty in being selective in applying his late brother's wishes. Thus, while an alleged alteration or codicil to Edward's will which hasn't been seen is completely relied on, explicit written confirmation by Edward of River's discretion in raising and directing the Prince of Wales and of Edward's complete faith in his brother-in-law is discounted. Richard is intellectually and morally already placing himself above his brother, his brother's family, and the rule of law.

8. Edmund Shaa (1434–1488) was a goldsmith who was engraver to the Royal Mint for twenty years. His brother, Ralph Shaa, preached against the legitimacy of Edward IV's marriage.

9. The Downs is a sheltered area of sea off the Kent Coast between Deal and Dover.

10. John Esteney was abbot of Westminster from 1474 until his death in 1498. He was born around 1418 of unmarried parents and entered monastic life in 1442. He permitted William Caxton to set up a printing press in the abbey precinct.

11. It has been asserted by some later historians that the absence from this meeting of some of the executors of the 1475 will, particularly Elizabeth, proves that a second will existed. This cannot be so. Elizabeth was in sanctuary and would have been at grave personal risk, as would her children, if she left the Abbey. Three of the executors named in the 1475 will had died: William, Bishop of Ely; Richard Fowler, Chancellor of the Duchy of Lancaster, and Richard Pygot. The naming of executors is a personal thing. It is not a responsibility or trust that 'goes with the job'. So as the 'new' Bishop of Ely, Morton would not have been an executor by right of that post. If he was an executor, he would have known of and agreed to his name being included in a new will, or in a codicil to the original. There is nothing to indicate this was the case. Thomas Rotherham remained an executor, even though he was no longer Bishop of Lincoln but was now Archbishop of York. He remained

an executor because he was Thomas Rotherham. Likewise, his replacement as Bishop of Lincoln did not become an executor of the will.

12. In 2022, that would be the equivalent of over £1.05 million or 50,000 days (approaching 150 years) wages for a skilled workman.

13. Buckingham had inherited a great deal of property from his great-great-grandmother, Eleanor de Bohun, wife of Thomas of Woodstock (youngest son of Edward III) and daughter of Humphrey de Bohun, Earl of Hereford, Essex and Northampton. Eleanor's younger sister and co-heir Mary de Bohun married Henry Bolingbroke, who became Henry IV, and her share of the de Bohun estates became incorporated into those of the House of Lancaster. When Henry VI was deposed by Edward IV, he then appropriated that half into the Crown estate. Henry of Buckingham claimed those lands should have devolved to him instead. Unsuccessful in regaining the property from King Edward, he now looks to Richard to help regain these lands. This is probably one of Buckingham's prime motives in supporting Richard's bid for the Crown.

14. John Gunthorpe became Dean of Wells cathedral in 1485 shortly after the accession of Henry VII. He died there in 1498.

15. Richard had moved out of his mother's residence at Baynard's Castle to Crosby Place pending the arrival of his wife, Anne. His son remained at Middleham. Crosby Place was the tallest residence in London at the time. Built around a courtyard, it had its own chapel, gardens, marble floors, and a great hall with oriel window.

16. Thomas Langton was chaplain to Edward IV and carried out several diplomatic missions. He will be promoted further under Richard's wing to the bishopric of Salisbury. Under Henry VII, he was moved to Winchester and in 1501 he was elected to succeed John Morton as Archbishop of Canterbury. He died of the plague just five days after his election.

Chapter 23

1. Charles Pilkington will receive substantial rewards from Richard III including Constable of Nottingham and Steward of Sherwood Forest. Robert Harrington is the brother of James Harrington, who has a long-standing relationship with Richard and a similarly lengthy feud with Stanley.

2. Oliver King (1432–1503) was a priest and lawyer who was fluent in written and spoken French. As well as carrying out diplomatic tasks for Edward IV, he was Clerk of the Signet and also Edward's

Secretary 'for the French tongue'. He became Bishop of Exeter in 1492 and was translated to Bishop of Bath and Wells in 1495.

3. For all his cries of 'Traitor', once crowned, Richard promised not to attaint Hastings but to give full protection to his widow, Katherine Neville, sister of 'The Kingmaker', together with her husband's property and the wardship of her son and her son-in-law the Earl of Shrewsbury. Given her husband's philandering ways, it is not inconceivable that Katherine was quite comfortable in receiving Richard's benevolence.

4. Elizabeth Shaw lived to be eighty-two, dying in 1527. On her release from prison she married Richard III's Solicitor General, Thomas Lynom.

5. Some versions of the story suggest the lady in question is Elizabeth Lucy, a mistress of Edward who bore him a son, Arthur Plantagenet, in 1461. That, of course, would not have helped Richard at all, since if there was a pre-contract with Elizabeth Lucy then Arthur had a potentially better claim to the throne than the Protector. As it is, Arthur went on to live until 1542.

6. The two sons of Edward IV were not formally disinherited from the throne until the following year, when Parliament passed Titulus Regius. So it follows that all Richard's actions as King in the intervening time were unlawful.

7. Six years on, an uprising occurs in York by some of its citizens angered at the raising of taxes by Henry VII. One of their acts of civil disobedience is the torching of Fishergate Bar, a gateway into the city, on 15 May 1489, carried out by Sir John Egremont and John Chambers. After the attack, it is Thomas Wrangwysh who is reprimanded for not keeping the Bar safe. The damage is such that the Bar is bricked up and will remain so until 1827.

8. Sir Robert Willoughby (1452–1502) held lands throughout the west country, becoming Under-Sheriff of Cornwall and Sheriff of Devon. He would join Buckingham's rebellion, flee to Henry Tudor, and secure several positions with him. Sir William Haute (1430–1497) is another landowner who joined Buckingham's revolt. He was Sheriff of Kent but relieved of the position by Richard III because he was a cousin of Earl Rivers. John Fogge (c.1417–1490) was a Kent MP and strong supporter of both Edward IV and Edward V, joining Buckingham's revolt and later fighting at the battle of Bosworth. Fogge was apparently reconciled to Richard on 26 June, a theatrical means of securing his release from sanctuary.

9. Stanley carried the constable's mace at the coronation.

Chapter 24

1. Dr Hutton was an alumnus of Cambridge, his doctorate in civil law. In 1474 he was Principal of Borden Hostel within Peterhouse College. During the reign of Henry VII, he gathered various ecclesiastical preferments becoming Archdeacon of Bedford 1489–1494, translating to Archdeacon of Huntingdon 1494–1496. He became rector of Girton, Cambridge, in 1498, and died in 1506.
2. The Earl Marshal, alongside the Lord High Constable, ran the Court of Chivalry that presided over matters of heraldry and genealogy, ransom, soldiers' wages, and the spoils of war. In addition, it was the court martial.
3. Berkeley's claim to fame is as the winner of the last battle between exclusively private armies in England. Known as the Battle of Nibley Green, it was fought in 1469 to determine the claim on the estate of the great-uncle of Thomas Talbot, Viscount Lisle. Thomas lost the battle and his life.
4. A pardoner could be a layman as well as an ecclesiastic who was licensed to sell pardons or indulgences on behalf of the Catholic Church.
5. Sir James Tyrell (1445–1502) had one of those 'classic' Wars of the Roses careers in that his father was beheaded for treason by Edward IV as one of a group of Lancastrians, including the 12th Earl of Oxford, plotting to murder their King. James then fought on the Yorkist side at Tewkesbury, after which he was knighted by Edward and entered the service of Richard of Gloucester. On Richard's accession to the throne, Tyrell was made Master of the King's Horse (also known as Master of the King's Henchmen) which made him responsible for horses, stabling, squires and grooms, the hench (horse) men. In 1484, the year after the Princes' disappearance, he was made High Sheriff of Cornwall and then Governor of Guines. Although pardoned by Henry VII when he gained the throne, Tyrell managed to get involved in treason with the exiled Duke of Suffolk. On his capture he confessed to his part in the murder of the two Princes. He then followed his father to the executioner's block. There is a tradition that Richard first sent one John Green to London from Gloucester with a letter to Robert Brackenbury requiring him to do away with the Princes. This Brackenbury refused to do, as it went against his duty as Constable of the Tower with special responsibility to keep his prisoners safe. But riding from Gloucester to London would take three to four days and then it would take four to five days to ride to Worcester, which is where More says he made contact

with Richard. It would then take Tyrell four to five days to get to London. So the best part of a fortnight to do the King's will – and Brackenbury not only keeps his job and his head but is rewarded in the following year with a knighthood? Brackenbury was a long-time employee of Richard and owed him his wealth and position. It is highly unlikely that he would refuse an order from Richard: indeed, he does eventually hand over the keys to Tyrell, knowing what for. He would have been no more or less complicit if he had enrolled others himself to do the deed. Bearing in mind that the bond between Brackenbury and Richard was so strong that he led the vanguard at Bosworth with Norfolk and died for his King, this again makes the refusal, and consequently Green's ride, look like a pantomime story. And would Richard dispatch two letters directly incriminating him? The story has gained some further credence though, in that a John Green (and it is a common name) of Warwickshire was granted a pardon by Richard for all (unspecified) offences on 20 September.

6. Reginald Bray (1440–1503) is a Worcester man who entered the service of Margaret Beaufort during the period of her marriage to Sir Henry Stafford and continued to work for her until his death. He will undertake great responsibilities under Henry VII. Married to Katherine Hussey, they had no children.

7. Lewis Caerleon was a Welsh physician with degrees in medicine from Cambridge and Oxford. But his prominence was as an astronomer with a particular interest in calculating the time of eclipses. He was arrested on suspicion of being the link between Margaret and Elizabeth in January 1484 and imprisoned in the Tower until his release after Bosworth. Henry VII granted him a pension and eventually a knighthood.

8. Nicholas Gaynesford (1427–1498) was several times MP and High Sheriff of Surrey and Sussex.

9. Sir William Norreys (1441–1507), an Esquire of the Body to Edward IV, was sometime Sheriff of Oxfordshire and Berkshire, and a Justice of the Peace. Sir William Stonor (1450 –1494) was Sheriff of Oxfordshire, Berkshire, & Devonshire, High Steward of Oxford University, Joint-Constable of Wallingford Castle, and a wealthy wool merchant.

10. Sir Thomas St Leger (1440–1483) was married to Anne, sister of Richard III, who died in childbirth 1476. He was a soldier and administrator for Edward IV. Famously, he was sentenced to have his hand cut off for brawling in the Palace of Westminster but was pardoned. He lost his position as Master of the Harthounds and Controller of the Mint on Richard's accession. He also lost the

wardship of his stepdaughter Anne to Buckingham. Sir Thomas Arundell (1454–1485) was a Cornish nobleman. Made a Knight of the Bath by Richard, he nevertheless joined Buckingham's revolt and was thereby attainted. His estate was passed to his step-sister Anne's husband, Sir James Tyrell (he does feature a lot). Reinstated by Henry VII, he died just weeks after the Battle of Bosworth. Sir Richard Nanfan (1445–1507) is another Cornishman, and past Sheriff of the county. He will become Deputy Lieutenant of Calais, recommending his chaplain, Thomas Wolsey to Henry VII.

11. Sir John Rame (referred to also as Thomas Rame or Thomas Rameney) would be executed by Richard at Exeter alongside Sir Thomas St Leger.

Chapter 25

1. Sir Ralph Ashton (also spelt Assheton) was born 1421 and died sometime before 1490. He was known as the Black Knight of Ashton and said to have rode around the countryside looking for peasants to torture and kill, a favourite method being to roll them downhill in a barrel spiked with nails. He became Sheriff of York and rose to become Vice-Constable of England under Richard III. He received a pardon for supporting Richard from Henry VII, but was reputedly murdered in 1486, his death being celebrated by the community of Ashton-under-Lyne for centuries after.

2. Sir Richard Huddleston (1441–1485) would die fighting for Richard at the battle of Bosworth. He was born in Cumberland. Thomas Tunstall (1433–1499) was the son of a Lancashire knight.

3. From research carried out in 2000, it was adjudged that Richard Ratcliffe was the 152nd richest man of all time to have lived in Britain, with a relative wealth today of £2.8 billion.

4. Walter Roberts was attainted by Parliament, following which Sir Edward Stanley (later Lord Monteagle) and Sir John Savage – both of whom would support Henry Tudor – went to arrest him at his manor of Glassenbury in Kent. The story goes that Walter wined and dined his would-be jailers so well that they had an afternoon nap while their catch escaped on knotted sheets out of a window, locking the doors both inside and out. He then found a place of sanctuary and hid there until Henry's invasion. Stanley and Savage returned to Richard with a thousand pounds of plate and treasures but no Walter Roberts. More likely they facilitated his escape from what would have been a visit to the executioner's block. It is also notable that the mother of Sir John Savage is Katherine, daughter of Thomas, Lord Stanley.

5. Thomas Barowe was a judge in the Court of Chancery. As well as being appointed Master of the Rolls by Richard III he was also Keeper of the Great Seal, which he delivered up to Henry VII after Bosworth.

6. Pierre Landois (1430–1485), sometimes referred to as 'Landais', was a politician hated by the Breton barons and was eventually overthrown by them, tortured, found guilty of corruption, and hanged four weeks before the death of Richard III.

7. Christopher Urswick (1444–1522) was a priest and confessor for Margaret Beaufort and was used by her as a go-between with John Morton. He held various ecclesiastical positions, the last of which was as Rector to the London parish of Hackney.

8. Charles VIII (1470–1498) was known as Charles the Affable. His sister's regency continued until he came of age at 21, during which time there was a revolt by nobles, called the 'Mad War' 1485–1488, which the royalists won. He then married Anne of Brittany in 1491, despite her being contracted to marry Maximilian I, Holy Roman Emperor. He died after hitting his head on the lintel of a doorway.

9. Richard's belligerent attitude at Picquigny was still remembered, characterising him as an aggressor.

10. Sir John Savage (1444–1492) fought for Edward IV at Tewkesbury and held the office of Royal Carver, and was a Knight of the Body, second in the order of precedence at Edward's burial.

Chapter 26

1. Giacomo Passarella is Bishop of Imola, Italy. He is translated to Bishop of Rimini in 1488, a post he holds until his death in 1495.

2. Cadwallader was a regional Welsh king of the seventh century who has achieved mythical status through the works of poets and bards. He was most likely a peaceful leader who patronised many churches and who did not achieve particular success in battle, succumbing eventually to plague.

3. Sir Walter Herbert (1452–1507) was Steward of Abergavenny. He was the brother of William Herbert, 2nd Earl of Pembroke then Earl of Huntingdon. then William died in 1490, Walter inherited Raglan and Chepstow Castles.

4. Richard Griffith (1456–1486) was the brother of William, Lord of Penrhyn Castle. Sir Evan Morgan of Tredegar (or John in the English form) was appointed Sheriff of Wentloog and Newport by Henry and Steward of Machen. Also joining Henry's army is David Cecil of

Alltyrynys, whose descendants will become famous serving Elizabeth I and James I.

5. Sir Gilbert Talbot (1452–1517) is a younger son of the 2nd Earl of Shrewsbury. He is given the Grafton estates in Worcestershire after the execution of Sir Humphrey Stafford in 1486.

6. Sir John Spooner also led the men of York to the battlefield, then returned to York with the news of Richard's death. York was the principal city supporting Richard and had received much preference as a result.

7. Sir Walter Hungerford (d. 1516) was a former Lancastrian supporter who received a pardon. Hungerford was arrested when news of Henry's landing reached London. At Bosworth, he killed Sir Robert Brackenbury in hand-to-hand combat. He served as a Privy Councillor to both Henry VII and Henry VIII.

8. Sir Brian Sanford (or Bryan Sandford) of Thorpe Salvin, Yorkshire, was rewarded by Henry with the stewardship of Caistor, Lincolnshire, Lieutenant of the Tower of London, and several other potentially lucrative positions of responsibility. Sir Simon Digby (d 1519) lost his father and four brothers at the battle of Towton. For his part at Bosworth he was given substantial lands in Rutland. He went on to become Lord of Coleshill, Warwickshire in 1495 when he was Deputy Constable of the Tower.

9. Recent researchers have suggested that the battlefield may have been as far as six miles away from the traditionally accepted site. This deduction has been made following the unearthing of documents setting out compensation payments by Henry for damage to land and crops as a consequence of the battle made to towns in the wider area and to Merevale Abbey. But such payments could have been made regarding camping or foraging sites rather than sites of battle.

Chapter 27

1. Henry removes John of Gloucester from his position at Calais but on 1 March 1486 awards him an income of £20 a year from the manor of Kingston Lacey in Dorset.

2. The sweating sickness seems to have arisen in England towards the end of the Wars of the Roses, later moving into Europe where it was known as the English sickness. Thomas, Lord Stanley pleaded absence from Richard's army because he had contracted it, which suggests that it was already known about before Henry's invasion. Its cause is unknown, and its last known outbreak was

in the middle of the sixteenth century. Henry's son Arthur and Catherine of Aragon contract it in 1502. Catherine survives, but Arthur dies.

3. As Constable of the Tower, Oxford was also responsible for keeping the lions and leopards that were in the Royal Menagerie, for which he received 12d a day plus 6d a day per animal for their expenses.

4. The Lord Chancellor is responsible for ensuring the independence of the courts and their smooth running. Alcock took over the position from Thomas Rotherham, Archbishop of York, on Henry's ascendancy to the throne. This was always a temporary role for Alcock and there was no ill-feeling when he was replaced by Morton. Translated from Worcester to Ely, Alcock continued to work closely with Henry and Morton thereafter. As for Archbishop Rotherham, he sat back from political life to concentrate on his ecclesiastical duties until his death from plague in 1500.

5. Parliaments are still rare and infrequent, only called when the King needs something that cannot be dealt with personally or with his Council. Usually, it is the right to raise taxes for the defence of the realm (the King's own expenses have to be raised from his retained estates) and increasingly parliament demands to know exactly what the taxes will be spent on and then to be assured that they have been spent on precisely that. In the whole of Richard III's 32 years of life, parliament only sat for 112 weeks.

6. Richard Woodville (1453-1491) became the 3rd Earl Rivers. He held no particular office. He died unmarried and the earldom became extinct.

7. 24 February 1486 to be precise.

8. Robert Morton obtains papal dispensation on 23 July to retain his other income producing benefices, including archdeacon of Gloucester and of Winchester, and prebends at St Paul's, Salisbury, York, Beverley, and Wherwell Abbey. He will be formally consecrated as Bishop of Worcester by John at Canterbury on 28 January 1487.

9. Among the marvels recorded are restoring sight to the blind, bringing the dead back to life, and even providing a ghostly hand to prevent an innocent man being hanged on the gallows.

10. Giles Daubeney (1451–1508), a Somerset man associated with Barrington Court outside Ilminster and South Petherton, Member of Parliament for Somerset, was knighted by Edward IV. He was a close confidant of Sir Reginald Bray in planning Buckingham's Revolt.

Under Henry VII he is a Privy Councillor, Master of the Mint, Lieutenant of Calais, and created Baron Daubeney.

11. William Celling was, like Morton, a member of All Souls' College, Oxford. He became Prior at Canterbury in 1472 where he stayed until his death in 1494, during which time he performed useful diplomatic services, also using these journeys to collect ancient Greek and Roman manuscripts.

Chapter 28

1. This story follows the outline provided in The Register of Archbishop Morton, written at the time. It differs from Polydore Vergil's version, who relates that Symonds is with Lambert Simnel at the Battle of Stoke, four months later. Vergil is writing some thirty years after events he did not witness, so here we are basing our account on the Church's memoranda.

2. Schwartz had experience fighting with Charles the Bold at the siege of Neuss and for Maximilian both against the French and against rebellion in Flanders.

3. The pillory was usually sited in the market square. Those in it would be jeered at and ridiculed but sometimes suffered physical abuse with rotten fruit and vegetables, offal, or worse. The punishment would normally be inflicted on drunks or prostitutes and would last for a couple of hours.

4. Richard Harliston was the first appointed Governor of Jersey. Following initial successes, he fell out of favour with the locals by seeking to acquire the status of 'Lord of the Islands', with the backing of Margaret of Burgundy and the French. He was blocked from this by Henry VII which led to him leaving the island to back the attempt to remove the English obstruction to his plans. He later backed Perkin Warbeck's claim and finally ended his days in the service of Margaret at her court.

5. In 1494, FitzGerald's enemies arrested him and had him sent to London where he was brought before Henry on a charge of treason. Such was his character that he used the trial to blacken those enemies and portray himself as a true friend of the Tudors. Famously, when the Archbishop of Cashel claimed that FitzGerald had burned down his cathedral, the Earl replied, 'I would not have done it had I not been told that My Lord Archbishop was inside.' This reportedly so amused Henry that he freed him immediately and reaffirmed his role as Lord Deputy of Ireland! He was ruthless towards his enemies – real and perceived – and was killed in a campaign against the O'Carrolls in 1513.

Chapter 29

1. One of those to gain advancement from the Archbishop was a young Thomas More, who joined Morton's staff in 1490 at the age of twelve as a page at Lambeth Palace. The future Lord Chancellor of Henry VIII and martyr to his faith, More was supported by Morton at Canterbury College, Oxford, and he praised his early mentor in his books *Utopia* and *The History of Richard III*.
2. *Sovereign* blows up in 1512 at Brest, taking with it the lives of Sir John Carew and Sir Thomas Knyvett.
3. Sir Robert Willoughby (1452–1502) was High Sheriff of Cornwall in 1479 and High Sheriff of Devon in 1480. Lord of the Manor of Callington (where he died and was buried) he was created Baron Willoughby de Broke in 1491. He will be one of Henry's principal commanders against the Cornish Rebellion of 1497.
4. Anne (1477–1514) would be married to Charles for the ten years until his death. They had six children, all of whom died very young. After Charles died, she returned to Brittany and attempted to lead it back to independence. However, Charles had been succeeded by his brother-in-law Louis XII, who promptly divorced his wife, Charles's sister Joan, and forced Anne into marrying him. After her death in 1514, the elder of her two daughters married cousin Francis I, thereby fully integrating France and Brittany.
5. Chamber was captured and hanged, not least because he seemed to be the ringleader of Northumberland's murderers. Egremont fled to the Low Countries where he joined the court of Duchess Margaret.

Chapter 30

1. Robert Chamberlain (1430–1491) fought on the Yorkist side at Towton, Barnet, and Tewkesbury. He was in exile with Edward IV and accompanied him on his French expedition in 1475. Under Richard III, Chamberlain was made Captain of Beaumaris Castle in 1485, Sheriff of Anglesey and Receiver of North Wales. It was therefore an embarrassing disappointment that he was totally ineffective against Henry's procession through Wales leading to Bosworth. He was arrested in 1488 for supporting the pretender Lambert Simnel.
2. Tournai was captured in 1513 by Henry VIII, the only Belgian city ever to have been ruled by England. It was actually represented in the English Parliament of 1515. The city was handed over to French rule in 1519.

3. This coincidence was more than enough for later speculation that Warbeck was a bastard son of Edward IV raised by Brampton, and even that he was the bastard son of Margaret of Burgundy.

4. Maurice Fitzgerald (1460–1520), the 9th Earl of Desmond, was disabled and usually travelled everywhere in a horse-drawn litter. Although a supporter of Warbeck, he submitted to and found favour with Henry VII. Though he treated his friends well, his enemies – or, indeed, anyone stepping out of line – saw a very different side to his character.

5. Robert Clifford (1448–1508) was an original supporter of Warbeck but was quickly turned by Henry's agents to divulge much intelligence about Perkin's pals and their plans. Simon Mountford was executed for his part in the rebellion. He had been found guilty of insurrection back in 1465 under Edward IV. It was another case of two strikes and you're out. Lord Fitzwalter (1452–1496), previously Henry's Lord Steward, was convicted of treason on 23 February 1495, his death sentence commuted to life imprisonment at Guines Castle. After trying to escape, he was beheaded in November 1496. Thomas Thwaites (1435–1503) was Chancellor of the Exchequer and Chancellor of the Duchy of Lancaster under Edward IV, and Treasurer of Calais under Richard III. Sentenced to death for his part in the Warbeck rebellion, this was commuted to imprisonment and a heavy fine. William Worsley (1435–1499) was spared execution because of his order and pardoned the following year. He retained all his ecclesiastical preferments until his death.

6. Lady Katherine Gordon (1474–1537) was the daughter of the Earl of Huntly by his third wife. Katherine became a favourite lady-in-waiting to Queen Elizabeth and managed to have four husbands in her sixty-three years.

7. An Gof is also known by his anglicised name Michael Joseph.

8. Reginald Bray (1440–1503) was a senior advisor to Margaret Beaufort for whom he had worked since her first marriage to Sir Henry Stafford and then to Henry VII. He married Katherine Hussey in 1475, who survived him by three years. They had no children.

9. James Tuchet (1463–1497) was a minor nobleman who had been involved in the 1492 siege of Boulogne. He was described by Francis Bacon as 'unquiet and popular and aspiring to ruin'.

Chapter 31

1. Henry Medwall (1462–1502) was educated at Eton and King's College Cambridge as a lawyer and had an ecclesiastical living at

Balinghem, Calais. He worked for some time for Morton at Lambeth Palace.

2. Richard Pynson (1449–1529) was born in Normandy, educated in Paris, and is first recorded as living in London in 1482 and running a print works in 1492. He was appointed King's Printer to Henry VII and Henry VIII.

3. A cap of maintenance is a ceremonial hat, usually of velvet, with fur turned up at the edge, often ermine.

4. Louis captured Milan within a month, and the City State remained in French hands for the next thirteen years. He then invaded Naples in 1501, which led to war with Ferdinand of Aragon, who expelled the French in 1504.

5. Avery Cornburgh held various parliamentary seats in Cornwall and Plymouth. He had a varied life as a sea captain, Keeper of the Great Wardrobe, Under-Treasurer of England, Controller of Mines in Cornwall, and was twice Sheriff of Cornwall. He also had terms as Sheriff of Essex and Hertfordshire.

Bibliography

Arthurson, Ian, *The Perkin Warbeck Conspiracy* (Sutton Publishing 1997)

Ashdown-Hill, John, *The Mythology of Richard III* (Amberley Publishing 2015)

Barker, Juliet, *Agincourt* (Little, Brown 2005)

Bennett, Michael, *Lambert Simnel and the Battle of Stoke* (Alan Sutton Publishing 1987)

Bradley, Stuart, *John Morton. Adversary of Richard III, Power behind the Tudors* (Amberley Publishing 2019)

Breverton, Terry, *Henry VII – The Maligned Tudor King* (Amberley Publishing 2019)

Brewer, Clifford, *The Death of Kings* (Abson Books 2000)

Broadberry, Stephen et al, *British Economic Growth 1270–1870* (Cambridge University Press 2015)

Brockliss, L W B, *The University of Oxford: A History* (Oxford Scholarship Online 2016)

Brooks, Mary et al, 'Fragments of Faith: Unpicking Archbishop John Morton's Vestments' (*The Antiquaries Journal* 2020)

Budden, John, *A Biographical Sketch of Cardinal Morton* (written c.1600, published by Dorset Natural History of Antiquaries Field Club 1879)

Bynum, Caroline W, *Material Continuity, Personal Survival, and the Resurrection of the Body: A Scholastic Discussion in its Mediaeval and Modern Contexts* (University of Chicago Press 1990)

Clapham, John, *A Concise Economic History of Britain* (Cambridge University Press 1966)

Cunningham, Sean, *Richard III, A Royal Enigma* (The National Archives 2003)

Davies, C S L, *John Morton, The Holy See, and the Accession of Henry VII* (English Historical Review January 1987)

Davis, H W Carless, *Balliol College* (F E Robinson & Co 1899)

Davis, J C, *More, Morton, and the Politics of Accommodation* (Cambridge University Press 1970)

Dockray, Keith, *Richard III: A Source Book* (Sutton Publishing 1997)

Fern, Susan, *The Man who Killed Richard III* (Amberley Publishing 2014)

Fleming, Peter, *Bristol and the War of the Roses* (Bristol Historical Association 2003)

Fletcher, Anthony, *Tudor Rebellions* (Longman 1983)

Goodman, Anthony, *The Wars of the Roses – the Soldiers' Experience* (Tempus Publishing 2005)

Goodwin, George, *Fatal Colours* (Weidenfeld and Nicholson 2011)

Harper-Bill, Christopher, *The Register of John Morton* 2 Volumes (Boydell Press 1991)

____, 'The Familia, Administrators and Patronage of Archbishop John Morton' (*Journal of Religious History*)

Harvey, John, *The Plantagenets* (Fontana 1967)

Hicks, Michael, *Edward V. The Prince in the Tower* (Tempus Publishing 2003)

____, *Richard III* (Tempus Publishing 2000)

Hillier, K, 'The Rebellion of 1483, A Study of Sources and Opinions' (*The Ricardian* March 1983)

Jacob, E F, *The Fifteenth Century* (Oxford University Press 1969)

Jones, Dan, *The Hollow Crown* (Faber and Faber 2014)

Jones E T and Condon M, 'Henry VII's letter to John Morton concerning William Weston's voyage to the new found land' (University of Bristol – Explore Bristol Research 2011)

Kendal, Paul Murray, *Richard II* (George Allen & Unwin 1955)

____, *Warwick the Kingmaker* (George Allen & Unwin 1957)

Kleineke, Hannes, 'Morton's Fork – Henry VII's "Forced Loan" of 1496' (*The Ricardian* Volume XIII)

Knott, Betty, 'Translation of John Morton's Will' (The Missing Princes Project 2018)

Logan, F Donald (Ed), *The Medieval Court of Arches* (Boydell Press 2005)

Mackie, J D, *The Earlier Tudors* (Oxford University Press 1988)

Maurer, Helen E, *Margaret of Anjou* (Boydell Press 2003)

More, Thomas, *The History of King Richard III* (Hesperus Press 2014)

Mortimer, Ian, *1415: Henry V's Year of Glory* (The Bodley Head 2009)

Paravicini, Frances de, *Early History of Balliol College* (Kegan Paul, Trench, Trubner 1891)

Penn, Thomas, *Winter King* (Penguin Books 2012)

Pidgeon, Lynda, *Brought Up of Nought, A History of the Woodville Family* (Fonthill 2019)

Pollard, A J, *Richard III and the Princes in the Tower* (Alan Sutton Publishing 1991)

_____, *The Wars of the Roses* (Macmillan Press 1995)

Ross, Charles, *Richard III* (Methuen London 1990)

Ross, James, *The Foremost Man of the Kingdom* (Boydell Press 2015)

Rowse, A L, *Bosworth Field and the War of the Roses* (Panther Books 1968)

Santiuste, David, *Edward IV and the Wars of the Roses* (Pen and Sword Books 2010)

Scofield, Cora L, *The Life and Reign of Edward the Fourth* (Fonthill 2016)

Sim, Alison, *Pleasures and Pastimes in Tudor England* (Sutton Publishing 1999)

Sim, Alison, *The Tudor Housewife* (Sutton Publishing 2005)

Skinner, Raymond J, 'The Life and Turbulent Times of Sir Roger Tocotes' (*Wiltshire Archaeological Magazine* 2002)

Thomas, Keith, *Religion and the Decline of Magic* (Weidenfeld & Nicolson 1971)

Van Loo, Bart, *The Burgundians: A Vanished Empire* (Head of Zeus 2021)

Weir, Alison, *The Princes in The Tower* (The Bodley Head 1992)

Wilkinson, Josephine, *Richard, The Young King to Be* (Amberley Publishing 2009)

Williamson, Audrey, *The Mystery of the Princes* (Sutton Publishing 2002)

Woodhouse, R I, *The Life of John Morton* (Longmans, Green & Co. 1895)

Index